W9-BBS-161

HUMAN EVOLUTION,
LANGUAGE AND MIND

HUMAN EVOLUTION, LANGUAGE AND MIND

A psychological and archaeological inquiry

WILLIAM NOBLE
Department of Psychology
University of New England

IAIN DAVIDSON
Department of Archaeology
and Palaeoanthropology
University of New England

Illustration   **D. Hobbs**

CAMBRIDGE
UNIVERSITY PRESS

Published by the Press Syndicate of the University of Cambridge
The Pitt Building, Trumpington Street, Cambridge CB2 1RP, UK
40 West 20th Street, New York, NY 10011–4211, USA
10 Stamford Road, Oakleigh, Melbourne 3166, Australia

© Cambridge University Press 1996
First published 1996

Printed in Hong Kong by Colorcraft

National Library of Australia cataloguing-in-publication data

Noble, William, 1944–
Human evolution, language and mind: a psychological and archaeological inquiry.
Bibliography.
Includes index.
1. Human evolution. 2. Sign language. 3. Language and
languages – Origin. 4. Perception. 5. Thought and
thinking. I. Davidson, Iain, 1948– . II. Title.
573.2

Library of Congress cataloguing-in-publication data

Noble, William, 1944–
Human evolution, language and mind: a psychological and archaeological
inquiry / William Noble. Iain Davidson.
        p.   cm.
Includes bibliographical references and index.
1. Human evolution. 2. Language and languages – Origin.
3. Signs and symbols. 4. Linguistic change. 5. Psycholinguistics.
I. Davidson, Iain. II. Title.
GN281.4.N63 1996
573.2–dc20   95-53827

A catalogue record for this book is available from the British Library.

ISBN 0 521 44502 7 Hardback
ISBN 0 521 57635 0 Paperback

CONTENTS

ILLUSTRATIONS

TABLES

PREFACE

Why is the topic of human evolution, language and mind of joint interest to a psychologist and an archaeologist? Noble (the psychologist) is primarily taken up with the issue of hearing impairment, hence in communication under conditions that make it impossible or hard to hear. Included in that, necessarily, is an interest in communication using visible signs. Davidson is an archaeologist primarily involved in the study of those prehistoric people in Europe and Australia who made and used stone tools, hunted animals, gathered plants, and painted and engraved on rocks and other materials. Our common interest, then, originates in communication using visible signs.

Among major influences on Noble's thinking has been the ecological theory of perception developed by James Gibson (1950; 1966; 1979). Gibson, throughout his life, was preoccupied with visual art, especially in the means it employs to achieve representation of objects in the world. Representation can take the form, for example, of fixing on a surface a two-dimensional image of a three-dimensional object, such as a human or other animal figure. The representation separates the object from its context and reduces it to a single frozen image, unchanging in space or time. Gibson theorised that whoever, in prehistoric times, first made a 'recognisable picture'—a concept we have since come to see as quite complex (Deregowski 1984)—would have experienced a major change in their conscious awareness, both of the world and of themselves. In Gibson's view (1966, 229), making such a thing would inevitably induce some kind of reflection on the image, the object, and the image-maker as creator of the image.

The interest in Sign language led to the work of Gordon Hewes (e.g., 1973; 1974) an anthropologist who stands in a distinguished tradition advancing the argument that human language was based, in evolution, on communication using gestures. These mimicked such everyday actions as would be involved in tool-making or food-preparing. Hewes proposed that somehow or other gestural communication was transferred to the vocal-auditory system, possibly through the involvement of the mouth and tongue in the making of indexical or similar gestures.

Was there some way that Hewes's ideas about mimetic gestures might relate to Gibson's ideas about picture-making; and further, given Gibson's talk about effects upon consciousness, might the point of origin of language lie somewhere in all that? On this matter Noble decided to inquire of archaeologist colleague Davidson what was known about the capacities and practices of the people who made the very first pictures. Unknown to him, Davidson was worrying about the fragmentary and inconsistent evidence for the earliest symbol-making; how, indeed, the earliest symbols could be recognised without the conventions of language—we take pains to sort out symbols in this text. Over a somewhat more than usually convivial lunch, we realised that we had been converging, from different starting places, on the same problem—the evolutionary emergence of language and its relation to the production of representation. Our journey from that lunch to the completion of the book has taken $8\frac{1}{2}$ years—a long voyage. On the way there have been several papers, which we found could not simply be rearranged to produce a book-length work. This is not, therefore, a mere recasting of those papers, but a new approach to the issues addressed in them.

Eric Higgs (Davidson's doctoral supervisor) once remarked that the future of archaeology lay with psychology. Davidson was suitably dismissive. At that time his interests were in how prehistoric people got their food, especially by the exploitation of animals. The interpretation of archaeological evidence concerning this form of activity seemed rather less speculative than interpretation of other forms—bones could, after all, be identified to parts of the body and type of the animal they helped constitute. 'Art' and 'symbols', let alone 'mind', seemed far away from anything he understood as reasonable subjects for inquiry. The turn-around began in 1989 with a paper on a minimalist interpretation of the 'art' of Parpalló. It gathered strength through collaboration with Noble because of the sceptical approach we each incline to adopt towards theory and permissible inter-pretations in our own (and each others') disciplines.

To elaborate on that point: this book, like several of the papers before it, has threatened to break up into at least two separate works. To prevent it doing so has required effort to clarify and understand meanings peculiar to the other's parent enterprise. We have been fascinated by the continual need for each to keep the other honest about claims made from within their own subject. The extent of our individual prejudices about our academic 'home ranges', as well as the ignorance of the nature of the other's, have been more clearly revealed by the exercise of trying to find common expression from both. The game is worth the effort, especially as a counter to the increasing speciation within disciplines, never mind the isolation of disciplines from each other.

Separately and jointly, in the unfolding of this project, we have benefited from discussions and arguments with many people, and it is a pleasant, if hazardous task (someone accidentally overlooked) to recollect and identify them here. For Noble the list includes Carolyn Baker, Alan Costall, Jeff Coulter, Eve Danziger, Helen Fraser, Ian Lubek, Don Mixon, David Olson, Ed Reed, Bruce Stevenson, Michael Tomasello and Bill Warren. For Davidson it includes Peter Brown, Bill Calvin, Rob Foley, Rob Gargett, Peter Hiscock, Simon Holdaway, Dietrich and Ursula Mania, Bill McGrew, Sue Savage-Rumbaugh and Tom Wynn. For both of us it includes Helen Arthurson, Whitney Davis, Jan Deregowski, Dean Falk, Clive Gamble, Tim Ingold, Peter Jarman, Alex Marshack, Nick Reid, David Rindos and Peter White. As always, none of these people may be charged as accessories to the intellectual offences we alone are responsible for committing.

We want to thank our students and colleagues who have tolerated our eccentric enthusiasms rather as indulgent parents. Davidson thanks the Wenner-Gren Foundation for opportunity to meet and discuss many issues with colleagues at a conference in Cascais.

Douglas Hobbs produced most of the final illustrations, and we acknowledge with thanks his painstaking skills and style, especially in the computer graphics. Several of the resultant figures (Figures 3, 4, 7, 24, 25, 26, 30, 37, 42, 45) are originally by Heather Burke, and we give special thanks to her for those outstanding pieces.

CHAPTER 1

AN EVOLUTIONARY APPROACH TO THE ORIGIN OF MIND

In the distant future I see open fields for far more important researches. Psychology will be based on a new foundation, that of the necessary acquirement of each mental power and capacity by gradation. Light will be thrown on the origin of man and his history.— Darwin, 1968[1859], 458

In speculating in this way about 'the necessary acquirement of each mental power and capacity', it is clear that Charles Darwin meant something like, 'how mental capacity emerged in humans through processes of evolution'. In the century-and-a-half since 1859, there has been much speculation upon this phenomenon, but little attempt to come to grips with the enlarging body of evidence about the behaviour of the creatures, ancestral to modern humans, in which this 'mental capacity' emerged.

Our book attempts to show how 'mental capacity' might best be conceived in the light of recent developments in psychology, social science (including philosophy), and animal ethology. Following that conceptual clarification we turn to consider the evidence of the archaeological record to evaluate how, in a context of natural selection, such a capacity did emerge. We begin with a foretaste of the arguments we will expand and defend throughout, to the effect that mindedness in human terms is inseparable from language use, and that gestures and fixed visual images have a key function in the origin of behaviour that today may be described as linguistic. We justify later our preference for calling linguistic behaviour communication using symbols.

Speaking and intentionality

Any discourse about language confronts us with an almost insurmountable problem. What would it be like for there not to be language? If this question were to have been asked a hundred years ago, the answer from most people engaged in debate about the matter would have been quite straightforward (Harris 1988). If there were no language, some other way would be found to communicate our ideas. For most of the length of time, historically, that any thought has been given to the matter, language has been considered by most theorists to be simply a mechanism whereby we transmit our thoughts to one another. Those thoughts (or ideas) were held to be independent entities, forms that were clothed in suits of words so that they might promenade in society in a recognisable manner.

Due to the efforts of people like Ferdinand de Saussure, Edward Sapir, Ludwig Wittgenstein, Lev Vygotsky and George Mead—a cast of characters we will encounter through several of the following chapters—the proposal was developed in this century that thinking and speaking cannot be detached from each other; that ideas are not to be found other than as the strings of words we utter. Words, indeed, *are* words insofar as they convey meanings. It was Saussure's insistent point that a word (as a sound image) and its meaning (as a concept) were as the face and back of the same sheet of paper. You could not cut one without cutting the other, and you could not have one without the other. So far from the view that words were merely like clothes, in which our ideas were dressed, ideas without words became considered an impossibility.

With this line of argument came a parallel recognition that to speak is to exercise intent. We rely upon aspects of a scheme for grappling with intention whose pedigree may be traced through the 19th century philosopher/psychologist Franz Brentano to the medieval scholar Thomas Aquinas (Gregory 1987), and which has been articulated more recently by Daniel Dennett and others (Dennett 1987). The term 'intention' means 'aboutness'. When anyone speaks, they speak *about* some thing, some one, or some event. What's more, we speak about matters *to* one another. This is best represented in the theorising of Mikhail Bakhtin who observed that '... the word is a two-sided act. It is determined equally by whose word it is and for whom it is meant.' (Holquist 1981, 170). Part of what it means to say someone speaks is that they are aware of what they do, and that they are addressing someone (even if only themselves). What they say may be mistaken; the person they say it to may not be listening, or may be other than the one they *suppose* they are saying it to; but, in all the conditions of everyday life, words are addressed knowingly by persons to others. To put it succinctly, to speak is to know that you mean something.

There is a danger when discoursing about language, which is to regard the words that are uttered in speaking as tokens of a more abstract system that lies behind and beyond any actual use of words. Because we can identify 'languages', we are able to consider the concept of 'language', and then to entertain the idea of 'language' as a more abstract system than any instance of speaking ('langue' in Saussure's terminology, as distinct from 'parole'). Saussure, who is usually held as a founder of present-day linguistics, never intended that language be seen as detached from human social existence. Nonetheless, reification of 'language' has intensified following his distinction between 'langue' and 'parole'. From Harris's treatment of Saussure (Harris 1987, xiv–xv) it may be taken that the reifying effort lies at the door of Chomsky (e.g., 1964, 52), who saw Saussurian 'langue' as equivalent to his 'linguistic competence', an abstract system innate to the human mind, and distinct from any actual 'linguistic performance'. The transformation of a form of conduct (speaking) into an abstract entity (language) in turn gives birth to almost mystical views about language, the mind, rationality, and aspects of human existence as standing outside of evolution.

In our view attention should be directed to what people *do* in their communicative interactions with each other; we should not be sidetracked by tendencies to abstraction. Here we suggest a parallel; indeed, one which is pertinent to our evolutionary story in several respects. Most people with two legs engage in a range of behaviours using them. Amongst other things, they use their legs to walk. Usually they do this effortlessly. Nonetheless, humans had an ancestor which walked on all fours—a gait we discuss in chapters 2 and 6. Walking bipedally emerged in our ancestors during their evolution. More closely tied to everyone's experience, infants and babies do not walk as adults do. They learn to walk that way. The way people walk varies within and between communities; it varies from time to time, and on different occasions, for individuals (Cutting et al. 1978; Patla 1991). There are many different ways of walking, yet communities, and persons within communities, have a characteristic way of doing it. We recognise people by the way they walk (Cutting & Kozlowski 1977), even from the *sounds* of their footsteps. How walking is done is quite complex; it involves the coordinated use of many sets of muscles. And by walking, many different things can be accomplished. We can appreciate all these things about walking without having to invoke a mysterious abstract entity called, say, 'ambulation', of which the more everyday activity of walking is somehow a material expression.

Saussure stated (1983[1916], 10) that 'it has not been established that the function of language, as manifested in speech, is entirely natural: that is to say, it is not clear that our vocal apparatus is made for speaking as our legs for walking.'. But we do not believe it is altogether clear that 'our legs [are made] for walking'. Photographic documents of the locomotor habits of some so-called feral children (MacLean 1979) suggest that bipedalism may not be an inevitable behaviour of modern human morphology. And contrariwise, Lieberman (1984) has argued for the recent evolution of the upper laryngeal airway system as being *for* speech. The only points that we want to read into these remarks are that, in typical cases, (only) the lower limbs in humans are *used* for locomotion, and the upper laryngeal airways are *used* for speaking.

We need only change one phoneme in the word 'walking' to show the parallel with talking. It is legitimate to consider the actual communicative (or ambulatory) behaviour of persons in real settings without inventing an abstract system that somehow enables or supports this behaviour. In the case of speaking, the behaviour may be said to support itself. Through being continually performed it is maintained as a form of communal conduct. But, as with walking, the behaviour is only available to organisms with morphologies that can express it. Equally with walking, however, that morphology had to have been naturally selected from a variable range.

The ancestors of modern human beings, for some period close to the branch point with other apes, did not habitually walk on their legs alone. In just the same way, those ancestors, for some time subsequent to the branching with other apes, did not talk. How either behaviour came to be expressed, and why it was selected, are intelligible questions within an evolutionary framework, and we aim to answer the second of them in this book. Of continual concern in the argument is to explain how human speaking (or its equivalent in Sign language), as a behaviour, is distinct from all other forms of communication. If we explain this properly we believe the nature of the human mind is made comprehensible.

A theorist we rely on initially to launch the argument is philosopher/psychologist George Herbert Mead (1934). He said that communication is *only* recognisable as a form of *behaviour*. Furthermore, behaviour can only be recognised as communicative in virtue of its evoking a response. A signal is not communicative if it is not responded to.

This scheme does not adjudicate upon questions of intentionality of communication or upon synergy (mutual communication). It also leaves the activity of certain forms of life unclear, and we need to be clearer. Behaviour is usually attributed to *animate* life, which thus excludes plants. Mead did not say anything about plants, though Darwin was very much concerned with them, and their various 'movements and habits' (Darwin 1875a; 1875b; Gruber & Barrett 1974). Mead would likely have said that as plants, for the most part, do not join in responding to communicative signs, they are largely outside his scheme of things. Here we can borrow a term from Gibson (1966), who speaks about objects *broadcasting* information about their presence. Plants, it may be said, exude chemicals, or reflect light, in ways that attract animate life, but they do not, typically, respond to signals within their vicinity. We say 'typically' and 'for the most part'. This is because the movements of, for instance, carnivorous, climbing or phototropic plants are due to reactions to forms of energy that equate with those eliciting sensory responses in animals (Shropshire 1979); and the mechanisms of reception in such plants are akin to those in animate life (Bentrup 1979). There are no sharp boundaries to be drawn here.

Bees that are attracted by the light or odour of plants do more obviously communicate, certainly among themselves (Frisch 1954); though perhaps not by 'language' conveyed in 'dancing' (Wenner 1971). What about with the rest of the animate world? Under Mead's scheme of things the bee's buzz as it drifts into the hearing of humans is communicative, for it brings about a response.

The question unresolved is whether, as in the case of the bee, there is an *intention* to communicate. Human beings necessarily come up with such a question because we know how to ascribe intentions to ourselves and other people. We are clear about the fact that human behaviour is (often) intentional in nature, and we can express ourselves on that point. The nature of the consciousness (hence intentionality) of creatures which do not speak is enigmatic. We return later in this chapter, and in Chapters 4 and 5, to the concept of 'consciousness'.

For the sake of forecasting the argument about mind and language it must be stipulated that we are, ultimately, telling a story about how communication became such that its intentional character is unquestionable. That state of affairs must stand in contrast to one in which communication does *not* have an intentional character. But this is where language actually gets in the way, for we are considering a circumstance we cannot possibly imagine, namely, a condition of being aware without the use of language as a feature of that awareness. 'Awareness' is another word for 'consciousness', and is hence taken up in later discussion. This chapter began with the question: 'what would it be like for there not to be language?' The answer is that, as language users, we cannot know what it would be like, even assuming that it would 'be like' anything. It may not be possible even to approach an answer, since the question, in being *posed*, can only be from the perspective of a language-using questioner (cf. Nagel 1974). Hence, as Wittgenstein remarks (1961[1922], 151 ¶7), 'What we cannot speak about we must consign to silence'.

Communication using symbols

Human communication of the form we call linguistic is communication using symbols. In our usage, a symbol is anything that, by custom or convention, stands for something else. A symbol is a representative of another thing; it is like an ambassador for that other thing. There are two important elements in this definition: (1) that the thing stands for something other than itself; (2) that it does so by convention, that is to say, by social custom. Anything can be a symbol and, in human life, almost anything is. Pictures are things that stand for other things. If you draw a house, what you have is a symbol for a house—although we will have to argue for that, and do so in Chapter 3. How we can come to see a mere set of lines as representing a house is an intriguing achievement (Gibson 1966); it is one, we argue, that points to the product as a symbol. The picture is a symbol, just as the words used to indicate it ('this is a house') are symbols. The word 'house' stands for the object it refers to. The meaning of the word (or the picture) depends upon social convention. No one can introduce an utterance others have never heard before and expect it, there and then, to be taken as standing for anything. The representations we make must at all times be tied communally to the objects they are made to represent.

A behaviour expressed by a (not so) close relative of modern human beings is the set of vocal utterances made by vervet monkeys in the face of different classes of predators. In response to the sight of snakes heading for them through the grass they make one sort of cry; in response to the sight of eagles flying overhead they make another sort. These calls have the effect of alerting other monkeys to the different sources (and whereabouts) of the different predators. The others look down in response to a 'snake cry' and up in response to an 'eagle cry'. We could call these utterances symbols if only we could be sure that the monkeys used them with intent; that they knew that one call stood for 'snake' and the other stood for 'eagle'. We do not know that; but it looks from all the evidence that the monkeys do not have these cries as symbols (Cheney & Seyfarth 1990).

What the monkeys could have is the makings of a symbol system, if they were to *notice*, to *discover*, that the different calls may be made to stand for objects in the world. We suspect that this is not a straightforward discovery to make, and we do not know how it was made prehistorically. In Chapter 8 we offer a chain of carefully constrained speculation about contexts for the expression of behaviour which might ultimately lead to such discovery: we outline it below. The reasoning we bring to bear on the matter is that it is legitimate to frame the problem as one of discovery, and, given that, to propose some feasible steps for making it.

There are several interesting features in the evolution of the ancestors of modern humans. (1) The brain gradually expanded over a period of about 2.5 million years; (2) stone was being flaked through most of the same period; (3) flaked stone was continually being used in association with scavenging food from dead animals; (4) over a period of at least 1.5 million years, little seemed to change in the behaviour of these creatures whose brain size was increasing. Many hypotheses have been put forward to account for the increase in brain size. Besides an hypothesis that accounts for some portion of the increase as a change in overall body scale, the further one we find plausible is that the hominids were increasing the refinement of their motor control, particularly their forelimb control. The archaeological record establishes the expression of bipedal locomotion by about 3.5 million years ago. The forelimbs were thus increasingly useable for the transport and breaking of stones. In the motor control hypothesis—proposed by Darlington (1975) and developed by Calvin (1982)—the particular capacity that was continuously improving was stone throwing. The capacity to throw further, faster, and with increasing accuracy, and thus to throw stones at rivals, at predators and at prey, would confer endless advantage over fellows who could not do this. Such an improvement can explain the expansion of the brain *and* the absence of any other change in the archaeological record.

We have argued that the aiming of missiles for successful throwing can in turn support aiming without throwing: what is called pointing in the modern world. Pointing is an intentional behaviour—one original meaning of the word 'intend' is 'point'—and it seems to be unique to humans (Butterworth 1991). In fact infant bonobos (pygmy chimpanzees) make a pointing gesture, but do so in contexts such that their natural caregivers cannot witness the behaviour, as when an infant is being carried on an adult's back (Savage-Rumbaugh 1984). Of course, even if this gesture were expressed in ways more visible to adults, it might not call forth a response from them. Uniquely human is that human infants witness older others pointing long before they themselves do it, and are keenly attended to and imitated by those adults whenever they start to. Children, and bonobos in certain laboratory arrangements, learn the efficacy of pointing through the attention paid to it by human experimenters, and themselves start to imitate such mimicking gestures. We return in Chapters 2 and 4 to contrasts in interaction between human adults and infants compared with other primate adults and infants.

To complete the synopsis of our evolutionary scenario: pointing can reveal the whereabouts of predators or prey to fellow creatures, and in silence, thus without warning of one's own presence. The refinement of control of the forelimbs allows for the possibility of their controlled movement in following the path of a prey or predator animal; it also allows for the possibility of making gestures that distinguish prey from predator.

We round off this story with the proposal that the leaving of a trace of such a gesture in a persistent form creates a meaningful object for perception. The trace of the gesture is meaningful because of the salient links among the gesture, the object that provoked it and the communicators. It is in this complex of behaviours and their products that we see the prospects for the sign itself (the trace of the gesture, hence the gesture itself) to become noticed, as against being simply the means for drawing attention to something else. The vervet calls draw the attention of the others to something significant in the landscape (Burling 1993). Inscriptions of analogous utterances, i.e., forelimb gestures, following the sort of evolution just outlined, may be the mechanism whereby such signs are discovered as objects that represent things other than themselves. Thus are symbols born.

Humans and language—some issues about definition

In order to proceed we need to define what it is we are going to talk about in this account of the evolutionary emergence of the distinctive uniqueness of human behaviour. Many of the features which we regard as unique are more or less direct consequences of the emergence of language, of communication using symbols. In order to make this argument we will cover territory unfamiliar to some parts of the audience which might be interested in our story. There will be archaeologists and prehistorians unfamiliar with the philosophical and psychological aspects of the account, and there will be philosophers and psychologists unfamiliar with the archaeological aspects. Much of the work will address these aspects and show how they are tied together.

Not all the possible definitions of what it means to be human can be reconciled. One approach is to look to the anatomy of modern humans to define human uniqueness, but this runs into problems arising from the variation existing in different populations around the world (e.g. Brown 1990). Moreover, for humans and our ancestors, there is an unparalleled record of fossil specimens which tends to emphasise the continuity of anatomical variation across geographical space and also through time—bearing in mind that variability in space and time must be considered together (e.g. Stringer 1988). Such definitions may, therefore, be practically unsuitable if we wish to identify the point in time, or the place at which, our ancestors became human.

One of the problems in defining 'human' in terms of anatomy is that the limits are not currently in dispute, but in evolutionary time they have been. Despite bestial metaphors for antisocial behaviour ('that person is a pig') there is less difficulty in adopting a social definition of 'human': humans are those organisms identified by other humans as human. (This approach has pragmatic limits: one way that prejudicial and even more unspeakable acts get sanctioned—so-called 'ethnic' so-called 'cleansing'—is to define victims as non-human.) But, in the main, most people have little difficulty in identifying the difference between humans and all other animals, including chimpanzees and bonobos, despite close similarity of anatomy (Huxley 1906), genetics (Rogers 1993) and behaviour (McGrew 1992).

At one time, a convenient behavioural limit identified humans as 'toolmakers'. Jane Goodall's (1964) documentation of chimpanzee tool-making was not the first observation of this ability of apes in the wild, but it was a timely one, given popular interest in the new discoveries of very early stone tools (e.g. Leakey 1966) and the fossilised remains of their makers. It effectively ended the use of this definition. Another approach, which we prefer, is to point to the widespread use of items external to the body (one way of conceptualising 'tools') among non-human and human animals, a matter discussed in the next chapter. In this way we avoid assuming that the making of stone tools, in and of itself, provides the fundamental distinction between humans and other animals.

We return to what we see as the only viable distinction, namely, that humans are unique, under natural conditions, in being creatures who communicate using symbols, thus, among other things, allowing tool manufacture to take the social (symbol-guided) forms that it does (Ingold 1993a; Reynolds 1993). Our criterion for symbol-based communication is 'all-or-none'; we have difficulty with notions of 'protolanguage', 'rudimentary language', or 'language as we know it'. Such ideas have been voiced to try to gradualise the development of symbol use. We do not think this can work. As with the notion of something having, or not having, 'meaning' (Noble & Davidson 1991), symbols are either present or absent, they cannot be halfway there. Such an argument is consistent with the idea expressed earlier of *discovery* of the property of one thing as able to stand for another. 'Discovery' is an achievement, a binary condition—something is discovered or it is not. Nothing can be 'half-discovered', though something may be discovered that turns out later to be but half of something larger, hence 'half-discovered' can make sense in that case.

The idea of 'language as we know it', with its implication of 'language as we do not (or not quite) know it', may be used to illustrate the conceptual difficulty that lies in wait for a gradualist approach on this sort of question. What might be 'language as we do *not* (or not quite) know it'? We are not talking about *a* language (such as Russian) that a native English speaker may not know, or not know too well ('not quite know'). We are concerned with some description of 'language' as a form of communication that is not fully like a language such as English or Russian (and, again, we are not talking about archaic or precursor versions of these languages, such as Anglo-Saxon or Old Slavic; nor, for that matter, about the limiting case, described in Chapter 8, when the very first symbolic sign/s occurred). To the question, 'what is language as we *do not* know it?', there is only one answer. There is no such thing as language as we do not know it, when what we are considering is the communicative use of symbolic signs. If something is not thus language as we (actually or potentially) know it then it is misleading to refer to it as language at all.

The conceptual difficulty for a gradualist approach can be seen by considering something that is not language yet might be thought of as 'protolanguage', namely, 'body language'. The proposition of those who refer to 'body language' is that bodily postures may be taken by an observer as communicating feelings or motivational states of the person posturing. As such they are what Liska (1986) would call 'symptoms' of the posturer's feelings or desires. An observer's response to those symptoms may be spontaneous, insofar as 'body language' is naturally expressive (Darwin 1981[1871]). But attention may be drawn to the possibility that there *is* a predictable set of postures expressive of such symptoms, and we may thus see the postures as the products of deliberate intent. Their original effect, in authentically communicating some feeling or desire, is dependent on their spontaneity. Once the posturer, likewise aware of the communicative possibilities of the posture, chooses to manipulate it to deliberately convey a symptom, the observer cannot rely on its authenticity, and it ceases to communicate anything reliably.

There are, of course, benign (and everyday) forms of 'inauthentic' expression of 'body language', such as when people imitate the non-verbal performances of another—an ability that, practised up, forms a key part of the activities of acting and miming. In everyday settings, gesticulations can function as metaphoric statements (the vulgar 'finger' sign indicating 'up yours'). The readiness of response to all such forms of 'body language' lies in the audience seeing them as contrived versions of spontaneous symptoms (as in mime), or as derivatives of bodily actions (as in the rude sign). They are responded to as *symbols*—deliberately made gestures and postures that either stand for spontaneous versions of those things, or that state something in place of words (Langacker 1987). There may thus be 'vocabularies' of such signs: conventionalised ways of gesturing and posturing (Kendon 1993, 50) that both performers and audiences are familiar with, hence know the meanings of. Body language, when thus 'linguistic', is symbolic, not proto-symbolic.

Where spoken or signed language is concerned, a community of language users, in learning the uses of language from their caregivers and peers, can *only* communicate by conforming to the conventions of the language, there being, nonetheless, a constant play of social and historical forces concerning conventional 'meanings' (Bakhtin 1981[1975]). Due to the constraint about conventionality, there is a fundamental opposition between language and spontaneous 'body language'. In natural 'body language', the communicative aspect of the posture depends on its being 'symptomatic'—neither symbol-guided nor symbolic. If it becomes self-consciously conventionalised, then its communication is untrustworthy, or (mere) art, or in lieu of spoken utterance, and in any such case is symbol-guided and/or itself symbolic. Language as we know it (the only form there can be), can only function communicatively under *any* conditions ('artful' or otherwise) if the arbitrary signs are conventionalised. The point about 'artfulness' in the context of language as we know it is to indicate that we are not so naive as to overlook the fact that natural language can also be used to deceive. Our point is that body language *only* becomes language-like when it is used to delight or deceive (or convey a common meaning); deception can *only* occur (successfully) with language if it is a rare use.

On this basis we can proceed to examine the story of the evolutionary emergence of humans by looking for the signs of language. Whilst not without potential to generate confusion, this definition of human-ness (language-using) can be made robust if we stick to the core point that signs of language are to be found in communication using symbols. There is a caution to be expressed here. Many experimental settings that involve chimpanzees manipulating plastic tokens, Sign language signs, or illustrated computer keys, could be described as 'communication using symbols'. That form of description may only be intelligible to the human participants in the experiments. Our main aim is to identify the emergence of symbols prehistorically.

Some recent approaches to the evolutionary origin of mind

Recent years have seen a spate of publications about the issues of the evolutionary emergence of mental capacity or its correlates, by psychologists, linguists, philosophers, biologists, biological or social anthropologists and archaeologists. These scholars differ among themselves about the nature of 'mind', whether it is synonymous with, more, or other than the brain, whether it can be said to exist at all, whether its characteristics are innate, or acquired during early life experience—a process known as ontogenetic development—and whether it is other than or synonymous with language. We will side with ontogenetic development, supported by evolutionary history, and align ourselves with the position that 'mind' is a term used to account for ways that humans go about their business, rather than a 'thing' for which we might search. This echoes an earlier point about 'language' as a conceptual abstraction from the behaviour of speaking, signing, writing or otherwise communicating with symbols.

All writers on this topic acknowledge that language is somehow important to 'mind', but they differ among themselves about the form this importance takes. We recognise that individual positions depend on particular definitions of language, and on particular understandings about what 'minds' are taken to accomplish. In broad terms we suggest that the activities humans engage upon as a consequence of their language use are central to the concept of 'mind' (Ryle 1949). This position has been argued by Saussure, Mead and others. The problem is displaced by such an argument, and it becomes essential to consider what language is, as well as to look at how language and 'mental activity' are related. Should the view of mind and language as co-extensive be persuasive, the payoff is that the evolutionary issue comes down to explaining the emergence of linguistic behaviour.

Writers on this topic differ in the weight given to the *evidence* of evolution, some ignoring it altogether in preference for thought experiments and ad hoc evolutionary scenarios (why let evidence get in the way of a good story?), some leaning solely on anatomical data as if 'mind' might have a physical relationship with that. Others depend on uncritical interpretation of the archaeological record. We will argue that there *is* good evolutionary evidence, but it is not in the fossilised remains of human ancestors; rather it is in the products of their behaviour. The interpretation of this evidence of ancestral products is made more difficult because, for much of the older evidence and for the standard story that has built up because of it, there has been little thought about the issues of the mental capacities of the makers. Interpretations reflect unrecognised assumptions that the mental capacities of ancestors were like those of the archaeologists and others who make the interpretations, as well as interpreters' ideological commitments to uncritically accepted views of 'mind'.

Central to the issues is the vernacular appreciation of what the mind 'is', especially in the context of a current vogue for communicating professional theorising about 'mind' to the popular psychology market. 'Mind' has been much discussed by psychologists and philosophers, especially since the work of Descartes in the seventeenth century. Descartes's position was informed by the belief that there might exist 'things', such as God, the soul or the mind, for which there was no material evidence. It is belief in the immaterial mind that forms the subject of the 'mind-body' problem which has preoccupied many scholars since that time. Twentieth century debates on these and related issues have largely untangled the questions about *minds* from those about *souls*, though some of the opinions defended most vehemently seem no less religious. There is the question about whether present day human abilities are innate or acquired during ontogenetic or experiential development. Views about this are well represented in recent literature; resolution of it is best made in terms of what are the inherited characteristics which enable the acquisition of particular abilities.

The view that crucial human abilities are innate has a long history which, in western thought, may go back to at least the Greek historian and mythologiser, Herodotus. Belief in the innateness of language lives on in the work of Chomsky and his followers, though now the definition is extended beyond vocabulary to grammar and syntax. Extended reification results in the belief that there is such a 'thing' as language, which has a 'life' of its own, somewhere inside the equally metaphorical mind. We briefly review a sample of contemporary writings on the evolutionary origin of 'mind'.

The concept of representation is central to contemporary evolution-based stories about the 'origin of mind'. In this context, 'representations' may be defined as including all forms of response in a biological system to energy impinging on it (e.g., sensory responses). 'Mental representations' are often characterised as activity in or states of cells in the central nervous system, analogous to various forms and levels of programming in a digital computer. We examine this analogy for 'the mind' in more detail in Chapters 4 and 5.

Bickerton (1990) sees language as the key to understanding human mentality. In his view it is the ultimate representational system and it evolved as a transformation from absence of language to the presence of what he calls 'protolanguage'. Bickerton illuminates protolanguage as akin to the sort of one-word utterance produced by very young children, or by chimpanzees in experimental settings such as those of Gardner and Gardner (e.g., 1980). Protolanguage evolves into language (as we know it), on the argument that children quickly move from the one-word phase to the syntactically ordered form of utterance more characteristic of adult speech (or Sign).

Bickerton's story has been criticised by Pinker (1992) on a number of grounds, including the absence of real evidence for the abrupt, two-stage evolution from no language to protolanguage to language as recognisable in contemporary human life. Pinker also criticises Bickerton for conflating what he terms 'natural language' with mental representation ('the language of thought', which we encounter in Chapter 4). He argues that the evolution of forms of mental representations—taken to be useable for more general cognitive purposes, such as perceiving, reasoning and remembering—may not be co-extensive with that of language. Pinker and Bloom (1990) have discussed ways in which 'natural language' may be considered to have evolved. Their account also posits intermediate forms of utterance analogous to Bickerton's 'protolanguage' idea, but more gradualist than that.

We asserted that gradualism cannot work when it comes to matters of meaning or symbol use. Pinker and Bloom would seek to counter that. They point out (1990, 722–723) that barely comprehensible utterances—the analogues of 'fractional' meanings—can nevertheless be made some sense of. They cite such things as the 'agrammatical' telegraphic style of newspaper headlines, malapropisms, and stories in a foreign language newspaper (for people with only a passing knowledge of the language in question). Bickerton uses the analogy of 'pidgins', contact languages among speakers of different native languages. Pidgins may have little in the way of grammatical structure, but serve basic communicative functions by adaptation of elements of the speakers' native languages for mutual contact purposes. Bickerton paints a picture of hominid ancestors struggling to make others understand their protolinguistic yet nonetheless referential mouthings, and both he and Pinker and Bloom invoke notions of selective pressure for hominids to keep applying effort toward extracting meaning from unpromising material.

Not noticed in the examples of fractional meaning is that the comprehensibility of not very comprehensible material is enabled by the fact that those exposed to the utterances are already language users, who can thus postulate likely meanings, by bringing the apparatus of language and related pragmatic and contextual knowledge to bear on the task. The scenarios of hominids struggling along similar-looking lines are illicit projections of that apparatus to creatures with no such resources.

Corballis (1991) invents a machine, the Generative Assembling Device (GAD), which enables everything in human experience to be mentally represented, including natural and manufactured objects. The generative basis of this representational capacity is argued as an ability to combine limited sets of simple elements into a seemingly limitless range of products: phonemes and morphemes are put together to form words, phrases and sentences. Corballis's GAD is thus allied with Chomsky's Language Acquisition Device (LAD), the mental machine which enables children to understand and generate grammatical utterances. The GAD seeks to be a more general brain-based computer, responsible for the ability to classify, for example, visible objects by generating representations based on a limited set of visual elements (so-called 'geons' [Biederman 1987]). For Corballis, the evolution of this capacity results from bipedalism, which 'freed' the hands to engage in manipulation and ultimately gesture. Critical to that was the taking over of generative function by the left hemisphere of the brain, with its claimed dominance for control of serial output such as language, and its contrast with the more 'holistic' propensities of the right hemisphere.

The question of hemispheric asymmetry is treated by Bradshaw and Rogers (1993), who review evidence for hemispheric lateralisation in the control of behavioural function, for example, in the form of limb preference and vocalising, in several species of mammals and birds. A recent report (Bauer 1993) shows similar asymmetry for vocal control in amphibians (frogs). The burden of the argument by Bradshaw and Rogers is an insistence on gradualism and continuity among at least anthropoid species as regards practical and intellectual capacities. They cite bipedalism, tool use and the gradual expansion of the brain as productive of the particular adaptations, including language, of modern humans. In that respect their position accords with Corballis, yet contrasts with his emphasis on the supposedly uniquely 'generative' human nervous system.

We believe there is no more evidence for such engines in the machinery of the human brain as Corballis's GAD (or Chomsky's LAD), than there is for souls or minds. Characterising human uniqueness will come down to an understanding of particular behavioural adaptations and their evolutionary consequences, in terms of selection from a variable range. On that score we do not diverge from any of the scholars whose work we mention in this section; we differ with respect to presuppositions about the phenomena to be accounted for.

Donald (1991) also relies on the idea of mental representation, and offers a three-stage story. The first stage saw the evolution in our hominid ancestors of a capacity for mimesis—the recollection and controlled reproduction of action patterns based on motor memories. The second stage takes the form of evolution of a capacity for lexical invention, which in turn provided the selective context for phonation. Finally, with the emergence of externalised representations, in the form of graphic images and other symbolic artefacts, the modern mind evolved, with its supposedly wide-ranging cognitive capacities. As one commentator (Chase 1993, 159) on a synopsis of Donald's text (Donald 1993) has noted, the archaeological record relied on for much of the story does not provide evidence of the inferred behaviours as clearly as Donald takes it to. Add to this the observation (Mills 1994) that 'Donald ... presents no convincing evidence (and in some cases no evidence at all) showing that particular brain structures or particular types of neurological functioning were correlated with his supposed stages.'

Chase closed his commentary on Donald's text (p.753) by remarking that, 'the meaning of archaeological data in psychological terms is either unclear or controversial or both. One reason is a lack of communication between archaeology and psychology.' Our enterprise is proof that such communication has begun to occur.

Some issues about 'minds', behaviours, consciousness and brains

Central to the 'modern mind' in Donald's account is a device he takes to be synonymous with 'consciousness', the executive mechanism for control and command of the rest of the cognitive system. Donald identifies this central executive (p.365) as a 'homunculus', a manikin or Tom Thumb, living inside the brain, who translates perceived signals into internal representations that can be understood, and gives orders for the carrying out of activity. The homunculus stands as the intentional agent running the mental enterprise.

The idleness of this notion can be shown by asking how the homunculus does what the person in whom it resides presumably cannot. As Palmer (1987, 61) remarks:

> It would indeed be an explanation of why I behave in the ways that I do, or of how I am able to do the things that I do, if it were discovered that inside my skull were a miniature genius who for purposes of his own moved my limbs around.

Such a creature must have a smaller homunculus inside its head and so on, like the big fleas that have little fleas, *ad infinitum,* forever postponing the problem of where consciousness resides.

The useful feature to appreciate about Donald's point is the recognition that consciousness entails intentionality (aboutness). Just as speaking is speaking *about* something, consciousness is consciousness *of* something. You cannot be conscious, as a human being, and not be aware *of* something. The position we develop in discussing 'mindedness' in Chapter 4 is that human consciousness *of* things is another way of describing human speech *about* things.

In developing that position we are aided by Toulmin's (1982) descriptive scheme, which distinguishes three levels of awareness: sensibility, attentiveness, and articulateness. The concept of consciousness can be applied at each level, as follows:

(1) Conscious sensibility is synonymous with awakeness (and unconsciousness with, for example, sleep). A conscious being at this level perceives environmental stimuli detected via its senses.

(2) Conscious attentiveness is a category Toulmin distinguishes from unconscious attentiveness, using the example of someone driving a car whilst being aware of what is unfolding before them, versus their being on 'automatic pilot'. We examine this particular contrast in detail in Chapter 5.

(3) Conscious articulateness Toulmin equates with fully self-conscious expression of, for example, thoughts, plans or intentions. (Unconscious articulateness is identified by Toulmin as something like activity that is 'unmotivated' yet able to be recollected and described).

Toulmin's scheme has elements in common with that of Edelman (1992), who distinguishes between 'primary consciousness' and 'higher-order consciousness'.

Primary consciousness is shared by many animate organisms, and hence is akin to conscious sensibility. Higher-order consciousness is consciousness in the human sense and involves something more than that routinely available to non-human animals. It has commonalities with Toulmin's categories of conscious attentiveness and articulateness. Certainly, Toulmin doubts that non-human animals, and human infants, can be more than '*un*consciously attentive' to surrounding events (Noble 1987). This may be seen as a statement on one side of a broader debate about the nature of non-human awareness, well summarised by Walker (1983). We identify absence of language as the feature that limits the consciousness of non-human animals to that of sensory sensitivity (conscious sensibility). Human mindedness is essentially marked by the conscious attentiveness and articulateness that language enables.

The core issue for this book is how that sort of mentality emerged in the course of human evolution, always given that what is being referred to here are particular forms of behaviour. These forms must have arisen at some time during the course of the evolutionary emergence of our species. But they are aspects of behaviour we share, in part, with other species (e.g. McGrew 1992) as is to be expected for characteristics which can only be argued to arise by evolutionary processes. We assume that a properly formulated evolutionary account outclasses any rival version of how humans and other living entities get to have the characteristics they do.

Cheney and Seyfarth (1990, 204–255), reviewed the data on attribution of mental states by other primates and found no conclusive evidence that apes or monkeys know *that* or *what* they know. Monkeys seem not to behave in ways that show they think other monkeys have states of mind. Apes, in Cheney and Seyfarth's judgement, do seem to assess the 'thinking' of another ape, but this can only be seen when one ape acts as if the other is thinking the same as them, which may not amount to much in the way of 'mindedness' at all. 'There is very little evidence that chimpanzees recognise a discrepancy between their own states of mind and the states of mind of others' (Cheney & Seyfarth 1990, 218). Human thinking and assessment of the minds of others may often seem no different from this, yet they are. As Cheney and Seyfarth (1990, 254–5) point out, much theatre involves the audience knowing that the character of the actor holds a false belief (as poignantly exemplified in the Romeo and Juliet story). Monkeys, and probably all apes, lack this ability to attribute to others a 'mental state' different from their own. 'Without such attribution there could be no tragedy or comedy, no irony and no paradox.' We will offer an account of how the attribution of mental states may best be understood, and in doing this will exemplify the assertion about apes and monkeys we have just made.

Most people will agree that dogs have perceptual experience (conscious sensibility); in the case of dogs there is rather surprisingly little more than fanciful anecdotes, as indulged in by Darwin (1981[1871], 46–48, 54) in his discussion of language origins, about what that perceptual experience might 'be like'. Because of a lack of documentation, and because of the lack of detachment engendered by the close relationship some people have with pets, it is rather difficult for anyone to judge what the perceptual experiences of these creatures might really be. Partly because of the 'social' engagement with this animal, such observers might even believe that their pet not only perceives, but also (contra Toulmin) knows what they perceive in a way akin to how the pet owner does.

On the other hand, there is outstanding documentation for vervet monkeys (Cheney & Seyfarth 1990) and a variety of ingenious observations of the abilities of chimpanzees (e.g. Boesch 1993) and bonobos (e.g. Savage-Rumbaugh & Rumbaugh 1993) which show abilities in our closer relatives which some take to blur the distinctions between human uniqueness and the abilities of other animals. The most remarkable successes in two-way communication with bonobos, and claimed as having features of language, have been achieved in a program which recognises language as 'the inevitable outcome of the social interaction of intelligent creatures' (Savage-Rumbaugh & Rumbaugh 1993, 106), where one of the partners in the social interaction is a native language user. We leave unanswered the question of how to determine whether and how a creature is 'intelligent'.

The view of language as an inevitable product of 'intelligent' interaction seems to run counter to the understanding that certain areas of the brain are specially related to speech production and perception (Falk 1992, 68–71). Loss of speech—aphasia—can result from a small lesion in what has become known as Broca's area in the fronto-temporal region of the left hemisphere of the brain (see Figure 1). The area is named after the Parisian surgeon and anthropologist, Paul Broca, who identified such a lesion in a patient who could only make one utterance. After the patient died, Broca dissected the man's brain and proposed a link between the loss of speech and what appeared to be a localised lesion.

People with 'Broca's aphasia' may often *understand* speech because the lesion is so localised. Lesion in another region can cause loss of speech comprehension, without grossly affecting speech production (Wernicke's aphasia). Subsequent research has led to similar claims for a mapping of specific functions to particular parts of the cerebral cortex. The status of these claims is open to question, as, indeed, is the idea that because features of speech production are associated with specific brain areas, it then follows that *language* is located in specific left hemisphere areas. Efron (1990) cites a range of evidence showing that equivalent right hemisphere areas, as well as areas beyond the fronto-temporal lobes, are implicated in production and comprehension of language (see also Lenneberg 1967, 61–2; Joanette et al. 1990). Deacon (1988) describes comparative studies of monkey and human brains which reveal widespread involvement, in equivalent (homologous) brain regions across the two species, in vocalising and related oral-laryngeal muscular control. He concludes (p.377): 'Although there is an immense discontinuity between linguistic and non-linguistic communication, there probably is no comparable dishomology of neural connectional organisation that underlies this difference.'

How might we reconcile the finding that there are nonetheless specific, even if widely distributed, areas of the brain implicated in the production and reception of speech, and which are broadly unvarying between individuals, with a view that

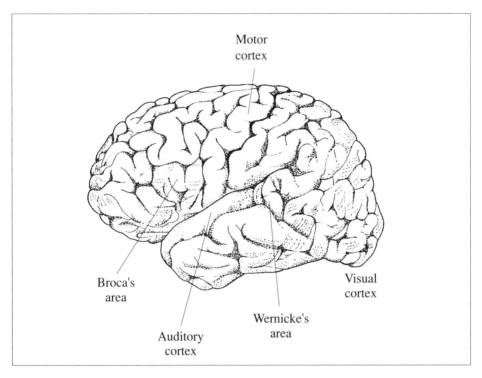

Motor
cortex

Broca's
area

Visual
cortex

Wernicke's
area

Auditory
cortex

Figure 1 Left hemisphere of a human brain showing Broca's and Wernicke's areas.

language is an outcome of social interaction? Edelman (1992, Chapter 9) has produced an argument that all such localised functions are the result of a process of natural selection operating on existing neuroanatomy in those particular locations, due to sensory inputs projected to them during ontogenetic development. Edelman referred to this process as somatic selection rather than the related but different scale process of evolutionary selection. His position seems to gain support from the observation that young children who suffer Broca's or Wernicke's aphasias can recover the functions of speech production or perception, presumably because other areas of the cortex are recruited to the functions previously performed in the damaged parts. This seems perfectly in accord with the claim by Savage-Rumbaugh and Rumbaugh (1993), given that language use in a social context will give equivalent sensory inputs to almost identical locations in the brains of all conspecific members of the social group. When such communication is cross-specific the situation is uncertain. Chimpanzees and bonobos do not have exactly the cortical regions corresponding to Broca's and Wernicke's areas, but do have homologous features.

A link between aspects of production and comprehension of vocalisations and areas in the left hemisphere of the brain is presumably what we would expect under a somatic selection model. Somatic selection would lead to localisation of relevant functions in similar cortical areas in other species even though they do not have the same form. Consistent with Deacon's conclusion, Galaburda and Pandya (1982) have shown that the connections between Broca's and Wernicke's areas in humans are matched by similar connections between the homologous parts of the brains of rhesus monkeys. Deacon's (1988) analysis of tracer and electrical stimulation studies showed that 'language functions have recruited cortical circuits which evolved for very different purposes'. He goes on to ask why, despite these similarities, monkeys and apes have such difficulty acquiring vocal skills and learning symbolic communications. We suspect this question is only raised because Deacon assumes that vocal skills and symbol-based communication abilities follow necessarily from the configuration of the brain. Our argument is that practices which happen to be unique to humans, and which we detail in the final chapters of this book, recruit the structures of the brain, rather than being determined by them. Such practices depend on prior structural evolution—bonobos cannot perform every behaviour common to humans. *Practices* interact with structures.

Most non-human animals communicate by many means, which include vocal utterances susceptible to analysis for their language-like properties. An early study of the vervet monkey calls suggested they had the characteristics of words (Seyfarth et al. 1980) but subsequent study reduced the scope of this interpretation (Cheney & Seyfarth 1990). Although the conclusion was that these communications fall short of language, there is no sign that they are not adequate to the survival of individual vervets. These animals' consciousness and their communications are part of what it is to be that animal.

There is agreement that the consciousness, the mental character, of our ancestors was probably transformed by the acquirement of language (e.g. Davidson & Noble 1989; Dennett 1991; Edelman 1992). The nature of that transformation is differently understood by different commentators; as is the problem of how the transformation occurred. A typical solution to the problem of 'how', takes the form of alterations in central nervous system circuitry, enabling connections previously unmade. One writer whose ideas are invoked in this context (Rozin 1976) has said that access is thus gained to the 'cognitive unconscious'. We note the absence of support for such a neuro-architectural solution in Deacon's statement quoted above. Nonetheless, subtle structural changes may be feasible which somehow bring about awareness of what is going on. But *what* is it that theorists take to occur?

For Jaynes (1977), 'consciousness' originates when a 'mental' voice, hitherto commanding the behaviour of some human being, is discovered to be one's own. For Dennett (1991), a fancied hominid practice of asking questions of and receiving answers from others, one day provokes a self-provided answer, and a new 'virtual' connection arises in the brain. For Burling (1993), utterance autonomously devised for addressing oneself, is spoken aloud (in Burling's case that event inaugurates social communication rather than 'consciousness'). We have already mentioned the schemes of Bickerton and Pinker. They at least include the idea that the business of getting the words together may not be straightforward. Notions such as Jaynes's or Dennett's could be mistaken for the very different point Vygotsky makes (e.g.,

1962[1934]; Wertsch 1985) about children's 'mentality' emerging in the form of self-addressed speech appropriated from their linguistic interactions in family and other social contexts, a matter we return to in Chapter 4. More to the point, in the accounts by Jaynes, Dennett or Burling, language has simply taken its place, homunculus-like, inside the human (or hominid) skull. 'Consciousness' is then 'awakened' when the rather 'matter-of-fact' activity of self-generated speaking gets connected to the rest of the mind or brain.

There is an unrecognised view informing all these stories, namely, that once there is a morphology approaching that of modern human beings, there just are functions, such as speaking (in what language?). We are actually no further, with these explanations, than the view of Chomsky that language is innate to human beings. Given *that* as 'solving' the matter of language origin, the real issue is taken to be something more mysterious still, namely, 'consciousness' itself. This makes the task look intriguing, but actually faces us with an impossibility. If the occurrence of language is taken for granted, the foundation issue has been stepped over and replaced with issues which are unfathomable. How is 'consciousness' to be conceived as separate from the linguistic activity that makes it manifest? Are we talking about some species of mystic spirituality or transcendent (godlike?) awareness?

Language

The process of evolutionary emergence of the phenomena of mind, language, and 'higher consciousness', can be considered in the light of the evidence of fossilised fragments of the skeletons of human ancestors, and in terms of the behavioural products of those ancestors. An increasing number of fossils document change of physical form which are subject to varying interpretation. At one level it would be convenient to assume that innateness rules, for then there is some hope that the material evidence of fossilised skeletons will indicate a cerebral or other skeletal rubicon which proves the emergence of language. This might be a change in the shape of the skull (inside or out) showing the production of language or thought in the brain; or it might be a change in the anatomy of the throat, showing the production of speech. But the argument we have been considering suggests that these are not likely to be useful lines of approach, since any animal will recruit whatever neuroanatomical *stuff* there is to the purposes it can achieve as an animal with that development and experience.

In the Savage-Rumbaugh model of language emergence the only problem that must be dealt with is how communications first became transformed into language. It is straightforward that modern human babies are born into families or other social groups where interaction is routinely conducted through spoken, signed or other language communication. One exception might seem to be provided in the context, reported on by Goldin-Meadow and Feldman (1977; Goldin-Meadow 1993), of children born deaf to hearing parents who are unwilling to have the children learn Sign. The contention is that the children construct their own gestural language as if language were innate to them. It is nonetheless the case that the caregivers of these children were engaging in some order of communication with them, and in the course of this interaction it is inevitable that gestural communication took place, from which the children could construct a set of 'home' signs (Fant 1972). All children thus have the opportunity for what Lock (1980) calls 'the guided reinvention of language'. The first appearance of language cannot, by definition, be any such reinvention. It must have occurred in another way.

There is a doctrine—'ontogeny recapitulates phylogeny'—discredited in its original formulation, by which it is understood that in the course of maturation to its own adult form, the maturing organism expresses the evolutionary history (phylogeny) of adult forms ancestral to it (Gould 1977). In the picture of language's evolution sketched so far, we have a clear case where ontogeny could not recapitulate phylogeny, where what happens in the development of the human child cannot be taken to give a picture of the evolution of capacities in adult creatures ancestral to that child. If the emergence of language for modern children depends on the presence of language users, the phylogenetic process has to be different. We cannot suppose that language-using offspring were born to non-language using parents under a model that language is reinvented from the guidance of the caregivers. There must have been an original *invention*, which has since gone on being guidedly reinvented. Moreover, the first inventors of language were primates and, as such, may be supposed uncontroversially to have been using vocal, gestural and other communications in their habitual interactions with their conspecifics.

Thus, the focus is on what happened when hominids first expressed themselves in ways of which they were aware. When we look at the assembly of elements introduced here to provide an understanding of this evolution, we see that the physical form of the ancestral skeleton may not have been so very important. Cranial capacity increased among our ancestors, hence presumably so did brain size, both absolutely and relative to body size, over the period from the time of the common ancestor between humans and chimpanzees and bonobos. Less is known about the changes in the skeleton of chimpanzees and bonobos since there are presently no skeletons or fossils from earlier than the seventeenth century, when Tyson (1699) dissected a chimpanzee to establish that this was not a human pygmy but a closely related animal.

We also know something about some of the changes in the shape of the inside of the cranium, from the time of the common ancestor, and there is good reason to suppose that this reflects some aspects of the shape of the brain (Falk 1992). One of the changes that occurred was the appearance of a shape which distinguishes humans from other primates in the region of Broca's area. Because of the association of that region with speech production, this is taken by some (Falk, for example 1987; Holloway, for example 1969; Tobias, for example 1988) as strong evidence that our ancestors 2 million years ago had language. We will argue (Chapter 6) that there is no other sign from this period of behaviour that would be expected to be associated with such a capacity.

What seems to be needed to argue for the timing of the earliest emergence of language is some sign in the archaeological record that our ancestors behaved in ways that allowed language reinvention among their infants or that could be expected to result from language use. Language reinvention, we suggest, requires a social context of learning (Chapters 2, 4 and 7); artefacts imbued with 'symbolic meaning', we suggest, result from language (Chapters 7 and 8). The next chapter introduces the empirical starting point for discussion of the evolutionary process of this feature of human behaviour. In it, we cover the relevant evidence from modern primates as a way of identifying the characteristics of the common ancestor of humans, chimpanzees and gorillas.

CHAPTER 2

THE COMMON ANCESTOR OF HUMANS AND OTHER APES

Once upon a time, there were no humans, gorillas or chimpanzees. All of these creatures, including the pygmy chimpanzee or bonobo, are descended from a single species of common ancestor of about between five and ten million years ago. This chapter discusses the nature of that common ancestor.

What are Primates?

The variation of organisms is not continuous but clumped in populations recognised by the natural tendency of individuals to interbreed with other members of the population and not to breed with members of other populations (see e.g. Mayr 1969). These reproductively isolated populations are called *species*. We will see in Chapter 6 that this definition causes some problems for our story, since we can never be certain of the interbreeding status of creatures identified to species only on the basis of fossils. Classification, even at the most basic level, has an element of hypothesis about it.

Zoologists use a hierarchy of groupings of species to show (hypotheses about) degrees of relatedness and patterns of evolutionary history. Humans are grouped together with a variety of other animals, most closely related to chimpanzees, bonobos and gorillas, but linked more remotely to monkeys, tarsiers, lorises and lemurs. This grouping of animals which share a common ancestor perhaps 80 million years ago (Martin 1990) is known as the Primates (a grouping zoologists call an order). Modern chimpanzees, bonobos, gorillas and humans are separate species, since in natural circumstances they do not interbreed with each other. But among these species, zoologists recognise that two of the animals are more closely related to each other than they are to either of the other two. They group chimpanzees and bonobos together into a single *genus* and give each species a name with two parts, the first for the genus and a second for the species within the genus. In this way, chimpanzees are in the genus *Pan* and the species *troglodytes*, and bonobos are *Pan paniscus*. The artificial nature of classification even at this simple level is illustrated by the fact that, although the majority of primatologists would call gorillas *Gorilla gorilla*, several authors (Groves 1970; 1989; Szalay & Delson 1979, 470; Tuttle 1986, 13) have suggested they should be in the genus *Pan*. Humans are in the genus *Homo* and the species *sapiens*.

The use of genetic evidence to reconstruct evolutionary relationships through the analysis of blood groups or DNA sequences allows many different accounts about the closeness of relationship (Martin 1990, Chapter 11), so that it is difficult to decide upon appropriate levels of naming beyond the genus. We, therefore, prefer a classification which allows the easy telling of the story, such as that in Figure 2, which shows evolutionary relationships among the group of creatures collectively known as Anthropoids (Anthropoidea in zoological nomenclature, a suborder within the order of Primates in the zoological systematic hierarchy). This suborder includes the monkeys of Old World (in the superfamily of Cercopithecoids [Cercopithecoidea]) and New World (in the superfamily of Ceboids [Ceboidea]), together with the apes (in the superfamily of Hominoids [Hominoidea]). Within the Hominoids, there are three families: the several species of gibbon in the family of Hylobatids (Hylobatidae), also known as lesser apes; the great apes in the family of Pongids (Pongidae), which includes the orang-utan (*Pongo pygmaeus*) with the African apes; and humans and their ancestors in the family of Hominids. So all Hominids and Pongids are also Hominoids. They are also Anthropoids and Primates, depending on the degree of generalisation needed. This classification is taken from Quiatt and Reynolds (1993) who follow Martin (1990). We recognise that Groves (1989) would group them differently (and call what we call Hominids

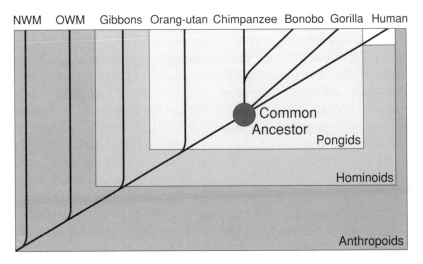

Figure 2 Tree of relationships among Anthropoids (NWM = New World Monkeys; OWM = Old World Monkeys) indicating position of the Common Ancestor.

'Hominins') but our classification is by no means eccentric. We modify it slightly in the light of a decision about appropriate naming, and reserve the name hominid for those members of the Hominids for which we have no general agreement that they were human (as we defined them in Chapter 1). It is not usual or convenient to call humans apes, though in this classification it would be correct.

This figure also represents an approximation to the likely evolutionary relationships of descent for these interrelated creatures. Most of the relationships are not of primary concern for our argument, but in order to show the context of the more recent events in human evolution, we give an approximate time-scale in Table 1.

There was a common ancestor of African pongids, hominids and humans. Some of the descendants of the common ancestor are modern humans, others are modern chimpanzees, bonobos and gorillas. Other descendants were the fossil hominids, ancestors of human beings, which we will consider in Chapter 6. The evolutionary emergence of humans, chimpanzees, bonobos, and gorillas involved a series of changes from the nature of the common ancestor. In investigating these changes, to understand how modern humans became as we are or how modern chimpanzees or gorillas became as they are, we might reasonably ask what the common ancestor was like. For the ancestors of humans we can answer the question by reference to fossilised parts of the skeleton from different periods after 4.5 million years ago (WoldeGabriel et al. 1994), and to the archaeological evidence of the products of their behaviour after about 2 million years ago. There are no fossil remains of the common ancestor (Wood 1994). There are also no fossils that can be attributed to creatures ancestral to gorillas, chimpanzees or bonobos (Szalay & Delson 1979, 469–470), nor archaeological traces of their behaviour. As a result, assessment of the nature of the common ancestor derived initially from comparative anatomy of modern animals, a process which formed an important part of the acceptance of the evidence of evolution through the lectures of Thomas Huxley (1906). More recently the interpretation has been refined as a result of genetic studies (Rogers 1993) of modern animals and humans.

Rogers (1993) summarises the genetic evidence from sequencing of nuclear or mitochondrial DNA and from other genetic studies. Five of the sequencing and three of the other studies show that chimpanzees are more closely related to humans than they are to gorillas, while two of the sequencing studies and two others show a closer relationship between chimpanzees and gorillas. One study shows humans most closely related to gorillas, and three sequencing studies and one other cannot separate the three sorts of animal. Rogers analysed the theoretical models for interpreting these results and concluded that the most likely hypothesis was that the divergence from a common ancestor took place relatively rapidly, probably over a period substantially less than 0.5 million years. For most of this period, Rogers (1993, 212) suggests, 'it is unlikely that the last common ancestor of humans and chimpanzees was a different species and hence fully isolated reproductively from the contemporaneous ancestor of gorillas'. Although this matter is still currently controversial (Goodman et al. 1994; Marks 1994; Rogers 1994; Ruvolo 1994),

Time	Geology	Ceboids	Cerco-pithecoids	Hominoids	Hylobatids	Pongids	Hominids
40 Myr	EOCENE						
		Fossils					
	OLIGOCENE						
35 Myr							
			Fossils				
30 Myr							
25 Myr							
	MIOCENE						
20 Myr							
				Fossils			
					?Fossil?		
15 Myr						Fossils (Pongo)	
10 Myr					Fossils		
						Common ancestor	
5 Myr	PLIOCENE						Fossils
	PLEISTOCENE						
1 Myr							
NOW	HOLOCENE						Humans

Table 1 Timescale of the last 40 million years of primate evolution.

Coruccini (1992) has shown that the three-way split is the best interpretation from the statistical analysis of these data. Similar data suggest that the bonobo and the common chimpanzee separated after the three-way split from the hominids and gorillas (Zihlman et al. 1978). From such studies, it is possible to construct not only a picture of evolutionary relationships among the African and other apes, but to make some statements about the behaviour of the common ancestor. This picture differs from that obtained by accepting an earlier separation of gorillas, and making comparison among humans, chimpanzees and bonobos (Cameron 1993).

Evidence from comparisons with chimpanzees, gorillas, and other primates

Mostly we can define what the common ancestor was not. Because it was a common ancestor of humans, chimpanzees and gorillas, we suspect that it was restricted in its distribution to Africa; was not bipedal; had a small brain; probably did not have a large meat component of its diet, and probably did not prey on vertebrates; did not make or use tools to any great extent, particularly not those requiring planning such as building shelters or making fire. We know nothing of its vocal or other communications, but we may be reasonably sure that it did not use signs as symbols. The next section deals with how we infer this set of negatives from the evidence of modern humans and other primates. We leave until Chapters 6 and 7 the story of the emergence of human characteristics in the course of the evolutionary emergence of humans: bipedalism; large brain size; dietary change and hunting; tool use, including shelter construction and the control and use of fire; distribution beyond Africa; language and other uses of symbols.

Distribution

Having established what the closest genetic relationships are among these primate species, we can repeat the process Huxley and Darwin applied to comparative anatomy and look at their geographical distribution to infer the likely distribution of the common ancestor. The modern distribution is summarised in Figure 3. For all species, modern distribution is undoubtedly restricted by competition with modern humans.

The lesser apes, the 5 to 7 kg gibbons (*Hylobates* spp.) and the 11 kg siamang (*Hylobates syndactylus*), live in the trees of the tropical rainforests of mainland and island Southeast Asia. There is little difference in weight between males and females, though males have rather larger canine teeth (Martin 1990, 31–32). Some isolated finds of fossil teeth suggest a slightly wider distribution in the past (Szalay & Delson 1979, 462–466), but the lesser apes were always confined to Asia, although there is a rather gibbon-like fossil, *Dryopithecus*, from Europe (Groves 1989).

Orang-utans, (*Pongo pygmaeus*), are now confined to the rainforests of Sumatra and Borneo, and are also primarily arboreal. Unlike the lesser apes, there is a marked difference in weight between males and females. With males sometimes reaching 70 kg and females 37 kg, they are the heaviest of all mammals living primarily in trees (Martin 1990, 32–33). Fossil teeth are known from the early Pleistocene onwards, and show a wider distribution into mainland Southeast Asia as far as central China, which became restricted into Indochina between 25 000 and 10 000 years ago, and subsequently to Sumatra and Borneo (Szalay & Delson 1979, 469).

Gorillas (*Gorilla gorilla*) live in two main populations in the rainforests of central Africa: a lowland population in an area north of the Zaire River, and a mountain population, further inland, in the mountains west of Lake Victoria (Schaller 1963, 25–36). Gorillas are primarily terrestrial in habit, and their body size is great, and greatly different between the sexes. Adult males have average body weights of 140–160 kg depending on the population, and females have weights of 70–100 kg (Tuttle 1986, 19). There are no fossil remains attributed to gorilla (Szalay & Delson 1979, 470), but Schaller (1963, 27–30) suggests that there must have been a continuous distribution between the two populations at some time in the past. These distributions are shown on the map of Africa in Figure 4.

Bonobos, (*Pan paniscus*), also known as pygmy chimpanzees, are distributed between the two main gorilla populations in the humid rainforests of Zaire (Kano 1979). The habitat is very heavily forested and bonobos are described as the 'most forest adapted of the African apes' (Susman 1987, 78). Average female body weight is 30 kg and average male body weight is 40 kg (Tuttle 1986, 17). There are no fossil remains attributed to bonobos (Szalay & Delson 1979, 470).

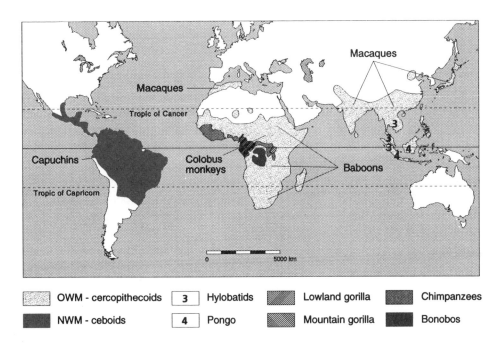

Figure 3 World wide distribution of primates shown in Figure 2.

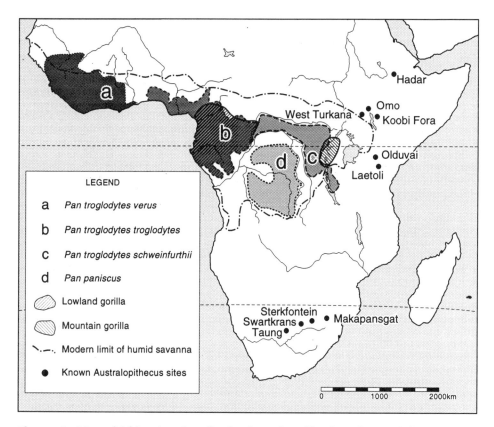

Figure 4 Map of Africa showing distribution of gorillas, bonobos and chimpanzees in relation to tropical forests and the distribution of finds of the earliest ancestors of humans.

Chimpanzees, (*Pan troglodytes*), are the best known of all the apes (see McGrew 1992, 15–39 for summary of detailed studies). Their distribution is wider than that of other African apes and the range of occupied habitats is greater. The best documented are those from the Gombe National Park in Tanzania, studied by Jane Goodall (1986), near the southern extreme of the range of distribution of chimpanzees. Many other sites are, like Gombe, on the eastern side of the western Rift Valley of equatorial Africa, but there are populations, with some sub-specific variations in anatomy and weight, near the Atlantic Ocean from Cabinda, north of the Zaire River, to Senegal. Their whole range covers more than 5000 km southeast from Senegal (McGrew 1992, 15). Habitats 'range from rain and montane forests to dry woodlands, and sometimes even savanna with widely scattered trees' (Goodall 1986, 44). Average male weight is 39–43 kg while average female weight is 30–34 kg (Tuttle 1986, 16). There are no fossil remains of chimpanzees or their ancestors (Szalay & Delson 1979, 470).

From this evidence, we might conclude, as Darwin did, that the common ancestor should have lived in Africa, and that the primitive condition for the ancestral great ape is to live in tropical forests, since all seem well able to survive there, whatever the effect of competition with humans. There is some sign of a derived condition shared by chimpanzees and humans (but not by gorillas) for living in the savanna. On this basis, the common ancestor of hominids and chimpanzees might have lived on the edge of the tropical forests in Africa.

Locomotion

Apes show adaptations to movement in forested environments. Gibbons and siamangs are, however, the only true brachiators among them (Martin 1990, 32, 489–490), with a pattern of movement through the trees by swinging from branch to branch with their arms only, and having a period of movement without contact with the tree. At other times they walk bipedally on branches or the ground, with their hands, despite the great length of their arms, held off the ground (Tuttle 1986, 36–40).

Orang-utans are also arboreal for most of their movement, though not in the manner of the gibbon and siamang. Rather, while in the trees, an orang-utan supports its massive body weight with any or all of its four limbs (Tuttle 1986, 40–43), and has a freedom of movement of the hind-limbs almost as great as that of the arms. When walking on the ground orang-utans are ungainly, folding their long fingers and toes under and placing the sides of their hands and feet on the ground (Schwartz 1987, 7–8).

If movement in trees is a problem for orang-utans due to their large body size, it is even more so for gorillas. Where orang-utans evolved specialised anatomy for moving in trees, mountain gorillas spend most of their time on the ground (Tuttle 1986, 48), a behavioural rather than an anatomical adaptation. Movement into trees for feeding, nesting and resting is rare and cautious, apparently with some reason, as they have been seen to fall or to attempt to walk on branches which do not support their weight (Schaller 1963, 81–85). Lowland gorillas, with more trees available, spend more time in them. Schaller prefers to call the pattern of locomotion in trees 'quadrupedal climbing'. The usual pattern of movement is quadrupedal and terrestrial, in a distinctive pattern known as knuckle-walking, in which the hands are formed into fists and the weight is borne on the middle bones of all the fingers. Bipedal walking or running is rare and limited to short distances (Schaller 1963, 82–83).

Bonobos are very versatile in their locomotion, being able to travel up to a kilometre in the trees, by any combination of using feet and hands to hold while climbing (quadrumanous climbing), quadrupedal walking, armswinging or bipedal walking (Tuttle 1986, 46–48). Knuckle-walking, as with the gorillas, is the usual means of movement on the ground (Doran 1993). They are rather more arboreal than chimpanzees (Doran 1993), and male bonobos hang with their arms more frequently than male chimpanzees. In captivity, bonobos are much more bipedal than common chimpanzees (Savage-Rumbaugh personal communication).

Chimpanzees are quite commonly terrestrial and use knuckle-walking, though younger chimpanzees move freely in the trees. Doran (1993) recorded that all but one episode of travel between feeding sites was terrestrial. They are commonly said to use bipedal stances for walking or standing (Hunt 1993), though the quantitative data on this have been rare (Tuttle 1986, 43–46). The subject is not even discussed, for example, by Goodall (1986). McGrew (1992, 41) points out that emphasis on bipedalism in apes may be misleading: 'apes rarely go bipedal ... Wild chimpanzees being artificially fed go bipedal to carry away their booty, but they rarely show upright locomotion at other times.'

On this evidence, it seems unlikely that the common ancestor was bipedal for anything more than occasional walking in trees and rare movements on the ground. The extent of movement or any other activity on the ground is more open to discussion. It might be tempting on this evidence to argue that the ancestral condition was terrestrial as in gorillas, chimpanzees and humans, with bonobo arboreality a derived condition. Against this is the arboreality of the Asian apes. If the common ancestor was arboreal for 80% of the time, then the extent of terrestrial movement of gorillas, chimpanzees and humans is something that has emerged during the course of evolution from the common ancestor for all three classes of animals.

But the behavioural labels mask much detail, of the anatomy of the foot (Gebo 1992) and in the movement of the centres of mass (Tardieu et al. 1993). Chimpanzees appear to have transferred to the ground the movement patterns of walking on branches; humans have a distinctive symmetry of movement when walking on the ground (Tardieu et al. 1993). Thus, we may conclude that the common ancestor had some bipedal activity, albeit distinct from that of humans, but it generally used all four limbs for locomotion.

What the common ancestor did with its hands in locomotion is more difficult to determine. On the basis of the sort of argument used here, the common ancestor was probably a knuckle-walker, although the absence of fossils of ancestral apes leaves us uninformed (see for example Begun 1993; Shea & Inouye 1993). It might be argued that, because gibbons and orang-utans do not knuckle-walk, this behaviour is a more recently derived feature of the African apes. But the forelimbs of gibbons and orang-utans are so specialised (e.g. Martin 1990, 489–491) that they may be irrelevant to understanding the common ancestor of apes and humans.

Brain size

Thus far we have considered features of modern apes as if they were discrete characteristics, despite the fact that there is some variation in them. When we turn to consider the brain, the most complex organ of the body, the problem of variation is more acute, since the variation is continuous in a huge number of features. Martin (1990, Chapter 8) has summarised the evidence from comparative anatomy of primates. Since our procedure here is to contrast what can be said from the study of modern animals with what can be said from the study of prehistoric evidence, we are limited in the range of features we can use. Here we will concentrate only on cranial capacity, which has a close relationship with brain size (see for example, Martin 1990, 365), because it is often measurable in fossil specimens.

We have chosen not to consider subdivisions of the brain as these are not directly observable for fossil specimens and the fossils cannot be contrasted with the evidence from modern animals. Various authors (e.g. Dunbar 1993) have considered the importance of the volume of one of the regions of the brain, the neocortex, in accounting for the variation of behaviour of primates. Sawaguchi (1992) showed that the relative size of the neocortex is significantly related to diet, social structure and group size. But given that relative size of neocortex has varied during the course of evolution, it would be adventurous to estimate it for past species without reference to the fossil record. It can never be measured directly for prehistoric specimens, so it is of little value for making inferences about the process of human evolution. The relative size of different parts of the brain may be an unreliable guide to the relationships among the various species of primates. Bauchot (1982) calculated the distances between different primate species when volumes of brain components (weighted for body mass) were compared. This showed that gorillas and chimpanzees were closer to monkeys than to humans, and that humans were closest to two species of New World monkeys in the genus *Cebus*, and to the Old World monkey, *Cercopithecus talapoin*. The pattern of evolution of the different regions of the brain is not simple.

The problem here is that which applies to any specific region of the cortex of the brain: their positions are difficult to specify for fossils, and, as the discussion (in Chapter 1) of Broca's and Wernicke's areas showed, the identification of such regions may be an unreliable guide to the functions with which they are associated. Perhaps the most that can be said is that the human brain appears to be more convoluted than that of other primates. Richman and colleagues (Richman et al. 1975) showed that much of the form of the convolutions is predictable from an understanding of the deformation of solids subject to differences of internal microstructure. That being so, some of the shapes said to have particular meaning in an understanding of brain function may be little more than the result of changes due to the expansion of the brain in relation to changes in the size of the cranium. Considering data from 48 species of mammals (not just primates), Jerison (1982) showed how, as brain size increases, the surface area of the brain increases beyond that expected if the successive brains were just larger versions of a single three-dimensional shape. The increase resulted from the production of sulci or gyri (see Figure 1, Chapter 1) which are seen on the distinctive convoluted surface of the brain.

Significantly, the human brain can be seen in this analysis as one among many: it does not have the greatest length of gyri either absolutely or in relation to brain volume, and does not have the largest brain volume. The extent of gyrification is very precisely determined by brain volume alone. Neither theoretically nor empirically do these features of the brain explain a uniqueness such as human language. Jerison (1982) goes further: 'Functional interpretation of *new* gyri such as a third frontal convolution (Broca's area), may, in fact carry no more information than interpretations in terms of cerebral rubicons that are based on brain sizes.' Recent analysis by Armstrong and colleagues (1993) has demonstrated that it is most plausible that cortical reorganisation went in step with brain expansion and did not precede it. This seems to imply that the functions now associated with particular cortical regions in humans were not originally as salient as they are now. In other words, the cortical reorganisation is exaptive (Gould 1991; Gould & Vrba 1982)— structures emerged before the functions they now seem dedicated to.

Much attention has been paid to the indicators of the organisation of the brain which might also be identifiable in fossils. In particular, several scholars have looked at the asymmetry between the left and right hemispheres of the brain or as inferred from endocasts of the interior of the skull, which tends to preserve some of the surface morphology of the brain. Bradshaw and Rogers (1993) have recently reviewed the published evidence. This suggests that asymmetry is a very wide-spread phenomenon, occurring to some degree in many vertebrates, including animals as distant from humans as chickens and frogs. Essentially the differences among the apes and humans are ones of degree. In humans, the right hemisphere is longer at the front and the left hemisphere longer at the back, also the pattern in chimpanzees and gorillas, but not in orang-utans. From this evidence, we might conclude that the common ancestor would have had this pattern. Human brains are wider at the back, a feature not seen in any other primate, but visible in the endocasts of fossil hominids. Bradshaw and Rogers (1993) suggest this may relate to right-handedness, a feature common in humans, but not among the great apes, although the data are so poor that this is still a matter for current research (Marchant & McGrew 1991). The handedness issue becomes involved in the question of language origins as Broca's and Wernicke's areas, closely associated with language reception and production, are located in the left hemisphere in most adult humans. Nevertheless, the widespread nature of cerebral asymmetry suggests that handedness may be a phenomenon associated with but not resulting from it. This is plausible given that chimpanzee and gorilla brains have lateral asymmetry, with little evidence for population bias in handedness as there is in humans (Byrne & Byrne 1991; McGrew & Marchant 1992). It is more appropriate to discuss handedness when we consider the archaeological evidence for its possible emergence in Chapter 6. We therefore limit this discussion to cranial capacity.

Figure 5 shows body weights and cranial capacity for selected Old World monkeys, the apes and humans. These average figures mask the observed variation. Nevertheless, there is some pattern of increase of cranial capacity with body size. Intuitively we expect that the brain of an elephant is larger than the brain of a mouse, whatever the ranges of functions of those brains.

Even so, the pattern is complicated. There appears to be a predictable relationship between body weights for this sample of Old World monkeys, gibbon, chimpanzee and orang-utan, but the gorilla data show exceptionally high body weight for its cranial capacity while humans have very high cranial capacity for their body weight.

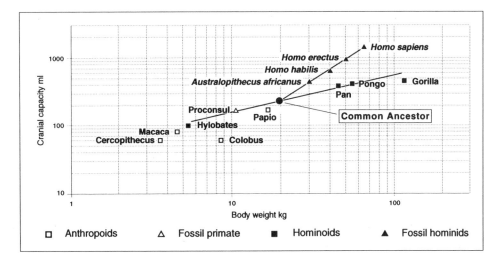

Figure 5 Body size and cranial capacity of primates and fossil hominids.

In line with the type of reasoning we have been engaged in, we suggest that the large body size of the gorilla is derived relative to the common ancestor, as is large cranial capacity for humans.

Through the course of hominid evolution of our ancestors, there was a tendency for increase in cranial capacity which allows us to estimate the brain and body sizes of the common ancestor. Figure 5 shows the regression lines for the brain size and body weight of modern primates (excluding humans) and for the averaged values for fossil hominids (taken from Martin 1990). These lines cross at values for body weight of approximately 19 kg and cranial capacity of approximately 210 ml, suggesting a creature a little larger in both dimensions than an olive baboon (*Papio anubis*). Given that there were changes in cranial capacity of all primates over this period, not just in human ancestors, this is likely an overestimate. We may take these as plausible upper limit estimates of the characteristics of the common ancestor.

Jerison (1973) explored the relation between brain size and body weight exhaustively, and constructed a measure he called Encephalisation Quotient (EQ) to describe the size of the brain of any particular species when compared with a typical mammal of the same body size. Various other measures have been devised which depend on different interpretations of essentially similar graphs of these two variables (see e.g. Martin 1990). It is convenient to retain Jerison's original calculation, in which Old World monkeys and apes have EQ of between 2.3 and 2.7, with leaf-eating species, colobus monkeys (EQ 1.2) and gorillas (EQ 1.6), much lower.

Using our estimates of the brain and body size of the common ancestor, the EQ would have been 2.5, about the same as a modern chimpanzee. This should give us pause before paying undue attention to the absolute or relative size of the brain (or its substitute, cranial capacity). The South America monkey, *Cebus apella*, the tufted capuchin, the most frequent tool-user of the monkeys (e.g. Gibson 1990; Visalberghi 1993; Westergaard & Suomi 1994) has been tested for its ability to learn by imitation (Visalberghi & Fragaszy 1990) and found to be less able than chimpanzees, bonobos and orang-utans (Visalberghi et al. n.d.). Further analysis of its performance suggested that, unlike the other animals, the capuchin failed to comprehend the way the experiment worked sufficiently to perform it adequately. Whatever the reasons for the lack of comprehension or performance, it seems unlikely to be attributable to the relative brain size as measured by the Encephalisation Quotient of 3.5, significantly above that of apes with which it was being compared. The closely related species *Cebus albifrons* has an even higher EQ of 4.8 (Jerison 1973, 392). Brain size, absolute or relative, does not seem to be a reliable or sufficient indicator of the sorts of abilities that might, in evolutionary terms, have led to the emergence of distinctively human behaviour.

Diet

The human brain, in waking or sleep states, is the most energy demanding organ of the body. It is estimated that, at 2% of body weight, it accounts for 20% of energy expenditure compared with 9% for macaques or chimpanzees and 3% for elephants (Hofman 1983; Sokoloff 1981). Foley and Lee (1991) argue that the change in cranial capacity during the course of the evolution of hominids and humans from the common ancestor required dietary and developmental strategies which would sustain the extra cost of a large brain. Moreover, Clutton-Brock and Harvey (1980) have shown that comparative brain size is strongly related to diet, folivores (leaf-eaters) having smaller brains, with proportionately less neocortex (Sawaguchi 1992), for their body size than frugivores (fruit-eaters). It is appropriate, therefore, to consider observations of diet among the primates to attempt to assess that of the common ancestor.

Leaves constitute the primary source of protein for most primates, and fruits provide easily digested carbohydrates, rich in energy (Waterman 1984). In addition, the standard view is that the original primates were probably insectivores (Cartmill 1974; Szalay 1975), so that it is no surprise that many apes and monkeys frequently include insects and other arthropods in their diets. These provide complementary amino-acid intake and lipids (Hladik 1977; Waterman 1984).

There are many difficulties in studying diet in free-living primates. In particular, there are problems of comparing diets of animals in habitats characterised by different food species; problems of identifying the relative importance of different dietary items; problems of dealing with individual and inter-population and inter-seasonal variation; and problems of converting the observations of feeding into data about nutrition. As with humans, so for the chimpanzees of Gombe, the problem is even more difficult: there are too many data. Since 1970 all animals at Gombe, followed for whatever purpose, have also had notes taken about the food eaten and the length of time spent feeding. Summarising that quantity of data in a few simple statistics cannot do justice to the variation observed. This is not the place to deal with these difficulties, and we will confine ourselves to the most general summaries of the issues.

To compare diets, we use data from Tuttle (1986, 55–113) (mostly percentages of time spent feeding on particular categories). We simplify these (already simplified) data in Figure 6 which shows the percentages of fruits, meat and other foods in the diet. The other foods are mostly leaves, but may include about 10% of bark or roots. The difficulty of the interpretation of these data is shown by the two points joined by a line. These are different observations of the same events: time spent feeding; and weight of food ingested. The major difference between the two ways of representing diet is the change in the relative importance of fruits and insects. Only 14.4% of the time was spent collecting fruits, and 36.8% on insects. But in terms of food ingested, 62.6% was fruit and only 4.1% insects. Given the small package size of all insects, it is likely that some adjustment of relative frequencies is quite generally necessary. Other data are obtained from faeces (Tutin et al. 1991), with all the problems of identifying completely or incompletely digested foods. Faeces provide a further indication of the uncertainties, particularly surrounding the eating of meat: McGrew (1992, 32–3) reported finding chimpanzee faeces with whole undigested bush baby limbs. The frenzied nature of chimpanzee meat eating might well prevent the digestion of some of the ingested meat.

Gorilla diet is not easily characterised. In the Virunga mountains they are specialised for leaf eating, with negligible amounts of fruit or meat (including insects) in their diet (Fossey & Harcourt 1977). In the lowland gorilla, overall diet is less dominated by leaves, although in bad fruit seasons they survive almost

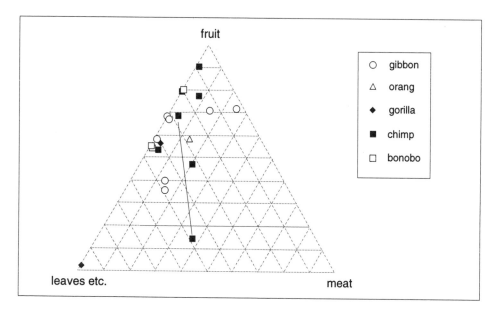

Figure 6 Graphic representation of the relative compositions of diet of the five main groups of apes.

exclusively on leaf diets, while the chimpanzees living in the same forest continue to seek fruits (Tutin et al. 1991). For gorillas, obtaining nutrition from leaves is promoted by abundant intestinal flora and fauna specialised at digesting cellulose.

Separation among the other groups is more difficult. All seem to combine fruits and leaves in their diets, with occasional studies showing substantial intake of insects or mammal protein. Figure 6 emphasises that most of the gibbons tend to combine more leaf eating with their fruit diet, and chimpanzees less. Orang-utans span the range of chimpanzees in the middle of the range for fruit. Bonobos, similarly, span the range, but some have a rather higher fruit component. The graph cell with 50–60% fruit, 40–50% leaves and 0–10% meat (including insects) shows one study for each of the apes being considered here. This strongly suggests that the common ancestor probably combined fruit and leaves in its diet, and that the extreme leaf-eating strategy of gorillas is a relatively recently acquired behaviour.

Several studies show that there is a close relationship between diet and gut morphology for any given body size (e.g. Chivers & Hladik 1984; Clutton-Brock & Harvey 1980; Martin 1990). While the guts of apes are adapted to leaf-eating (gorillas) or fruit-eating (chimpanzees and the Asian apes), human guts seem well adapted to meat-eating or, at least, high energy diets. In this, humans are like the South American monkey, *Cebus*, which we have already seen has the highest encephalisation of non-human primates. It seems the high energy costs of large brains and changes in diet should be considered together.

Clutton-Brock and Harvey (1980) showed a significant independent relationship between their measure of Comparative Brain Size and home range size, a result *not* echoed in the study of relative size of neocortex. Clutton-Brock and Harvey related these two significant correlations to the possibility that folivores may not require such extensive memory for the efficient exploitation of their food sources. The general pattern for small-bodied animals in a single order is a requirement for high energy foods which are often clumped in space (Jarman 1974). As they must range widely to encounter these clumps, natural selection should favour those better able to find their way back to locations of high energy food. If this is a reliable rule, it should apply within other orders (such as the orders of bovids, or primates): the smallest species within an order should be those for which high encephalisation is most advantageous, if remembering how to reach resource locations is enhanced by encephalisation. But Byrne (1994) has pointed out that:

> Even in animals with simple stomachs, eating mature leaves requires a large gut for efficient fermentation, and hence a large body to support it; but since mature leaves are relatively abundant in most primate habitats, only a small range is needed. By contrast, frugivory requires a larger range area for year-round access to a variety of fruit species, but the high sugar content allows digestion by a shorter gut, and thus smaller body size.

On this argument, the relatively low encephalisation (EQ) of gorillas (and colobus monkeys) reflects a comparatively large body size to support a big gut for processing large quantities of leaves. At the very least, this argument demonstrates the systemic relationship among many factors, including brain size. We disagree with Gibson's (1986) argument that brain size increases independently and thus permits a range of new abilities, including the exploitation of new niches.

Chimpanzees' consumption of invertebrates, mostly termites or ants, has been characterised as a staple of their diet (McGrew 1992, 155), in contrast to gorillas which seem to consume them only in tiny amounts (Fossey's 1983; Fossey & Harcourt 1977; Tutin et al. 1991; Watts 1989). It is 'insectivory' that has stimulated the most involvement with tools by chimpanzees, different populations using sticks or grass stems to fish or dip for termites or ants. Orang-utans and gibbons, however, eat varying quantities of invertebrates without recourse to tools (with rare exceptions, Lesley Rogers personal communication). The common ancestor seems likely to have been an eater of insects or other invertebrates, probably without the assistance of tools. Chimpanzee tool-use seems likely to have been an independent invention.

There are several recent studies of the eating of meat from vertebrates among chimpanzees (e.g. Boesch & Boesch 1989; Chivers & Hladik 1984; McGrew 1992; Oates 1986; Stanford et al. 1994; Teleki 1973; Tutin et al. 1991; Wrangham 1977; Wrangham & Riss 1990). Gorillas (Goodall 1977; Schaller 1963; Tutin et al. 1991) and orang-utans (Rodman 1977) do not seem to consume vertebrates in the wild, although there is one reference to orang-utan meat eating (Sugarjito & Nuhuda 1981), in which a female ate an infant gibbon; her male companion showing no interest in the activity. On this basis, unless there are more reports of meat-eating among orang-utans, the eating of meat by both humans and chimpanzees may be a relatively recent adaptation. This is in keeping with the eating of vertebrates (or their eggs) among other primates. Although about one third of all primates for which there are adequate records consume parts of animals (Harding 1981), the relative importance is very variable, and the distribution by type of animal is inconsistent. It would be difficult to infer anything other than that these behaviours have no consistent evolutionary pattern. The high incidence of predation among some baboons (Strum 1981) suggests that in appropriate circumstances many primates may acquire the habit of pursuing and killing vertebrates. It would seem, on this basis, that both chimpanzees and baboons are best considered to provide analogies for hominid meat-eating rather than having a shared evolutionary background.

When we turn to the means of acquiring food, there are problems of definition. Words get attached to behaviours or events in such a way as to determine how the facts are viewed. We will encounter this widespread tendency when talking about the evolution of hominid and human behaviour and whether Neanderthals 'buried' their dead (Chapter 7). The problem comes to have political importance when hunter-gatherers are said to 'roam' the country, as if they had not sufficient purpose or understanding of their land to be allowed the right to keep it. In talking about diet, we encounter this problem of association in many ways, none more potent than in talking about 'hunting'. It would be vain to try to stem the tide of common usage that chimpanzees 'hunt', Neanderthals 'buried' and fisher-gatherer-hunters 'roam', but we may wish to be more specific about what the behaviours thus identified really constituted.

Goodall (1986) suggests that 'The hunting, killing, and eating of medium-sized mammals is probably a characteristic behavior of chimpanzees throughout their range', and she documents more than 20 prey species in seven different study areas. At Gombe, she documents, during 22 years of observations (over 246 months) the catching and/or eating of 221 colobus monkeys, and 194 other animals, an average of just less than one colobus and one other per month (Goodall does not state how many individual chimpanzees were involved, but the Gombe community is usually described as between 40 and 50 individuals). These predations had marked effect on colobus numbers in the Gombe region (cf. Wrangham 1977; Stanford et al 1994). More recent data (from 1982–1991) show that patterns of predation vary between study periods, study populations, individuals, ages, sexes, and seasons (Stanford et al 1994). In these studies, individual chimpanzees were followed for nearly 14 000 hours, and killed a colobus monkey every 40 hours—a much higher rate.

Goodall (1986, 270–312) observes that 'To some extent all hunting may be opportunistic and happen only after the sighting of suitable prey', though this may involve long pursuit. The exact circumstances of the initiation of actions to obtain a prey animal are obscure because, unlike human hunters, the chimpanzees cannot tell us anything about their motives. Predation on baboons reached a peak at Gombe during the years when provisioning was being used as a means of increasing the opportunities for observation. Wrangham (1974) and Teleki (1973, 108) suggested that this created more opportunities for chimpanzees to predate on baboons. But sighting does not seem to be a sufficient stimulus to predation either on baboons or on colobus monkeys. This is even more clearly demonstrated in the cases of infanticide, cannibalism and inter-community violence (Goodall 1986,. 283–4, 313–57, 503–34). Teleki (1973) suggests that hunger was not a sufficient explanation of predatory events either.

There seems to be no sign that chimpanzees seek out prey which is not visible to them, such as by the use of visual cues (e.g. tracks) of the earlier presence of an animal. Vervet monkeys, for example, similarly show no sign of recognition of the significance of tracks of pythons (Cheney & Seyfarth 1990, 285–6). But lack of reports may not be a reliable guide to reality. Christophe Boesch (personal communication) has spoken of such tracking, but not published his observations. It would in any case be difficult to distinguish between animals following visual cues and those relying on the invisible, olfactory cues that might also accompany the track.

The question arises about the strategies used in hunting, in particular whether chimpanzees cooperate in the hunt. This is certainly the view of Teleki (1973). Busse (1978) showed that success at killing by any individual chimpanzee *decreases* as group size increases, but more recent studies at Gombe (Stanford et al. 1994) as well as Taï (Boesch 1994) reverse this conclusion. Goodall (1986, 285) suggests that the actions of the chimpanzees can be more simply interpreted as maximising their individual chances of obtaining the prey. Their simultaneous individual actions might also increase the chance that either or any of them will obtain food, and the subsequent competitive squabble for a share usually ensures that more than one individual will benefit. This seems an adequate description of cooperation in pragmatic terms, though it is more doubtful whether it should be regarded as similar to cooperative hunting by humans in which an ideology of sharing ensures patterns of reciprocal distribution in most communities.

Tools

A further question about how food is obtained relates to the use of tools. Humans use tools in food acquisition in almost all types of societies. Beck's (1980) definition of a tool seems to us the most useful: 'to be a tool, an external object must be free of any fixed attachment to the substrate and must be held, carried, or manipulated by the user'. It would appear that among present day non-human primates, only chimpanzees use tools for subsistence, and then almost exclusively for obtaining insects and other invertebrates (McGrew 1992) and for nut-cracking (Boesch & Boesch 1981). There is some evidence that Japanese macaques (monkeys not apes) move stones around in play and with no suggestion of use as tools (Quiatt & Huffman 1993).

McGrew (1992) gives exhaustive consideration to the question of tool-making and use by primates. There are two situations to be considered whose difference is encapsulated by a distinction between 'can do' and 'do do'. There are many things that apes are able to do when given the opportunity (or denied others) in captivity or when in close proximity to human communities. Kortlandt (1986), for example, has suggested that it would be valuable to research further the suggestion that all instances of stone tool use by chimpanzees in the wild result from opportunities to observe similar behaviour among humans. McGrew (personal communication) suggests it is equally plausible that hominids could have learned from chimpanzee ancestors.

Among free-living apes (and capuchin monkeys), only chimpanzees have *frequently* been observed using tools without human stimulus, with less evidence from orang-utans, gibbons and capuchin monkeys (McGrew 1992, Table 2.2).

Nests are somewhat difficult as a category of tool. Nests made by apes from leaves and branches may include detached material, but are not themselves detached from the material of which they are constructed (e.g. Groves & Sabater Pí 1985), and might be disqualified under Beck's definition (e.g. Boesch & Boesch 1990). If nests are included, wild orang-utans come into the class of tool-makers and users (Galdikas 1982), as do gorillas and bonobos. Otherwise, despite extensive study of free-living gorillas, there have never been observations of tool-use. Observations of free-living bonobos are relatively less intensive, but despite careful scrutiny, tool-use other than nests has rarely been reported. Groves and Sabater Pí (1985) are in no doubt that nest-building was a behaviour of the common ancestor of orang-utans as well as the African apes.

The second point from McGrew's synthesis is that among captive animals, good quality data are available spontaneously from chimpanzees, orang-utans and bonobos, as well as capuchin monkeys, with minor evidence of tool-use by captive gorillas and gibbons.

What interpretation can be placed on the different quality of evidence between the free-living and captive situations? One interpretation could be that there is some innate ability for tool-using, even tool-making if nests are included, in all of the relevant primates, which can be realised by the stimulus of captivity. More simply, we could argue that the context of captivity usually provides more time and opportunities for activities which are called tool-use. At times this is because the captive environment is not full of the components and resources that are usual in the lives of chimpanzees in the wild, so captive animals occupy their time in other ways. McGrew has a criterion for tool-using of spontaneity of use, but this may be rather misleading in captivity, given that that environment for chimpanzees is frequently full of objects which would be called tools given *any* use of them. So the use of tools in captivity may be a product of the ready availability of things that observers class as tools. We note that the opportunities afforded by captivity are rarely considered in a matter such as diet, since it is straightforward that M&Ms are not naturally available to wild primates. Tool-use in captivity should be treated with caution.

McGrew (1989b) considered the issue of tool-use in a similar way to that presented here. He postulated that the confusing data on tool-use can be resolved into two alternative models of ancestral hominoids: one model ancestor gave rise to all apes other than gibbons. This earlier ancestor, in McGrew's view, was an opportunistic tool-user (to account for the use of tools in captivity); wild orang-utans and gorillas lost the habitual use of tools as they became more specialised to life in the tropical forest. McGrew's alternative model is of a common ancestor as late as a postulated separation between hominids and the two species of *Pan*. This creature was as little involved with tools as bonobos are in the wild. On this model, *Pan troglodytes* and humans both independently discovered the use of tools. We suggest choice between these alternatives depends on the interpretation of nest-building, and on the extent of belief in innateness of tool-using ability unrealised in modern orang-utans and bonobos until they enter the laboratory.

Acceptance of nests as tools suggests that tool-use is not a major issue. And as all nests must be constructed, the making of tools is not an issue either. It seems most plausible, then, that the common ancestor of humans and African apes had a capacity, realised or not, to make and use tools. It would be tempting to combine McGrew's two models and suggest that, other than for nests, the capacity was not realised in practice, and only became realised by chimpanzees and hominids.

But there is another way to look at tools, which is the conclusion reached by Beck (1980). After a catalogue of reported animal tool-use, claimed as exhaustive, Beck concluded that tool-use is widespread among animals, even given the restrictions placed on its recognition. Tool-use alone, therefore, is not uniquely human, nor even unique to chimpanzees and humans. What does seem distinctive to chimpanzees and humans is the variety of tools (McGrew 1993). In Beck's analysis, apes as a category are only matched for their diversity of tool use by birds as a category. But when individual species are considered, chimpanzees (and not bonobos, still less gorillas) exhibit more variety than any other species: and this variety has a geographic dimension (Figure 7).

McGrew and others have pointed to regionally distinct patterns of tool use among chimpanzees, and discussed whether the variations should be attributed to ecological differences between the locations where the distinctive tools were used, or whether there is a case for what they call 'cultural' transmission. The conclusion is that, while ecology is a sufficient explanation for some but not all the variation, the patterns and variations cannot straightforwardly be called 'cultural'. Tomasello (1990, 305) is most explicit in this regard:

> My overall conclusion is thus that chimpanzees have 'culture' in a very different sense than do humans. Much of the continuity across generations in chimpanzee tool use and communication is maintained by the continuity of learning experiences available to individuals—which 'shape' individual learning. Very little of the learning comes from observing and reproducing the behavior of conspecifics, which, in the current account, is a defining feature of cultural transmission.

We will cite confusion of meanings for 'culture' in Chapter 3 as a reason for avoiding the term altogether. As the majority of definitions of culture start from the notion that it is identifiably a human characteristic, it becomes increasingly difficult to understand why behaviour that is so different from that of humans should be

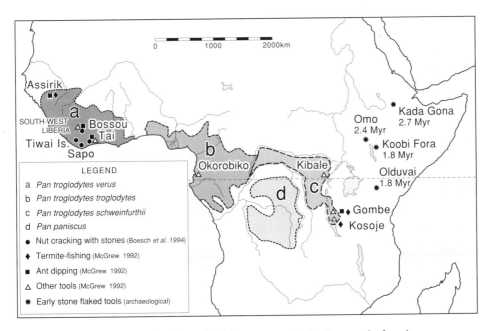

Figure 7 Distribution of tool-use in chimpanzee study sites, and of early archaeological stone flaked tools.

called 'culture'. It is quite possible to discuss transmission of behaviour between individuals of the same or different generations without being concerned about whether it should be called cultural (e.g. Tomasello 1990). Despite earlier claims, there is now considerable doubt about the extent to which any monkeys or apes have been shown to *imitate* behaviour outside a context of social interaction with humans (Tomasello et al. 1993; Visalberghi & Fragaszy 1990). This lack of imitation is central to the difficulty wild chimpanzees have in transmitting behaviours between individuals. It is nowhere better illustrated than in the best documented claim of 'teaching' of an infant chimpanzee by adult caregivers (Boesch 1991b; 1993).

Boesch reported several instances of mothers seeming to intervene in the attempts by infants to crack nuts to obtain the nutritious meat within. Altogether, 977 interventions were recorded during 4137 minutes of observations. Almost all of these were what Caro and Hauser (1992) call 'opportunity teaching', where infants were stimulated or facilitated (Boesch's words) to use tools to crack nuts. Two instances might be called 'teaching' if witnessed among humans, because the adult female demonstrated the appropriate tactic to an infant who subsequently adopted that behaviour. This is what Caro and Hauser call 'coaching'. One of the instances is said by Boesch (1993) to involve imitation. Tomasello et al. (1993) dismiss these two instances as teaching, on the grounds that neither intervention appeared to continue until there was a sufficiently successful outcome. There might well be fewer teachers if we were all judged by such criteria, but the important point here is not so much the degree of success as the persistence (a criterion by which we might escape).

Two observations seem to be in order: first, the age range of infants involved in these observations (from <1 year to 8 years), suggests a very long apprenticeship among chimpanzee nut-crackers, which may, of course, be due to the lack of persistence. Longitudinal data showing a developmental sequence are needed. The infant chimpanzees may benefit immediately from the demonstration of appropriate tactics, but take a long time to incorporate them into their general approach. Boesch (1993) suggests one reason for the apparently slow learning is that nut-cracking requires strength, and the apprenticeship continues until the animals are strong enough to succeed. Caro and Hauser (1992) point out that there is no evidence that taught infants acquire the skill earlier than untaught. If strength is indeed the criterion for success, it is unlikely that the process can be speeded up by teaching. There may well be little selective pressure for teaching in this sort of context.

Secondly, we expect to witness rare instances of behaviours which, while unimportant, could be favoured by natural selection under different conditions. The two instances of behaviour which look like teaching can be understood in this way. The rudiments of 'showing a procedure' may represent a chance variation that, when expressed in a context of further behavioural evolution, is then selected for. Such an opportunity could arise from the nut-cracking example if the rare 'teaching' behaviour continued to be exhibited when the shells of the nuts were more brittle or the demonstrated procedure involved less force than for nut-cracking. We will suggest in Chapter 7 that the making of flaked stone tools provided such a selective context.

The common ancestor, then, was probably a nest builder, and unlikely to have been a teacher of tool use. Apes and their ancestors behave and behaved like their conspecifics because they lived among them and were exposed to similar contingencies.

Vocal and non-vocal communication

Almost all of the senses of animals guide them, members of the same species, their predators, or their prey to determine their friendly and unfriendly interactions (Wilson 1975, Chapter 10). Many of these sensory occurrences communicate about potential mates, others about the nature of the environment, perhaps about the presence of food sources or about predators. Others serve to deter or deceive predators to enhance survival. We discuss these matters in Chapter 5.

There is little to be gained, in the present context, from casting our net so wide as to include all aspects of communication, and we will confine ourselves to those that seem most like human speech, namely the vocal utterances of the modern primates. There are many forms of communication, verbal and non-verbal in all primates including humans, and these are frequently enmeshed in complex ways (Kendon 1993). Much of human speech can be considered to carry the message at the level of the meaning of the words (the semantic level). Voice quality (intonation and prosody) may convey messages quite separate from that meaning, though, as in our discussion of body language, it is not clear that there can be such a separation of meanings unless one of the communication modes is language.

This book is concerned with how any such signals came to be used as symbolic signs. We cover the concept of symbol in Chapter 3. Humans seem to be the only creatures who use signs symbolically (cf. Pinker 1994), and the majority of such utterance is in speech or graphic systems derived from it (writing, typing). Burling (1993) has argued that, in evolutionary terms, language emerged from some other form of signs than non-symbolic vocal utterances (which he describes as part of a 'gesture-call' system). We return to Burling's argument later in this chapter and in Chapter 8, because he draws particular attention to iconic calls and gestures, but without apparently seeing the significance in them that we do (Davidson & Noble 1993b).

To sustain or dismiss an argument about continuity between vocal utterances of non-human and human primates, we must first understand what vocal utterances there are among the non-human primates, and what the vocal utterances of the common ancestor might have been like. In the most detailed study of communication among non-human primates, Cheney and Seyfarth (1990) describe and analyse those of vervet monkeys (one of the Cercopithecoids), particularly by recording their utterances and playing them back to observe the reactions when context is controlled. Most remarkable, and best known, are the calls vervets utter in the presence of predators. These are commonly referred to as alarm calls, though there is a risk in accepting uncritically that they can only be interpreted as alarms (see Chapter 5). Other vervets hearing the calls respond in an appropriate fashion to avoid or escape predation. The system works very efficiently, a product of infant learning presumably honed by natural selection (vervets which do not run for cover get killed). Other vocalisations, grunts and *wrrs*, seem to communicate information about conspecifics, with some suggestion that individuals can be recognised and associated with their usual foraging range. Few studies of communication in other primates have such a detailed array of observations, experiments, analyses or theoretical insights.

It seems unlikely that the call given in the presence of a leopard could 'mean' 'leopard'. As Burling (1993) points out, the call is not given in any other context except of a threat of predation, and, as Cheney and Seyfarth (1990) document, only when there is an audience for the call. This makes evolutionary sense; a monkey calling when alone would achieve little except to draw attention to itself and increase its own vulnerability.

These data may be interpreted in two ways. Given that the Cercopithecoids are distinguishable by 30 million years ago, at least 10 million years before the first Hominoids are identifiable (Table 1), such calls must either be a very common attribute of apes and monkeys, or they must be a parallel evolution in these monkeys. If a common attribute, we would expect similar specificity of communication in the lesser and greater apes, including the common ancestor. If a parallel evolution, then we must argue that the forces of natural selection have worked to favour similar communication systems where circumstances of predation and ecology are suitable (data suggest that such circumstances selected similar patterns of call use among chickens [Evans et al. 1993]). The common ancestor might have had an analogous call system in those parts of its habitat similar to that of vervets.

One of the problems in distinguishing between the alternatives of commonality or parallel selection is that few other primates have yet been studied in the same detail as the vervets (but see Mitani in press). It would deny the commonality case if it were found that vervets were unique among monkeys. The parallel case is more difficult to discuss. The vervet monkeys were chosen for the research precisely because they have an ecology of feeding in open areas on the ground where they can be seen, heard and studied by human investigators. Establishing the nature of the communication system for any other primate is likely to require some of the same circumstances for the study to be done at all; hence, constraints on feasibility may produce observations of limited generality. Nevertheless, we consider the limited data on vocal and non-vocal communication by hominoids.

The vocalisations of gibbons in the wild were reviewed by Haimoff (1984). These consist of elaborate, repetitive and stereotyped 'song' bouts, often near dawn, frequently involving both members of a monogamous pair 'singing' together. They are commonly said to involve the advertisement of tenure of a territory by the pair. All species of gibbon have this behaviour (with some variation), and each species has distinctive and consistent sequences of utterances. Brockelman (1984) suggests there is increasing doubt that the calls can be said to carry 'meaning'; rather they seem to be an end in themselves. Repetition of the practice in captivity suggests that the calls are not straightforwardly territorial. An alternative approach suggests they may indicate the state of the callers' stamina or strength or of the attachment between them (Leighton 1986).

Gibbon calls entered significantly into one of Hockett's discussions of the design features of language (Hockett & Ascher 1964). In a series of papers, Hockett defined 13 features of language which have proved valuable in describing the language-like elements of non-language communication. In terms of these features, Hockett and Ascher claimed that gibbon calls and language show several similarities, such that we might take them as characteristic of a common ancestor of gibbons and the African apes (including humans).

More recent work in primatology and in assessing the significance of these design features may produce slightly different interpretations from those of Hockett and Ascher (e.g. Jolly 1972; Boehm 1992). The analysis of vervet calls (Cheney & Seyfarth 1990) to try to assess their semanticity has shown that it is very difficult to identify this even in apparently very clear-cut circumstances. We suspect that analysis of more recent studies of gibbon calls would eliminate Hockett's claim of gibbon semanticity. In addition, the notion of arbitrariness is probably more complex than Hockett (e.g. 1960) originally expected. As Saussure (1983[1916]) noted, the arbitrariness of linguistic signs is not unlimited. For signs to have meaning they must be constrained by conventional usage in a community of users. There is no evidence that the aspects of gibbon calls which Hockett claims as arbitrary are shared by a community. Rather they are unique to individuals or monogamous pairs of animals. They may also not be arbitrary if they are the only such calls the animals can make.

Boehm (1992) discussed recent detailed descriptions of chimpanzee vocalisations in the context of Hockett's more extended list of design features. His interpretations differ somewhat from ours, as seen again through discussion of arbitrariness. Chimpanzees make an arm-wave gesture commonly interpreted as a threat. Boehm (1992, 332) suggests this gesture is not arbitrary because 'it seems to suggest hitting as a likely consequence of noncompliance'. But this still involves arbitrariness, since the full threat display involves more actions than hitting, such as glaring, swaggering, drumming, throwing, and mock charges (e.g. Tomasello 1990). Arm-waving could be said to be an arbitrary choice from this range of options. On the other hand, it is difficult to determine whether this is arbitrary in the sense of involving a choice by the animal of the particular gesture to achieve the desired result. Boehm goes on to suggest that a *cough-threat* can serve the same function, but we suspect further analysis is needed to determine whether these apparently similar communications are used interchangeably or whether different contingencies can define the nature of the choice being made. We have attempted to summarise design features of the vocalisations of other apes (and humans and vervets) in Table 2.

Not all of the studies have been described in the same detail, so it is difficult to determine the status of the vocal utterances of some species for some features. We include data from the bonobo 'Kanzi' (e.g. Greenfield & Savage-Rumbaugh 1990; 1993; Savage-Rumbaugh & Rumbaugh 1993a; 1993b), the most remarkable of the apes with language experiment experience (see our assessment in Noble & Davidson 1991). We have tended to be conservative about accepting whether the communications described have particular design features. In doing this, we have adhered to the principles employed throughout this book.

As Hockett (1960) claimed, some features of communication systems in non-human primates are common to those systems and to human linguistic communication. But the most fundamental feature, the vocal-auditory channel, is not a necessary condition for language. All writing and Sign languages do not involve this channel. By the same token, 'Kanzi' understands some spoken English but communicates using a computer whose keyboard is illustrated with distinctive signs. Audible synthesised words are generated when an appropriate key is pressed (Savage-Rumbaugh et al. 1989). The really important differences in this table, we suggest, are the lack, among non-human primates, of four sets of features: (1) semanticity and arbitrariness; (2) discreteness, productivity, and duality of patterning; (3) displacement; and, (4) (probably) traditional transmission.

We have already discussed semanticity and arbitrariness, and will return to them again at different points in the book, and we will discuss displacement after our theoretical discussion of symbols, language and communication. These data suggest that semanticity and arbitrariness were probably not properties of the communication system of the common ancestor. The fact that 'Kanzi' communicates in a manner which suggests semanticity, and may even involve some arbitrariness, we attribute to the fact of this animal having been involved in a relationship of communication with humans, and one that has had practical consequences, almost since birth. We return to this sort of issue in Chapter 4.

The three design features of discreteness, productivity and duality of patterning are closely related and fundamental properties of language. Language can be used productively because words, arbitrarily (but conventionally) related to their referents, are composed of discrete elements. While the words are 'meaningful' the discrete elements are, in general, individually meaningless (duality of patterning). For this to be possible, the elements of the utterance must be distinguishable. In humans, vocal utterances can be split up into units known as phonemes which can be recognised by showing the distinct meanings of words occasioned by the change of one of these elements. /P/ and /b/ are separate phonemes because 'pad' and 'bad' have separate meanings. In chimpanzees and gorillas utterances are 'graded', meaning that one call gradually changes into another (Marler 1976). Of course, many human utterances grade also, not having such distinct boundaries as their written counterparts would suggest. This is partly due to coarticulation (e.g. Miller 1981), the phenomenon whereby the actual sound of a phoneme is influenced by the one that precedes or follows it. The similarity between apes and humans in this

	Vervet	Gibbons	Orang-utan	Gorilla	Wild chimpanzee	Wild bonobo	Kanzi	Human
Vocal-auditory	Y	Y	Y	Y	Y	Y	Y/?	Y
Broadcast/directional	Y	Y	Y	Y	Y	Y	Y	Y
Rapid fading	Y	Y	Y	Y	Y	Y	Y	Y
Interchangeable	Y	?	?	?	?	?	?	Y
Total feedback	Y	Y	Y	Y	Y	Y	N	Y
Specialised	Y	Y	Y	Y	Y	Y	Y	Y
Semanticity	?	Y/?	N	N	N	N	Y	Y
Arbitrariness	?	Y/?	N	N	N	?	?	Y
Discreteness	Y	Y	?	N	N	?	Y	Y
Displacement	N	N	N	N	N	N	?	Y
Productivity	N	N	N	N	N	?	?	Y
Traditional transmission	Y	?	?	?	N/?	?	Y	Y
Duality of patterning	?	N/?	N	N	N	N	?	Y
Sources	(1)	(2)	(3)	(4)	(5)	(6)	(7)	(8)

Table 2 Classification of vocal utterances of apes (and vervet monkeys) in terms of Hockett's design features of language.
Sources: (1) Cheney and Seyfarth 1990. (2) Hockett and Ascher 1964, Mitani 1992. (3)Tuttle 1986, MacKinnon 1974. (4) Tuttle 1986, Marler 1976, Fossey 1972, Mitani in press. (5) Tuttle 1986, Goodall 1986, Marler 1976, Boehm 1992, Mitani in press. (6) Tuttle 1986, Kano 1979, Mitani in press. (7) Hopkins and Savage-Rumbaugh 1991. (8) Hockett 1960.

regard is, however, superficial. It is as if the apes had calls composed of vowels, while humans have vowels and consonants. The consonants split up the sound stream in a way which ensures much more certain boundaries of phonemes (Perkins & Kent 1986).

The lack of boundary markers is feasibly one reason why the number of identifiable vocal utterances in non-human primates is relatively small. Goodall (Goodall 1986; Lawick-Goodall 1968a) described 34 calls, but spectrographic analysis of them led to the lumping of several into a smaller number of calls (Marler 1976). Boehm (1992) suggested that further work may lead to a greater number of calls being recognised. The problem of recognition, of course, is partly due to the lack of boundary markers; it is also due to the lack of contextual cues. Snowdon (1990) summarised experimental results suggesting that marmosets (one of the New World monkeys) can respond in different ways to calls made by different individuals. This suggests that the perception of vocal utterance is finely tuned to the variation made in the utterances. Categorical perception (as it is called) seems to be a widespread phenomenon in systems of communication involving vocal utterance. This is hardly surprising, as presumably the systems for receiving calls have evolved in step with the systems for emitting them.

Nevertheless, the number of communicative forms in the vocal utterances of pongids seems small when compared with human speech. In Table 3 we summarise some estimates of the numbers of communicative utterance (including what Burling would call gesture-calls, or non-verbal communications).

Even admitting the richer repertoire described by Goodall, and not Marler's restricted list, there are fewer vocal utterance types among chimpanzees than there are among the phonemes common in human speech. But the essence of our

	Gibbons	Orang-utan	Gorilla	Chimpanzee	Bonobo	Human
Vocalisations	11	21	17	34	14	>40 phonemes
Non-vocal, facial	12	17	8	11	47	136
Non-vocal, postural	19	3	?	26	included with facial	included with facial
Sources	Marler 1987 Tuttle1986	MacKinnon 1974 Tuttle 1986 Kaplan & Rogers 1994	Fossey 1972 Schaller 1963 Tuttle 1986	Boehm 1992 Goodall 1986 Marler 1976 Tuttle 1986	Tuttle 1986	Brannigan and Humphries 1972 Crystal 1987

Table 3 Numbers of types of vocal and non-vocal communicative utterance in pongids and humans.

argument here is that phonemes are rarely used alone and rarely have meaning as single utterances. They are typically used in combinations of from 2 to at least 27 (in English, 'antidisestablishmentarianism', once the schoolchild's favourite longest word, presumably has 27 phonemes). One survey showed that there are 429 monosyllabic words in English ending with /-d/, and 3884 monosyllables ending with a consonant (Crystal 1987). Whilst it seems likely that there is more to be discovered about hominoid vocalisation, these statistics about a human language suggest that it is quite fundamentally different from the communication systems of any other free-living primates. The common ancestor probably had a restricted range of vocal utterances.

'Kanzi' has a wider range of communicative utterances than a wild bonobo through access to the indexical signs on the computer keyboard. 'Kanzi' may have an expanded vocal range in these experiments (Hopkins & Savage-Rumbaugh 1991), compared with wild bonobos and other captive bonobos. Hopkins and Savage-Rumbaugh argue that the changes have resulted from the learning environment in which 'Kanzi' has been reared, specifically that they may result from exposure to human speech, since all four of the novel vocalisations are produced in response to vocal or gestural utterance by humans. These experimental results seem to confirm the importance of learning context in the acquisition of communicative vocal utterances. What inhibits such learning in wild primates, and presumably in the common ancestor, is (or was) limitation of contexts.

Burling (1993) makes a valuable distinction between language and language-like behaviour on the one hand and gesture-call systems on the other. He would include with language-like utterances conventional non-linguistic spoken expression (what he calls *oh-oh* expressions) and conventional gestures. In his view, the calls of vervet monkeys are part of a gesture-call system which has more in common with human gestures and body 'language' than it does with language and language-like behaviour. No doubt the common ancestor used non-vocal communication, but this had little in common with language-like communication.

Burling also identifies a distinct system of communication among humans which he calls iconic calls and gestures. These calls usually evade classification by linguists and yet are rare in primates while common among humans. We have suggested (Davidson & Noble 1993b) that it is this class of communication which could have been the source of the evolution of more language-like behaviour among early non-human primates. We have consistently emphasised the evolutionary emergence of throwing and pointing, leading to iconic gestures, and how these had a role in the transformation of communication into language (Davidson & Noble 1989; Noble & Davidson 1989; 1991; 1993a).

Symbols?

Claims for the use of symbols by non-human primates are extremely rare, yet every utterance in language is symbolic, as we shall argue in the next three chapters. There are, so far as we know, no claims for anything resembling symbol use in natural conditions by any primates other than humans and chimpanzees. It seems highly unlikely that the common ancestor used symbols. On this interpretation, even if the chimpanzee examples discussed below are accepted as symbol use, the behaviour was one that emerged independently after the divergence from the common ancestor, just as human use of symbols did.

Do wild chimpanzees use symbols? There are three questions here. (1) What is a symbol? (2) How can we detect symbols? (3) What is the relevance of outcomes from experiments with captive chimpanzees?

The first question is addressed in the next chapter. Sufficient to say here that a symbol is something that stands for something else. We should state that we do not believe that symbol-use has been (or will be) demonstrated for any non-human animal, at least outside contexts of human intervention. Here we discuss the contrary claims. King (1991) defines a symbol as 'an arbitrary, noniconic signal', though she admits that some iconic signs can be symbolic. By concentrating on arbitrariness, she finds many cases similar to the vervets, where calls appear to refer to objects with no obvious relationship between the call and the referent (except their co-occurrence). But they are not arbitrary in the sense that there is any choice about the calls that may make this reference. We believe that more care is needed with the definition of primate (or any other animal) calls as symbolic (cf. Snowdon 1990).

There is one case study which claims to provide the evidence of something approaching symbols: the leaf-clipping display first described, among provisioned wild chimpanzees in the Mahale area, by Nishida (1980, 117) as an 'expressive gesture':

> A chimpanzee picks off one to five stiff leaves, grasps the petiole between the thumb and index finger, repeatedly pulls it from side to side while removing the leaf-blade with the incisors, and thus bites the leaf to pieces. In removing the leaf-blade with the incisors, a ripping sound is conspicuously and distinctly produced.

The gesture is made in three contexts: (1) courtship, being followed by copulation within 30 seconds in half of the cases; (2) demanding food from human provisioners; (3) other contexts of frustration. This may very well constitute a signal. It seems to have an arbitrary relationship with the context. It has been seen in only a limited number of populations, twice at Gombe and several times at Bossou in Guinea (Nishida 1986). In the examples from Bossou, there is no suggestion of courtship display. Under these circumstances some of the elements for this to be a symbolic gesture are undoubtedly present. But, we doubt that all of them are. There does not seem to be any sign that leaf-clipping could indicate a desire for copulation outside the immediate context of some chance of doing it.

Elsewhere, McGrew and Tutin (1978) observed chimpanzees in the Mahale study area engage in what they called 'the grooming hand-clasp'. This involved a paired movement facilitating grooming of underarms by partners in the actions (McGrew 1992, 68). The practice was frequent in Mahale, but has never been observed in the adjacent study area of Gombe. It has been observed subsequently in another study region, and there, too, it was absent from the adjacent study area. McGrew and Tutin originally referred to this pattern of behaviour and accounted for its variable occurrence as a 'social custom'. McGrew is in no doubt that this pattern of consistent occurrence in one area with absence in an adjacent area, if found among humans, would 'be accorded cultural status'. While the authors do not claim that this gesture is symbolic, considering whether it is 'cultural' suggests that its symbolic status needs to be assessed.

At Gombe, chimpanzees engage in underarm grooming, but they may do this with the arm of one participant clinging to a branch. It seems plausible that the grooming hand-clasp is, at least in part, a response to the contingencies of grooming underarms where there are no suitable branches. It might be said that the arm of the groomer stands in for a branch, but it seems far simpler to say that this is a case of pragmatics rather than symbolism. Tomasello (1990) suggests that the behaviour is one of conventionalisation, where the learning of an individual is determined by the interaction with other individuals.

The second question is about our ability to detect the presence of symbols. Here, we have to acknowledge the limitations of existing methods. When we identify symbols among humans we can ask someone about them to determine whether or not they stand for something else. But we cannot do that for chimpanzees. The vervet study shows that playback experiments can serve to elucidate some of the contexts in which calls are made, and, on the whole, they do not support an interpretation of the calls as symbolic. Similarly, playback experiments with orang-utans were able to show that the 'long-calls' emitted by males serve to mediate spacing of high-ranking males, but not to attract female orang-utans (Mitani 1985). We cannot judge from the published evidence whether such calls should be considered symbolic. We suspect the case is overwhelming that they are not, given the restricted contexts in which they are performed.

Aside from playback experiments, there are two avenues for determining the symbolic (or other) nature of animal communication: anecdotes or scientific analyses. Anecdotal claims are always problematic, as the discussion on deception in primates shows (Byrne & Whiten 1988), and run the risk at all times of anthropomorphism. Boesch (1991a) reported combinations of vocalisations with drumming on trees among chimpanzees in the Taï forest. Sometimes these seemed to indicate indexically (Boesch claims it is iconic) that the drummer was changing direction. On other occasions, Boesch interpreted the drumming to indicate a rest period of a particular duration. The claim is based on 23 observations of a single individual over a 16 month period. At the end of the period the chimpanzee stopped communicating in this way. We are not certain that the data show this to be symbolic indication of either rest or duration (though duration seems unlikely in the absence of timepieces).

The alternative to anecdotes is to describe the calls and their contexts as objectively as possible. In vocal utterance, this has led to the use of spectrographic

analysis of the acoustic properties of calls. Such analysis has permitted the identification of individual and population variation in particular chimpanzee calls (the
'pant-hoot') but the interpretation of these differences remains difficult (Mitani et
al. 1992). A moment's reflection shows that this weights the description against
symbolic interpretation. Figure 8 displays spectrograms of a human saying 'carrot',
and 'symbol'. We include the first of these because it is a word which symbolises
part of a plant, which is also a food for humans and laboratory bonobos. 'Kanzi'
produced one of his novel vocalisations ('ii-angh') in response to the question 'Do
you want a peanut?' (Hopkins & Savage-Rumbaugh 1991), and the vocalisation
illustrated here was made as he opened a bag of carrots. 'Symbol' is the ultimate
symbol, a word that stands for the concept of 'symbol'. None of these spectrograms
shows anything to identify them as symbols. We are looking in the wrong place.
Any attempt to objectivate 'meanings' by discussing the distinct acoustics of
different utterances (such as words) fails precisely at the symbolic level of analysis
(Noble 1993a). Word meaning is context-dependent, as we show in the following
three chapters.

Thirdly, what is the relevance of the experimental work with laboratory apes?
There is no doubt that some of this work, particularly that with 'Kanzi', has involved
animals hearing, or otherwise perceiving, and understanding the symbols of spoken
English and communicating coherently with their human partners using an illustrated computer keyboard (Savage-Rumbaugh et al. 1986), American Sign Language (Gardner & Gardner 1968; Miles 1990; Patterson & Linden 1981) or plastic
tokens (Premack 1976). Some part of this communication undoubtedly involves the
use of symbols, though not perhaps the production of new ones. We do not
underestimate what has been learned from these experiments, and recognise that for
some of the problems we have been referring to here the possibilities of controlling
experimental conditions allow much more detail of behaviour to be observed. But
these are of more relevance to the story we are telling if the experimental animals are
thought to have innate abilities, some of which are not realised in the wild. How any
unused cognitive capacities might have emerged in evolution is difficult to contemplate. The alternative view is that they are a result of the human-ape interaction, just
as language emergence in infant humans is a result of human-human interaction. For
our endeavour to identify the prehistoric origins of symbols and language, we must
try to understand how a quite different process occurred. How did non-symbolic
utterances of the type found commonly among other primates become symbolic?

Social context of learning

Society

Hitherto, we have paid little heed to the interactions between individual animals in
what are frequently called 'social' interactions. Ingold (1989) properly draws a
distinction between definitions of 'society' either as emphasising interaction between individual animals (applicable to any animals), or as essentially concerned

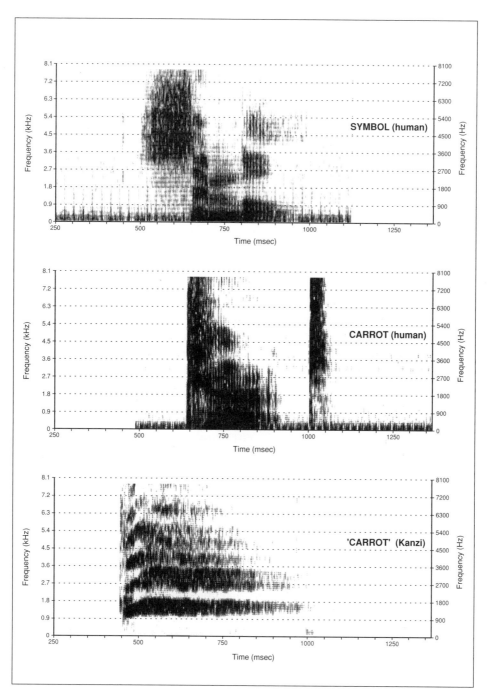

Figure 8 Spectrograms of 'Kanzi' uttering a sound when opening a bag of carrots (from videotape supplied by Sue Savage-Rumbaugh) and of humans saying 'carrot' and 'symbol'.

with rules and relationships (and applicable only to humans). Whilst (with Ingold) we recognise that there must be some continuities of patterns of inter-individual interaction during the course of evolution, we also recognise (with Ingold) the fundamental importance of language in defining rules. In a discussion that seeks to understand the evolutionary emergence of language, we find it most convenient to limit the word 'social' to humans, lest we slither from one understanding to another and trick ourselves into seeing social rules where there were none. There are several other reasons for not addressing the inter-individual interactions of other animals. The existing literature is already comprehensive (e.g. Dunbar 1988; Fedigan 1982; Foley 1989; Foley & Lee 1989; Quiatt & Reynolds 1993; Smuts et al. 1986), and often used to model the behaviour of early hominids. As Wrangham (1987) points out, such modelling often assumes that early hominids were similar in their behaviour to a living species of non-humans, and one or other primate may well provide the best model (McGrew 1991). Testing the veracity of any model of inter-individual living arrangements for long-dead hominids would go beyond plausible limits of archaeological interpretation. We are, therefore, happy to leave primate 'social' systems to others. We may identify the best model, but any model based on a living primate runs the risk of leaving chimpanzees (bonobos or baboons, depending on the model) as somehow 'failed' hominids which did not scale the evolutionary ladder of progress to become humans, rather than seeing them as the most successful chimpanzees (bonobos or baboons), so far, compared with which humans are the breakaway group who could not make it as that sort of ancestral primate.

Wrangham (1987) adopts the strategy we have been using here, comparing what he calls social organisation of African apes against a tree of relationships similar to Figure 2 in order to make inferences about the common ancestor (though he generally does not consider orang-utans or gibbons in his analysis). The diversity of arrangement among the pongids makes generalisation either very complex (Foley & Lee 1989) or potentially fruitless. Gibbons are monogamous; orang-utans are solitary; gorilla males keep harems; chimpanzees have alliances among males; compared with chimpanzees, bonobos may have weaker alliances among males and stronger ones among females; and some humans have various ideologies of monogamy which are sometimes observed. (Different human groups, of course, also have ideologies of polygyny, polyandry and other customs about inter-individual arrangement which are more or less commonly observed.) This characterisation emphasises the fact that people may tell sociologists they are monogamous, ignoring their temporary liaisons, while ethologists have no similar disparities to resolve.

Wrangham (1987) opted to consider more specific traits of interaction. His characterisation of the common ancestor was that it had closed social networks; males were sometimes solitary; females moved out of their birth group for mating (exogamy); females did not form alliances, but did associate in groups based on tolerance; males did not have single mates; groups were probably hostile towards other groups and males were probably aggressive in intergroup encounters, including pre-emptive attacks. Ghiglieri (1989) makes similar comparisons (isolating the group human, chimpanzee and bonobo from gorilla) and includes an assessment of the extent of parental investment by males. He finds that orang-utan males spend no time caring for infants, while those of mountain gorillas and chimpanzees do little more than protect infants from other males. Goodall's (1986, Chapter 7) figures are the most detailed record. She discusses data over up to 8 years on the patterns of association between adult males and others and adult females and others. None of the adult males (including 27 chimp-years of observations for 4 individuals) had constant companionship (measured as an association for more than 90% of the times of observation). By contrast, all observed females (29 chimp-years for 4 individuals) had one or more adolescents or juveniles with them at all times, with the exception of one year for one individual after the death of her offspring. Bonobo males invest rather more time, including some food sharing and grooming. On this basis, the common ancestor probably had small amounts of male parental investment in offspring.

Learning

We take it for granted that learning is a normal part of the social development of primates. Our primary concern is for the context of infant learning, which Wrangham (1987) and Foley (1989) do not cover. There are some studies of how it is achieved in vervet monkeys, and wild or captive chimpanzees, though, as interpretation of the phenomenon of sweet-potato washing by Japanese macaques shows, there is much disagreement (contrast Visalberghi & Fragaszy 1990 with Nishida 1986).

There are two kinds of learning of relevance here: observational learning (including local enhancement, emulation and imitation); and teaching (including opportunity teaching, encouragement and discouragement) (Caro & Hauser 1992; Nishida 1986). Vervet monkeys seem to make their distinctive vocalisations without coaching, but learn to be more precise in the contexts in which they use them, eliminating calls at falling leaves, and refining their 'identification' of genuine predators (Cheney & Seyfarth 1990). In addition, they learn appropriate responses to hearing the calls of others by observational learning of how others respond (Seyfarth 1986). These learning effects were achieved through both encouragement and punishment by adult vervets (Caro & Hauser 1992). But what is learned is not how to make the sounds (as we might teach an infant to say 'thirty' instead of 'firty') but the appropriate context for their production; not how to respond but when to respond in the appropriate way. If this is classified as teaching, then not only may observational learning be widespread among animals, but teaching must be expected among Anthropoids (see Figure 2) as well as among Hominoids.

Tomasello (1993) is more conservative about teaching: 'it may be said that in their natural habitats chimpanzees do not actively instruct their young ... they prevent them from doing certain things' or facilitate them (the Boesch nut-cracking example). Elsewhere, Tomasello (1990) suggested that individual chimpanzees learn tool-use by environmental shaping, and communication by conventionalisation. Most of the sorts of tool-making we will see in the hominid archaeological record can be learned by some combination of observational learning in a social context and conventionalisation of actions (Wynn & McGrew 1989). Teaching requires an understanding by the teacher that the knowledge held by the student is different from theirs (Tomasello et al. 1993). The careful analysis by Cheney and Seyfarth (1990) suggests that all apes lack the ability for such understanding. The common ancestor probably lacked this ability too.

Language experiments with apes suggest that in a context where the environment is rich in stimuli that are alien to the chimpanzee's natural environment, captive animals can acquire skills quite readily, provided they are exposed to the new environment at a (very) young age (Rumbaugh et al. 1991). We reiterate the point made above, that wild apes don't learn much that is like human communication, because they don't have much of such matter to learn.

We conclude that if the common ancestor had been put into a language experiment, it too, given the right conditions created by its descendants, would have learned to do far more than it did alone. The issue is how those descendants became so very different. In the next three chapters we analyse the nature of the differences to provide a framework for understanding the archaeological record of the period when those differences emerged.

CHAPTER 3

SYMBOLS AND THEIR SIGNIFICANCE

Our endeavour is to account for how human beings evolved to become minded in the ways that they are. In opening that account (Chapter 1) we identified communication using symbols, the defining feature of language, as the key to understanding the concept of mind. In Chapter 2 various aspects of other present-day apes were examined to develop an assessment of the likely characters of the ancestor common to them and modern humans. We identified a range of behavioural ingredients, ancestral to humans, that emerged after the common ancestor. These ingredients include bipedalism, the flaking of stone and its use in throwing, opportunities for joint perceptual attention and imitation due to changing forms of adult-infant interaction from birth. Effects would arise from and constraints apply to these characteristics in the evolution and development of the hominid brain. The communications of the common ancestor were probably primarily non-vocal, with a limited range of vocal utterances. It seems unlikely that symbols were part of these communications.

In this chapter we address what a symbol is, how something can be a symbol, and how symbols are created and sustained. Covering those topics is critical in itself; it is also important in gaining an understanding of archaeological materials. The issue of symbol use leads us to the issue of mind (Chapter 4). Then, in Chapter 5, we move to the question of the nature of human awareness, the phenomenon for which we seek an evolutionary explanation. This takes the form of a general theory of perceiving, communication and symbol use, of which language is the foundational form. In consequence of this argument about mind, perception and symbol-based communication, a fundamental question for us—and for students of behavioural evolution in general—is the identification of the presence of symbols in the material record of hominid evolution.

Tackling these issues involves not only biology and archaeology but also psychology, since we have to justify the position that humans are the only creatures who use language. To do that satisfactorily involves explaining what language is. In the present day, almost all people we call human are, naturally, language users. It is difficult to stand back and appreciate what language *is*, in a way that allows us to think about what it might be or have been like to experience the world without it. We begin by analogy with the closely related (though *not* natural) abilities of reading and writing.

Arbitrariness and code-making

The production of this book depends on capacities we as writers share with our readers, namely, to read and to write (normally, people who can do one can do the other). For almost anyone who has got to the position of using books for reference, education, or amusement, the capacities to read and write are taken for granted. We may need to be reminded that, in contrast to the normal acquisition of a native spoken or signed language, learning to read is a hard-won, and far from universal, skill.

Reading depends upon the existence of written texts, and there are various kinds of writing systems (orthographies) that are used to generate such texts. For readers of texts based on alphabetic script, reading means decoding an orthography, the function of which is to convey meanings via words and their relationships (syntax). Nonetheless it also involves attention, especially in the acquisition phase, to the link between the inscribed form of the alphabetic characters as such, called *graphemes*, and the small speech sound units, *phonemes*, which they encode. There is not a one-to-one mapping between the graphemes used to spell English words, and the phonemes that can be analysed out of the sounds of those words, though the mapping is not haphazard: the two levels of description, words and phonemes/graphemes, exemplify the design feature of 'duality of patterning' defined by Hockett (1960), mentioned in the previous chapter. To illustrate the mapping problem: the word 'grapheme' contains two graphemes, 'p' and 'h', neither of which, alone, sounds anything like the 'eff' sound they signal together in this context. Other graphemes in the word behave more like the sounds they signal individually (and in the context of the word 'hap*h*azard', ironically, 'p' and 'h' do not misbehave). Because there are sufficient regularities between sound and appearance—'p' and 'h' together are always either sounded separately or as 'eff'—the system works despite its odd features, and in defiance of strenuous efforts to revise it (Shaw 1948).

Reading also involves seeing how words with quite different *meanings* (pat, bat, pad, bad) are nonetheless made up of combinations from a common set of phonemes/graphemes (Byrne 1991). Because, by themselves, these small elements are meaningless, this point about how an alphabet-based written code works does not occur with ready intuition, and approaches to reading which overlook or ignore these sub-lexical encoding principles can be counterproductive (Byrne 1992).

Indeed, major arguments surround the issue of how best to instruct people in mastery of reading (e.g., Liberman & Liberman 1992; Adams & Bruck 1993).

The difficulty—and the arguments—arise because writing, in contrast to speaking or signing, is a technology (Ong 1982, 84), an invented practice rather than the expression of a natural capacity. To do it depends upon knowledge of how to encode, for example, sounds into an arbitrary visual form. We say, 'for example, sounds', because sound-based utterance is not necessary to form language. Language can occur as a system of visual signs, such as American Sign Language, used in some Deaf communities (Baker & Battison 1980). We will use the word 'sign' for the moment to refer to any form of expression (e.g., audible as in spoken utterance, visible as in manual gesture) that has a communicative function. We will later introduce a classification scheme that broadens the concept of 'sign' to include entities and occurrences other than bodily expressions. To distinguish this use of the word 'sign' from the language of a Deaf community we always refer to that as Sign or Sign language.

The contrast between the invented character of reading/writing and the naturalness of speaking (or using Sign language) might be used to support an argument that language, understood as a 'faculty', is a unique and innate 'organ' inhabiting the human mind (e.g., Chomsky 1980; 1986). It is not our intention to engage directly with those sorts of arguments; we will return to the conceptual link between language and mind in the next chapter. Here we say that, whatever else the existence of language may be taken to imply about human nature, in most members of the human species we witness the expression of a behaviour ('talking'—using larynx or hands) which evolved from a set of prior conditions in which the behaviour could not be identified as language. (Exceptional cases occur with children born deaf/blind or brain-impaired [Goode 1980].) The tasks we set ourselves are to explain the nature of that behaviour, what it depends upon, and what are its consequences. Once that is understood we can explore the evidence of how it evolved, and how its emergence accounts for certain features of the archaeological record of our human ancestry.

The reference to arbitrariness of encoding is the first matter that needs to be explained. We use orthography (writing systems) to give some examples. Both written English and written Russian rely on alphabets. Other writing systems, such as Japanese, use marks that correspond to different speech segments, at about the level of syllables (Fromkin & Rodman 1978, 365); others, like Chinese, encode meaning units, or morphemes (Liberman & Liberman 1992). The sound, in English, which typically goes with the visible arrangement of marks making up the (Roman) alphabetic character 'b' involves closure of the lips, either in part accompanied or immediately followed by partial closure of the vocal chords, or 'voicing' (Ladefoged 1975). This sound is broadly invariant across different spelling contexts—*b*ad, a*b*le, com*b*ine, distur*b*. The sound a reader of Russian would make in response to the same visual arrangement 'b' occurring in that (Cyrillic) alphabet is quite different, involving the tongue and the roof of the mouth, something like the way these are used when saying the italicised part of the English word o*ni*on. And whereas, in the

Roman alphabet the visible arrangements 'b' and 'B' are lower and upper case versions of the same character (hence pronounced identically), the visual shape 'B' in Russian represents a different character to 'b' and is pronounced like 'v' in English (Folomkina and Weiser 1963).

These examples demonstrate the arbitrary nature of the relationship between visual and auditory codes. The arbitrariness in this case lies at the point of connection between appearance and sound. Another arbitrary connection is between either vocal or visual forms of expression and what these forms refer to. This second kind of arbitrariness is illustrated more readily using a word rather than an alphabetic character. A common object of reference of the word 'dog' in English is an animal, usually hairy, with sharp teeth (canines) which are used in aggressive display and for tearing meat. This animal is closely related, (pre)historically, to wolves, but is unlike them in its attachment to human caregivers. Other objects may be referred to using the word 'dog'. A mechanic may use the word to refer to the sort of tooth-shaped device that engages and holds a ratchet-wheel. The word can be used to refer to an action, such as that of one person pesteringly attending to the activities of another. The second and third of these uses might be metaphoric extensions of the first, such that the tooth for the ratchet-wheel looks a bit like a dog's tooth, and the person who 'dogs' is one who persistently follows you around. This shows a way in which language expands and changes. It could be said that 'to dog' another is to act in imitation of 'a dog'; and the 'dog'-tooth looks like the tooth (a canine) which is distinctive of, and comes to be named after, the animal. In the end, though, there is nothing about the *word* 'dog' that imitates or resembles the animal, the mechanical device, or the action, to which it refers.

This is the second sort of arbitrariness, observed in all spoken languages. The 'dog' of the ratchet is not so called because it is hairy or aggressive, shows attachment or is used on meat; the act of 'dogging' is not related to hairiness, teeth, devotedness, or meat (though it could be aggressive). In these two examples of 'metaphoric extension', the word 'dog' takes its meaning by reference to particular and different features of the original animal from which it is derived; yet the word may well have lost those connotations in everyday usage (by a mechanic or a commentator on someone's action). In this way the reference has become cryptic, and new meaning is encoded.

The conceptual basis of code-making

Codes can be seen most clearly *as* codes when they are patently cryptic. Some codes, such as Morse code and semaphore, were initiated as methods of signalling over great distances. Morse code was devised about 160 years ago and used to communicate over the newly perfected electro-magnetic telegraph by means of patterns of impulses (the 'dots' and 'dashes') standing for each alphabetic character (Friedman 1977). Semaphore, invented during Napoleon's campaigns (Macksey 1986), uses one or two arms displaced relative to each other to stand for each alphabetic character.

The devising of such codes depends on all users being able to appreciate that a specific, *newly* founded visual or auditory pattern stands for an already familiar linguistic entity. Secret codes are simply ones to which the number of users is restricted, thus making it difficult for those who do not know the key—the translation rules—to understand what is being communicated. Seeing that one thing can stand for another underpins the code-making practice. The capacity to see that X stands for Y is not readily observed in nature. The vervet monkeys, whose cries we have described in previous chapters, show no signs of seeing *that* those signs stand for ... whatever they do stand for. Hesitation about identifying what they may stand for is precisely because the vervets cannot advise us what (if anything) they 'stand for'. We take up that matter in Chapter 5, mentioning it here to emphasise the unusual capacity required for 'encoding'.

The most critical ability required for code-making is that of manipulating things at a conceptual level. Take morse code. In this system there is physical substitution of one thing (e.g., a graphic or phonemic pattern such as that forming the letter 'b' [/b/]) with another (one long and three short sound bursts, i.e., 'dash-dot-dot-dot'). Critical for users, however, is to be able to keep seeing the commonality of *reference* ('this dash and these dots now stand for that alphabetic character') sustained throughout the substitution. That is a purely conceptual issue—no physical act need represent it. We are dealing with a subtle point, obvious once grasped, easy to overlook. It would be in order to say, 'The letter 'b' is now represented by this dash and these dots'. This means more than saying: 'these now substitute for 'b', i.e., that visible shape or audible sound'. What is meant by the sentence 'The letter 'b' is now represented by this dash and these dots' is as follows: 'This visible shape (b) or this sound /b/ represent the letter 'b'. The letter 'b' is understood to mean what may be written out as 'bee' in the dictionary, and, among many other things, it stands for the 2nd letter of the Roman alphabet. *Now*, the letter 'b' is represented by this dash and these dots'.

The common object of reference, for the written shape, the spoken sound, or for the succession of dash-and-dots, is the alphabetic character. That there *is* an object of reference is an indication of the conceptual level of the operation we are describing. To put it in practical terms, anyone who appreciates (understands) the reference understands the concept, although the character of this understanding will vary between people and may change for any one person. Evidence of understanding the reference, hence the concept, would lie, for example, in being able to elaborate intelligibly—as above—on a meaning of the phrase 'the letter 'b''. The operation of concepts is language-dependent; to appreciate a concept is to be able to engage in the sort of elaboration made above. It could be said that the physical act of uttering English or American Sign Language forms the expression of conceptual knowledge, but we do not need to undertake physically expressive acts in order to operate conceptually. We can think things through as well as talk them through. In saying this we should emphasise that we take the thinking in question to be an unexpressed use of language. Its achievement depends on prior exposure to (and, normally, expression of) physically expressed talk. In the next chapter we take up this point in more detail, with reference in particular to analyses by the social psychologist George Mead and the developmental psychologist Lev Vygotsky.

As a contrast to all the foregoing, consider a classical experiment of the sort inaugurated by Ivan Pavlov and his associates in the early years of this century (e.g., Pavlov 1927). From direct measurements in dogs of the quantity of secreted saliva, Pavlov observed that the 'alimentary' reflex of increased salivation in response to oral contact with food is also provoked by the sight of the food, i.e., prior to its actual contact with the salivary organs. He further found that, 'the vessel from which the food has been given is sufficient to evoke an alimentary reflex ... the secretion may be provoked even by the sight of the person who brought the vessel, or by the sound of his footsteps' (p.13). These findings led to a long series of experiments to investigate the ways in which natural bodily reflexes become 'conditioned' by signals other than the ones to which they are naturally adapted. It was quickly established that the alimentary reflex could be provoked by the occurrence of previously neutral stimuli (like the sound of a metronome), even when the sound was eventually *not* followed by the natural stimulus. If the natural stimulus did not follow the formerly neutral one, in time, the strength of this 'conditioned' reflex response diminished.

Pavlov's initial observation suggests that conditioning of natural reflexes can occur using sequences of arbitrary signals. Several different signals might be presented in succession for a few seconds each, and to more than one of the senses— different patterns of sound along with different visual patterns (Razran 1965, 228). Thus it would be possible, using the conditioning paradigm, to present a visual signal, say a stick and circle visual pattern (looking like the letter 'b') to a hungry dog, followed by presentation of food. The dog soon learns to expect the food on presentation of the pattern, and starts salivating. The visual pattern is then preceded by a sound pattern (say, one long plus three short bursts of sound), such that the animal starts to show anticipation of the food on hearing the sound. The visual pattern could now be withdrawn, for the sound pattern would be as effective in inducing the anticipatory behaviour. Thus we have a circumstance of physical substitution of one pattern for another, in just the same way as the morse code 'dash, dot, dot, dot' is a physical substitution for the graphic pattern 'b'. But is the substitution of an auditory for a graphic pattern in relation to the food in the conditioning setting really the same as the relationship of the auditory sequence 'dash, dot, dot, dot' or visual pattern 'b' to 'the letter 'b''?

The answer is 'no'. First, logically, the preceding signals do not stand for the food in the same way as the coded signs stand for the alphabetic letter. This is because they do not function as equivalents for the food; the dog cannot be *fed* with sounds or sights (which is why the conditioned reflex wanes if the conditioning signal alone is presented). The end point of the sequence in the conditioning experiment is not a sign but a material object. The relationships we have been describing regarding morse code and alphabetic characters are purely conceptual, they are relationships among signs such that any sign could in principle be substituted for any other, and the *referential* function would be maintained. (In principle: in practice, mixtures of signs cannot be used as a code. It would be impracticable to have a code comprising combinations of morse-type sound pulses and graphemes.) The answer to the question is 'no' on another count, empirical rather than logical. There is no evidence that the dog in the experiment can (or could) appreciate that it is looking at a visual or auditory representation of 'the letter 'b''. The conceptual resources for perceiving the patterns in that way are not accessible to it (nor to children who speak a language that has an alphabet-based writing system before they understand something of the written constituents of that language).

Thus, the physical substitution of one pattern for another is not the whole story (or even a critical part of the story) in referential substitution. The critical part is in knowing what any of these arbitrarily constructed signs ultimately stands for; knowledge that entails being able to *understand* that one thing could stand for another. It is this which characterises children's ability to engage in play in which objects are used to represent other things—a bench becomes 'a horse' (Olson 1988). Premack and Premack (1983) report on the impossibility of getting chimpanzee 'Sarah' to see that, for example, a miniature of a house could be related to a house itself.

Symbols

The example of substitution of signals that we have worked through helps to illustrate a key element in the sense of the term 'symbol'. A symbol is defined, for instance in Chambers dictionary, as 'that which, by custom or convention, *represents* something else' (our emphasis). The relationship of 'representing' is a purely referential one, not a practical one. The word 'food' may stand for (represent) what a dog, for example, can be nourished by; but it cannot stand *in* for it. It will not do, as a substitute for feeding the dog, to write the words 'fresh meat' on a piece of paper and put it in the dog's bowl. It is because the relationship is *only* referential that one (symbolic) sign can, in principle, be substituted for another with no loss of functional utility, provided that all relevant sign users are aware of the substitution. This is the force of the 'custom or convention' phrase in the dictionary definition of symbol.

Edward Sapir (1921, 20) was very clear in his nomination of language as a system of symbols, originally vocal-auditory, subsequently elaborated by the symbols used for writing (he identified Morse code as 'a symbol of a symbol of a symbol'). By contrast, that other influential figure in linguistics, Ferdinand de Saussure, thought the word 'symbol' was awkward when used to refer to linguistic signs, and argued (1983[1916], 68) for a degree of 'natural connection' between symbols and what they represent. Saussure cites the case of balanced scales as a symbol representative of justice, and which, he says, 'could hardly be replaced by a chariot'. Reserving the concept 'symbol' for objects invested with what may be characterised as prominent force within a community could have some pernicious consequences, as we will analyse in the next section. So, given the generality of the dictionary definition, and the support of Sapir, we retain the term symbol in the context of linguistic signs (see also Elias 1989).

One question to address before proceeding: If the dog in the conditioning experiment cannot perceive the visual or auditory signals as symbols, what does it perceive them as? What is their status with reference to the animal? That question cannot be readily answered, because the dog cannot be asked about the nature of its experience—a matter we take up again in Chapter 5. We can say that the signals in the experiment are *signs* for the animal because they are visible or audible expressions, made by the experimenter, and which function communicatively. They indicate to the dog that food is on its way. The indicative signs in this instance are arbitrary in their *form* relative to what they indicate, and only get linked to the occurrence of food by the deliberate actions of the experimenter. The reason such signs function at all is because, though the forms of the signs bear an arbitrary relation to the food, the timing of their occurrence is invariant in relation to its subsequent appearance. Signs of food for a dog in the natural environment are likely to be sight or smell, and will have the same order of invariant occurrence with respect to what is edible (Gibson 1966, 73). In that context the invariance of the 'timing' of these signs is due to the fact that they are natural accompaniments of the form and make-up of the food, and are detected in advance of its consumption in virtue of that natural connection.

In the context of the natural world, signs of food can be identified as *indexical*. This term is derived from Charles Peirce's (1955[1931]) scheme of classification of the forms of signs, a scheme we will rely on again in Chapter 5. From Peirce, the three main forms of sign that we concentrate on are icons, indexes and symbols. Icons resemble what they refer to, as in the case of a representative depiction such as a pantomime, photograph or ('realistic') painting; indexes are constrained in their form by the nature of what they indicate (for example, smoke as an index of fire, the smell of meat as an index of food). Symbols, as we have been stressing, stand in arbitrary relation to their referents, needing neither to resemble nor to be constrained in their form by their referents. We might hesitate about saying the sign of food for the dog in the conditioning experiment is an indexical sign because its *form* is not constrained in the way those signs are in the natural world (though its timing is). Such a sign might be called an 'arbitrary index', and we will have more to say about that sort of sign later.

So far the discussion has been about encoding of existing codes into other ones (alphabetic letters into morse). This has enabled us to show how symbolic signs function. As well, it shows that alphabetic characters are also symbols. They stand in conventional relationship to what they refer to, and could easily be thought of as being, themselves, substitutes for some earlier system of signs—pictographs, for instance. What, then, of the key referential relationship: that between sign and object? This is territory long inhabited by philosophy and linguistics (see, e.g., Harris 1988) and we do not attempt to offer final answers to the question. The matter comes up for discussion more than once, and in different ways, over this and the following two chapters, for it is an issue of central concern to our topic. Thus, we need to arrive at a position that is at least satisfactory with respect to arguments made in the final chapter about requisite conditions for the evolutionary expression of symbolic signs.

The word 'dog' can be used to refer to one of a class of animals; in the example we gave before it might be described as a 'domesticated canine'. In a sense that is not much different from saying that a dash and three dots can be used to refer to 'the letter 'b''. For 'domesticated canine' is simply a set of signs elaborating a concept, one whose function is to explain the sort of reference that 'dog' could be used for. No real journey has been made from sign to object in saying 'dog' can refer to 'domesticated canine'. Ultimately, the point must be arrived at where an actual object is indicated that answers to the descriptor of 'dog'. Let us say you introduce an actual live creature at this point having the formal characteristics associated with 'a dog' in, say, the middle-class Australian context. Its unfortunate habit of urinating on the carpet leads to a challenge that this is not a '*domesticated* canine'. Now there is room for dispute about what the word 'domesticated' amounts to. To an archaeologist the term 'domesticated' distinguishes dogs from wolves, the process of 'domestication' involving change in selective pressure in the production and survival of offspring (Clutton-Brock 1987; Davis 1987), rather than training in approved behaviours in middle-class households. To the householder, the archaeologist's definition may have less relevance than one which stresses such training (though the house-trainability owes part of its existence to the results of selection pressures that interest the archaeologist).

The word 'domesticated' is a symbol that refers, not to an object, but to a set of behaviours, be these generally affiliative or more particularly to do with 'house training'. Thus, it is a word that can have different conventions of meaning, depending on its contexts of use (for example, by archaeologists and pet-owners), hence it can have disputed meanings. There may be disputes among zoologists about what constitutes a 'dog', domesticated (by anyone's definition) or otherwise. Similarly, an innocent-looking word like 'food' could get people into difficulty. If, say, a biologist were to discuss such a term with the chef de cuisine, pointing out that a bale of hay in a barn is food (for a horse), or cowdung in a field (for a larva), just as is the cordon bleu dish coming from the kitchen, the exchange might become quite heated.

Theorists of language take these sorts of facts about words to indicate two things:
(1) a word for an object is not something that stands for the object as such, or any particular exemplar of the category named by the word; rather a word stands for a general concept of the object (Saussure 1983[1916], 66; Kendon 1991, 206);
(2) language is necessarily ambiguous and fuzzy (Lieberman 1984, 80–82).
The first point emphasises the idea that words are not 'representations' (like pictures) of objects, such that entities in the world are waiting to take their 'natural' names (Harris 1987, 56–58). The second point is what enables metaphoric extension, the exploitation of these very properties to allow new meanings to be encoded

in existing words, and new words ('dogging') to be devised to further exploit those new meanings.

We see the force and logic of these observations, but it is not clear that they exactly capture how language functions in everyday settings. If it were the case that people spoke in headlines ('man bites pigeon'; 'famous author falls') then there might be grounds for going along with the proposals about words as invariably standing for general concepts, and as being ambiguous. But everyday talk is specific in its reference. In a conversation about someone's family, for instance, no one would agree the speaker was operating with 'general concepts' when using the phrase 'my cousin Mary'. In such a conversation, words used like that could only be heard as referring to a particular person, a specific object, without ambiguity. These same words, in isolation, could be described as expressions of general concepts (such as, of pronominality, kinship and personal identity). Furthermore, any user of such a phrase would be thought not to understand what they had said if they could not switch to a conceptual level and explain what they meant by the words in question, supposing such an interrogation itself made any sense. In the circumstance of actual use, words are made to function with whatever degree of precision the context requires (see also Noble 1992, 639). (Headlines only work because the convention underlying their use includes a guarantee that the non-specific, attention-getting phrase will be supported by specifying text.)

Lieberman (1984, 81–2) argues that a word like 'table', when referring to the item of furniture, looks as though it is quite unambiguous in its reference, except that a context can arise where someone says, 'I'll use this chair as a table', thereby, seemingly, rendering uncertain the set of things that can be considered tables. But the problem is actually handled by the language used, and with no risk on this occasion as to what should count as what. In this circumstance you do not say (unless to be heard as weakly joking): 'We'll have to call this chair a table for the time being because I'm going to put my dinner plate on it'. The phrase employed, 'I'll use this chair as a table' precisely acknowledges the unconventionality of the use under the (broad) immutability of the object's identity.

In this argument we are not trying to say that language faultlessly reflects every nuance of interaction between symbols and their referents. In the example of 'domestication' given earlier it may be seen that there is room for misunderstanding and dispute in what parties to an interaction might take to be the topic of reference. But there is nothing in principle to prevent arrival at a common understanding of exactly what is being referred to (the only point we are seeking to illuminate). Clarity of reference does not then mean absence of profound disputation about what that implies (although, as it happens, many disputes do resolve upon just this sort of clarification, just as others stem from it).

What we have seen to this point is that the arbitrariness which characterises referential signs allows for substitutability of such signs, that such signs function as symbols, and, further, that there is potential for precise specification of referents using such symbols.

Referential signs as the basic symbols

Are there other kinds of symbols? We do not believe there are other kinds so much as that symbols come to be used for different purposes than the achievement of everyday reference. Words are typically used as tools in everyday life (O'Connell 1988): for instance, by means of words, individual persons, objects and places are differentiated; questions get asked and answered; states of affairs are described, gossip and lies get told. Some words come to be used ritually, or in restricted ways; they become vested with significance for overall community life. Certain objects and places get similarly imbued with significance. The condition which enables this is as follows: whatever the reason/s people imbue something with significance, they do so by telling stories which explain what that significance is. Nothing can be made an object of communal reverence without the prior establishment of communal reference. It is the shared use of signs for referential purposes that enables the social construction of everything else.

What gets socially constructed as a 'significant' entity does not, thereby, leave the symbolic realm—indeed, in many contexts of use, 'the symbolic' refers precisely to this category of the 'significant', often with particular reference to religious significance (e.g., Jung 1976). Chambers dictionary, which we invoked to give us the 'custom and convention' definition of symbol, goes on to define the term as referring to 'creed, compendium of doctrine, or a typical religious rite'. All human communities construct 'symbolic universes' (Berger & Luckmann 1966) where 'the symbolic' is taken to refer to the forms of abstraction about and explanation/ legitimation of 'the meanings' of things. This is what becomes developed as religious creeds. The use of the term 'symbol' to cover both the workaday notion of 'something that represents something else' and the more elaborate one of 'creed or religious rite' makes for difficulties in the analysis of the archaeological record of human evolution, as the following discussion explains.

Our position is that words as symbols enable construction of symbolic (including religious symbolic) universes. In this we rely on the argument of Berger and Luckmann (1966, 49–61), who observe that human expressions are able to be made objective. Such objectification contrasts with expressions, occurring more universally, of what they call 'subjective' states: states of arousal giving rise to such things as cries or howls. Cries and howls are what Burling (1993) has styled 'gesture-calls'. A unique feature of human life is that devices can be created which allow subjective states to be made objective. For example, an adversary might make a mark on another's door as a sign of hostile feelings toward that person. Such a sign may be made in anger, but its very persistence detaches it from the immediate expression of that anger. The mark persists as an objectively available record of a state of affairs; it is detached from the emotion which animated its production. By this is not meant that the mark *induces* detachment; its presence may stir great emotion. Rather, the mark is separate from the emotional expression of the person who made it whilst going on conveying that expression.

Berger and Luckmann identify linguistic signs as the system of similarly detachable expressions, and which have paramount place in human life. Thus, the word 'anger' refers meaningfully to an emotional state and does not require the speaker of the word to be in that state for its meaning, as a word, to be understood. The word may be used to refer to an earlier experienced state or to one that could eventuate. The detachability and objectifying force of linguistic signs enables reference to what is not immediately present.

An inevitable result is that words function to make real what is *not* perceivable. 'Anger' is a real emotional state that can be referred to by that word, and yet it may not be being currently experienced by anyone using the word in a conversation. One of the everyday powers of words, as symbols, is to enable reference to what exists, be these emotional states or material entities, but that are not immediately in sight— Hockett's design feature of 'displacement'. That same power enables reference to what is out of sight and is *imagined* to exist, such as 'the gods', 'ghosts', 'spirits' or 'the wind'. It is here, we impress, that symbols as 'simple' things cannot help allowing the emergence of, for example, superstitious beliefs to account for the conjunctions of inexplicable events (famines, fires, floods) and their disastrous consequences, leading ultimately to religious creeds. From this perspective we inevitably see it as the case that human beings create their gods to explain the inexplicable and to justify their own lives, including their conduct as 'explainers'. In the beginning it only was the word.

The case of the mark, in Berger and Luckmann's example, is one of the recording of a meaning ('I hate you') expressible in words, using a visible symbol in their place. Examples of religious or ritual symbol-use take various forms: a word may be taken to *be* (not just name) the spirit of a dead ancestor, and perhaps only be spoken under special circumstances; or an object may identify the status of a priest; or a place may be used to commemorate a major event and be protected from other uses. All these are instances of symbols which stand for things other than themselves: the mark for the hostile feeling, the word for the spirit, the object for the office, the place for the event. They may be prominent in their symbolic function, but to function at all requires workaday words that can be used to explain and justify their status. They may be held as esteemed (or feared, or despised), or at any rate as *distinctive* items; it is, nevertheless, the capacity enabling construction of the symbolic signs forming any community's language which thereby enables use of that language to construct its more prominent symbolic signs. The mark as a sign of hostility could not so function unless it were already appreciated in the linguistic community in question that such a mark in such a context had that meaning.

The example given by Saussure of his seeing a 'natural connection' between justice and balanced scales depends upon his and his readers' shared appreciation of the idea, which can only be elaborated through deployment of linguistic signs, that 'justice should be even-handed'. A way to characterise even-handedness is the joining of a symbol for justice, the blindfolded figure of the classical goddess Justitia, with a symbol for equal weightedness in the form of balanced scales—both the goddess and the implement being artefacts that have their own further explanations. Thus, what looks like an effortless perception is one built on the back of a lengthy history and education reliant on the use of language to explicate the various meanings that allow the link to be seen. A different history and education might even lead to a chariot symbolising a system or justice—Saussure's doubts notwithstanding. If it were taken as paramount that 'justice delayed is justice denied', a chariot might symbolise, by 'natural connection', the need to keep things moving. Justice is often characterised by a sword: a chariot could be 'the means of conveying the condemned to the gallows'. With enough imagination we expect anything could be made to 'naturally' connect with 'justice'.

Chase and Dibble on symbols

The concept of 'symbol' used to refer to those things which figure in ritual of one sort or another includes the foregoing symbol for justice, a symbol involved in the legal rituals of 'Western' societies. The ubiquity of these more prominent forms of symbol can lead to possibilities for debate about what evolved from what. In our argument, the symbolic signs making up (and ongoingly productive of) a language are the basis for more elaborate forms of symboling. By contrast, Chase (1991) who gives similar prominence to symbols, argues a position that makes 'symboling' a form of creative behaviour from which others, such as linguistic behaviour, derive. For Chase, the key point which characterises a symbol, using the Peircian perspective we outlined earlier, is the *arbitrariness of the relation* (Chapter 2) between sign and referent. Thus, he notes (1991, 195) that the phenomenon of interest is 'the kind of arbitrary relationship between a sign and its referent that forms the foundation of human language ... although it is broader because it is not confined to the context of language'. Elsewhere (p. 193) he states that 'language ... owes its very existence to symbols'. Chase and Dibble (1987, 264) list language along with 'religion and symbolic thought, and culturally defined social systems'. The existence of language thus appears either to rest on or to emerge in concert with a more general capacity (for 'symboling'). If symboling is either precursor to or contemporaneous with linguistic behaviour, then from an evolutionary perspective the emergence of this general capacity for symboling becomes in need of explanation.

Chase, and Chase and Dibble (1987), are concerned to show what may or may not be legitimately said about the presence of symboling in relation to the Palaeolithic archaeological record, a matter we return to in Chapters 6 and 7. What we need to deal with here is a case for supporting 'the creation of arbitrary relations' as a foundational behaviour from which symbol-making behaviour of various kinds flows, versus a case for the particular kind of symboling behaviour, identified as linguistic, as the foundation for other symbol-making and use. Chase and Dibble have not aimed at providing theory or speculation about how symboling—be it general or particular—may have emerged. In one sense, their refraining from engagement with such a question might be taken as a sign of scientific prudence (our exploration of it equally a sign of folly). In another sense, though, it means that analysis of and evidence for the behaviour being considered is left without guidance. For instance, a consequence of making arbitrariness the central issue in symbol production is to create puzzles over the status of representational depiction. Chase says (p.196) that icons and indexes stand in some kind of natural relation with their referents: relations of resemblance or symptomatology.

> For both icons and indexes, the relationship between sign and object need only be *perceived*. In the case of the icon one recognises the resemblance between it and its referent*, and in the case of the index, one observes and recognises the association between them. By contrast, the relationship between symbol and referent must be *created*. (Chase 1991, 201–2, emphases in original).

In a footnote at * Chase concedes that icons in the form of representational images must be created, but does not elaborate on the creativity involved in this case, as against that needed for making symbols. Elsewhere (p. 200), Chase states that icons representing 'things that do not exist in nature' (therianthropic, i.e., half-human/half-beast figures such as that shown in Figure 9) could be evidence of symboling because they may be understood as icons of items that are themselves

Figure 9 Carving of imaginary figure found at Hohlenstein-Stadel, dated about 32 000 years ago (see Figure 40 for site location). *Courtesy:* Ulm Museum.

Figure 10 Engravings on limestone blocks from La Ferrassie (see Figure 40). *Courtesy:* Les Eyzies Museum.

symbolic (i.e., to do with creeds and ritual). In that same context he cites an argument made by Halverson (e.g., 1987), among others, that Palaeolithic representational depiction, at its inception, is *non*-symbolic (see also Chase 1994). This argument is precisely that the depiction may not have been made as part of religious or other totemic activity. The repeated engravings at sites near and including La Ferrassie (Delluc & Delluc 1978)—see Figure 10—are among the earliest artefacts (from about 32 000 years ago) that may be taken to be symbols (Bahn 1986; Davidson 1990). Chase and Dibble (1992, 44) cite the stylised and standardised form of these engravings as the basis for so classifying them, adding: 'even if they were also iconic'. Thus, the sense of the 'symbolic' from these statements is that 'symboling' has the character of ritual or related socially 'significant' conduct and that the making of icons and the making of symbols are distinct achievements.

We find a similar appreciation of symbols in the earlier, and, within anthropology, influential writing of Raymond Firth (e.g. 1973). Firth is not satisfied that words are symbols, contrasting the imprecision of the words of a language with the symbols used in mathematical analysis. He invokes the Peircian scheme; and also takes it that symbol making implies complex conceptual content. For example (pp. 64–5), the red flag that *symbolises* 'revolutionary politics' may be, physically, the same red flag that *indexes* road works ahead. In the first case the social context of use of the sign makes us 'conceive the idea it presents', in the second 'it serves to make us notice the object or situation it bespeaks'. Whatever the validity of this distinction, the point we stress is that language is entailed in either case. The red flag on the road may be thought to act as an index, in the way a conditioning signal does in the Pavlovian experiment. But the connection is not discovered in the way it is in that analogy. We do not learn by direct association, through running the car into piles of rubble a few times, that the flag indexes danger ahead. Rather, the flag is an arbitrary index whose meaning is understood through a socially constructed convention explained in the code book governing rules about road use. The same physical object subserves distinct purposes in the two situations Firth describes; the character of either (any) sort of meaning for the flag is in the form of a linguistic elaboration.

The sense of the 'symbolic' evoked by Firth, Chase (and Saussure), is theoretically impenetrable—how could a capacity for such 'symboling' emerge? We have already elaborated how this special use of 'symbol' arises from the very nature of language as a symbolic medium—able to be used to fashion fanciful meanings from those more mundane. The notion of 'symboling' these scholars introduce also presents insurmountable problems when we try to operationalise it in contexts beyond our own community of shared understanding.

Chase (1991) lists, as potential signs of prehistoric symbol-making: style, arbitrary form, and standardisation. We would argue that any evidence of these would also be evidence of language (Davidson 1992, 55). It is notable that to distinguish the presence of 'symboling' in each case Chase does rely on such evidence. He cites a claim for style in the form of the consistently different plant stems used by three different groups of chimpanzees in the course of their termite fishing (McGrew et al. 1979). These differences in form are non-symbolic, Chase argues, because language is not involved. With arbitrary form, the distinction Chase relies upon is specifically between the non-symbolic operations for producing flaked stone as against the regularities that constitute language. Standardisation, Chase states (1991, 207), will show evidence of symboling only if it is 'dictated by a concept related to a non-physical (i.e., communicative) function'. Whilst seeming to want the behaviour of symbol production to have broader than linguistic implications, Chase cannot avoid the fact that to detect symbolic conduct is to detect the behaviour—linguistic—which we argue underpins all other symbol construction.

Icons as symbols

Still left as a puzzle is the status of representational depiction, which, because it is understood as iconic, is somehow not symbolic. We could invoke the dictionary definition once again and say simply that because a picture is an object that represents something else (a picture of a bison represents a bison), then such an entity is a symbol (see Noble 1993, 70). It turns out that there are larger issues at stake, because concepts descriptive of various psychological functions are involved in this analysis. Chase says that, in the case of icons and indexes, 'the relationship between sign and object need only be perceived'. With an icon 'one recognises the resemblance between it and its referent', with an index 'one ... recognises the association between them'. We need to scrutinise the meanings of the concepts 'perceiving' and 'recognising of resemblance' being invoked here. Other analysts of prehistoric icons have relied on versions of perceiving and recognising to account for the production or pre-production of such depictive imagery. The various ways these concepts are characterised will be examined after discussion of the icon-as-symbol issue.

The making of iconic depictions is an intentional practice in its own right. A behaviour whose deliberateness is less easy to specify, but which is an inevitable *precursor* to that which at some point takes the form of such deliberate production, has very great significance in the account we will ultimately offer of the evolutionary emergence of language. Icons arise by means of mimicry—a gesture that copies, for example, a contour of an object traces it in imitation. The centrality of icons to our theorising, and the critical role of imitation in producing them, means that instead of seeking to establish iconic images as symbols simply by appeal to the dictionary, the analytic task is aimed at showing how the deliberate, i.e., self-consciously planned, production of such representation entails language, and is itself unambiguously symbolic. In Chapter 8 we argue that (and how) communicative symbols are bootstrapped on behaviour precursory to the self-consciously planned production of iconic representation.

Halverson (1987) suggests that the absence of corroborating evidence for links between the earliest known depictive images and 'hunting magic' or religious ritual leaves open the possibility that no 'symbolic' function need attend their production. At the same time he speculates (p. 70) on a scenario for their production thus: 'For hunters ... there is much indeed to occupy the mind in planning, preparing, tracking, trapping, stalking, chasing, killing, butchering, transporting, distributing, eating, celebrating, reminiscing, and dreaming.'

Some of these terms (chasing, killing, eating), as we saw in the last chapter, could describe the activities of some other primates (McGrew 1992, 99–105); some, such as planning and reminiscing, as we discuss in various places throughout this book, are behaviours involving language. Halverson imagines Upper Palaeolithic life as 'embedded in the concrete and action'. There is, though, an assumption: that linguistic behaviour (symbols used communicatively) forms part of that life. Halverson may speculate that the 'higher order' symbols associated with religious or totemic practices are absent, though we doubt whether there is any method for establishing the validity (or invalidity) of that assumption. He believes that what gets depicted is the projection of a 'mental image', in part stimulated by cues from features of the landscape itself that are witnessed as resembling other features (a crack in a rock that looks like the outline of an animal). He takes it (1992a, 228–9) that 'there were art critics as soon as there was art', and sees their first question as, 'What's it supposed to be?'. From evidence such as that of repeat attempts at delineation, he also takes it (1992a, 229) that those making depictions would 'pause from time to time to ask themselves if they were getting it right'. So, even if the practice is assumed to be a direct reproduction/projection of mental content, it is also assumed to be embedded in a language-using community.

Similar assumptions inform Lewis-Williams and Dowson's speculations (1988). The earliest depictions, in their view, are of sensory impressions (rather than 'mental images') resident in the visual nervous system as such, including the nervous systems of other primates. These impressions take the form either of disturbances of vision ('entoptics') of the sort that can occur with migraine headaches, or of iconic hallucinations that may occur under various types of altered consciousness. As part of their account, Lewis-Williams and Dowson offer a description of perceptual recognition, namely, as a process whereby visual impressions arising from external stimulation of the eye by light are matched against stored images in the brain. An impression is 'recognised' if a fit is achieved between such an impression and an already stored image. With internally generated impressions (entoptics or hallucinations), '[t]he brain attempts to recognise ... these forms as it does impressions supplied by the nervous system in a normal state of consciousness' (p. 203). As we pointed out previously (Noble & Davidson 1993, 130–1), even in Lewis-Williams and Dowson's own account, the seeing of such phenomena critically depends on language-guided induction and training procedures. Despite the invocation of the brain as a putative mechanism for 'recognising' the impressions, *social* procedures are needed to allow the person to focus attention on and try to make sense of what is experienced.

Davis (1986) turns the recognition/resemblance matter the other way around. He questions (1986) the classically-held view (such as expressed by Halverson and Lewis-Williams and Dowson) that the origin of image making can be understood as the copying or projection on to surfaces of mental representations of some sort. As Davis says (1986, 199) there is no prehistoric evidence for the *cognitive* capacities underwriting any such projective capacity. There is no sign in other primate behaviour for exteriorising whatever interior imagery might occur in their minds (or brains/nervous systems), even though the nervous systems of hominids and our close primate relatives can be presumed to be similar. Instead, Davis speculates that originators recognised (iconic) similarity between physical marks they themselves made, incidentally in or on surfaces, and natural environmental features.

Significantly, in Davis's argument, the status of mark-making which results in the production of forms recognisable as other things is perforce a *semantic* activity. At Figure 11 we reproduce the scheme he devises (Davis 1986, Figure 6) to distinguish a form of marking which he calls 'semiotic' from that which is 'semantic'. He makes the distinction thus (197):

> The term *semiotic* is ... applied ... to any marking produced deliberately and for its own sake... A semiotic mark only has *semantic value*, is *referential*, if it stands for an object besides or beyond itself. (emphasis in original)

Thus, Davis explicitly expresses the view that iconic marks are semantic. Conkey

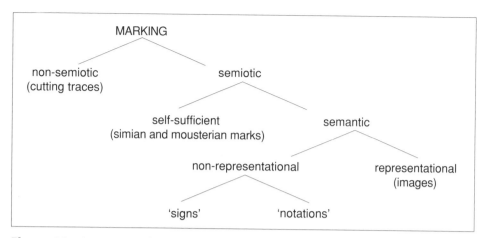

Figure 11 Categories of marking showing iconic (representational) marks as a sub-aspect of the semantic category. *From* Davis 1986.

(1987) has advocated that universalising accounts of 'the meaning' of prehistoric depiction are better replaced with ones sensitive to the varying contexts of its production; but she is in no doubt that 'meaning' (semantic value) is there in the imagery. Seeing resemblance in marks, made up or noticed as things that look like other things, is of necessity *referential*. In being iconic the referent may be readily appreciated—or it may not, a matter we analyse in the ensuing section. Whether or not the referent is self-evident, the fact of a relation between entity (referent) and representation (icon) means they share certain properties with words.

What is it for something to be an icon?

Chase's statement about the ready perceiving of relations between iconic signs and that which they are signs of makes their (contrived) nature deceptively straightforward. It sounds uncomplicated to say icons are things that resemble other things, but there is more to it than that. Icons are identified by human investigators: they are picked out because they resemble something else, or they are objects/surfaces modified by human agents to look like something else. Consider the object reported upon by Goren-Inbar (1986) found at the Lower Palaeolithic site of Berekhat Ram, pictured here as Figure 12a, and dated to older than 270 000 years ago (Feraud et al. 1983). This was picked out by the archaeologist because it resembled something else, akin to the 20 000—30 000 year-old 'Venus figurines' (e.g., Gamble 1986) of the European Upper Palaeolithic (Figure 12b). There is no evidence that the Berekhat Ram object was formed by human agency rather than by natural forces (Davidson 1990), a point supported by Pelcin (1994), hence we cannot say that it was a thing *made* to resemble anything. The fact that it was picked out by archaeologists means that this object now remains iconic because archaeologists (and perhaps others) continue to perceive the resemblance. We have no way of knowing whether it was perceived *as* anything at any other time.

a   b

0   5 cm

Figure 12 **a** Berekhat Ram object (see Figure 42). *Courtesy:* Israel Museum;
b 'Venus figurine' from Dolni Vestonice (see Figure 40). *From* Marshack 1972.

Icons do not 'present themselves'. In speaking of them as being picked out note
must be made of the fact that to pick something out is to exercise a choice about what
it is that resembles what. In the case of the Berekhat Ram object, the resemblance is
with the arrangement of certain human bodily features, an arrangement to which the
archaeologist is primed through familiarity with the archaeologically well-known
(much) later figurines. Lorblanchet (1977) notes the prevalence in Upper Palaeolithic
depictions of what is unhesitatingly called 'partial' or 'incomplete' representation
(Halverson 1992b). Images of animals frequently show only certain parts, like
heads or the line of the back (Figure 13). As we have pointed out before (Davidson
& Noble 1989, 149) it is impossible to define completeness for an image; indeed, all
representations are incomplete, since the only way they could be otherwise is if they

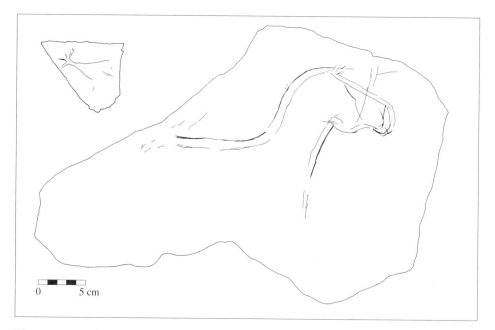

Figure 13 Palaeolithic depictions from Parpalló (see Figure 40) showing parts of animals. *From* Villaverde Bonilla 1994.

were the objects represented. The intention to portray some general or specific aspect of something leads to its 'complete' depiction once the conventionally defined image of that feature is fashioned. Deregowski (1972) records the case of drawings of domestic cattle being seen as incomplete by viewers among a group of Ethiopian people because the detail of a dewlap, held as highly salient for distinguishing this animal, was missing.

It becomes feasible that images are iconic whose reference nevertheless cannot be simply 'perceived', because what has been picked out for representation makes the image unintelligible for any who are unused to attending to that feature *in depicted form*. Deregowski (1980, 112–118) describes the extraordinary difficulty people have, who are unfamiliar with conventions of 'Western' depiction, in making out anything meaningful in pictures whose content is readily identified by those who are familiar with those conventions. In the background of almost anyone reading this book is a lifelong exposure to single-point-of-view perspective depiction, in the form of photographs and other imagery, all of which maintain and modify conventions dating to Ancient Greek and Roman times (White 1967). The concept of the 'iconic' is primed for typical members of 'Westernised' communities to match such depiction. We are seduced by the photograph, a mechanically provided image, into believing that this somehow provides *the* way of representing things. The photograph is itself a consequence of historical pictorial conventions involving fixed viewpoints, the invention of the *camera obscura* and centuries of experiments with optical instruments (Costall 1985). It takes a moment's reflection

Figure 14 Depictions characteristic of the style used by Northwest coast Native American people. *From* Boas 1955.

to see that iconicity varies from the conventions people are used to in Westernised communities. Figure 14 shows examples of imagery whose referents are variably recognisable by people with the sort of backgrounds we take most of our readers to have. Different viewers may disagree on the very question of whether these images *are* iconic.

This observation does not amount to an argument that photographs have only an *incidental* connection with what they are photographs of. Clearly, the structure of reflected light that gets focused by an artificial lens onto photosensitive material is of the same order as input to a *camera obscura* or a chambered eye (Gibson 1950; 1971). What we are stressing is that the technological achievement called the camera is itself the result of historical processes of selection of modes of iconic representation which captured ever more effectively—namely, in the classical Greek and Renaissance Italian styles—the appearance provided by the overall convention of single-point-of-view perspective (Hagen 1980; 1986). In text below we refer to the idea of survival of effective forms of representation. The convention of single-point-of-view speaks to postural attitudes of static contemplation of stationary environmental features (Wartofsky 1980). Such postures and acts do not guarantee the convention of single-viewpoint *depiction*; they are doubtless a critical ingredient.

We are not aware of any documented cases of non-human primates making icons outside of a context of human captivity and tutelage. Even within that context it is not clear what such animals produce. Gardner and Gardner (1980) claim an example of image-making for a captive chimpanzee, called 'Moja', trained with American Sign Language signs. We quote from an earlier work in which we said that the animal: 'made a trace with chalk on paper, and after the research assistant's signed 'what that?' made a gesture taken by the research assistant to mean *bird*' (Noble &

Figure 15 Mark made by chimpanzee 'Moja' and taken by a research assistant to have been identified by the chimpanzee as a 'bird' . *From* Gardner & Gardner 1980.

Davidson 1991, 244). Figure 15 reproduces the trace from the Gardners' report. Our earlier characterisation of this scenario was designed to signal caution about what conceptual resources the chimpanzee was bringing to it, as against those supplied by the research assistant on its behalf. Let us suppose the animal was attempting to depict a bird. We do not know what we are faced with because it is not clear whether some part of the object was picked out for picturing (the body, the eye, for instance). The limits on conversational interaction prevent inquiry about 'what it's supposed to be'. Critical to this analysis is that such interaction would be necessary, not only here, but universally. How is this so?

Moja's 'drawing of a bird' would be recognisable as such an icon only because it conformed to the conventions of some style of representation with which we were already familiar. In that case the ape would have had to have been trained in this style, an unlikely possibility. On the assumption that Moja was producing an 'untrained' or 'primitive' attempt at depiction, we would be back to the other impossible-looking task of seeking to discover, through interrogation, what aspect of the object the picture stood for. This point generalises to any icon produced outside of familiar conventions. Halverson's (1992a) off-the-cuff remark about critics emerging simultaneously with artists needs to be reconceptualised in the following terms. Any attempt at iconic representation must be sustained in a conventionalising context, such that what has been picked out for the icon to resemble is made apparent to oneself and to others. Critical judgments, by the icon-maker or others, take two yoked forms: (1) Does the depiction match the object—is it recognisable as representing it—according to prevailing criteria of similarity; thus (2) does it do it as well as variant depictions made by oneself or others?

Variation among depictors/depictions will be bound to occur as there must be variation in the bodily (sensorimotor) coordination and control abilities of different group members and from time to time. Anything judged to improve on a resemblance, with respect to whatever is being picked out, sets a new standard of acceptability and thereby extends competitive criteria. It may be postulated that the historical selection of conventions occurs through competition among variants which are necessarily set in social contexts of shifting criteria. Depictions that persist within a community are feasibly those which distinguish more effectively among salient objects or features. What is judged as salient (and effective) will vary through space and time. As a technical accomplishment, the production of iconic signs is well characterised as resulting from adaptation, selection and duplication within contexts of education and training whose formality will also vary (Gombrich 1960, especially Chapter V)

By whatever means conventions survive to be duplicated and modified, the *communication* of what any form is created to (try to) represent is integral to its production as a representation. The simple perceiving of resemblance in icons is starting to look like the conceptually, hence socially, sustained achievement that it indeed is. Icons are referential and in that sense have something in common with words. The meaning of an icon, in the sense of what it is a representation of, is witnessed through the linguistic elaborations that serve to convey the relation between image and referent. As Goody remarks (1987, 9–10):

> [O]ne is never engaged simply in making an icon of an object as such: a horse standing in a field is a horse viewed in terms of a language that places the animal in a system of categories.

The works of the scholars we have been referring to in this and the previous section have language as explicitly or implicitly bound in with depictive practices. We hope the foregoing analyses allow appreciation of why this has to be so. Icons are symbolic in being referential; and their meanings, in terms of what they represent (and, need it be said, their significance if used as totems or religious sacraments), are sustained within the symbol system of language.

What is involved in 'recognising' or 'perceiving resemblance'?

It begins to look as though 'recognising' and 'perceiving of resemblance' involve more than meets the eye (and the central neural tissue to which it is linked). Lewis-Williams and Dowson (1988) suggest the brain recognises things through comparing current input with stored memory. Davis (1986, 200) says that 'For thousands of millennia, the primate and hominid *visual systems* had experienced perceptual ambiguity ... and had recognised identities and similarities', and that '*perception* will construe ambiguous information erroneously—will see edges or depth where edges and depth do not exist' (our emphases). Chase does not commit himself to any version of recognising, but does make it clear that the perceiving of resemblance in icons is more-or-less automatic: 'A viewer associates a picture of a bison with a bison because it looks like one ... for both icon and index, there is something natural about the relationship between sign and referent'. We do not dispute Chase's points; we do argue that the achievement of this evidentness and naturalness is historical. Chase also appreciates that people do the perceiving and recognising, not their brains or eyes (Coulter 1979a; Noble & Davidson 1991).

These characterisations by Chase contrast with our earlier point about the production/identification of icons, where we argued that icons do not simply 'present themselves'; rather they are picked out by human observers, hence judgements are being made about what resembles what. In the texts we have examined, the terms 'recognise' and 'perceive resemblance' are used roughly interchangeably. In fact, in their ordinary meaning, these terms do not reduce to each other. The reason they get conflated is precisely because of the ideas expressed by Lewis-Williams and Dowson and by Davis that 'recognition' is routinely what perceiving is about, and that the 'process of recognising' is one in which a matching-up is made between an image and a memory, thus, that a resemblance between them is perceived.

The following brief analysis derives from an earlier one (Davidson & Noble 1989, 129–130) as further informed by Jeff Coulter's discussion of Wittgenstein's treatment of the concept of 'recognising' (Coulter 1987). It needs a moment's reflection to see that, in ordinary usage, to recognise something/someone is to make a claim to *familiarity* with that thing/person. To see a resemblance is to lay claim to some form of *similarity* between one thing/person and another. Common to both of these slightly but distinctly different activities is the claim-making feature. This need not be a publicly expressed avowal, but it no less takes the form of a claim (to oneself) for all that. Either of these types of claim is recognisable as such by the fact that it may be defeated or be the subject of modification. Asserting familiarity may turn out to be a mistake (the person you thought you *recognised* as X turns out merely to *resemble* X). It may be that the resemblance you think you can see from a far distance breaks down when you get closer, and make out more details; thus, the relation of resemblance is unstable. Thus, finally, as Gilbert Ryle (1949) pointed out, the term 'recognise' refers to an achievement. The achievement of recognition occurs when a claim is confirmed.

Recognition would be described as having been '*thought* to have been achieved' if the claim is vetoed—'I thought I recognised it as one of Mozart's string quartets, but my partner said "no, it's Haydn...".' That too can change if the initial claim is upheld—'...then the announcer confirmed I'd been right'. Goren-Inbar (1986) claimed to recognise the pebble from Berekhat Ram as a model of a hominid female, but others (e.g., Davidson 1990; Pelcin 1994) dispute the achievement. Confirmation of the recognition will be difficult in this case, but would, at least, require some independent evidence, such as signs of modelling. The research assistant claimed to recognise that Moja had represented something, and Moja was taken to confirm this. It is doubtful whether criteria for such confirmation have been adequately defined or described. Which reinforces the general point that the achievement of recognition or of seeing resemblance is criteria-dependent: either one requires ratification for its acceptance or rejection.

Recognising and seeing resemblance thus entail use of language (and a social context) for their achievement. They are occurrences which only arise in the claim-making practices of community members. The perceptual achievements of non-language users, in the face of entities they detect (and might be described by Lewis-Williams and Dowson as 'recognising'), reveal only part of what is involved. That part—the capacity to detect and respond to environmental events—is critical. We noted in an earlier analysis (Davidson & Noble 1989), that a hungry toad will predate in the face of experimental simulations of prey, namely, purely optical modulations that give the appearance of a wriggling worm (McFarland 1985). The toad cannot be said to recognise (or fail to recognise) 'the worm' because there are no criteria by which its action can be judged to involve success or failure in *recognition*.

We will return to considerations of these sorts of issues in the next chapter, as this is an example of a 'mental predicate'—the attribution or otherwise of a 'state of mind' to a perceiving being. The final function of the analysis undertaken here is to reveal the apparatus of a human community which is needed to support taken-for-granted features of individual conduct such as the production and perception of symbols. It is this same nexus, of individual and community, that may be used to make sense of the notion of mind.

Some notes about 'culture'

We have argued, as with the example of the chimpanzee 'Moja', that seeing what something represents exemplifies common knowledge, shared appreciation of the convention which supports this or that *meaning* of the thing. It is well documented in present-day societies that 'meaning' is crucially dependent on the circumstances of an individual's membership of a social group (Morphy 1991). The present analysis examines the support structure of that fact. The definition of symbol involves the role of shared knowledge—'that which, by custom or convention, represents something else'. Nothing is 'customary' or 'conventional' outside of groups whose coordinated actions make it so, as may be seen in the example of spelling conventions we used at the start. This puts a critical constraint on any attempt to explain the origin of symbol use—the origin must involve the coordinated actions of at least two community members.

Symbol-guided behaviour was identified by the anthropologist Leslie White (e.g.1942; 1959) as the key to distinguishing human from other forms of life. The word White (1959) sought thereby to define, and which would naturally suggest itself as relevant to all this, is 'culture', a term often reserved to identify behaviour constrained by articulable conventions of one sort or another. 'Culture' has a status rather like 'mind'—it might even be thought of as 'the mind' of a 'group' of people. It is a reification of an abstract concept, derived from observation of a person's behaviour as constrained by that of others they interact with during their lifetimes. It is a category which may repay analysis, but it cannot be invoked as a causal mechanism. Defining 'culture' in this or any other way will probably not be generally assented to, and insofar as this is true it is a term likelier to confuse than to clarify.

Kroeber and Kluckhohn (1954) assembled more than 150 definitions of the term 'culture', showing that, even though most definitions have assumed the term refers exclusively to human conduct, there is much scope for dispute. McGrew (1992) and McGrew and colleagues (1979) selected one definition, that put forward by Kroeber

(1928), with a view to seeing whether it might apply to the behaviour of other primates, particularly chimpanzees. McGrew's conclusion (1992, 82; 230) could be taken as definitive about the *lack* of culture in chimpanzees; and it could be seen as raising questions about the cultural nature of some human behaviour. By selecting a different definition, a different sort of conclusion could be arrived at. With respect to the range of primates captive to (or domesticated by) human investigators, Tomasello and colleagues (1993) conclude that those thus 'enculturated' behave distinctively differently from those they term 'wild'. Kortlandt (1986) has pointed out that some behaviours expressed by 'wild' chimpanzees, such as the use of stone for nut-cracking, may emulate that of modern human use. If so, and if we were to retain the term 'culture' as a framework for considering all this, then some 'wild' chimpanzees may be 'enculturated'. If culture is also taken to be exclusively human (e.g., Holloway 1969), then some chimpanzees may be human or human-like.

We are faced with something akin to the matter raised concerning tables and chairs. Are some chairs sometimes tables when found in some behavioural contexts? Are some chimpanzees humans when their behaviour exhibits cultural features? Is 'Kanzi' human? Rather than wear ourselves out with these peculiar questions we prefer an approach which looks to behaviours of organisms that do or do not show evidence of being guided by language use. Provided we can gain clarity about what we mean by language (which we can: language is the symbolic use of communicative signs) we can avoid essentialism about how the organism is to be defined—this relates to the social definition of humanness introduced in Chapter 1. We will, for convenience and convention's sake, identify as 'chimpanzees', 'bonobos' and the like, creatures whose species names have been thus assigned to them by 'modern humans', recognising that definitional work about species (and culture) can continue forever.

Another problem with the term 'culture' is that it suffers a fate precisely like that of the term 'symbol'—which is not surprising, given the convergence of the two terms in definitions of culture by White (1959), Geertz (1964), and ultimately Kroeber and Kluckhohn (1954). Both terms have humdrum meanings (symbol = language; culture = symbol-use), and both have highbrow meanings (symbol = ritual; culture = the Sydney Opera House). This shows up in McGrew's discussion (1992, 82) of a supposed burial of a Neanderthal with flowers (Solecki 1961). McGrew suggests that it would be 'excessive' to deny that this was cultural. If the scepticism (Gargett 1989; Noble & Davidson 1989) about interpreting this collection of archaeological evidence as such a burial is well-founded (see Chapter 7), then McGrew is wrong. More to the point in this context, McGrew does not say *why* such denial would be excessive. It seems likely that McGrew has foregone his careful analytical approach to chimpanzee behaviour, which used value-neutral criteria for 'culture' derived from Kroeber, in favour of a Sydney Opera House one. Under such a reading, dismissal would be 'excessive' because, in the romantic reading, the archaeological record here seems to show evidence of the origins of 'flower arranging', 'floral tributes' or 'wreaths'.

The occurrence of flowers in the absence of any other evidence can only provoke more questions than it answers. If humans do or do not use flowers in association with some behaviour; if other creatures do or do not, we are no closer to determining the cultural basis or otherwise of any of the behaviours in question. We have decided not to employ the term 'culture' at all from now on, simply to get around the sort of linguistic minefield of assumptions about the nature of human and other animal conduct revealed by the foregoing analyses. The vital element to retain is the fact of interaction among community members as the basis for expression of uniquely human characteristics, including, as we proceed to argue, the social construction of mind.

CHAPTER 4

CONSTRUCTING 'THE MIND'

We closed the previous chapter by saying that 'culture' might be another word for 'group mind'. After considering the concept of 'culture' we explained why, for present purposes, we dispense with the term. In this chapter certain features of the term 'mind' are examined, so as to reach a position about its meaning appropriate to our enterprise. This needs to be done because the evolution of modern human behaviour may be taken to be the evolution of 'mindedness', and the sense of that statement must be carefully scrutinised. Some current approaches to the evolutionary *origin* of 'mind' were considered in Chapter 1; here, 'mind' or 'mindedness' needs to be more clearly understood. In the end we will dispense with the term 'mind' as referring to any sort of natural *entity*, whilst arriving at a position which shows that behaviour understood as 'minded' is essentially interactive. Claims for extra-sensory perception aside, we are unaware of any candidates for forms of interpersonal exchange of minded productions other than those based on symbolic use of communicative signs. Considered this way, 'minded' behaviour is linguistic in nature; thus, human minds are socially constructed. Such a position turns out to be particularly apt for an account of the emergence of modern human behaviour grounded in evolution and archaeological evidence.

There are efforts currently to explore the nature of the mindedness of creatures other than humans (e.g. Whiten, 1993), as well as continuing debate over whether the term is applicable beyond the normal human case (e.g. Premack & Woodruff, 1978; Premack, 1988; Cheney & Seyfarth, 1990). We have considered some elements of this issue in earlier chapters, and will continue to touch upon it in this and the next one. It follows from the opening paragraph that what counts as mindedness in these contexts will involve symbol-based interactions.

Discussion of the 'mental' always threatens to be complex and messy. We cannot possibly expect to settle the questions that others have raised about appropriate ways to conceptualise 'mind'. It has been one of the major topics of 'Western' analysis, featuring especially in the writing of the pre-Christian era Greek philosopher Plato and, more recently, in the work of Descartes. 'Mind' itself may thus be considered a product of philosophical and related practices of the 'ancient and modern Western world'. It has, we suppose, even been considered a mark of membership, such that those living in communities beyond the realm of the 'Western world' are characterised by 'savage' (Lévi-Strauss 1966), or 'primitive' (Godelier 1977[1971]) minds. Such notions may be held as patronising, racist, or whatever; they are unexceptionable if used to point to the fact that what is thinkable in one historical or geographical context differs, maybe markedly, from what is thinkable in another. Once mindedness is seen as co-extensive with symbol-based communication, it is a characteristic of nearly all creatures identifiable as human (among exceptions being children born deaf/blind or brain impaired, as noted in Chapter 3). The 'Western mind' is then shorthand for ways of thinking we (writers and readers of books like this) broadly comprehend since we are familiar with the 'forms of life' which have developed those ways. The concept of 'form of life' is Wittgenstein's (1958); it refers to common ways of acting and understanding among members of the same community, and we use it in that sense in this chapter. It might be thought by some to be synonymous with 'culture'; we read it as a more general term.

A 'social construct' position takes 'minded' to denote those forms of conduct that exhibit signs of planning or forethought. Planning, as the term is ordinarily understood, implicates language in the guidance of skilled action. Parker and Milbrath (1993) include as 'planning', instances of behaviour characterised by continuous bodily adjustments, such as reaching and grasping. They term this 'planning in action' or 'procedural planning', though we believe such behaviour would be better described as controlled action, rather than as an instance of a 'plan'. Be that as it may, these authors go on to identify as 'planned activity' the kind of behaviour which shows evidence of the pre-arrangement of objects for subsequent action upon them, and the pre-selection, segregation from contexts, and encoding, of action elements. Parker and Milbrath point out that such behaviour ('declarative planning') cannot occur independently of language. The terms *procedural* and *declarative*, borrowed from Anderson (1985), are related to the concepts devised by Ryle (1949) of 'knowing how' to do something and 'knowing that' so-and-so is the case. As Parker and Milbrath state in conclusion (p.320): 'the transition from plans as procedures to declarative plans develops with linguistic event representation from the codification of a procedure, to the decontextualization of its parts, resulting in increased potential for plan modification and regulation.'

Bloch argues (1991) an apparently contrary point, namely, that action of this kind is independent of language. He suggests this is because some skilled actions can be acquired without words, and because much skilled action does not require words for its maintenance in the practised actor, and, further, because skilled action is not the same as its description. The two sorts of behaviour (procedural and declarative actions) are certainly not to be confused with each other, yet, for humans at any rate, they are unavoidably interdependent. People who suffer alcohol-induced amnesia ('Korsakoff's Syndrome') can exercise skilled behaviour that entails sensorimotor control (keeping a pointer aimed at a moving target), but cannot learn tasks that require verbal mediation, such as how to get through a simple maze, a task that depends on planning, on remembering sequences of self-instruction, for its acquisition and maintenance (Butters & Cermak 1980, 48–49). Thus, people with amnesia may be able to perform what Parker and Milbrath call procedural plans, but not declarative ones. Amnesia does not affect the capacity to remember *how* to do things; it impairs the capacity to retain propositions *about* things, hence, including propositions about how to do something novel (Cohen & Squire 1980).

As people raised in literate societies we are accustomed to the expression of ideas about the unusual nature of human awareness (e.g. Dennett 1991; Flanagan 1992). The mention of '*literate* society' is more than incidental. Part of how the 'mind' is understood, in the kind of community which includes the production of writing about that very topic, reflects an influence of mass literacy (Olson 1986; 1994). The unusual nature of human awareness lies in the fact that not only do humans, under normal conditions, 'know' all sorts of things ('water is wet', 'blood is thicker than water'), we also know *that* we know such things. We can reflect on the fact that we know things; we can 'monitor our self-monitorings' (Harré & Secord 1972). Even among advocates of the view that non-human animals are 'minded', and know many things in the way humans do, few would advance the further claim to the effect that those other animals can reflect on the fact of their knowing. It might be said that the inauguration of the practice of philosophy, a practice dedicated to reflection, corresponds to the making of statements about what there is to know about and what is involved in knowing about it (Russell 1993[1946]).

Our intention in this chapter does not include a retracing of the history or philosophy of mind. That task is monumental, and several recent texts, in addition to those mentioned above, have been addressed to the subject of mind (e.g. Gardner 1985; Priest 1991). There is even an 'Oxford Companion' to it (Gregory 1987). We will limit our attention to a contrast between two current approaches: the 'social construct' story we prefer, and the 'representational' story. The basic idea in the 'representational' approach is that mental activity is the forming of 'interior' items of knowledge which represent entities and events 'exterior' to the knowing subject. It can be considered to hold a dominant position in contemporary discourse, and to have a lengthy pedigree. The 'social construct ' story stands in radical contrast to the 'representational' one, and ultimately undermines it, as we will indicate later.

The 'representational' story

In one form or another, the 'representational' view of mind is more widespread than the less orthodox 'social construct' story. The following treatment does not pretend to be exhaustive, nor do we cover internal disputes among contemporary theorists (e.g. Churchland 1986; Stich 1992). We point to some conceptual limitations of the representational story when we turn in more detail to the social construction approach.

The contemporary model that animates the representational approach is the digital computer. The power of this analogy is very great, and whilst it is recognised by its adherents *as* an analogy, the consequences of its adoption give rise to (sometimes unrecognised) assumptions about cognitive abilities that only make sense when understood against that model. Fodor (1975) is explicit in invocation of the computer model, and uses it to support his claim for a language ('Mentalese') innate to the human and, supposedly, other higher primate central nervous systems. This is the 'language of thought'. The nature of this 'language' may be understood in terms analogous to the software that can be implemented at ever higher levels of sophistication in a mechanical or electronic computing device. Necessarily, a final description of such an 'interior language' is the 'machine-language' metaphor used to describe the lowest (*bi*nary dig*it*, or bit) level of computation executed in such a machine. The binary system is so-called because it is based on a procedure using only two conditions, symbolised by 0's and 1's, to represent 'off' and 'on' (or 'open' and 'closed') states of an electrical circuit. A basic computer screen can be thought of as a field of tiny individual points ('pixels') each of which can be blank (off) or activated (on). Any pattern displayed on such a screen is describable by a string of bits (0's and 1's), hence a computation in the form of the production of such a list in the central processing unit of the computer, determines what appears on the screen. Any pattern made on the screen is equally able to be given as such a list.

Dennett (1991), similarly, describes 'consciousness' as a 'virtual machine' of the sort constructible by layers of software—'software' being the instructions (programs) that operate to bring about various kinds of computation. Displayed on the screen of a computer used for writing a letter or a book are images of words and numbers. These images result from the operation of programs which translate what to human users are intelligible strings of letters and numbers. The translations turn the input entered by the user (keystrokes), via various intermediate steps, into binary digital form at the machine-language level. The intermediate steps use codes (compilers and assemblers) to make the input 'readable' by the circuitry of the machine (Capron 1987). 'Virtual machines', in Dennett's usage, are such things as games, calculators, and word-processing devices.

Subtler influences of the computer metaphor occur in writing which makes no explicit appeal to it. Crain (1991), for example, following Chomsky (e.g., 1986), argues for the innateness in humans of 'rules for syntax'. Syntax may be understood as any system of conventions by which symbols are related to each other in connected utterance. In one argument, such regularities, being conventional, are themselves symbolic (Langacker 1987). Crain states (p. 597) that the 'universality of language in our species stands in glaring contrast to the much more selective attainment of *comparable* cognitive skills, such as the ability to perform arithmetic calculations' (our emphasis). The assumption that language and arithmetic calculation are comparable only makes sense if the computer model of the brain/mind is taken for granted as a background condition. Since computers handle numeric and alphabetic strings on exactly the same machine-language principles, a human mind taken to work like a computer might be expected to be 'hardwired' for both. That arithmetic needs to be taught, whereas language appears to require no special tutelage, is taken by Crain as evidence that language alone is 'hardwired'.

Certain events in animals' nervous systems look 'binary'. There are nerve cells that connect sensory receptor cells in the retina (in the eye) or the cochlea (in the ear) to 'higher-order' cells in different specialist areas of the central nervous system. These connecting cells and higher order cells are called 'neurons'. As fluctuating energy from the environment stimulates retinal or cochlear receptor cells, this gives rise to electrochemical changes in such cells. That energy is transferred to neurons. The form of electrochemical energy observed in neurons is qualitatively different from that in receptor cells: it occurs as pulsed electrical discharges, called 'action

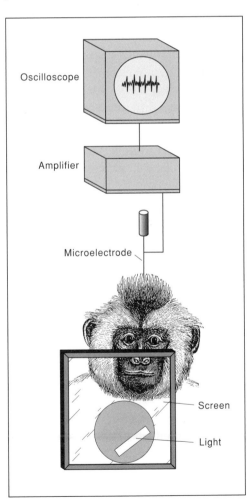

Figure 16 Experimental arrangement for recording neural pulses ('action potentials') from a single cell of a monkey's visual system and representing them on an oscilloscope screen. *From* Atkinson et al. 1993; monkey from Darwin 1872.

potentials' (see Figure 16 for an example of such pulsed energy due to stimulation of a monkey's visual system). Action potentials are like a series of discrete on-off-on-off (i.e., binary) events occurring in the nerve. They are always about the same magnitude, but vary in their recurrence rate (per second) as a function of changes in external energy level. Action potentials arise as a result of transient voltage differences between the interior and exterior of the neuron (Stevens 1973). Environmental energy levels change perpetually, and they often do so in a continuous way—e.g., as the sun rises or sets so the level of light (electromagnetic energy) gradually increases or decreases. The response in sensory neurons to such a continuous change in energy level is nonetheless in the form of an increase or decrease in the *rate* of discharge of uniformly sized action potentials. Such a form of neural encoding can be thought of as equivalent to analog-to-digital (continuous-to-discrete) conversion in an electronic circuit (Rosen & Howell 1991), hence as plausibly akin to binary digit computations.

Whatever the fidelity of the computer model to events in an actual nervous system, one attraction of the model is that it furnishes a material analogy for mental processes, and thus supposedly overcomes what many commentators see as a serious difficulty in Descartes' speculations about the immaterial 'mind' (Chapter 1). In the 'modern Western' context it was Descartes (e.g. 1988[1644] Pt 1 ¶53) who most specifically propounded the ideas of the unavoidable reality of the mind, and of a categorical difference between mind and body:

> A substance may ... be known through any attribute ... but each substance has one principal property which constitutes its nature and essence ... Thus extension in length, breadth and depth constitutes the nature of corporeal substance; and thought constitutes the nature of thinking substance. Everything ... which can be attributed to body presupposes extension ... whatever we find in the mind is simply one of the various modes of thinking.

The mind, in this characterisation, is substantial but immaterial. In Descartes' system, indeed, thinking is the one feature of existence of which one can, despite initial uncertainty, begin not to doubt, and the essence of humans is that they are thinking things. Mind is also indestructible, hence immortal, and in this sense the equivalent of the 'soul' (Descartes 1988[1641]). For many in the contemporary world who seek to engage in the 'scientific' study of mind, its character as proposed by Descartes is troublesome. To retain the reality of mind whilst seeing its realisation in a material (computer) model, feels more secure than a position which has mind in a category of mysterious substance.

The 'representational' nature of mental events can also be traced to the Cartesian (from Des*cartes*) system, although the concept can be seen as the result of a more ancient legacy from the reflections of Plato. Plato accepted a doctrine, more ancient yet, that the products of the senses are an unreliable basis for knowledge. He argued that the reason we can nonetheless apply names and judgements coherently is because there are, usually unrecognised by us, pure, and unvarying versions of things which allow us to make one general term apply to various particular instances. Those pure versions are identified by Plato as Forms (Flew 1971, 50), which Priest (1991, 10) has described as 'quasi-mathematical, non-spatio-temporal, general ideas'.

Plato used the doctrine about Forms to argue for a non-corporeal (and immortal) soul, as that by which the Forms are known. One argument, for example, states that the Forms must have been known to souls before any one of us is born, else how otherwise could we correctly know the application of the general to the particular, given the unreliability of what is sensed (Flew 1971, 53–54, quoting from Plato's *Phaedo*). The foundation is laid thus by Plato for a clear distinction between the bodily and the mental, and for the soul (or mind) to be endowed with pure forms of knowledge, in effect, innately. The pure Forms of things, being unconnected with the flux of the merely perceivable, are also 'representations' of things—they stand in our minds for what exists in the world.

Descartes (and, for that matter, Plato) figure significantly in ongoing debate, not only for their historical priority, but also because their views continue to influence contemporary discourse, at least under a representational story of mind. The 'representation' idea in Descartes has a different character from Plato's idea about Forms, whilst partaking of some of its features. In his *Optics*, published along with *Discourse on the Method* (1637), Descartes objected to the idea that, in perceiving, we have little, identical *versions* of things in our heads. Instead he argued that we should think of perception as the formation of images which represent those things, in the way that engravings can intelligibly represent objects in the landscape, whilst not being identical with what they represent.

The nature of representations as not mere copies of what they represent is used by Descartes to argue for the active function of mind. He makes the point (1988[1637], 63) that, to be faithful to the rules of perspective, pictures 'often represent circles by ovals better than by other circles; squares by rhombuses better than by other squares'. He went on to observe that 'in order to be more perfect as an image and to represent an object better, an engraving ought not to resemble it'. In not resembling it, just as a word does not resemble its referent, Descartes saw the activity of the mind in fashioning its knowledge of what exists. The Cartesian imagery has been described (Dennett 1991) in theatrical terms, such that appearances 'in the mind' are as players on a stage; the mind's 'owner' is cast in the role of spectator to this representational show.

Through these and several other arguments, Descartes, like Plato, and modern-day 'representation' theorists, have defined the mind as a device (be it material or otherwise) for performing mental operations, such as perceiving, recognising, knowing, deciding, remembering, speaking and understanding. These sorts of terms are ones that people readily identify as characteristic of 'mindedness'. It is on the basis of such abilities that people plan, execute and recollect the acts which structure their lives. It is also from these bases that people attribute mentality (or its absence) to others. In our argument it is more straightforward to dispense with 'mind' as the source of such capacities, and to recognise that it is *people* who perceive, recognise, know, remember, speak and understand (Coulter 1979a). Introducing 'mind' to do these is to allow an abstraction to stand as an agent.

Abstraction (and reification)

Abstraction is a vital feature in the formation of concepts. To acquire the concept of 'a word', or 'a bird' involves seeing that *examples* of these things can be talked about as just that, *as* examples (Bolton 1977; Piaget 1959). Thus a young child may point and say 'bird' on sighting one or another version of this order of animal. We would not be inclined to say they have 'the concept of 'bird'' as an abstract class; rather, they have a name for a number of similar things which have yet to be distinguished. Indeed, it is a well-known phenomenon that children, in the course of learning the use of language, are overinclusive (by adult standards) in what they will call 'doggie' or 'birdie' (Bates et al. 1991). When children learn to separately identify different sorts of birds, we are likely to agree that their use of the word 'bird'—say in answer to the question: 'What is the name for all these feathered friends?'—now stands for that abstract concept.

We peddle in abstractions constantly. This text is no exception to that; it would be impossible to compose otherwise. Terms like 'language', 'tool', 'diet', 'nest', 'communication', 'mind', and the thousands of others we rely on to construct our discussion, are abstractions. Where the propensity for abstraction becomes a problem is when we start to believe that any of these abstractions, vital for the setting forth of argument, has a reality outside discursive activities. Some may: others cannot. The term 'acid' or 'tool' is an abstraction derived from theory, yet there may indeed exist entities that properly answer to those names. Something can be said to be an acid which behaves in a predictable way with respect to other parts of a chemical system (Hacking 1983). A piece of stone or wood may be called a tool if it answers to certain criteria of production or use (Davidson & Noble 1993a). Entities of this sort may be called 'natural kinds' of things (Quine 1969); their existence is, in a material sense, independent of human fancy. That does not mean they are independent of human representation. The definition of either an 'acid' or a 'tool' may be adjusted (by people) across historical time periods, or across different paradigms (Kuhn 1970), as further considerations come into play. Ape nests are tools by some definitions, not by others, as we discussed in Chapter 2. What was understood as describable (or not describable) under the term for one discussion may be excluded in another. Coulter (1989, 45) cites an example (from Place [personal communication]) of whales defined as fish. The medieval category for whales as fish holds good under a description for fish which takes features of living in water and propulsion through it using fins and tail as definitive of fish. A definition which includes cold-bloodedness and egg-laying excludes whales as fish. The natural existence of these creatures is not in doubt at any point.

There is no naturally-occurring entity that answers to the term 'language' or 'mind'. These are abstractions pure and simple (perhaps neither so pure nor so simple). They are terms whose meaningfulness derives from being short-hand ways of referring to certain practices, for example, speaking or signing, in the case of 'language'; solving problems or acting with intent, in the case of 'mind'. As Coulter (1991b, 329) points out:

> A 'language', a 'word', a 'phrase', a 'sentence', are in a crucial sense *abstractions* from arrays of practical communicative activities in social interactions. Like any other abstraction, these have their uses. Where we go wrong is if, having effected any such abstraction, we relocate it *behind* or in back of actually situated forms of conduct as a kind of invariantly present and omnirelevantly informing phenomenon. (emphasis in original)

The issues raised in this section may be quite foreign to some readers. In discussing with each other the sort of problems this chapter could pose, we saw that we may not succeed in 'engaging the minds' of some readers. That very phrase—'to engage the mind'—reveals the insidious matters being considered, for it would not be hard to take it that there was indeed an entity, an agent, to be engaged with. The phrase is actually short-hand for the interpersonal interaction going on here. The reader is being addressed by a (two-headed) author at 'long distance'. Because the text is printed, hence mute, and you are likely reading silently, we could all begin to think a sort of 'mind-to-mind' transfer is happening. That belief may be bolstered by the notion that the ideas are 'on the page', '*in* the book', as they might be lodged '*in* the mind'. But none of this is so. We are people who have inscribed a series of documented arguments and findings. The reader is a person, engaged, say, in weighing their worth. This is an interactive event between persons, as would be all the clearer were authors and reader talking to each other directly. Abstraction can help to mask that plain point.

This brings us to the related (inevitable) problem, that of the entification or reification of the abstraction: the turning of it from a noun as short-hand for certain kinds of behaviour, into an object. The contemporary use of the notion of 'mind' can be seen in textbooks of Psychology. Atkinson et al. (1993) state, 'cognitive psychologists often rely on an analogy between the mind and a computer' (p.10). Since computers are objects, minds become objects too. The concept has become part of the lexicon—a recent manifestation is reproduced in part as Figure 17. The problem of reification needs to be confronted because it creates serious difficulties for any scientific analysis of behavioural evolution. Confounding occurs in the writing of some theorists (e.g. Bickerton 1990) who try to hunt the snark of 'the mind' because they believe in its efficacy as a sufficient ('innate') cause of representing, categorising and conceptualising. It occurs in other accounts (e.g. Corballis 1991; Donald 1991) where the analysts believe that mental evolution can occur independently of behavioural.

None of our arguments seeks to avoid commitment to the idea that central nervous systems ('brains') are inevitably implicated in the production of language, hence 'mindedness'. Just so, legs are implicated in bipedal ambulation, as are hands in piano-playing (Noble & Davidson 1991). But just as these practices also require several other components, including communities of fellow humans, so too does

Figure 17 Part of an unsolicited mailing to one of the authors inviting him to try to get more from his mind.

language. And as piano playing is not to be found 'in' the hands, nor walking 'in' the legs, so, we will conclude, forms of thinking are not to be found 'in' the brain.

Some problems about mental representation

What is represented in the representational story about mind? For Plato, innate knowledge of existence is represented in the mind; for Descartes, represented 'in mind' is an innate capacity to produce representations of everything that may stand for what exists. Appealing as these notions may be, they are hardly adequate as explanatory of anything (for example, how did they get there?).

In its present-day computational rendering, the representations are strings of symbols (ultimately, series of 0's and 1's) which various programming levels engage with so as to enable the machine (the brain) to handle input and deliver output. Fodor (1975, 67) characterises 'understanding' of a sentence as akin to the processes which occur in a computer when the sentence as it appears on the screen is 'read' at several program levels (the equivalents of semantic and syntactic 'analyses', and a mechanistic level). Ultimately, the sentence may be stored, i.e., recorded as an alteration in the physical state of a device (say, a virtual or hard disc). Fraser (1992) notes a problem that this picture introduces, namely the point at which the sentence's *meaning* is grasped—a point not reached by the computer (Costall 1991). From Fraser's account (pp. 59–61), this problem is tackled in various ways. One seeming solution is that 'understanding' occurs by matching the input sentence to a model held in memory. This, of course, merely postpones the matter, besides raising the question of what it means to speak of a 'remembered model'. The matching of one sentence with another still needs something (or someone) to recognise that a match has been made, leaving aside the question of whether it is intelligible to count as 'understanding' any procedure of matching. If the matching/recognising activity is held to occur 'in' the mind then we have a species of the 'homunculus' problem mentioned in Chapter 1 (see also Searle 1992).

Alternative solutions, such as those proposed by Dennett (1979) and Pylyshyn (1984), in effect, assert that the computations assign aspects of representations to decreasingly complex levels, such that they are ultimately 'self-understanding', or that, because they are 'mental symbols' residing in and expressed by physical systems, they are 'intrinsically meaningful', so the question of meaning in the socially conventional sense of 'the meaning of a symbol' does not apply. Such propositions sweep the problem out of sight, and beyond comprehension (see also Erneling 1993, 59–80).

Though not greeted with universal enthusiasm, the underlying hope which sustains the computational approach to 'mind' is that computers can (or eventually will) act in ways that humans do. Among other things, if computers ever could so act, then the 'understanding' problem might be resolved. A consistent critic, the philosopher Hubert Dreyfus (1972; also Searle 1980) analysed various of the reasons which make that ambition unrealisable. In a recent revision, Dreyfus (1993) shows how his predictions about the failure of 'artificial intelligence' research, when applied to the simulation of human conduct, have been borne out. His basic argument is that human action is embodied, skilful and 'encultured'. The computer does not operate with these features, and can only work with (ever larger) data bases containing fixed 'facts' and 'rules' about the nature of situations in which persons might find themselves. Thus, in programs designed to simulate the activity of 'going to a restaurant', a list of plausible operations—looking for a table, ordering from the menu, devouring the meal, paying the bill—may be written as a 'script' (Schank & Abelson 1977). But this fails to address the point that 'going to a restaurant' cannot be pinned down as any sort of uniform activity. As Dreyfus puts it (1993, 44):

> [M]aking a phone call, answering a call for help, retrieving a lost object, looking for a job, getting signatures for a petition, repairing equipment, coming to work, doing an inspection, leaving a bomb, arranging a banquet, collecting for the Mafia, looking for change for the meter, buying cigarettes, hiding from the police, etc., etc., might lead one to enter a restaurant...

Even the nature of an action so apparently singular as 'going to a restaurant *for a meal*' cannot be uniformly scripted, since conduct is necessarily sensitive to the details that vary from one occasion to another. Besides effects due to the kind of place one is going *to* (Maxim's, Hungry Joe's Bar and Grill), going to a restaurant: with the new boss, one's bosom pals, aged aunt, alone, on a blind date, not feeling too well, may all be occasions of 'a meal', but the event is substantially different under different institutional, social and personal contexts.

It has been claimed that another approach to software design, known as parallel distributed processing, should enable computers to be more flexible in response to contextual nuance (McClelland et al. 1986). Besides internal disputation (e.g. Fodor & Pylyshyn 1988; Rowlands 1994) about the plausibility of claimed advantage for the new approach, there are no signs of it offering an empirical edge over the original, serial approach, as regards the simulation of human behaviour (Dreyfus 1993).

Despite the widespread support for it, we think the computer analogy is inappropriate as a model for the mindedness of human conduct (actually, we think it is fundamentally misconceived—see also Heil [1981]—but the present context is not the platform for polemic on this matter). A more relevant point is that, in addition to being inappropriate as a model, what the computer model seeks to be analogical *of* is systematically misrepresented. We arrive at that position following an account of the basis for a 'social construct' approach to mind.

The 'social construct' story

Wittgenstein

The Cartesian view of mind has been radically undermined by two related developments in philosophy: Wittgenstein's investigations (1961[1922]; 1958) into meaningful uses of language, and Ryle's (1949) explicit critique of the Cartesian mind as any sort of meaningful entity. Wittgenstein examined the use of language in both general (everyday) and specialist (scientific, logical) activities. Even more critically, he showed ways in which the ill-use of language can lead us astray in our appreciation of how to understand various phenomena of experience. Ryle, following Wittgenstein, proposed that mindedness can be understood as witnessed (only) in forms of conduct. Descartes' system throws in doubt the existence of everything except the contents of one's own mind. The effect of reaching such a position is to give everybody privileged, indeed, exclusive access to their own minds—the existence of all else being in doubt. By the same token, everybody is denied access to the content of minds other than their own. The effect from Ludwig Wittgenstein's work is to overturn the idea of mind as in any significant sense *private* to individuals.

Part of Wittgenstein's point is that speaking and thinking are of a piece with each other. The terms may be used in application to different forms of activity (for example, uttering aloud vs silent self-address), but it is not possible to divide out the thought from its expression, whether or not the 'thinking is done aloud' (thinking could not *be* 'done aloud' without words). Wittgenstein remarks that 'When I think in language there aren't 'meanings' going through my mind in addition to the verbal expressions: the language is itself the vehicle of thought' (1958 ¶329). As to the privacy of individual experience, he offers several proposals on how to make best sense of this (and how not). One image (1958 ¶293) is of a group of people, each holding a box which only the holder can look into. No one can look into anyone else's box, and each person states that what is in theirs is 'a beetle', a fact confirmed by each looking at whatever it is that is in their own box—supposing there is anything in it, and supposing that whatever *is* in any given box stays the same from one observation to the next.

Wittgenstein poses the question, if there was motivation to make the word 'beetle' have *actual* referential function among this group of people, then the 'private' verification procedure gets them nowhere. There being no shared appreciation of what the word can possibly mean, it cannot be used by anyone to refer to anything. You might object, saying 'well, at least each would know, idiosyncratically, what the word referred to'. But by what means could anyone confirm, even to themselves, this idiosyncratic knowledge? They could only do so by use of the conventions of their already shared language. As we have been stressing, for anything to be a symbolic sign it must be conventionally understood; nothing is 'conventional' that is idiosyncratic.

A more complex point concerns personally experienced states such as 'being in pain' or 'having a pain'. Surely this is a prime candidate for privacy of experience? Yet here we see that the pain anyone experiences is not some 'thing' that only that person 'inwardly' *knows* of, and others are in the dark about. We note that the very term 'pain', being a noun, can lead to our thinking of it as naming an entity, hence may lead us astray in the way the word 'mind' does—another example of reification. Pains can be localised (in your leg or in your head, etc.) and described (as shooting, hammering, etc.), but these are characterisations of states of 'hurting', not names for things residing in your body. As regards the issue of the privacy of this experience, Wittgenstein points out that we do not 'know' our own pain, in the same sense that we know (or don't know) what day it is. It could not be intelligibly said that 'I am in pain *and* I know (or don't know) it'. Pain is not something its experiencer knows; it is something they are going through, the state they are in. Others are appropriately described as knowing (or not knowing) you are in pain (Chapman & Dixon 1987).

Of someone it may intelligibly be said that 'they are in trouble', 'and they know it' (or 'they don't know it [yet]'). It cannot be said of them that 'they are in pain and they (don't) know it'. The knowledge other people have about a person's pain is made known to those others through expressions everyone recognises as *criterial* of pain experience. Behaviours that express pain experience are ones whose significance we learn, in the course of growing up. There may be occasions when others have cause to doubt a pain claim, as when parents suspect a child is seeking to avoid school; or to suspect its concealment, as when those same parents are faced with what looks like a sick child who desperately wants to play outdoors. As Chapman says, (p.107), '*the possibility* that others can hide their feelings from us does not mean that the feelings of others are *necessarily* hidden from public view' (emphases in original).

The intelligibility of everyday interaction entails that the thoughts and feelings of people who share what Wittgenstein called the same 'language games', hence the same 'forms of life' (Margolis 1987) are, in principle, transparent to each other. The principled nature of that point does not deny the fact that people can withhold expression of their thoughts and feelings and may be strongly motivated on occasions to do so. Indeed, transparency is guaranteed only because of practice in its opposite. We argue in Chapter 8 that the capacity to withhold expression of a feeling or thought helps to account for why language was selected (in evolution) prehistorically. Under normal circumstances, nonetheless, public availability of any person's thoughts is what enables the pursuit of mundane practical affairs within communities.

The acquisition of the artless ability to 'show what you're thinking' (or its artful variants: simulation or concealment of a thought), arises through exposure to various contexts of social learning. We have already discussed such artless and artful behaviour in relation to 'body language' (Chapter 1). Here we consider its relation to 'mind'. Sacks (1992[1966]) describes a form of game played by children of around 5 to 10 years, in which they take turns at passing (or pretending to pass) a small object like a button to each member of the group, with one member actually given it. The aim of the game is for the rest to figure which person the button was really passed to. As Sacks says (p.364):

> one sees the button by seeing that they know they have the button ... [a]nd this phenomenon of seeing other people's thoughts is really an important thing... [I]t's nonsense to say that thoughts are things that can't be seen ... since [people] certainly do take it that one can see what anybody is thinking. Not in every case, certainly, but you can see what people are thinking, and there are ways of doing it. And you must learn to do it.

The very existence of the button game is both evidence of, and training ground for acquiring, such fundamental human abilities as that of switching strategies so as to appear to have/not-have, and thus to build a repertoire of deception skills (and deception-detection skills). Sacks's qualifier about 'not in every case' supports the point that concealment can sometimes be carried off. If it could not, the game, and the related game of poker, and social, commercial or political 'games' dependent upon provision of misleading cues, would not exist. Almost all competitive games depend on players being able to instruct themselves on appropriate deception strategies, and discovering their efficacy when put into practice.

The question of transparency or otherwise of other people's thoughts also bears critically on the issue of 'mindedness' of non-human primates, since claims have been made about their capacity for deceptive behaviour (e.g. Whiten & Byrne 1988). The significance of such a claim, were it substantiated, lies in the sort of 'mindedness' that would have to be at work if the 'deception' in question were akin to what goes on in the button game. The evidence for deception in non-human primates, based upon 'seeing/not seeing what the other is thinking', is indeterminate. There are stories told of chimpanzees and baboons acting stealthily in the course of grooming or copulation, which can have the effect of not drawing the attention of rivals to what they are doing. Commenting on these sorts of accounts, Cheney and Seyfarth (1991) point out (p.193) that acting out of the line of sight of a more dominant animal does not entail appreciation of the other's perspective and 'state of knowledge'; it may as readily be explained as a learned response to the contingencies that attack from the other animal depends on being in its sight, and is avoided when out of its sight. The conclusion of a recent review on this topic (Heyes 1994, 299) is that 'there is currently no compelling evidence for mental state attribution in nonhuman primates'.

Cheney and Seyfarth offered their comment in the course of reporting on studies with rhesus and Japanese macaques, concluding (pp.193–4) that 'monkeys are sensitive to the composition of their audience and ... are astute observers of each others' behaviour and apparent attentiveness. They may be less astute observers of each others' minds'. We take the view that in the absence of signs of language use among these animals, the requisite 'mindedness' to read or be read is also unavailable. This position is actually supported by Whiten and Byrne (1988, 235). These authors appreciate that the use of what they call 'psychological' terms (to do with interpretation of 'states of mind' in others) could be thought to breach a canon of scientific objectivity.

> But we would appeal here to Wittgenstein ... who argues that a child, as an apprentice language user, must gain an understanding of a psychological term by noticing which aspects of *behaviour* are picked out publicly by the language-using community as being relevant to that term. On this model ... the attribution of mental states to others should not be regarded as a subjective affair. (emphasis in original)

Without the apparatus of a language-using community it is not clear how 'mental states' could be manifested by and to anyone.

Ryle

Gilbert Ryle (1949), addresses matters that relate to the concern expressed by Whiten and Byrne. Specifically, he examines the question of an 'inner' mental world versus an 'outer' world of behaviour, with respect to what he terms the Cartesian myth of 'mind'. A myth arises due to 'the presentation of facts belonging to one category in the idioms appropriate to another' (p.10). Since what Descartes described, concerning thoughts and feelings, are perfectly intelligible, Ryle sees his task as one that explodes the myth, not by denying those facts, but by correctly positioning them as to their category. The Cartesian division of body and mind introduces notions of an inner, private 'mental' reality of the sort touched on in the discussion of pain, and an entirely separate outer, 'public' physical reality. For readers whose background is in psychology, the long-standing division between the 'introspected', subjective world of 'mental life' and the 'observable', objective world of 'behaviour' can be traced to this Cartesian division. From Wittgenstein we may begin to discern the 'dissolution' of this duality.

Ryle's exposure to Wittgenstein's investigations (Ryle 1967[1951]) places the crux of his analysis in the infelicitous use of terms in the language. He gives the example (1949, 17–18) of someone being shown around 'a University', hence seeing a succession of libraries, residential colleges, laboratories, and the like, but then asking to be shown 'the University'. The problem here is that the visitor has mistakenly taken it that 'university' is another in the same kind or category of thing as 'library' or 'laboratory'. If the ill-use is not corrected, the person is at risk of being heard as referring to a further *entity*, yet one which is mysteriously unlike the entities listed so far. Through such errors of usage, 'ghosts' are created. The particular ghost Ryle stalks is the one he dubbed the 'ghost (of the mind) in the machine (of the body)'. Because thoughts, feelings, intentions and the like do not belong in the category of the physical, yet are real enough, there must be a further entity (the equivalent of the 'University'), unlike those that come under a physical description, but which these things *do* come under, namely, the mind.

Ryle offers the thought that the form of the Cartesian myth came about because of the highly satisfactory explanations based on purely mechanical principles for the working of the Universe, such as those by Galileo Galilei (1953[1632]) which Descartes himself refers to (1988[1637]). But the evidently *non*-mechanical quality of the workings of the mind needed to be rescued from such physical determinations. In the absence of any candidate accounts for a scientifically-based story, the default was to a sort of obverse of the mechanical.

> The workings of minds had to be described by the mere negatives of the specific descriptions given to bodies; they are not in space, they are not motions, they are not modifications of matter, they are not accessible to public observation. Minds are not bits of clockwork, they are just bits of not-clockwork. (Ryle 1949, 21)

Ryle goes on to observe how no one seemed to see that the system being developed was hopeless from the outset. By rescuing the mind through putting it in a category inaccessible to any but the individual thinker, *common* criteria for judging the worth or appropriateness of public conduct would have to be relinquished. Mechanical theories which were successful in accounting for physical phenomena (in terms of causes and effects) could not explain how we judge, in our everyday affairs, for example, intelligent from unintelligent conduct. Therefore some other set of theories, yet based on some other cause-effect principles, would have to be entertained. Ryle notes, 'Not unnaturally, psychology is often cast for just this role.'

The sort of 'psychology' Ryle is referring to is any of the various versions of inquiry into 'mental mechanism' which continue to honour one form or other of Cartesian body-mind dualism. The continued honour is actually expressed by seeking to *deny* a significant role for one or other term of the dyad. The behaviourist tradition eschews 'mind', the cognitivist eschews 'body'. There are some forms of psychology which try to transcend the mind-body division. Gibson's ecological approach includes a principle of animal-environment mutualism (Costall 1984; Michaels & Carello 1981; Still & Costall 1991). Aspects of Gibson's theorising feature in the next chapter. In undertaking our own analysis of how to approach the issue of 'mindedness' we prefer to dissolve (better, ignore) the Cartesian distinction.

Ryle proceeds to consider various ways in which language use in everyday settings gives clear guidance to the nature and extent of the intelligence of human conduct. This intelligence is appreciated through the conduct being undertaken 'carefully', 'skilfully' or 'sagely'; as against its being performed 'thoughtlessly', 'clumsily' or 'stupidly'. People vary in their judgements about the worth or quality of their own or someone else's conduct or performance. In turn, this has the effect of provoking questions about their grounds for holding such views. By means of such conversational interaction, publicly expressed frameworks of expectations, standards and criteria emerge for ongoing appraisal. Everyday life is replete with such commentary on conduct, and critique of that commentary (e.g. Goffman 1955; 1956; Jayyusi 1984). In the previous chapter we cited Halverson's remark (1992a, 228–9) that 'there were art critics as soon as there was art'. Among the many functions of language in everyday life is its use in expressing evaluations of relative worth.

The point Ryle insists upon is that the bases of all evaluations are the actions, products and utterances which constitute items or sets of behaviours. Items of behaviour and of the material objects (such as tools or other artefacts) which may persist from such behaviour, are the seats of intelligent (thoughtful, practised, well-planned) or unintelligent (careless, stumbling, ill-conceived) conduct. There are no other identifiable items that enable evaluation. Furthermore, any act or product up for evaluation of its relative worth (its quality of 'mindedness') can only be a target of judgement insofar as there are *criteria* held as relevant or applicable in the given circumstance. Presumably, evaluations against criteria occur because comparative performances are made, and their relative effectiveness gets tested against their judged respective consequences. To continue the 'art critic' example, an evaluation may take the form: 'this painting is a better likeness of so-and-so than that one', with the returning comment, 'it is not meant as a likeness, but as an expression of human pain', and the retort, 'Well, in that case it's not as good as this other picture, which is also meant to express pain', and so on, perhaps for ever.

These observations tell us that two things are unavoidable in consideration of 'mind'. (1) We are not witnessing performances 'down-stage' (to borrow the Cartesian theatre image), under the *control* of an unknowable mental apparatus that is behind it all yet out of sight. (2) Criteria used to appraise conduct (like Wittgenstein's criteria for pain expression) are sustained within linguistic communities by social interaction between people. A spy might act with appropriate secretiveness, such that their conduct is out of all sight; unless and until the fruits of their clandestine actions are available to be judged against some appropriate standard, the 'intelligence' of their 'intelligence' is enigmatic. You might say, the cunning-ness of the spy's action can be watched on a TV show, as they operate all alone. But watching a TV show is not 'watching a spy all alone'; if someone is being '*watched*' they are not 'all alone'. There are also criteria which bear upon seeing the action on TV as that of 'someone spying'. As pointed out in Chapter 1, the audience only sees these actions as those of a spy because a set of conventions of what it is to act as (hence, for the moment, to 'be') a spy has been established between actors and audiences.

In this analysis we have sought to show that 'mindedness' is not a name for activity by some occult organ: it is witnessed in the occasions of interpersonal conduct among those with shared 'language games'.

Coulter

Our earlier argument against the representational approach was that the computer is inappropriate as a model of mind. We turn now to problems with what the representational story is aimed at being a model *of*. Coulter (1979b) relies specifi-cally on Wittgenstein, to a lesser extent on Ryle, to focus his broader analytic attention on mind as 'socially constructed'. Our initial point of departure is Coulter's critique (1983, 6–23) of Fodor's concept, mentioned earlier, of 'the language of thought'. This concept is a cornerstone of the contemporary represen-tational story. The upshot of Coulter's critique is that the conduct modelled by the computations representing various 'mental acts' is itself misrepresented. He uses the example of 'deciding', which Fodor characterises as a 'process' in which a set of hypothetical states is somehow realised in the central nervous system. These states broadly correspond to the proposition: if a given behavioural option is performed in a given setting then a given consequence will ensue with a given probability. To engage the 'process of deciding', a set of such options, together with a set of priority orderings for outcomes for that setting, must all be presumed to be represented in the central nervous system.

The problem is that 'deciding' is not well described as a *process*. In Ryle's terms (1949), deciding is an achievement verb, like 'winning', not a process verb (like 'walking'). To say of someone or some body of persons (a committee) that they decided on a course of action is to describe the *outcome* of their deliberations, the end-point (statement of intent, vote taken). In reaching a decision, efforts may be engaged, such as 'deliberating on different options'. This is not 'deciding', though it might, under some circumstances, be described as 'having trouble trying to decide'; under other circumstances it may be described as 'looking judiciously at various possibilities'. Loosely—and this is where ill-use can lead us astray as to the phenomenon to be analysed—the meeting of a committee might be spoken of as 'they're deciding right now', and have that be thought of (by a child, perhaps) as a process. On closer consideration there are no elements besides moments of coming to conclusions that are candidates for 'deciding'. The phrase, 'they're meeting *so as* to (try to) decide' is a more precise way to capture what's going on. Various procedures will be exercised in reaching that decision, such that the whole thing may be described as a 'decision-making process' (constituted by numerous elements, one or two of which are acts of decision).

A different example of 'deciding' can be in the case where someone does no more than express hesitation about doing something they had been intending to do, yet entertains *no* other options besides what was planned, and then decides to go ahead and undertake it even so.

'Deciding' is also subject to publicly expressible criteria for its accomplishment. People may assert that they decided, thereby seeking to identify their action as autonomous. This may be challenged by someone who holds that they had no choice but to act in the way they did, or that they acted without serious attention to alternatives.

Fodor gives an equally inaccurate account of 'understanding' (Coulter 1983, 10–11). He considers 'understanding a sentence' to be analogous to the computations undertaken in a computer when it 'understands' (transforms into machine language) a string of grouped letters forming the sentence. We leave aside the question, noted earlier, of how to align what takes place in the computer with what 'understanding a sentence' can mean in everyday terms. The problem to face here is that the phenomenon is misrepresented: 'understanding' is no more a process (not even a rapid process) than 'deciding'. As with 'recognising', a matter we mentioned briefly in the last chapter, 'understanding' is also an achievement. Its nature as an achievement is readily appreciated when we consider that any claim to understanding has to be ratified. A claim to understand may be defeated if the person so doing cannot meet appropriate criteria for demonstrating that understanding.

This takes us to the conceptual heart of the representational story and the broader treatment of mind under a 'social construct' approach (Coulter 1989, 64–65). Once the Cartesian mind is invented it may be spoken of as the inner agent ('homunculus') undertaking achievements which, because it is 'inside' you, is mistakenly thought to be engaged in processes that cannot be seen. Or it may be mistakenly thought of as the inner space ('theatre') where these obscure processes occur. Concepts such as understanding are taken to describe a process such as 'hearing sounds and interpreting (computing?) them as words'. It is supposed that there are phonological, syntactic and semantic channels or modules (Fodor 1983) in this putative mind, and that these engage in the process of turning acoustic input into something intelligible. In the representational account it becomes legitimate to ask 'how do you understand what I am saying?' and for this to mean something *other* than 'what do you take me to be saying—how would you paraphrase it?'. Rather, in the representational framework, the question means something like, 'what process in your brain/mind takes place that allows you to *represent the sounds I'm making as words and phrases* that have meanings for you, and which are the same as, or at least akin to, the meanings they have for me?'

The following observation is drawn in part from Baker and Hacker (1984): No device for generating understanding—thought of as the turning of sounds into meaningful words and phrases—is needed here. In the ordinary course of events, if you and I are speakers of the same language, we *already* understand the words and phrases each says when we speak. (We come back to 'failure to understand' in such a case in a moment.) If we are not in a relation of belonging to the same language community, then we are not likely to understand, in a mundane practical sense, what each other is saying, though we are likely to understand that, when observing the other's conduct, what either one is doing is 'speaking in a language we do not speak' (as against making funny noises).

For it to be the case that, at the level of meaning in our shared language, 'I don't understand you', then either you are using words and phrases beyond my comprehension, or perhaps you are not making yourself very clear. If what you say is 'beyond my comprehension' it may be that while we are each identifiable as speakers of the same language, we are not, on this occasion, engaging a shared 'language game' hence a common 'form of life'. If you are 'not making yourself very clear', that might amount to the same thing as being 'beyond my comprehension', or it might mean you haven't chosen your words carefully enough on this occasion. The times have been many when the present authors, speakers of the same *everyday* language, have got into severe wrangles over the understandability of 'language games' derived from our respective academic 'forms of life'. At no stage in any of our respective claims not to understand the other has there been a 'process of understanding' such that we hear the other one making sounds and then we go through a process of recognising (or not) these sounds as words (even unfamiliar words) of some common language.

There are, of course, *acoustically* limiting cases: of muffled words being mistaken for the sound of something else, and only gradually recognised as 'the sound of someone speaking'.

In the 'social construct' story, understanding is an achievement, and as such there are criteria for its accomplishment. I can assert that 'I understand you' yet fail to paraphrase to your satisfaction what you have said: my claim to achievement is not ratified. I might hesitate and say, 'I'm not sure if I understand', but go on to have my paraphrase accepted as showing that I did—again according to whatever criterion is relevant in the circumstances. Such acceptance may be revised ('I thought he understood what I said to him, but I see now that really he didn't'), a parallel to the 'recognise'/'fail to recognise' illustration we gave in Chapter 3. 'Understanding' is a matter of avowal and application of criteria to the avowal. There are, as it were, symptoms of understanding (or not understanding) *X*, and criteria for judging symptoms as amounting to understanding (or not understanding) *X*.

A supporter of the mental representation picture of mind might well ask whether we are denying any part for brains or activity going on in them, in this account. As previously, the answer is 'no'; but we certainly doubt that 'an understanding claim' or 'criteria for its evaluation', are to be found 'in' brains or the activity occurring among brain cells. Where, then, *are* these items to be found? Our answer is that claims and their evaluation against criteria are not to be *found*; rather, they occur, and as part of the actions and reactions of persons in their various practical dealings with each other in the various realms of their daily lives. This is where the 'social construct' story radically challenges the 'representational' story. For we are not suggesting that there are matters occurring in brains that get *translated* into 'understandings' among persons (that would simply be a re-statement of the representational account). We are asserting that 'understanding' describes an interpersonal achievement, full stop. Brains are needed for this, but they are not where understanding occurs.

None of the foregoing denies for a moment that people may decide things and see and understand things, and engage in all the other minded activities characteristic of normal humans, all on their own. This passage was first drafted by one of us whilst at home alone, in the course of which texts had to be consulted, arguments grasped and paraphrased, decisions taken, and so forth. The exercise of these capacities under *self-guidance* is the result of years of socialisation in general and particular ways. Even so, these assertions still represent claims to understanding or decision-making, claims that are in principle and in practice open to challenge from others.

All the activities characteristic of mindedness that we have been talking about are varieties of the use of language in the production of human life. The 'social construct' story is that 'mental life' is an ongoing interpersonal activity. Far from 'mind' as personal possession, it is better characterised as *socially* distributed. As against the 'monologue' image of the individual mind sitting under the bonnet, as it were, of the individual's skull, we offer a picture of mind as perpetually 'dialogic' (Wertsch 1991), in which the dialogue may be in the form of self-address, yet in which the discourses forming it are taken from and contribute to the surrounding 'social ecology' (Noble 1993b). We say a little more about that in the next chapter. By characterising minded conduct as that which occurs in linguistic interaction, and observable through products fashioned according to plan, we establish criteria for 'signs of mind' that may be found in the archaeological record.

How do people get like this?

The ultimate aim of this book is to explain how people have evolved to become minded in the sense of being aware of their experience and knowledge, able to make plans and form judgements on that basis, and thus be in a position of control and foresight relative to their circumstances. These powers partially release people from the immediate contingencies of the natural environment. In the closing sections of this chapter we examine the questions of how people get that way ontogenetically, and whether other primates can.

As with the stories told so far, our treatment makes no claim to be exhaustive. The field of human development is as vast as that of 'the mind', and we do not even go so far in this part as to contrast one sort of story with another, except by mention of the following point. An inference the reader can safely make is that since mindedness and adult linguistic mastery are co-extensive in our analyses, we take it that such mindedness develops with the growth of such mastery in children, through their immersion in whatever language community they are born into. Such a way of putting things suggests that we learn to be minded, and learn that through linguistic and related forms of interaction with already minded tutors. By contrast, a strong form of the representational picture is that humans have an 'innate' mental 'language organ' (Chomsky 1986) which, while requiring exposure to the elements of the 'local' natural language, matures under its own developmental program, as might a physical organ. It is not part of our purpose to examine that claim. We note that it is not susceptible to ready evolutionary explanation (*pace* Bickerton; Pinker & Bloom, Chapter 1) insofar as a 'mental mutation' is hard to picture. And if not mental, a physical mutation for 'linguistic competence' (presumably coincidentally in more than one individual in the same group) seems like a fairly tall order (see Toulmin 1972, 457–460). Instead, we introduce theoretical proposals consistent with the 'social construct' approach and outline empirical observations relevant to that.

Two independent, yet compatible theoretical views emerged in the early years of this century, one in Russia the other in the USA, building respectively on the 19th century philosophical movements of Marxism and pragmatism. The proposals of Vygotsky (e.g. 1962[1934]) and of Mead (e.g. 1934) take language and related communicative activity as the medium for the construction, through interaction, of minded behaviour. Such interactions are the means whereby the child's actions and reactions get remarked upon, noticed and otherwise elaborated. These procedures increasingly provide the child with its *own* means of self-attention, remark, and self-involving orientation to features of its surroundings. Consciousness ('mindedness') is thus an 'emergent property' of talk directed by others to the child. This talk, for instance about plans and goals, hence about capacities to plan, becomes increasingly useable by the child as self-directed utterance. In Vygotsky's terms, the 'inter-mental' is appropriated by the child, becoming, thus, 'intra-mental'. In ordinary terms, through the conversations between older speakers and children acquiring the habits of speech, the children begin to practice the habit of speaking to themselves. With the suppression of vocalising (silent self-address) comes the appearance of conduct called 'thinking'.

Olson (1989) has characterised the interactive events between children and older others as the 'making up' of 'mind' on behalf of the child, until such time as the child can 'make up its own'. The transition can be seen in the form of activity by the infant which is constrained by immediate contexts, as against activity guided by its own propositions about non-immediate states of affairs. Central to the transition is the child's *discovery* of the power of symbols to enable the world to be 'represented' (rather than merely responded to), such as in pretend-play (Olson 1988), and in various forms of declarative plan-based episodes (Greenfield 1980).

The ideas articulated by Mead and Vygotsky have been elaborated by theorists such as Bruner (e.g. 1983), who speaks of the adult or older person as a 'vicarious form of consciousness' for the child, providing 'scaffolding' which the child can rely upon in the pursuit of various activities until such time as its own language skills enable self-guidance (Bruner 1985). Lock (1978; 1980) documents ways in which caregivers 'complete' actions for children, actions they cannot at first undertake wholly for themselves. With continuing exposure to the various contexts in which interaction occurs, infants learn ways to communicate their needs more specifically. In doing this, and with the adult thus able to complete 'intentions' for the infant more precisely, the child *discovers*, as Lock puts it, the scope and utility of its own communicative productions. The adult provides the kind of scaffolding Bruner refers to, a structure that can be progressively dismantled as the child becomes increasingly autonomous (self-guiding) in pursuit of its goals.

Zukow (1990) reviews several of the problems for an innatist account of language ability, and goes on to report studies that reveal the intricate ways infants' attention is directed by caregivers to salient perceptual features of their environment. Simple expedients can be observed, and across different human communities, such as throwing a stone toward the region of the visible environment to which the child's attention is, at the same time, being verbally directed. By the use of such aids to attention, caregivers provide 'scaffolding' at the level of perceptual distinctions that are simultaneously marked by linguistic reference. Zukow documents numerous 'show-and-tell' routines that occur in infant-adult interactions; for instance, the manipulation of objects and parts of objects in the infant's field of view, with correlated emphasis on relevant identifying names. Such activity involves a wide range of entities, both animate and inanimate, and serves to direct the child's notice to the features of different environmental objects, and to actions they undertake or that may be taken with them.

What Zukow (from Vygotsky) calls the 'socializing' of attention that is achieved through these interactions, rests on certain fundamental, and apparently universal, ways human caregivers engage with newborn offspring and infants. One significant phenomenon related to the guiding of coordinated activity is 'infant directed speech' (Fernald & Simon 1984). This takes various forms, but generally has the character of exaggeration of tonal line, higher pitch, and lengthening of speech elements, all serving to capture the infant's attention. It has been observed in various forms of the world's languages, and its chief function, universally, seems to be for eliciting turn-taking in interaction, through the use of rising vocal inflection (Papousek & Papousek 1991). A parallel phenomenon has been documented in the shape of infant-directed Sign (Masataka 1992); and, again universally, a related form of infant-directed behaviour occurs as song, especially in the form of lullaby (Trehub et al. 1993). Even in communities that do not appear to rely on specialised *forms* of infant-directed utterance (e.g., Schieffelin 1979), there is nonetheless clear evidence of attention-directing strategies based on language routines specific to infant-adult interaction episodes.

These phenomena are part of a broader structure for the organisation of interaction, two of whose key features are the co-ordination of attention, and matching of behaviour through imitation. These are features whose significance we indicated in Chapter 2, when discussing the implications, for hominid descendants of the common ancestor, of a lengthening period of infant dependency, together with postural and behavioural adaptations that enhanced opportunities for joint attention, imitation, and teaching. Butterworth (1991) observes (p.224) that

> adults monitor very closely the focus of the infant's attention and adjust their own gaze to maintain shared experience. Mothers vocalize at suitable moments when they see that the baby is attending to a particular object or event and by establishing joint visual attention they create a suitable tutorial environment.

By means of joint attentional manœuvres, the infant's orientations to its surroundings are channelled by caregivers toward goals understood, at first, by the adult alone. The capacity of the infant to join in the pursuit of those goals is borne along by a further integral feature of its life, namely, the ready, one might say 'reflex', imitation by adult caregivers of its emotional (Malatesta & Haviland 1982) and facial (Moran et al. 1987) expressions. By these expedients, particular behaviours—smiling, eye-widening, mouth and tongue movements—are differentially attended to, modelled and reflected back and the infant begins to express return matchings of its own. There are reports of neonatal imitative ability (e.g., Meltzoff & Moore 1983), although claims about that are disputed (McKenzie & Over 1983). In any event, the real signs of imitative behaviour occur after the first several months of life, following the infant's routine exposure to caregivers' imitations of its behaviour. Through these interactions, the association of different, imitated, expressions with different emotional states provides the infant with meanings for those expressions as signals for various grades of pleasure or misery.

The exception to the near-simultaneous matching of expression by adult caregivers is in the area of vocalising. As distinct from the conformance of adult-to-infant facial behaviour, Moran and colleagues observed that vocalisings are occasions for turn-taking (as in infant-directed speech). Meltzoff and Gopnik (1993) found that infants prefer attending to an adult model who imitates their bodily actions (for example, in playing with a toy) than to one whose actions are of the same order, but uncorrelated with their own. These authors note that co-attentive actions of caregivers, together with the turn-taking feature of what they call the 'conversational dance', enable the infant to distinguish actors from objects, and 'like me' from 'different', which in turn enables empathic appreciation of self in relation to other.

Can other primates get like this?

The critical nature of all these forms of interaction between 'minded' human adults and their maturing offspring can be better appreciated when comparisons are made among human-human, human-chimpanzee (chimpanzees taken to include bonobos), and chimpanzee-chimpanzee adult-infant forms of rearing. The evidence from work reported by Tomasello and colleagues (e.g., Tomasello et al. 1993; Carpenter et al. 1995) demonstrates that what they call 'enculturated' chimpanzees are significantly different in the behaviours they display from chimpanzees raised in natural conditions.

Tomasello et al. (1993) distinguish 'emulative' from 'imitative' learning. In emulating, by exposure to the performance of a model, an observer may see that a tool can be used to achieve a goal, and go on to perform by so using it. In imitating, an observer not only sees this, but also reproduces the way/s the tool is used by the model. These authors report that in natural conditions, chimpanzee infants are not the object of adult attention that human children are; their actions are rarely, if ever, responded to in the various and detailed ways we described in the previous section (see the discussion in Chapter 2 of the rarity of instances among chimpanzees of behaviour corresponding to 'teaching'). For young chimpanzees in their own ecologies, gaining the knack of termiting or nut-cracking arises through exposure to a model, and access to materials located in appropriate environmental contexts. Unlike in human children, it is not gained by copying (imitating) how the other performed (Nagell et al. 1993; Tomasello et al. 1987). Thus, the scope for diversification of skilled action is limited.

In contrast to this, there have been cases of infant chimpanzees raised in conditions of human or combined human and conspecific care, thus exposed to the sort of joint-attentional and reflective regimes we described in the previous section. These conditions contrast with ones in which such animals may be closely attended to by human keepers, and, for example, trained to associate signs with referents, but are not otherwise involved in the *human* agenda. An early study in which a chimpanzee was involved as 'part of the family' (Hayes & Hayes 1952), revealed signs of imitation learning. The somewhat more systematic studies of Tomasello, Carpenter and colleagues, show that such enculturated chimpanzees are indistinguishable from young children of 1.5 to 2.5 years old, both in the extent of joint attentional orientation to and actions upon objects, and in the degree of imitation used in performance of novel actions from observation of a model. By contrast, chimpanzees in their own ecologies show little or no signs of such behaviour. These researchers have concluded that the variable of adult human interactive engagement with their own offspring, and with the offspring of our genetically closest neighbours, is critical in the cognitive development of both. In contrast to the more indeterminate outcomes of 'language training' experiments (which generally have not involved human-like rearing), chimpanzees exposed to the everyday forms of human life show evidence of spontaneous expression of the communicative use of symbols (Savage-Rumbaugh et al. 1986), as well as signs of 'grammatical' regularity in the deployment of symbol-gesture pairs (Greenfield & Savage-Rumbaugh 1990; Greenfield & Savage-Rumbaugh 1993). Aspects of the capacity for linguistic behaviour are clearly there in creatures whose biology is most similar to humans. It appears that a further, interactive, ingredient would be needed in their own 'form of life' to allow expression of that capacity.

Andrew Lock (1978, 4) once posed what he called the 'supernatural' question, in reference to human-induced symbol use by apes, namely, 'Who were the friends who gave language to us?' As we have pointed out before (Noble & Davidson 1993, 135–6), behaviours expressible but not showing signs of consistent expression (which may be termed 'exaptive'), are vital for evolution to occur. That said, there can be no assumptions about the 'inevitable' prehistoric expression of expressible behaviours where their current expression relies on human tutelage (it is inevitable only in the sense that it happened). An argument trying to escape that stricture could surmise the prehistoric presence of now extinct 'friends'.' This simply postpones the problem, for any such tale must face the question of how the behaviour presumed to have been expressed by these extinct tutors gained its selection in the absence of tutors for *them*.

We conclude this way: at the base of the representational story is a Platonic/ Cartesian mind which either has innate knowledge or can generate it for itself. At the base of the social construct story is a language community, such that mindedness is socially distributed through a set of language games, and knowledge is acquired through interaction, only the capacity to acquire it being innate. Given the conceptual problems with the representational story, and the evidence supporting the social construct one, we consider that the question facing us is to account for how humans became speaking creatures. Before getting to that matter we must complete the theoretical picture by showing how communication, perceiving, and symbol-using can be brought together to describe our characterisation of modern human mentality.

CHAPTER 5

COMMUNICATION, PERCEPTION AND SYMBOL USE: THE PLACE OF MEANING

In this chapter we aim to tie together the various theoretical issues addressed so far, and to present them in a way that bears directly on inquiry into hominid and human evolution. Our first purpose is to consider the nature of perceptual experience. Perceptual experience is the bedrock form of contact all sentient creatures have with their surroundings, and it is valuable to appreciate its nature. Our second purpose is to account for how perceptual experience is linked with communicative activity. Our final aim is to specify the particular nature of human perceptual experience, given the existence of symbol-based communication in human life. Human life alone, we argue, introduces the question of the *meaning* of what is perceived, due to the self-consciousness delivered by communication based on language. Meaning, in this treatment, is understood in everyday terms—'what does this mean'; 'I (don't) know what you mean'—and we aim to account for how it may be understood. Among other implications of that feature of human life is the construction and interpretation (the 'meaning') of an archaeological record of human evolution.

All of what comprises an archaeological record can be brought under the one heading, namely, *signs*. Fossils and other relics are signs persisting in the environment of existences and practices from the past. We rely on two schemes for defining and understanding signs—one, already introduced (Chapter 3), is directly from Peirce (1955[1931]); the other derives from Saussure (1983[1916]). The concepts developed by these theorists allow an approach to the question of signs that fits the problem of how to consider the 'sign-character' of an archaeological record. We also discuss how signs function in communicative behaviour; how they work as *gestures* or as *emblems*.

Human observers of communicative and other behaviour in the natural world may achieve agreement among themselves about the state of things they observe. Care is needed, though, not to assume that this is the state of things for the communicators. Here we confront the problem of *meaning*: what (if anything) someone understands something to be about; what (if anything) others do. We have already analysed what the term 'symbol' can be understood to mean, and stated that 'mindedness' arises on the basis of language, which in turn is definable as the symbolic use of communicative signs. In this chapter we develop an argument which says that the concept of 'meaning' (or meaningfulness) only becomes an issue once the symbolic use of signs has emerged as a practice. Understanding the meaning of anything in an archaeological record—the problem of interpretation— is a keystone of archaeological practice; and is a matter demanding caution, as analysis in the next two chapters shows. Trying to determine if a piece of flaked stone might have been a tool, if so, what sort of tool, and what that might signify about behaviour, are interpretive activities, resting on empirical bases of variable robustness. Interpretive activity of any kind, we conclude, depends on the capacity for symbolic use of signs.

Peirce's sign scheme

Peirce offered a number of ideas about the concept of 'sign': the one concerning the *forms* of signs is perhaps his most enduring. *Iconic* signs are those linked by resemblance to the things they are signs of—a picture of a zebra is an iconic sign. *Indexical* (indicative) signs are constrained in their form to what they indicate. Smoke is generated by many forms of combustion: it both indicates and is constrained in its form by the presence and nature of fire. Smoke does not resemble fire. A mouse rustling in the undergrowth is producing an indexical acoustic sign of itself. The sign (the rustling) does not resemble the mouse, but its form, as an acoustic event, is constrained by the size and movement of the mouse. *Symbolic* signs are in arbitrary relation to what they stand for; they need neither resemble nor be constrained in their form by those things. The form of symbolic signs is the result of convention. Most words in most languages are symbolic signs in terms of their form. Their *meaning/s*—what they are understood to refer to—are given by convention. Some words are 'onomatopoeic' (echoic); they resemble or imitate what they refer to ('moo' or 'miaow'), and hence are iconic in form.

The form of a sign is one matter; its function is another. All words in a language, be they (Peircian) iconic or arbitrary, are, by nature, symbols, in virtue of *being* words (rather than nonverbal sounds). Words are symbols because they have referential function. Iconic signs can function in place of words. The road-sign picture of a traffic light functions in place of the word 'traffic-light' to refer to an up-coming feature of the roadway—as a red flag functions in place of the words 'traffic hazard' (Chapter 3). In this context, the picture, flag or word cannot have intelligible functions to a creature that does not engage in reference. It should be noted that visible forms of gestural signs are constrained by the size and shape, hence the possible sorts of movement, of the utterer's body, just as the physical forms of the mouth, teeth, tongue, larynx and lungs constrain the acoustic form of spoken words.

Thus, at one level of analysis (Verbrugge 1985), the forms of words or gestures are indexical signs of aspects of the sign-maker's physical form.

What sort of signs, in Peirce's terms, are archaeological remains? It would be a mistake to see a fossil as an iconic sign (something cannot resemble itself); it is better understood as an indexical sign of a deceased organism or extinct species. A stone tool, is an *indexical* sign of human practice because the form of the sign relates to the capacities of the originator/s, or the magnitudes of the implements they can wield. If marks on clay artefacts were to become a form of writing (Schmandt-Besserat 1978)—a popular but not a reliable interpretation of these archaeological signs (Lieberman 1980; Zimansky 1993)—their nature would be such that they inhabit the category of symbolic as well as indexical sign. If an object is made in the shape of a recognisable figure, for example, a Venus figurine (see Figure 12b in Chapter 3), its *form* may be iconic, in that it resembles its referent. Its *nature* as a sign means that it occupies iconic, indexical (constraints on maker's capacities) and symbolic ('meaning/s') categories.

A Venus figurine may be taken as a symbol in both of the ways we discussed in Chapter 3 ('simple' and 'socially significant'). It may be understood ('simply') as symbolic at the semantic level, as standing for, say, 'human female'. Whoever made such an object may have conceived of it in those terms. Whoever sees it, if they too have the conjoint concept of 'human' and 'female' (if they share this 'language game' with the maker), can see the object for what it was made to represent. Thus, a 'successful' communicative exchange has occurred in which it could be said that the maker and the perceiver understand each other. Notice the care needed in stating what conceptual category/ies the Venus figurine, as a 'simple' symbolic sign, is placed in. Because no one *now* shares the conventions of symbol-making with the originators of this object it is not straightforward to say what it represents. The originators may not have had a concept equivalent to the present-day one of 'human female', with its connotations of 'person' and 'gender' as larger categories to which the specific concept could be further referred (Conroy 1993).

This goes for the second way in which the Venus figurine could be 'a symbol', namely, in the sense of its being imbued with some further significance within a community. This figure has been interpreted (Gimbutas 1982) as religious, a 'Mother goddess'. If it was, then it may have functioned in ritual activities, and perhaps have been taken as conferring divinely derived power on its worshippers. If there was never such a goddess, then, although a 'successful' communicative exchange may be said to occur among present-day interpreters, no such exchange has occurred between the originators and the present-day interpreters. The reasons motivating the original production of this sign are not understood by present-day witnesses. Instead, those witnesses are applying their own concepts, derived from other language games, and other forms of life, to the sign.

Users of Sign language, when coining novel references, often rely on forms of sign that undergo rapid transformation from iconic to arbitrary—not one of the categories being discussed here, but related to symbol, as we analysed in Chapter 3.

(The transformation from icon-to-arbitrary sign is of particular interest for our theorising about language origin.) In Sign, an iconic sign may be needed to establish what novel item is being referred to. But Sign languages, just as spoken languages, operate syntactically (Klima & Bellugi 1979). There are equivalent regularities as in spoken languages constraining the ways these visible symbols are related to each other in connected utterance. For example, the 'signing space' may be a confined area in front of the torso. Gestures outside of that space are thus taken as non-formal signs (pantomime). In visible sign coinage, the iconic original is quickly reduced to a short-hand form of the original, and one that conforms to the syntactic rules of the language common to its users. DeMatteo (1977, 128) has described an example of this process in American Sign Language, regarding coinage of a sign for 'whale', that included a pantomime of this animal's water spout.

> The informant first signed BIG FISH and then ... traced a line over the back of his head from the base of his skull to a point high above his forehead in a giant C-shape. The line was traced with a claw hand, palm facing forward.

This informant then repeated the FISH sign and superimposed, *within* the signing space, a miniature of the gesture imitating the whale's water spout, but now made that gesture over 'the head' of the formal Sign Language sign.

> [T]he signer, having given us a clear idea of what the claw hand represented, moved that claw hand into the signing space in its appropriate location in relation to the fish, and thus, created a sign.

The mode of production of this sign shows how a form can migrate across Peircian categories—in this case, from icon to symbol. It could be that the Venus figurine migrated from being an icon (and symbol, perhaps in the first sense) related to a specific social context, to becoming a symbol (in both the first and second senses) functioning in a different sort of context. This object has certainly *now* migrated insofar as its identification as a 'Venus figurine' in modern-day communities gives it social significance. It may be observed that 'the archaeological record', by virtue of *being* such a 'record', entirely consists of signs that are symbolic, be they also iconic and/or indexical. Even a collection of pollen grain comes to symbolise, for archaeologists, the 'era' from which it survives. The problem we will have to approach in the next two chapters is whether any of those same signs had (any) symbolic meaning to prehistoric sign makers. The pollen presumably did not, whatever archaeologists and others may now make of it. In the scenario we describe in Chapter 8, migration of gestures from iconic to symbolic signs is taken to be part of the process in the inaugural production of arbitrary symbols prehistorically (a mechanism of which Peirce would approve).

Another term that occurs in talk about signs is the derivative one of 'signal' (such as semaphore). It may be said that signs are made, whilst signals are sent. So, a sign can be understood as something that arises in the (even inadvertent) sending of a signal—the rustling of a mouse. If the production is more deliberate, a sign may be used (BIG FISH) in the fashioning of a signal. In either event, a signal is a message that is being broadcast. This distinction will be used presently in our discussion of communication.

Saussure's distinction

Saussure insisted that language must be understood as a whole system; any part of it achieves its function only in relation to the whole, the sense of any term lies in how it contrasts with the sense of any other. Saussure is very much in the 'mental representation' tradition. In his view, behind any linguistic sign is a mental concept, of which the linguistic sign is its means of conveyance. We are not committed to the view that this sort of notion is invariably entailed in speaking (or using Sign), and introduce it only to explain a general feature of Saussure's system. The categories we are interested in using derive from an argument he made about the composition of the linguistic sign, namely, as comprising *signifier* and *signified*. In his system (Saussure 1983[1916]) 'signifier' and 'signified' are abstract, referring respectively to mental concepts representative of 'the carrier of meaning' (or 'sound-image') and 'the meaning as such' (or 'concept').

Saussure was concerned to emphasise that meaningfulness is an inseparable aspect of linguistic signs. There are problems, though, with his 'signifier/signified' distinction (Harris 1987, 5561), and we have opted for a move attributed by Hodge and Kress (1988) to Voloshinov (1973[1929]), dispensing with the abstract character of Saussure's system. We said in Chapter 1 that we see no need for an abstract item like 'language' as underlying the behaviour of speaking (Dewart 1989), any more than we need an abstract item such as 'ambulation' to account for the various forms of walking. Thus, the terms 'signifier' and 'signified', in our hands, refer respectively to actual signs and actual entities to which they refer.

An 'entity' in this treatment is anything that may attract a name. An entity can be any material object, for instance, a detached thing like a flake of stone. Equally, an entity can be a place in the landscape, such as a hearth or a shelter. Entities can be features of the biophysical environment, such as the edge of a cliff, a piece of fruit, a river, or a living (or dead) creature. Entities may be imaginary, such as a Mother goddess, or the famous unicorn at Lascaux (there being always the possibility for material representations of imaginary creatures). In our treatment, an entity could be a kinship category, like 'mother's brother', or a moral one, like 'justice', or an affective one like 'anger', since these terms derive from relations and practices among people. Hence, entities can be words (when they are in use—see later), texts or discourses. Signs of any sort may be used to refer to entities; signs themselves can be witnessed as entities ('this is the sign for 'traffic hazard''). We will focus our discussion in this chapter on material entities, but including words, texts and discourses as material entities. The key point is that of the referential link between symbolic signs and the entities they name—between signifiers and signifieds. The foundational nature of 'naming', of applying a signifier to a signified, and which

forms the distinction between verbal and nonverbal communication, will be discussed in Chapter 8.

Energy, information and (nonverbal) communication

Among humans, many natural signs fall under the heading of nonverbal communication. We noted in Chapter 2 that these were much more prevalent among humans
than other apes. All non-human communication, whether vocal or non-vocal, is
nonverbal in form (Burling 1993). Background concepts useful for approaching the
matter of any communication, verbal or nonverbal, are those of 'energy', and
'information'. Kendon (1981) identified an inspiration for the study of nonverbal
communication in information theory (Shannon & Weaver 1949), which is a
formalised account of energy transfer in any physical communication system, such
as a computer. The perspective gained from information theory was the abstracted
notion of 'information' considered irrespective of the nature or method of its
transmission. This allowed appreciation of the varieties of information sources,
both verbal and nonverbal, that may be available in interpersonal or interorganism
encounters.

Coulter (1991a) reviews some recent applications of information theory to
matters of human perceiving and knowing about the environment, and points out
that the everyday concept of 'information' has become confused with the physical
issue of energy transmission through electronic or neural systems. The hope of
some theorists who continue to employ the information theory model (e.g., Dretske
1981) is that perceiving and knowing, understood in terms of meaningful encounters in the everyday world ('information' in the ordinary sense of the term), will
somehow be derivable from talk about the encoding of electromagnetic or acoustic
waveforms among sensory nerves. We suggested in Chapter 2 that where this sort
of approach is taken, as in spectrographic studies of different animals' calls, the
informativeness (ordinary sense) of the utterance cannot be discerned. This point
will recur when we consider the nature of perceptual experience.

The concept of energy, as physical activity in a neural pathway, can be seen to
underlie all forms of information (verbal and nonverbal) transmitted within a
natural ecosystem. Living creatures exhibit a range of sensory sensitivities, in being
able to see, hear, touch, taste, smell, or in other ways connect with their surroundings. These sensitivities are the result of interaction between specialist receptor
surfaces (e.g., retinas and cochleas) and forms of electromagnetic, mechanical
(including acoustic) or chemical energy. Such energy is either reflected or radiated
from the surfaces that constitute the layout of material entities. In many species,
vision is enabled in virtue of collections of photosensitive cells located within a
chambered eye. Hearing occurs due to the movement of hair cells in the cochlea in
response to oscillating pressure changes in atmosphere or fluid. Touch takes the
form of mechanical deformation of an animal's soft surface tissue by the resistive
surfaces of objects; taste and smell are due to electro-chemical interactions between

molecules of volatile substances and micro-hairs in receptor pits located in the nose, mouth and tongue (Gibson 1966).

Energy can be said to be informative when detecting it by means of the senses affects the behaviour of the detecting organism. Hopkins (1983) describes a range of sensory systems that have been studied in insects, birds and mammals. One finding is that some systems are tuned specifically to features of the signals produced by conspecifics. For individuals of such species, what they can detect is largely confined to the acoustic productions of other such individuals. In one species of cricket, the 'song' of the male has definite peaks at 4 kHz and 16 kHz; the auditory sensitivity of females is largely confined to these two regions. Such calls can be said to be indexical signs, insofar as the caller is pointing out its presence to other species members. These signs are also communicative, in that one animal's signal has the effect of attracting another. It is the liaison of sign expressed and response made, as Mead (1934) argued, which allows human observers to identify the gesture as communicative, although there is dispute about what should count as 'communication', as we will consider presently.

Human observers, being human, can readily attribute a meaning to these sorts of signals we have been describing. Ethologists may observe that female crickets make their way toward calling males. Hence they may gloss the communicative event as one in which the male 'sings so as to attract a mate'. But they may also take it that this is how the cricket 'understands what is going on'. This is an example of the anthropomorphism—seeing the cricket as like a little person—which makes for so much difficulty and confusion in thinking about the nature of non-language-based experience.

Slater (1983) has argued that communication cannot be confined to activity which is construed as mutually beneficial (synergistic). Plovers, ground-nesting birds, make a 'broken-wing' display in the presence of potential predators when they are nesting (Ristau 1992). The bird walks away from the nest, dragging one wing, which distracts the intruder's attention from the nest. The benefit of such behaviour may not be considered mutual—it could be said to benefit the bird at the expense of the other animal. It also seems a clear instance of communication, though some would disagree, as we note below. Such behaviour can be characterised as an alternative evolutionary strategy to the production of signals and displays (such as those by nesting ducks or geese) which scare intruders off. Thus, as a first approximation, communication could be understood to include *anything* which is done to affect the behaviour of another creature, as Mead (1934) would argue. The situation is made complex because environmental habitats are occupied by many organisms. The same utterance may be responded to quite differently by different recipients, depending on their ecological relationship with the producer of the utterance (Figure 18, reproduced from Slater [1983], illustrates this point). Crickets and frogs produce calls which attract mates; these also have the effect of increasing their risk of being preyed upon. Vervet monkeys' calls may provoke a response that reduces the risk of predation, but they also may serve to alert the predator.

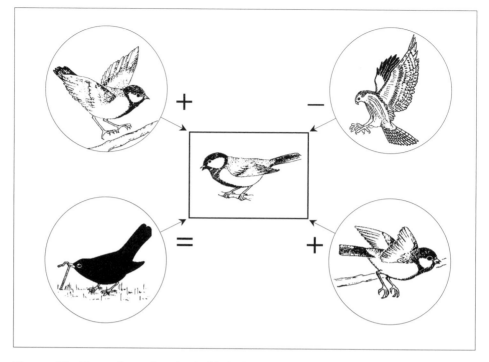

Figure 18 The variety of ecological links between organisms, as shown by responses to the song of a bird (centre). Positive form an attracted mate (top left), or a driven-off rival (bottom right); neutral from another bird which ignores the song (bottom left), and negative from an alerted predator (top right). *From* Slater 1983.

According to Krebs & Dawkins (1984) it is generally held among ethologists that attracting predators is not to be counted as a form of communicative act, but rather as an 'incidental effect'. Such calls are nonetheless indexical signs, comparable with the noise of a rustling mouse.

Marler (1967) excludes from communication signs whose benefit is not mutual, as well as 'incidental effects'. He singles out the rustling mouse as distinctly *not* communicating with the predatory owl. Slater (1983) leaves the case of the mouse indeterminate, seeing part of the problem as lying in the issue of intent. The mouse may be said not to intend communicating with the owl, which is why ethologists exclude the case. But as Slater says, intent is not readily determinable for non-human species, because they cannot be *asked* about such things. This is another example of anthropomorphism creating problems for analysis. We introduced the matter of 'intention' in Chapter 1, and discussed it in terms of 'planning' in the previous chapter. If it is assumed that intention, with its connotation of 'meaning something', has to be involved in communication, this will guide the approach to what is and is not to be classified as communicative. For some analysts, only those signals that *look* intentional (to them) will be counted. We offer the following resolution of the question.

The bulk of non-human animal signals have the effect of warding off same-species or other-species rivals and have the effect of identifying and/or attracting mates and offspring. Some species concatenate both functions in the same utterance (see, e.g., Narins & Capranica 1976). Considered in terms of nonverbal communication (Kendon 1981) such signals may be seen as gestural, as in the case of an acoustic or visual display, or as emblematic, as in the case of coloration or plumage. Furthermore, any incidental effects of such signalling *can* be considered as communicative using the distinction Goffman makes (1963) between 'information given' and 'information given off'. Information given may be thought of as intended communication, or that which is under the control of the communicator; information 'given off' may be thought of as whatever cannot be controlled by the organism, whatever 'leaks out' as it were. Goffman's analysis was focused on human communication, and he principally thought of leakage as expressed through items such as clothing, gait or general demeanour, which, whether or not the individual exhibiting these things appreciates it, can indicate type of occupation, social class, degree of sobriety, etc. A human analogy with the case of signalling crickets and frogs might be the production of a message to an acquaintance (the 'information given') which informs an eavesdropper about one's circumstances (the 'given off'). In the case of the mouse, there is simply information 'given off'.

Still unresolved in this way of talking about different communications is the issue of intent. We believe it can be left unresolved, with no harm coming to the analytic task. In this respect we note recent debates in animal ethology and related literature (Blumberg & Alberts 1992; Dennett 1983; Guilford & Dawkins 1991; Guilford & Dawkins 1992) about what considerations are relevant to the identification of sources of selective pressure in the evolution of communicative signals. The arguments turn significantly upon the appropriateness of introducing a role for purpose or intentionality in such communication.

The reason arguments arise here is because discussion forever risks *eliding* 'opaque' as distinct from 'transparent' versions of events. Coulter (1983, 108) takes these terms from Quine (1960) and applies them specifically to the issue of awareness in non-linguistic contexts. He gives the following example:

> If I were to say of my pre-linguistic infant that he is watching the President on television, it is clear that I am describing the object of his watching from an *adult* point of view, which is one that he cannot literally be said to have ... I am conflating the way it is with the child with the way it is for me... (emphasis in original).

The 'way it is with the child' may be described as 'opaque' for the adult observer of the child, the opacity being due to the fact that the pre-linguistic child's 'experience' cannot actually be characterised. The 'way it is' for the concept-using adult is always potentially 'transparent', because other, similar concept-users (participants in the same 'language game') can clearly understand the description of the adult's experience—'watching the President on TV'. Transparency here is exactly the 'transparency' discussed in Chapter 4. The (typically) effortless nature of the adult description risks an elision—the 'transparent' version offered by the adult may be taken as also 'opaquely' true (as a true account of the 'way it is with the child'). It is only among language-using humans that opaque versions of experience can be transformed into transparent ones, through observers asking perceivers what it is they perceive, or what it is they are doing. Between humans and non-humans (or pre-linguistic humans) such a move is unavailable.

A non-human animal's intentions, if indeed it has any, are undeterminable, because the opacity-to-transparency transformation is unavailable. There thus arises the same risk of *elision* between opaque and transparent versions, as might occur in the case of the pre-linguistic child. Instead of risking this elision (which is another way of describing anthropomorphism) it may be wiser to leave the matter unresolved. The studies of vervet monkey calls by Cheney and Seyfarth (1990) may be seen as investigations into the possibility of achieving transparency despite the absence of the vehicle—language—humans take for granted as enabling transparency among themselves.

The nature of perceiving

The apparently simple way to achieve transparency—by asking others what they see or hear—belies a fundamental feature in the annals of theory-making with respect to perception. From the time of Aristotle, contemporary of Plato, and reinforced by Hobbes, the 17th century philosopher, and Helmholtz, the 19th century physical scientist (Gibson 1966), perception has been understood as a process such that whatever may constitute the universe, perceivers have access solely to the result of activity in nerve cells. This tradition has combined with the Cartesian doctrine we discussed in the previous chapter that splits mind and matter, and throws doubt on the reality of anything but one's own self as a thinking (mental) thing. The result has been to make the apparent simplicity of the questioning of another person about their perceptual experience seem in fact like an invitation to delusion. Costall (1984, 110) cites one contemporary form of the traditional position, as expressed by Gregory (1974):

> Perceptions are constructed, by complex brain processes, from fleeting fragmentary scraps of data signalled by the senses and drawn from the brain's memory banks—themselves snippets from the past ... On this view all perceptions are essentially fictions; fictions based on past experience selected by present sensory data.

A standard textbook account (Schiffman 1990, 5–6) puts the position thus:

> [T]he perception of the physical world of objects and events is a constructive achievement, perhaps even an inference, based on the interpretation of the stimulation. Central to this view is that there is some internal constructive process that is held to occur on the part of the observer that mediates between the environmental stimulation and its perception...

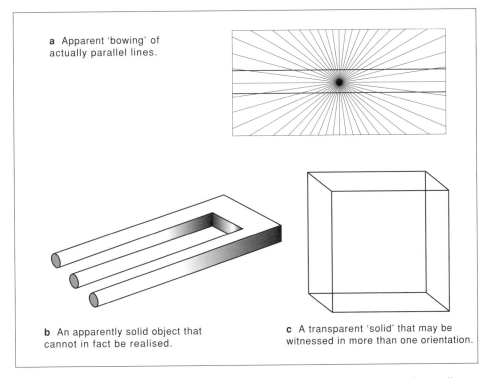

a Apparent 'bowing' of actually parallel lines.

b An apparently solid object that cannot in fact be realised.

c A transparent 'solid' that may be witnessed in more than one orientation.

Figure 19 Examples of odd visual effects. **a** shows apparent 'bowing' of actually parallel lines. **b** depicts an apparently solid object that cannot in fact be realised. **c** shows a transparent 'solid' that may be witnessed in more than one orientation.

Classic examples taken as supportive of this view are the distorted, ambiguous and impossible appearances that may be realised in various two-dimensional visual displays (Figure 19a–c). Because of these so-called illusions, dual possibility figures, and representations of entities that could not logically exist in nature, it is held that our perceptions cannot be taken at face value, they may not faithfully capture reality.

Another standard textbook account (Sekuler & Blake 1990, 3), offers a description of how the internal representational processes we discussed in the previous chapter might allow perception to be conceived as a 'symbolic' process:

Each of your percepts is associated with some characteristic activity in your brain ... Suppose you look at some object. Your experience, the percept, is certainly not the same as the object itself; however, the percept does represent that object. In this case, the symbols are not the sort we usually think of—a country's flag, a traffic sign, printed words. Instead, the symbols are the various brain states that stand for objects ... however, the properties of these symbols are not the same as the properties of the things being symbolized.

The 'internal representation' view of perception assumes the construction of mental 'pictures' (or brain 'states') from component elements of stimulus energy (coupled with previously stored material from within the brain itself). The energy originates in the environment, but is encoded into patterns of electrical activity (action potentials) in the nervous system. These microscopic events can be recorded by means of tiny electrodes implanted in individual nerve cells, the resulting signal then amplified, and displayed on an oscilloscope screen (e.g., Hubel & Wiesel 1968; 1970), in the way illustrated in Figure 16 (Chapter 4).

As can be appreciated, such coded neural patterns displayed on the oscilloscope screen correspond to nothing resembling (at least human) phenomenal experience. Thus, in the traditional account, some sort of internal brain (or 'mental') transformation must take place which re-presents (i.e., *represents*) and forms inferences from some combination of input and stored data ('memories') about what might plausibly be the nature of 'what's there', and in a manner intelligible to the organism. Sekuler and Blake go on to characterise such transformations as the 'computations', consistent with the computer metaphor, derived from information theory, that underwrites the contemporary form of the 'representational' picture we discussed in Chapter 4.

Schiffman's (1990) account quoted above is given in contrast to an approach that opposes the traditional one. Schiffman identifies the fact that perception rests upon sensory sensitivity to environmental energy, then goes on to say (1990, 6) that there 'currently flourish' two main approaches to the issue of what happens as a result. In contrast to the internal construction view is that of Gibson, described by Schiffman as the theorist:

> [who] proposed that inner mental processes play little or no role in perception: the stimuli themselves (e.g., the optic array) contain and specify the necessary and sufficient information for the perception of the physical world *directly*, without recourse to additional stages of processing on the part of the organism. (emphasis in original)

Gibson (1966; 1979) dubbed his approach ecological, to reflect his commitment to a 'realist' position (Gibson 1967; Turvey et al. 1981) in which perceiving is the direct accessing of structures of environmental energy by organisms with appropriate sensory sensitivities and motor capacities. The illusions and ambiguities which help the traditional view are seen in this approach as contrivances that exploit certain features of picture-making, and that have less relevance for perception in the real world. In an ecological model, when we confront an oddity in a two-dimensional display, this is far from indicating that perceiving is a mental construct. Rather, we accurately perceive a curious pictorial contrivance. An example is the appearance of 'ghost' contours where none is physically present (Figure 20a, from Kanizsa 1974). This has been taken (Coren & Porac 1983) to indicate that a contour is 'mentally constructed' because we see the display as portraying an opaque triangular object, of the same hue and reflectance as the background, partly masking some circles and another triangle that lie beneath it.

Another, perhaps simpler, way to characterise things is to say we respond to the

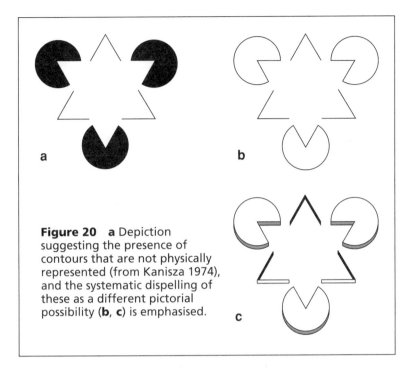

Figure 20 **a** Depiction suggesting the presence of contours that are not physically represented (from Kanisza 1974), and the systematic dispelling of these as a different pictorial possibility (**b, c**) is emphasised.

pictorial possibilities in the image (it is a picture, after all). It is certainly the case that once the components are made to look like individual items, a pictorial possibility that can be enhanced by making them appear more three-dimensional, the effect is dispelled (Figure 20b, c).

The Gibsonian approach to perception relies on the attunement of sensory systems, and their refinement in being so tuned over evolutionary time spans, to patterns already structured in the environment. Neural encoding, understood as trains of action potentials, may be better understood, through an ecological approach, as a product of the activity of physiological investigation. What is seen on the oscilloscope screen, as amplified from the miniature electrode in a nerve cell, is a new environmental entity, contrived through the application of complex technologies, not an expanded version of entities which some inner perceiver (the 'homunculus'?) inspects, with a view to figuring out what they could possibly represent. In this way of thinking about perceiving, action potentials do not stand as entities between the structure of the environment and the perceptual 'experience' of organisms in response to aspects of that structure. To see them thus is to give way to the confusion Coulter (1991a) refers to when pointing to the distinction between information understood as 'bits' along a computer wire and information understood in everyday terms. Such bits might be construable via a particular way of inspecting the machine (equivalent to tapping into a neuron with an electrode), but they are not displayed on the computer screen as a list of 0's and 1's for us to try to figure out what they might stand for.

Field studies by ethologists have produced results that are consistent with the Gibsonian approach. Halliday (1983) describes entomologists' observations of different species of firefly which show that each species maintains separation from the others (hence avoids trying to mate with them) through exhibiting different temporal patterns of light flashes radiated from the surface of their bodies (Lloyd 1971). This is illustrated in Figure 21 (derived from Lloyd). Halliday also mentions how individuals in a group of mongooses may be identified by the others through secretion by each of a unique combination of different relative amounts of a limited set of volatile compounds, a complex form of pheromone-based communication (Shorey 1976). These examples, from visual and olfactory sense modalities, point to energy *structures* as a property of what is available to be perceived. Furthermore, they suggest these structures being perceived, in virtue of their patterning, by organisms whose behaviours or central nervous systems are not easily thought of as including or enabling the making of inferences (the capacity entailed in the first quote from Schiffman).

In the acoustic arena, with human listeners, Warren and Verbrugge (1984) isolated the feature that distinguished two audible events. One was the disintegration of a fragile object upon impact with a hard surface (in this case, the sound of a glass bottle hitting the floor); the other was the sound of its repeated bouncing, intact, on such a surface. These authors found that the unfolding in time of the two events was the critical aspect distinguishing them, rather than their different audio-frequency spectra, or the markedly different first few milliseconds of each event. That is to say, when the spectral content of the events was made identical, and when the explosive impulse due to initial breaking was removed from recordings, listeners who did not know the experimental purpose could nonetheless judge what was being specified. Warren and Verbrugge observed that listeners could identify an event as something disintegrating, by being provided only with a set of synthe-

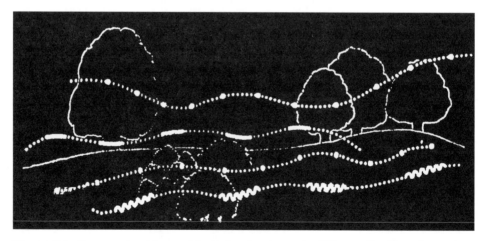

Figure 21 Temporal patterns of body luminescence in different fireflies, shown by composite time-lapse imaging. *From* Lloyd 1966.

sised acoustic pulses that were 'damped' (i.e., increasingly squeezed up in time, and of descending loudness) and also *asynchronous*. Such a temporal train acts as a model for the 'uncorrelated' bouncings of separate pieces of broken bottle. The event of bouncing, on the other hand, was able to be specified by use of a *synchronous* train of damped pulses, this being analogous to the bouncing of an intact object. The two patterns are shown in Figure 22.

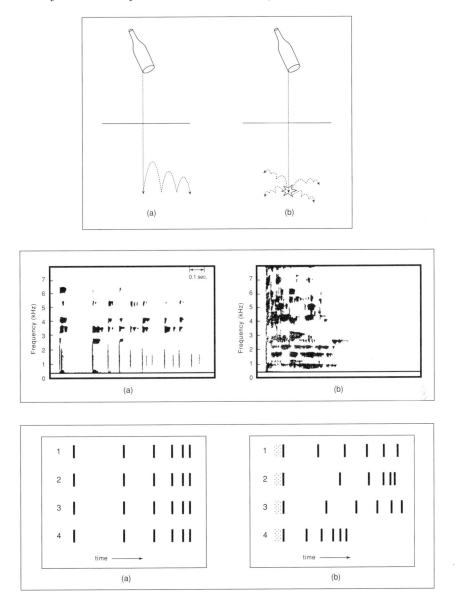

Figure 22 Recorded and synthesised spectrograms of the temporal patterns specifying the events of 'bouncing' vs 'breaking'. *From* Warren and Verbrugge 1984.

One may see this sort of investigation as showing how the different temporal structures of two similar events govern their perceived distinctiveness. The fact that critical aspects of these two events could be isolated, and the difference between them simulated using synthetic acoustic pulses, is in keeping with the proposal that structures of energy (in this case, temporal patterns) do function in perceptual discrimination.

Perception and meaning

A critical matter serving to distinguish the responses of fireflies and humans is that fireflies reveal their discriminatory capacity through selective attention to one temporal pattern of light flashes; that selectivity, in turn, being revealed through their behaviour. The human listeners of Warren and Verbrugge's experiment not only differentiate, they identify for the experimenter what they hear by referring to it in words. What they hear can thus be said to have meaning for them; it specifies an event that can be described. Human listeners are *aware*—conscious of the fact— that they have auditory 'experiences', and they are aware of what those experiences could mean. This is evidenced by the forms of reference they make ('that sounded like a bottle breaking'). The matter of human awareness—of the fact that people perceive, and can see the meaning of what they perceive—gives rise to many conceptual problems about what any sense-possessing organism actually experiences. We are apt to attribute a sort of 'wordless' version of human awareness to other creatures, another example of the anthropomorphising tendency considered earlier.

Cheney and Seyfarth (1990, pp. 102–110) detail the temporal and spectral structures of the calls made by vervet monkeys in response to different predator classes (referred to in Chapters 1 and 2). In the presence of other monkeys, a male vervet will (typically) produce a series of barking sounds on spotting a leopard or similar predatory cat; by contrast, it produces a single cough-like sound on spotting an eagle or similar predatory bird. By further contrast it will produce what these authors describe as a 'chuttering' sound on spotting a python or similar predatory snake. Figure 23 illustrates spectrograms of the different calls. These utterances have been the object of so much attention by human investigators precisely because they throw the issue of meaning into high relief. Cheney and Seyfarth devoted detailed attention (1990, pp. 139–174) to the question of what these and other vervet calls might 'mean', though they could find no firm answer. The different calls look (to us, humans) as though they convey meanings because they are specific to certain classes of environmental occurrence, or possibly different environmental entities, and other vervets within earshot react appropriately.

In order to approach the issue of 'meaning' with respect to the vervet calls we need first to expand on a characteristic of human awareness we noted in the last chapter. When humans refer to what they experience perceptually they are expressing a capacity to reflect upon what they see or hear. Harré and Secord (1972, 84–85), whom we referred to in Chapter 4, speak about the capacity to perceive as being that of monitoring one's surroundings. They go on to observe that humans have a further capacity: 'People, alone among animals, possess the power to monitor their monitorings'. This second capacity is that of reflection upon (hence being able to refer to) the outcome of the first. We suggest that it is the act of monitoring one's perceptual monitorings which provides humans *with* so-called 'perceptual experiences'. The very having of 'experiences' of our surroundings may *occur* because we can speak about them, and hence get them fixed in awareness. We suggest this because it may be necessary that in order 'to have the experience of something' one must be (referentially) aware of what that 'something' is, even if it is only describable as 'an unfamiliar thing'. This point follows from the argument about mind as a 'social construct' which we presented in Chapter 4. If mindedness is not 'innate', but rather emerges as the socialising of attention, then 'consciousness of perceptual experience' forms part of that emerging mentality.

Caution is needed in advancing this line of argument. Menzel (1971; 1974) exposed individual chimpanzees, on different occasions, either to a desirable entity

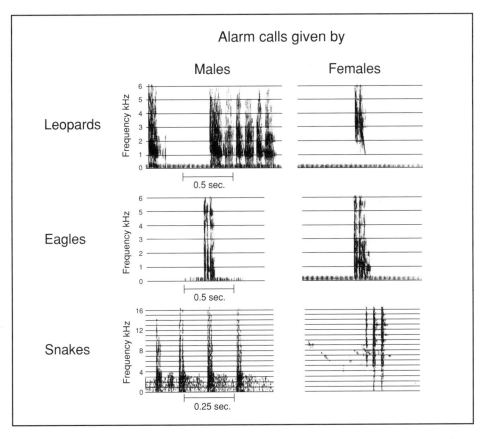

Figure 23 Spectrograms of three calls made by vervet monkeys in response to the sight of different predator classes while in the presence of other vervets. *From* Cheney and Seyfarth 1990.

(food) or to a potentially threatening one (plastic snake), then concealed the item in question, returning the chimpanzees to their holding cages. Upon release a few minutes later, the chimpanzees who had been shown one or other type, expressed distinct reactions (interpretable as desire or apprehension) throughout their approach to each. This could be taken to suggest they went on knowing there was something desirable/threatening, yet out of sight, 'over there'. Vauclair (1990) summarises experimental evidence which supports a view that chimpanzees particularly seem able to acquire 'some form of internal representation' (p. 314) of external objects/events. The capacity of chimpanzees to use and manipulate objects, as well as to mimic others' uses, under particular conditions, suggests that these animals may somehow retain images of high-salience objects (like foods, nutting stones, allies and potential threats). Those capacities are less readily observed in monkeys (Chapter 2). Thus, rather than assume an all-or-none distinction on this matter, it may be best to conclude, at least for the moment, that, in comparison with other apes, the human 'experience' of the environment is more highly elaborated, due to the form of monitoring (i.e., linguistic) which humans can recruit.

Walker (1983, 254–260) reviews experimental evidence to show that pigeons can be trained to respond to classes of visual displays, for example, alphabetic characters varying in font; or to photographs containing—or not containing—certain types of object (e.g., humans, trees). This indicates that these animals are sensitive to assemblages of features at a higher order than geometric elements; that they perceive salient environmental features as whole entities. However, this does not amount to saying that they 'have a representation of an object' in a way that might be argued from the above-mentioned observations with chimpanzees. Birds, generally, have rapidly fading memories for perceived entities (Walker 1983, 300–304). Hence, though their nervous systems are constructed in such a way that higher-order characteristics of environmental features can be discriminated, these animals seem not to have any means for 'retaining a representation' of what they see. By this we mean more than the phenomena known as 'iconic' and 'echoic' memory (Neisser 1967), which are forms of continuation of visual or auditory occurrences for brief intervals (fractions of a second or so) after cessation of the occurrence—a sort of nervous system 'resonance'. Being a property of nervous system activity, this is very likely something pigeons do have, and is captured by the 'rapidly fading memory' term. The retention we are speaking about has more to do with what has been called 'episodic memory' (Cohen & Squire 1980), a form of remembering that relies on rehearsal of what has been experienced, allowing for later recollection. The distinction between procedural (knowing how) and declarative (knowing that) skills was introduced in Chapter 4; there is loss of declarative knowledge in cases of amnesia. Episodic memory can be aligned with declarative ability.

The notion of 'representation' that we are trying to capture in this discussion carries an element of 'ongoingness'. Being able to keep a representation going after the passing of its cause is a logically necessary background element for the achievement of reflection. Infants up to about eight months will not search for an object they have been shown, which is then hidden from them. They do not exhibit what Piaget (1954) called 'object constancy', something he saw as a foundation stone for any reflection (Butterworth & Grover 1988). (We observe that infants might need to learn that 'searching' for things is appropriate as a *behaviour*, whatever 'way it may be with them' in terms of 'object constancy'.) Nonetheless, the expression of behaviour indicating a continued understanding of an object's existence is evidence of the 'perceptual' becoming increasingly imbued with the 'conceptual' (Premack 1988).

The chimpanzees in Menzel's studies expressed the same reaction to the plastic snake *each time* they were exposed to it, suggesting that whatever the 'representation' which sustained their fearfulness over the short term faded out in the longer term, and was not fixed as an episode in their lives. The behaviour may be captured by the point Wittgenstein (1958, ¶650) made: 'We say a dog is afraid his master will beat him; but not, he is afraid his master will beat him tomorrow'. Like dogs, chimpanzees under (more or less) natural conditions have no known means of representing things to themselves at a conceptual level. It may be that the 'representation' in the case of Menzel's chimpanzees was not some non-rapidly fading visual image of the environmental entity but their own more slowly dissipating emotion, hence, not 'representational' at all.

Reflection

Theorists other than Harré and Secord may prefer to keep open the question of the exclusiveness to humans of a capacity for reflection. There does seem to be general agreement, though, that what is needed to give meaning to entities or to recognise them is the ability to reflect, hence refer to something in one's experience. Dennett (1983; 1987) uses Grice's (1969) scheme, which relies on the notion of 'orders of intentionality'. First-order intentionality he has termed 'having beliefs and desires' about something. Second-order intentionality is the having of 'beliefs and desires' *about* those 'beliefs and desires'. Dennett has stated the case (1983, p. 346) for allowing that 'second order' intentionality is (minimally) sufficient for reflection upon perceptual experience so as to enable a creature to 'mean what it says'—to be aware that its utterance refers to something in its experience—as against produce a signal in response to a circumstance. To us, Dennett's talk of second-order 'belief and desire' is another (and less clear) way of referring to 'monitoring one's monitorings'. It is less clear because it begs the question of reflectivity in the use of a term like 'belief' throughout; how a creature can have an unreflecting (first-order) 'belief' about anything is incomprehensible. Be that as it may, living creatures can be characterised in terms of the 'order of intentionality' which they exhibit in their conduct.

Cheney and Seyfarth refer to this scheme and, after careful analysis of what the vervets' calls might signify about the animals' level of awareness, state:

> [W]e conclude that vervet communication is most consistent with ... first-order intention-ality; monkeys give leopard alarms because they want others to run into trees, not necessarily because they want others to think that there is a leopard nearby (Cheney & Seyfarth, 1990, p. 174).

These authors go on to point out the difficulty in trying to specify what the calls might 'mean'. Are they denotative ('names' for different predators) or propositional ('commandments' about ways to respond)? Nothing in the observations allows a conclusion, nor provides means to determine if these are the only alternatives.

If the vervet calling behaviour is correctly characterised as exhibiting less than 'second order intentionality', then it seems not to have reached a point at which meaning, in the sense of reference, becomes an issue. This is also suggested by the hesitancy with which Cheney and Seyfarth approach the problem of how (referen-tial) meaning is to be characterised for these utterances at all. We are not even sure if those authors have warrant to say that the monkeys 'want others to run into trees'; as against that the monkeys 'want' something else, or 'want' nothing at all. We turn once more to Burling's (1993) classification of different kinds of human utterance (see Chapter 2): language, language-like and gesture-call. He draws a parallel between the vervet calls and the subset of human nonverbal utterance he calls gesture-calling, pointing out that:

> [t]he leopard alarm call cannot be extended to a context where it would mean 'have you seen any leopards?' or 'don't worry, the leopard has gone.' ... We interpret an English word like 'leopard' to be a label for a particular kind of object precisely because it can be used in a great many different situations and to build a great many different meanings.

Giggles, gasps, grunts, laughs, sobs, screams, snorts and yelps are among many sorts of human 'gesture calls' that Burling mentions. He also notes the variety of forms of visual bodily and facial 'gesture-calls' (smiles, scowls, gaze shifts, etc.) and points out that, in contrast to verbal utterances, the meanings of all of these travel quite well across different communities, a point investigated at length by Darwin (1872). Human gesture-calls in everyday settings are typically indexical rather than symbolic, but, like the vervet calls, they also have the power to make a perceiver of such a call aware of something else occurring in the environment. Burling proposes that the vervet calls may be best understood as gesture-calls.

Where does this leave us in the matter of meaning and perception? Even if the vervets calls are not meaning-making in the referential symbolic sense, they are surely still meaningful in some sense? This sort of issue has to be treated with care, and the remainder of this chapter is devoted to that exercise. The payoff for taking pains over what we are to make of this and other features of communication, perception and symbol use is that we achieve a workable theory of how they relate to each other, and therefore what it is that demands explanation in the evolutionary emergence of modern human behaviour. There is the closely related payoff of how, as analysts, we are to perceive and interpret the archaeological record that may be used to inform us about that evolutionary emergence.

The earlier quotation from Sekuler and Blake would lead to the conclusion that if perceiving is a symbolic process (the symbols being in the form of brain 'states') then the meanings of things arise (and arise, presumably, for any creature) insofar as such symbols are made to refer to perceived environmental signals. Since the symbols in question *are* 'brain states' then meaning-making takes place within the brain or mind of the perceiver. This we would anticipate as a conclusion, given the contemporary representational orientation of those authors. If instead we follow a Gibsonian 'direct perception' line, in which pre-figured structures of energy are detected directly, without the involvement of symbols in the mind/brain, then this might suggest that the meanings of things are 'out there' in the environment.

Gibson has indicated just such a conclusion. In his view, material entities in the environment are specified for organisms with appropriately tuned sensory systems, in virtue of the way that the composition and layout of their surfaces reflect or generate structures of energy to which organisms are sensitive. The examples we gave earlier, about how fireflies and mongooses identify each other, and about how people distinguish breaking from bouncing glassware, support this argument. Gibson (1979) advances his theory to a further position, with the proposal that material entities exhibit what he terms 'affordances'. These are properties which entities offer to organisms by way of such things as: support for locomotion, climbability, shelter, edibility, and so forth. Gibson poses the question as to whether one can go from the direct perception of surfaces to the direct perception of 'affordances', suggesting that:

> [p]erhaps the composition and layout of surfaces *constitute* what they afford. If so, to perceive them is to perceive what they afford. This is a radical hypothesis, for it implies that the 'values' and 'meanings' of things in the environment can be directly perceived. Moreover, it would explain the sense in which values and meanings are external to the perceiver. (1979, 127; emphasis in original)

In Chapter 4 we were unwilling to accept the commitments of either a classical or modern 'representational' theory of 'the mind'; just so we are unwilling to accept the tenets of a 'brain-based' theory about 'where meaning arises'. But neither do we accept the Gibsonian 'external' alternative. In concluding the last chapter we arrived at a view of mind which, following Wittgenstein and features of theory within a 'social construction' tradition, took 'mind' to be a term descriptive of certain kinds of conduct, and dependent on social interaction for its realisation. A similar move, it turns out, can be made with the problem of 'meaning'. We argue that meanings do not reside in environmental entities (any more than 'affordances' do, but that is a separate argument, pursued in Noble [1993b]). It follows that meanings are not perceived directly, as part-and-parcel of what animals perceive. Nor do meanings arise inside individuals' heads. The position we come to, indeed, is that there is no need for meaning to be involved in perceiving *at all*. Exceptionally, meaning may, from time to time, enter the picture as part of, and as exclusive to, human perception.

That conclusion seems to fly in the face of a position we might be expected to arrive at in the light of Burling's (1993) analysis. If the vervet monkey calls are best thought of as akin to human gesture-calls, then those calls are still meaningful. We all know the meaning of a scowl or a howl. Our point is that we (humans) can lay claim to 'know the meanings' of these things only in virtue of the linguistic behaviour we can engage in with reference to them. Humans and other primates know how to react to these things; natural selection has seen to that. Only humans know how to reflect on them.

Humans with language, others, and perceiving

If it is only among humans that meaning is a feature of what is perceived it follows, in the terms of this argument, that it is not a feature of what vervets perceive. So, what *do* non-human animals perceive? The question phrased that way, in principle, cannot be answered. It may well be determinable what non-human animals can differentiate, and along what dimensions (witness the improving discriminations of infant vervets as they gradually cease to give 'eagle alarms' to leaves, small birds and other non-predators). Discrimination abilities can also be revealed through experiments like those with birds and chimpanzees mentioned earlier (and the hungry toad referred to in Chapter 3). But no one can say for certain what makes up the *content* of the perceived experience of any of these creatures (cf., Coulter, 1983, 115–6). It is undeniable *that* animals other than humans perceive—in the Gibsonian sense of being sensitive to structures of environmental energy. What they experience is another matter. The vervet monkeys might be distinguishing 'occurrences', or 'event forms', or 'objects', in the different responses they make to the energetic structures human observers denote as different types of predators. The earlier quotation from Cheney and Seyfarth shows the difficulty of specifying 'the stuff', the content, of the monkeys' perceptual world. This is even assuming there *is* content, as against an unreflected-upon flow of energy—what we referred to in Chapter 1, from Toulmin, as operating on 'automatic pilot' (Noble 1987; 1993a).

The name suggests that automatic pilot perceiving is the sort that gets done by humans when they are *not* monitoring their own monitorings. As a reminder: Toulmin (1982) characterised automatic pilot perceiving as 'unconscious attentive-ness', distinct from 'articulateness'—the state of full awareness of 'what's going on'. Instances of 'automatic pilot' functioning, when driving a car, are notable because it seems remarkable that you can control a speeding vehicle yet not be aware of that fact. Nonetheless, 'automatic-pilot' functioning is routinely part of how people operate, for example, in everyday locomotion. Toulmin distinguishes three levels of awareness—sensitivity, attentiveness and articulateness—at each of which one can speak about conscious and unconscious forms. Practised car drivers can, from time to time, be unconsciously attentive, that is, monitor their surround-ings without attending to what they are doing (without monitoring those monitorings). Toulmin asks whether pre-linguistic infants or non-human animals are other than *un*consciously attentive, as their highest level of consciousness. What this implies is that *conscious* attentiveness is the 'narrative-production' (Bruner 1990) condition of the monitoring of one's monitorings.

A question can be raised as to whether the automatic-pilot driving example is really an instance of unconscious attentiveness. Dennett (1991) for one, has claimed that, if probed, you could say what had occurred during a stretch of such driving. He goes on to argue that the case is better seen as 'rolling consciousness with swift memory loss'. This is the issue raised earlier in the chapter, about the forms of 'memory' to be found in different creatures, but revisited here with a view to commenting on the content of perceptual awareness. The status of 'unconscious attentiveness' may, indeed, be characterised as Dennett has done, and be a description of the life of the pigeons we talked about before, with their various capacities including that of seeing salient objects whole, together with a continuously and rapidly fading memory. In the human case, an analogue of sorts to the pigeon example can be witnessed in those cases of amnesia which give rise to continuous loss of episodic memory—forgetting *that* something or other is the case—whilst preserving its procedural form—remembering *how* to do something (Cohen and Squire 1980). In either example, we have 'an unreflected-upon flow of energy' (or 'rolling consciousness with swift memory loss'). But in neither case will a probe be effective. This *need* not mean the rolling state of existence is alien to the automatic-pilot case. The difference in the automatic-pilot case is that, if probed, the non-amnesic person has the resources of 'articulateness' which may be recruited to reflect upon, or at least make up a version of, what has just rolled by. With the amnesia sufferer we can presume (given prior commonalities of experience, language, etc.) what would have rolled by for that person, were they able to articulate it. In the case of the pigeon, we just do not have any means at our disposal to know *what* (if any *thing*) rolled by for it.

Pigeons are not people with amnesia: nor are amnesiacs pigeons! The 'actualité' cinematography that lets humans see 'what the world looks like through the eyes of a pigeon' is a falsehood in this important respect; what we are looking at is the world through our *own* eyes (as given to us through the imaginative eyes-plus-technology of the cinematographer). The actualité example is a good illustration of the anthropomorphising attribution problem mentioned earlier.

This issue has significance within archaeology (and all regions of ethology). Consider the sorts of conceptual and theory-laden resources brought to bear by present-day archaeologists to the making of, for instance, stone tools that resemble those remaining from the prehistoric past. Toth (1985) has made stone tools like those found in early hominid sites with a view to 'discovering' what our ancestors took themselves to be doing. But we cannot know that the concepts guiding his actions and reflected-upon perceptions bear any relation to those that supported the production of the originals, nor indeed whether any conceptual (as against visuo-motor) resources were needed for the original productions at all.

We will presumably never know about non-human and pre-linguistic human perceptual experience for we cannot ask monkeys, babies or our prehistoric ancestors prior to the emergence of language, what (if anything) forms or formed the stuff of their phenomenal worlds. We may be able to suggest, by experiment or with an effort of imagination, how it is *not* likely to be constituted. By contrast, there are numerous ways people compare with other people their perceptual experiences, most of them arising incidentally, such as when someone draws another's attention to something, and its identity is confirmed or questioned. Deliberate comparison occurs in the numerous contexts of instruction engaged in by social members, most notably parents, older siblings, tutors of various kinds. By inquiring about, seeking explanations for, and, indeed, challenging each other's categories and experiences in the language common to us, we discover and refine the terms and concepts to be employed in giving an account of or describing that experience; we achieve 'transparency' of mind (Coulter 1983). As we noted in Chapter 4, such activity, in the view of theorists like Mead and Vygotsky, is not only built into the business of becoming *self*-conscious, but of becoming conscious *in general* about the constitution of one's living, perceptual experience.

Ryle (1949) noted that the word 'perceive' (like 'understand') is best thought of as an achievement verb. Such verbs are in contrast to activity or process verbs like 'read' or 'play' (see Chapter 4). When 'something is seen', that is a claim to an achievement, not a description of a process. This alone casts doubt on the enterprise of characterising perception as activity inside the brain or mind. Gibson's (1979) alternative characterisation is, at first, strange to consider, but ultimately more satisfactory. For Gibson, perceiving is certainly an achievement, and it occurs, not in brains or minds, but at points of view. Furthermore, this being the case, perceiving is public, not private; for a point of view occupied by one organism can later be occupied by another. As with our disclaimer about language, none of these arguments seeks to deny the *involvement* of central nervous systems ('brains') in the achievement of perceiving. It is to argue that grappling with the fact of 'perceptual experience' takes in the whole system of human life.

Human perceiving is peculiar in having an incontestably self-conscious element. Human perceptual achievement is affected by the products of linguistic and related representational behaviour (Coulter & Parsons 1990; Noble 1987; 1993a). In the use of language, and other systems of representation that derive from it, such as the making of pictures (Noble & Davidson 1993), actions are undertaken in which the very achievement of seeing or hearing is taken notice of. To take notice of anything is to interrupt ongoing activity so as to scrutinise it, for instance, or listen more closely to it. In human visual awareness the flow of structured energy becomes 'arrested' when one stops to consider or contemplate what is seen (Wartofsky 1980). Doing these things is to bring a conceptual apparatus to bear on what is perceived.

Coulter and Parsons (1990) speak about the numerous different ways in which humans visually orient toward their surroundings as a result of the countless different kinds of practical action they undertake, action which is almost always 'concept-bound'. These authors draw attention to the 'staggered' quality of human perceptual consciousness:

> Just because, in the case of taking a walk or strolling to work, we are not normally inclined to describe someone as 'oblivious of their surroundings', we should not make the inference that, therefore, he *must* see *something*. We regard this as a fundamental characteristic of (visual) perception, and ... speak of it as the *staggered* quality of our visual relationship to the world. *One cannot deduce a continuity of visual orientation from a continuity of photon-photoreceptor interaction.* (263, emphasis in original)

This description captures well the switch from perception which is un(self-)consciously attentive (automatic pilot) to perception which *is* (self-)consciously attentive (articulate). When that switch is made, narrative occurs (Bruner 1990), if only self-addressed, to do with what is going on. Among matters that may be narrated are questions about what such-and-such in our surroundings could amount to or imply—what it might mean. 'Consciousness of meaning' in this argument is the expression of language-dependent knowledge. Thus it is an unnecessary category when considering the perceptual achievements or communicative activities of non-language-using creatures. We deal with the place of meaning in human life, first of all, and seek to clinch the argument about meaning and non-human life in the final part of this chapter.

Meaning: Linguistic entities

We begin with the most obvious field of reference for meaning: the meaning/s of words. It is possible to undertake highly 'technical' approaches to word meaning, as is done by some linguists and philosophers, but that is not appropriate here. We note the destructively critical treatment of all such 'technical' efforts by Baker and Hacker (1984). Our approach is non-technical, of the 'ordinary-language' variety (Austin 1961), namely, 'what does this word mean?', 'I don't understand what you mean', etc. Thus, we rely chiefly on Wittgenstein (1958) to help make sense of the concept in everyday terms.

Wittgenstein argues that a word's meaning is to be found in its use in the environment of other words. The meaning of a word is not a fixed (or any other sort of) *property* of it which can be brought out and inspected, or in some other way examined as a separable item. This point has much in common with Saussure's insistence on the indivisibility of sign and meaning. Rather, meaning is anchored in the ongoing conversational and other discursive activity of the members of a language community. As did Saussure, Wittgenstein suggests the analogy of a game, such as chess; in just the way that moves are intelligible *as* the game is played out (and there can be no 'moves' separate from the game), so the meanings of words and phrases are intelligible in (and only in) their actual uses. The meaning of the word 'clutch' in English is not contained *in* its isolated utterance, nor does it lie behind it (the word, in any case, has numerous meanings). Meaning is *in the use* of the word in a particular context for a particular purpose ('Keep your foot on the clutch until you've changed gear'). Meaning is in the use of the word in another particular context for another particular purpose ('The clutch needs changing'). In the first case 'clutch' is understood as a pedal you put your foot on; in the second as a mechanism linking an engine to a drive-shaft. Only from the context of use is there no possibility that reference is being made to a nest full of eggs.

To argue that meaning is *in* use is not to argue that meanings are invented as you go along, or that they are perpetually changing, or continuously negotiated (although one of the discoveries children make is the very negotiability of such things, leading to playful exploitation of words and rules). People do not routinely construct or negotiate meanings (or rules of play) as they proceed. Such activities will occur, at times *must* occur, but need not do so, particularly when interactants are familiar with each other in terms of shared 'forms of life' and 'language games' (Chapter 4).

By anchoring meanings or moves in ongoing conversation or play it may be said that the activities of conversation, discourse and play themselves provide contexts of regulation, such that meaning (or appropriate play) may be witnessed through the effective conduct of conversation or game; it is by these means that children become familiar with common meanings and practices. What this also says is that meaning is occasional, not perpetual. Meaning is not there as a constant element of play or discourse; it enters only when practically relevant. Indeed, typically, meaning comes into play only when it is a problem. And in saying 'meaning comes into play' we are not to be understood as saying that when meaning is *not* 'in play' it is either 'absent', or 'waiting in the wings'. People do not take it, when they stop to ask each other what they mean, that prior to the rupture they were speaking *without* meaning, and are now insisting on it being introduced. The meaningfulness of conversational activity is precisely shown by its smoothness of running; the meaning is 'taken for granted'. It is in this sense that 'meaning' is not an issue—it is not the topic of conversational attention.

We have been relying on images of automobile driving; these can help to bring home the point here. Occasions of use of words are occasions when they are 'engaged', just as gears and clutch in a car may be engaged to get us somewhere, when they form part of a working vehicle. Such a vehicle is a metaphor for a living language; but we do not see any particular part of this vehicle as being like any particular part of a language. Clutch and gears can be manipulated when the car is not taking us anywhere. Sometimes such activity may be instructive; as novices we can experience for ourselves something about the action of the clutch and gears. Sometimes it may be a necessary part of learning to drive (we are shown by a tutor how to act with such components). The point is that we can distinguish actual (real) use from idle manipulation. Wittgenstein's point is to emphasise that meaning is *really* only found in use. As against real use (or a sort of halfway position—tutelage—which can also occur with language, as when we are learning correct usage), idle manipulation is the equivalent of language being 'on holiday' (Wittgenstein 1958, ¶38).

Meaning: Non-linguistic entities

Non-linguistic entities are things such as material objects, and what we have to say bears closely on a matter central to the current enterprise, namely, interpretation of an archaeological record. It may seem feasible to extend the Wittgensteinian approach to analysis of 'the meaning' of objects. But it turns out that the concept of meaning does not apply in the same ways when we consider non-linguistic entities. If we ask, faced with flakes of stone and the bones of many dead animals, 'what does this mean?', we are not seeking a semantic elaboration, in the way such a question functions when we encounter an unfamiliar word. The question, rather, is to do with the significance of the material, its import with respect to a body of knowledge. It is the sort of question Sherlock Holmes poses when faced with an item that might be a clue.

We can ask that order of question about matters that appear more purely linguistic. If the patient says 'what does this mean?' when the physician announces 'your cholesterol count has risen 20%', in part a semantic elaboration is sought, but in larger part a statement about implications is being requested. Often, and in various social settings, seeking 'the meaning' of utterances is a quest for interpretation of motive ('what did he really mean saying that to me?'), or for the implications for unfolding action ('does this mean *I* have to pick up the kids?'), and so on. In our treatment of meaning with respect to words we were not proceeding to that form of analysis. We here acknowledge the reality of that aspect of language-based social behaviour. At that level of 'meaning', it is not the meaning of words as such we seek to clarify; it is the implications for our lives.

Archaeology is an interpretive practice, and the seeking of meaning in the sense of import or significance is part of its agenda. All scholarly practices have relevant interpretive domains, and interpretive work is also carried out in civil society in a number of ways. The physician interprets indexical signs (symptoms) to achieve a diagnosis; the bureaucrat interprets symbolic signs (an application to enter the country) to achieve a classification. At the end of these enterprises what is obtained is an identification ('this is what you're suffering from'; 'this is your visa status'). Entities are identified ('this is a handaxe'; 'these are pencil shavings' [cf. Ingold 1993, 340]).

The procedure of identification can apply to linguistic entities. Indeed, we will see that anything that can be done with regard to non-linguistic entities can be done with linguistic ones, but *not* vice versa, and that is the significant conclusion we will come to in this section. Acts of identification in relation to linguistic entities occur with such questions as: 'Is "ork" a word?' What needs to be clarified is the status of the sign; is it identifiable as belonging to the class of symbolic signs? Further elaboration about meaning, in the semantic sense we discussed earlier, would be inevitable, of course, if the answer to the initial question about 'ork' turned out to be 'yes'.

Beneath the more elaborate procedures of interpretation to arrive at identities and saliences is the commonest sort of activity with all entities, and that is *use*. Words and objects within the environment are simply used by people in the conduct of their everyday practical activities. As we mentioned in explaining Wittgenstein's argument that the meaning of words is in their use, such use is unremarkable (unremarked upon) in the course of most action and interaction. The same holds for the use of non-linguistic entities. We all use artefacts in the course of everyday routines (toothbrush, newspaper), and typically give them no further thought, unless their use is somehow problematic.

Entities that are named (identified) carry titles which, in principle, function to control how they are used (Noble 1981; 1993b). We identify 'naming' (Chapter 8) as the foundational feature of the symbolic use of signs. There is the risk that we give an overly 'rationalistic' flavour to what is involved here: but people do not blankly deal with life. Naming is not a 'cognitive activity' done by zombies. Our utterances are not strings of grammatically arranged words; they are expressions of our 'forms of life', where that concept refers to the way people in communities live and aspire to live (Margolis 1987). Naming a part of the landscape as a 'sacred site'; naming a building as a 'church' or 'school' delimits the uses for which it is sanctioned. This is because names are titles, in the sense that the entity carries certain entitlements bestowed upon it by its namers (and namers are always plural, as we saw in Chapter 4, because language cannot be private).

Because of entitlement, which goes hand-in-hand with significance in the sense of import, uses of non-linguistic entities can be disputed. There is room for *abuse* when entities carry titles, because deviant uses by the untutored or the wayward may attract censure from those who honour the title the entity carries. Linguistic entities can also be titles. Most words in most contexts are cheap, but as Salman Rushdie knows, the use of some words in certain ways can be very expensive indeed.

Do non-linguistic entities have meanings? As with linguistic entities, they can have significance, identity, entitlement, and use. Do they have meanings, in the sense that words have meanings? The answer seems to be negative. If an object, such as an iconic sign for 'traffic-light', is made to function as a symbolic sign in a traffic system it has no real non-linguistic identity; it functions solely as an advisory or stipulative symbol. When we speak of the 'meaning' of a non-linguistic entity we are only addressing its socially-constructed significance.

How does meaning come in?

The utterances of vervet monkeys can be identified as communicative gestures. Such gestures can be said (by us as human observers of them) to be meaning*ful* insofar as they provoke a meaning*ful* (coherent) response. But in the case of the vervet monkeys we do not seem licensed to say 'the meaning' is perceived by them, because, among other things, we have no licence to identify (define) what '*the meaning*' is. Cheney and Seyfarth (1990) describe the predator-context calls as 'alarms'. Yet several of their observations yielding descriptive accounts could lead one to describe the calls as threats to the predator, or as rallying cries to the rest of the troop, a point borne out in the earlier quotation from them.

Vervets' vocal gestures are meaning*ful* insofar as they are communicative, even though 'meanings' for them cannot be determined because no interpretive work can be done between sign-maker and observers of the sign. *Identifying* a meaning for a meaningful sign *is* an interpretive act, and as such it is subject to ratification and challenge (see Coulter, 1979b, e.g., 105–6). The only parties to the interpretation of the vervets' utterances are human observers and commentators. The type of interpretive activity enabled in this context is not the same as in linguistic communities. When Cheney and Seyfarth seek to know what the calls mean, the quest is exclusively human. No challenge to an interpretation can be elicited conceptually from the communicators in question (certain possibilities may be ruled out through behavioural test, but any ruling still leaves the reference opaque). The matter of meaning thus remains indeterminate, and the assumption that meaning is there *for* the communicators is just that; an assumption. Good sense can be made of what is going on among the vervets without that assumption being made. In the lives of these monkeys, discriminable events (or objects, or occurrences) can be observed which call forth different vocal responses, which in turn provoke different adaptive outcomes. The monkeys are attuned to structures of energy in the environment; they are sensitive to the contingencies that these structures specify, and their behaviour is explicable in terms of natural selection. Any meanings that human observers impute to these behaviours are interpretive acts dependent on language use, and neither such meanings nor meanings *as such* need be part of the scenario for the protagonists. Saying this is not saying 'the lives of these monkeys are meaning*less*', in the sense of being 'without significance'.

In the end, though, the 'significance' of the lives of these animals is its significance for human observers. It is the human capacity for making entities have significance that underwrites all the activity of ethologists, archaeologists, physicians, psychologists and the rest of us. The capacity to imbue entities with significance rests upon the capacity to signify. The evolutionary emergence of the capacity to signify, to name, is thus still the bedrock question to be answered. Meaningfulness is but one product of that emergence.

The issue, therefore, is how meaning-making of any kind could have emerged in human evolution. What is discovered in evolutionary terms is the *propensity* for meaning. Discovered is the power to make, send, receive and understand propositions about environmental entities, hence to control their form and distribution, and ultimately the entities to which they refer. ('Proposition' covers any form of utterance having meaningful content, such as, 'statement', 'assertion', 'message', 'question', 'complaint', 'command'.) Further, and to reiterate, 'meaning' comes up when propositions are misunderstood, or are unclear, confusing, or misleading, and attention and work are needed to unravel what the proposition is communicating (cf. Coulter, 1984). Then (only then) the matter of meaning is identified as an issue.

When 'meaning' gets to be an identified issue (becomes a topic subject to the discursive activity of a community) we may eventually see the emergence of thoughts about thinking—the construction of propositions addressed to the construction of propositions as such. The historically specific condition of 'Western-world' abstract thinking, developed upon generations of mathematical, natural science, and philosophical discourses (Toulmin 1972), is *not* the inescapable condition of human life. A form of the 'psychologist's fallacy' (James 1981[1890]), is to take the abstracted description of a phenomenon and mistake it for the phenomenon itself—thus, descriptions of the elaborate constructs about knowledge and mind that were thinkable by a seventeenth century French scholar like Descartes, are held as accounts of what underpins the capacity to perceive anything in a conceptually-bound way.

Sticks and stones etc., do not display any meaning, nor in any other way offer meaning; for meaning does not reside in such entities; meaning *occurs* via the discursive practices of human communities. Gibson's concern to exteriorise meanings, to get them out of our heads, mistakenly tried to make them resident in the entities to which humans refer. But since meaning occurs among us, and resides nowhere, then it is not to be found in our heads nor in what we use our heads (and the rest of our bodies) communally to refer to. With the features and inter-relationship of symbols, mindedness, and meaning straightened out, the task now is to scrutinise the archaeological record of hominid and human existence with a view to discerning the signs of meaning-making via the appearance of signs used symbolically.

CHAPTER 6

THE EARLY SIGNS OF MEANING IN PREHISTORIC BEHAVIOUR

Interpreting the archaeological record in terms of meaning and behaviour is not straightforward. It involves conventions and levels of analogy from the behaviour of modern people (Binford 1983; Davidson 1988) or other animals, and can be interpreted in different ways depending on the theoretical position of the interpreter (Noble & Davidson 1991; 1993). Material objects of the record— hominid fossils, stone tools, animal bones, pollen grains and many other things—were produced or occurred with or without meaning at the time they occurred. Other objects such as clay figurines, painted cave walls, Stonehenge or the Pyramids clearly had meaning for their producers. The difficult task is to identify from the objects whether the producers were involved in behaviour they understood to be meaningful.

Our view (Davidson & Noble 1992) is that there are no signs of meaning for the producers earlier than the first colonisation of Australia about 60 thousand years ago (Roberts et al. 1991). We discuss that in the next Chapter; here, we assess a highly influential alternative position, namely, that there is an origin of language, hence meaning, about 2 million years ago. This origin is said to be identifiable through increases in cranial capacity and through the first production of stone tools. Our conclusion will be that the evidence does not support the presence of language as claimed, yet does suggest the presence of critical precursor abilities that allowed linguistic behaviour to emerge. Our argument is that the changes which occurred were cumulative products of contexts for the selection of behaviours such as bipedalism, increased meat-eating, stone tool making, and throwing; not that expansion of absolute or relative cranial capacity filled up the space inside the head with qualitatively new stuff, like meaning, language or culture. In making this argument we carry the story of the evolution of our ancestors from the common ancestor, described in Chapter 2, through to the creature which had the anatomical and behavioural repertoire to produce meaning by communicating using symbols.

The common ancestor more than five million years ago, lived and nested in trees on the edge of the tropical forests of Africa, was rarely bipedal, and had a small brain but, for its small body size, one similar in size to chimpanzees'. The diet of this creature was fruit and leaves, with some invertebrates but little meat. Communication was primarily non-vocal, this and limited vocal utterances being honed through observational learning and conditioning. Symbols were not part of either form of communication. Females associated with each other but did not form alliances, and males were sometimes solitary, and little involved in rearing offspring.

How did this creature become bipedal, much larger brained, omnivorous, language-using and capable of surviving in almost any environment in almost any pattern of social relationship? How are these various changes related to each other?

The 'actors' in the hominid fossil record

Basing his argument on comparative anatomy and biogeography, Darwin predicted 'it is somewhat more probable that our early progenitors lived on the African continent than elsewhere' (Darwin 1889, 155), going on 'but it is useless to speculate on this subject'. Partly as a result of this prediction, the search for human origins has overwhelmingly been concentrated in Africa, and it is no longer necessary to be limited to speculation. It is a widely agreed consensus that Darwin was right (Gamble 1993; Tuttle 1988), to a greater extent than he could have known: progenitors at all the taxonomic levels we discussed in Chapter 2 (Anthropoids, Hominoids, hominids, *Homo*, and *Homo sapiens*) first appeared in Africa (Tuttle 1988). More fossil hominids have been found, from earlier dates, in Africa than anywhere else, and, with the slight possibility of an exception in Pakistan (Dennell et al. 1988a; 1988b), African stone artefacts are also earlier than those elsewhere.

Fossil classification

The most familiar accounts of the evolutionary story of our ancestors are based on the skeletal evidence of fossils. The popular literature is dominated by these accounts (Diamond 1991; Falk 1992; Johanson & Shreeve 1991; Johanson & Edey 1981; Leakey & Lewin 1992; Lewin 1989; Reader 1981), yet there are good reasons why the fossils alone do not tell the story we are interested in. The central assumption is the expectation that once the skeletal morphology looks like us then these creatures should be behaving like us. This has always been unlikely. In evolution: new variation arises by chance mutation or genetic recombination, not through selective pressure. Natural selection operates to change the relative frequency of pre-existing variable characteristics. The question is why one part of the range of variation of a species with a variable morphology should have become more successful than another. Looked at in this way, we can expect that the earliest appearance of a particular morphology will generally be earlier than the signs of the behaviour which made it successful. On some other occasions, morphological change and behavioural selection will be so immediate as to appear coeval.

Modern human morphology has been recognised at dates earlier than the evidence for modern human behaviour (Foley & Lahr 1992). This behaviour, when it emerged, was a major factor restricting the range of variation of morphology (Chapter 1). No single new behaviour can account for the modernness of behaviour or morphology. There was no 'Cerebral Rubicon' or other equivalent anatomical marker the crossing of which suddenly transformed hominids into humans. Rather, an accumulation of anatomical and behavioural changes created conditions for the selection of a further particular behaviour. Of all the range that existed when this novel, modern human, behaviour emerged, the range of anatomy most suited to it was that we now recognise as modern. Here we define a way of talking about the ancestors of modern humans which led to that state of affairs.

The first task is to establish what sorts of creatures we are talking about as the ancestors of humans, subsequent to the common ancestor. There are many different classifications of specimens of fossil hominids and of the relationships among them which can cause confusion among all but specialists. Since we do not give great priority to the importance of anatomy, we will not dwell on anatomical features that are used to distinguish the different specimens or used to group them into higher units of classification for the purpose of establishing relationships (Chamberlain & Wood 1987; Falk 1992; Groves 1989; Rightmire 1993; Skelton & McHenry 1992; Stringer 1987; Wood 1992a). The following discussion leads to reasons why the argument for an early origin for language is unsound. At issue is the use made by all sorts of scholars of the biological names given to the fossilised bones of hominid descendants of the common ancestor.

These biological names (genus and species) are classifications made by physical anthropologists, and may not reflect biological realities (specifically, interbreeding) of the past time from which those specimens have survived. The specimens are tiny samples from variable populations of different times and places. Estimates of evolutionary relationships among these samples are even more perilous interpretations, liable to be disturbed by a single newly discovered fossil. Taxonomists adopt some principles about the classification of fossils that involve estimates of similarity or numbers of similar characteristics. Empirical evidence from a living primate species, lemurs, is that more species can be recognised among extant populations (where actual breeding, which defines species, can be observed) than can be identified from morphological variation of the skeleton. Thus if one set of fossils is distinguishable from another morphologically, it is highly likely that 'we will not be overestimating species abundance' (Tattersall 1992, 345).

As against this view, everyday experience shows the human ability to make fine discriminations about the morphological characteristics of fellow humans, beyond the colour of hair, eyes or skin. We comment, favourably or unfavourably, on the prominence of chins or noses, or on the size and shape of other parts, some of which do, and some of which do not, reflect skeletal differences. Yet people with such distinguishable forms do interbreed. Unless we wish to argue (and we do not) that humans are fundamentally different in this aspect of biology, we may conclude that

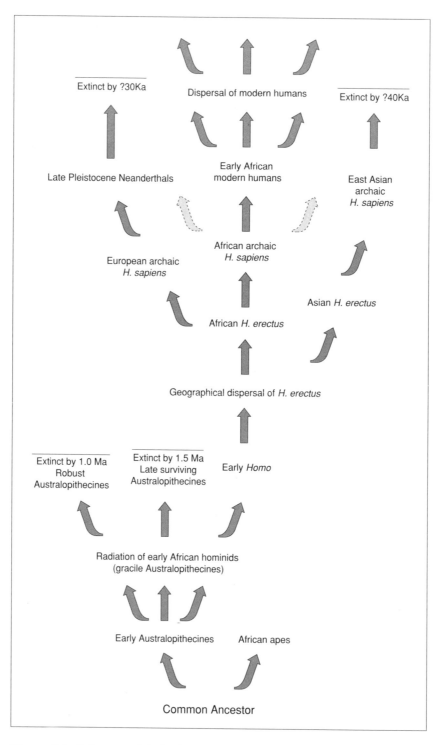

Figure 24 Foley's model of adaptive radiation. *From* Foley 1992.

morphology alone is an unreliable guide to species identification.

The fossil specimens from Hadar, in Ethiopia, including those known popularly as 'Lucy' and the 'First Family' (Johanson & Edey 1981; Johanson & Shreeve 1991) provide an illustration of the classification problem because of the controversy surrounding their ascription to one or more species. The original classification by the excavator was to two or possibly three species (Johanson & Taieb 1976) but this was replaced by a classification into one (Johanson et al. 1978). Subsequently, several authors have shown that the single species identification is unsound (e.g. Groves 1989; Olson 1985; Senut & Tardieu 1985; Zihlman 1985). Nevertheless, many analyses continue to consider relationships among species with the Hadar specimens included as a single species (e.g. Skelton & McHenry 1992). New discoveries in Hadar (Kimbel et al. 1994) have been interpreted to show that the variation in these early fossils is not so great as to disallow the single species identification (Aiello 1994). Since these specimens, dated between 2.8 million years and 3.3 million years ago (Brown 1982), are amongst the earliest known that clearly relate to the evolution of hominids, these interpretations are fundamental to the shape of the tree of relationships that can be constructed.

Pardoe (1991) has recently illustrated the nature of the problem with the procedure of naming species. By ignoring variability within a species and assigning specimens to species on the basis of morphology, a story can be told which will inevitably tend to be about one species replacing another. The genera and species being talked about are artefacts of the processes of classification used by the scientists concerned. Naming appears to give an entity sharper definition than it has: a hazard for language-users. In the typology of hominid fossils, separateness from other similar entities is reinforced by the sharp boundaries of the names, however much we remind ourselves that these are artefacts of classification. For this reason, we prefer Foley's (1992) model of adaptive radiations of hominids as a way of conceptualising hominid evolution (Figure 24).

In this model, it is emphasised that at any time there is a range of variation and that different parts of that variation are recognised as distinct species by palaeoanthropologists. We can never be certain of the potential, still less the reality, for these species to interbreed to produce fertile offspring.

The names of our ancestors

Table 4 shows nine subdivisions of hominids since about 4.4 million years ago: earliest hominids (Andrews 1995); *Australopithecus afarensis*; *Australopithecus africanus*; *Paranthropus* (two or three species, *P. robustus*, *P. boisei* and *P. crassidens*, often referred to the genus *Australopithecus*); *Homo habilis* (now widely thought to include three species, *H. habilis*, *H. rudolfensis*, and *H. ergaster*); *Homo erectus*; Archaic *Homo sapiens* (including *Homo heidelbergensis*); *Homo neanderthalensis*; anatomically modern *Homo sapiens*. Given the rapid pace of recent discovery and reassessment of the earliest hominids (Wood 1994; Andrews 1995) we do not give them further consideration here.

Date Myr	Specific name used here	Common name	Other names	Sites
4.4-3.9	Earliest Australo-pithecines	Early Australopithecines		Middle Awash, Ethiopia
3.8-2.9	Australopithecus afarensis			Hadar
3.0-2.0	Australopithecus africanus	Gracile Australopithecines		Olduvai Sterkfontein Makapansgat
2.5-1.0	Paranthropus	Robust Australopithecines	Australopithecus robustus; A. boisei	Olduvai Koobi Fora Swartkrans
1.9-1.5	Homo habilis	Early Homo	Homo rudolfensis; Homo ergaster	Olduvai Koobi Fora
1.8-0.25	Homo erectus	Archaics	Homo heidelbergensis	Olduvai Koobi Fora Nariokotome Sangiran Zhoukoudian
0.4-0.09	Archaic Homo sapiens			
0.12-0.04	Homo neanderthalensis	Neanderthals	"Man"	La Ferrassie Krapina Shanidar
0.1-0	Anatomically modern Homo sapiens	Humans		Lake Mungo Qafzeh Skhul Where you are

Table 4 Species of hominid since the common ancestor, their characteristics and problems (references in text).

In referring to these genera and species we will attempt wherever possible to avoid the alphabet soup of these names. For *Australopithecus*, we will use the general name 'Australopithecines', referring to earliest hominids and *A. afarensis* as Early Australopithecines, *A. africanus* as Gracile Australopithecines or graciles, and *Paranthropus* as Robust Australopithecines or robusts. We will refer to the three possible earliest species in our genus together as Early *Homo*; Archaic *Homo sapiens* as Archaics; *Homo neanderthalensis* as Neanderthals; and anatomically modern *Homo sapiens* as humans. But we will argue that the shape of the skeletons of some fossils makes them identifiable as anatomically modern *Homo sapiens*, at a date earlier than any evidence that they behaved in a way distinguishable from *Homo neanderthalensis*. This entails continued use of the cumbersome phrase

Problems	Key specimens	Biped-alism	Cranial capacity ml	Meat in diet	Tools
Closeness to chimpanzee ancestor? Habitat forested?	ARA-VP-6/1	?	?	?	N
One, two or three species? If more than one, how related to successors?	"Lucy" - AL288-1 "First Family" - AL333-xx AL444-2	Y	400-500	No evidence	N
Relationship to A. afarensis and H. habilis?	Taung "Mrs Ples"	Y	428-500	No evidence	
Diet? Toolmaking?	WT17000 OH5 ER407	Y	410-530	Some	?
Nought, one, two or three species?	OH7 ER1470 ?ER1813	Y	509-752	Not much	Y
Did all Homo erectus populations evolve into Homo sapiens, or only African Homo erectus?	OH9 ER3733 ER3883 WT15000 Petralona Atapuerca	Y	China 780-1225 Java 813-1251 Africa 750-1067	Becoming important	
Are the Africans the ancestors of all modern humans?	Kabwe Dali Omo	Y	1100-1430	Yes generally	
Did Neanderthals contribute genes to modern humans? Vocal ability	Kebara	Y	1200-1750	Yes generally	
Figuring out how they got like this	Qafzeh Skhul Cro-Magnon Us	Y	Male 1500+/-125 Female 1300+/-105 Fossil 1520-1600	Yes generally	Y

'anatomically modern *Homo sapiens*' to refer to that early group of creatures, human-like in appearance, but not yet in behaviour. The process of emergence of behaviour after anatomy can be identified because there is a relatively precise chronology. A similar process probably applied to earlier transitions between recognisable species, but the archaeological record is not sufficiently detailed as the scale of the boldest chronology for early hominid occurrences uses 50 thousand year time-spans (Feibel et al. 1989) as if they were events. The whole history of our species, anatomically modern *Homo sapiens*, would be confined by such chronology to a tale of two such events, ignoring all detail of the differences between our ancestors 49 000 years ago and ourselves.

We make few judgements about the phylogenetic relationships among these

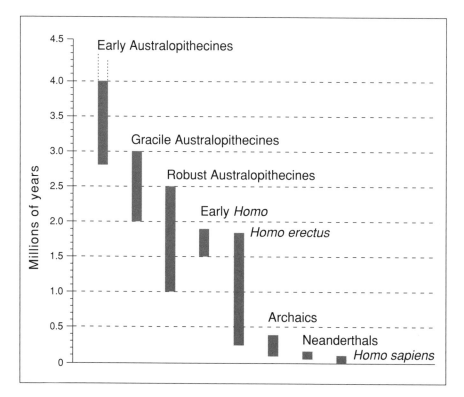

Figure 25 Chronological distribution of named species of fossil hominid referred to in this book.

fossils for the reasons already expressed. The evidence does not support an argument for some 'ladder of progress' from more primitive to more sophisticated hominids. For any period before one species became the sole hominid at a particular time, there is a claim that there was an earlier period when there were at least two contemporary species (Figure 25). This seems unexceptional if evolution happens through selection from a range of variation. A similar process of selection may account for the apparently large range of variation in the early Australopithecines which gave rise to the original (and more recent [Andrews 1995]) suggestion that there may be more than one species. Some parts of the range of variation were more chimpanzee-like, presumably closer to the common ancestor, and others more like later Australopithecines. One sort of selection favoured the Australopithecine range of variation, and another the chimpanzee range.

Contexts of human evolution

The major events and evidences in the last four million years are shown in Table 5, which is a ten-fold expansion of the most recent part of Table 1. The table covers climatic changes as well as the evidence of hominids and their behaviour.

Time	Geology	Climate	Stone tools	Other artefacts	Fossils	Ages	Colonisation
4 Myr	PLIOCENE				?hominid Kanapoi		
3.5 Myr			None	Laetoli trails	*Australopithecus afarensis*		
3 Myr					First Family "Lucy"		Hominids only in Africa
2.5 Myr			?Kada Gona?		*Australopithecus & Paranthropus*		
			?Omo?				
		Onset of glaciation					
2.0 Myr			? West Turkana		*Homo habilis & Paranthropus* *H. habilis & H. rudolfensis* *H. erectus* *H. ergaster*	PALAEO-LITHIC	
1.5 Myr	PLEISTO-CENE		Oldowan				?Out of Africa ?Java
				???Fire???	*H. erectus & H. heidelbergensis*		
1.0 Myr					last *Paranthropus*	Lower	Jordan Valley
							Europe
700 000 yr			Acheulean				
500 000 yr	Middle		More Acheulean	??Fire??			China
				?Spear? Fire	*Homo sapiens*		
100 000 yr	Upper		Acheulean ending	Tata tooth	Neanderthals and fully moderns		Out of Africa again
Present	HOLO-CENE	Interglacial	Lots of stuff	Lots	Fully moderns only	Middle, Upper etc	Australia, Americas

Table 5 Timescale of the last 4 million years of hominid evolution.

The period from 1.6 million years ago (Myr), which geologists call the Pleistocene, is generally regarded as one of unusual climatic and environmental change, although climatic change has a much longer history. Climatic fluctuations (Figure 26) are partly explained by well-documented variations in the situation of the earth and its orbit around the Sun (its aspect) (Martinson et al. 1987). The cold fluctuations are generally called glacial periods, and the warmer ones interglacials, though in many parts of the world (such as the bulk of Africa and Australia) there were no glaciers even in glacial periods. Some people have speculated about the importance of the cyclical fluctuation between cold and warm climate for the apparently rapid pace of human evolution (Calvin 1991; Vrba 1988). The link seems unlikely since climate has always been in a state of change, the record of change simply being more detailed for the most recent period. A general temperature decline before the Pleistocene seems likely to have been accompanied by fluctuations of lesser magnitude, but these are less easily, and less well, documented. Foley (1994) has recently shown that there is little correlation between climatic events and speciation events. Association between climatic and behavioural evidence remains to be explored, though we suspect little will be found.

The fluctuations of climate produced environmental changes which were dramatic in some parts of the world. The best known of these were the periodic expansions of glaciers at the poles and over large tracts of the European, Asian and North American landmasses. The evidence of these glacial expansions gave rise to the naming of the Pleistocene period as the Ice Ages. But there were collateral events of equally dramatic effect in human evolution, most notably changes in sea-level, with reductions of up to 150 m in periods of maximum ice-volume, and occasionally higher than modern sea-level in interglacial periods. The general decline of temperature for the many millions of years before the Pleistocene period was a major factor in the environmental changes that created the savannas of Africa. It is commonly suggested that it was in these savannas that our ancestors first adopted habitual bipedal gait.

Bipedalism and its consequences

Darwin (1889, 51) placed great emphasis on the important advantage of bipedalism in human evolution. Explanations of the emergence of bipedalism are highly varied, ranging from sex (Lovejoy 1981) to violence (Jablonski & Chaplin 1992). We are reasonably confident that this behaviour did not emerge as a consequence of language emergence; some small causality may go the other way. Bipedalism is the beginning of our story because one group of hominids adapted physiologically to the gravitational effects on blood in veins and arteries by natural selection of a system of blood flow around the skull which, through its cooling effect on the brain, had consequences for expansion of brain size (Falk 1992).

There is some evidence that all, except some of the earliest, hominids listed in Table 5 were bipedal in some degree. A remarkable item of evidence about the

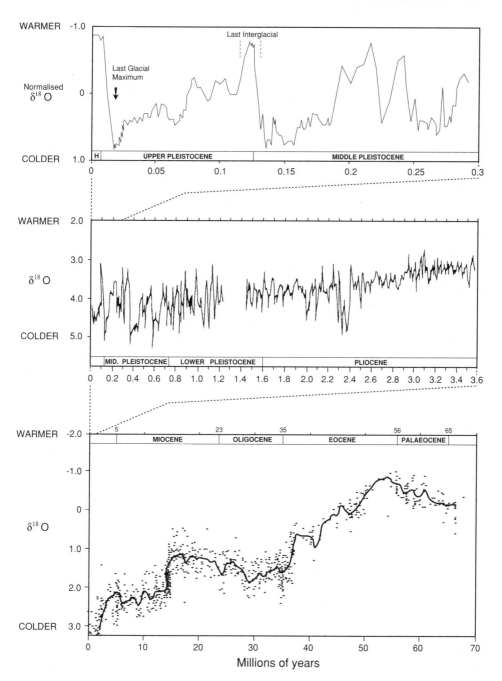

Figure 26   Climatic variation associated with fluctuations in temperature, ice volume (hence sea level) and precipitation, at different time-scales. *From* Martinson et al. 1987; Miller & Fairbanks 1985; Shackleton et al. 1984.

evolution and behaviour of our ancestors is the tracks of Laetoli (in Tanzania) (Leakey & Hay 1979). About 3.56 million years ago volcanic eruptions near Laetoli deposited a series of fine ash layers (known as tuffs) at the end of the dry season, and beginning of the rainy season. These ashes were quickly covered, preserving in their surfaces the imprints of raindrops, and the footprints of animals from 17 different families.

At site G, in addition to the tracks of guinea fowl, rabbits or hares, Hipparion (a horse-like creature), carnivores, giraffes and bovids, were found two trails unmistakably those of bipedal hominids, walking at the speed and with the stride length of (very) young modern human children (Tuttle 1987). There is no sign of a knuckle print such as might be expected if these were like chimpanzees or gorillas. On closer inspection, there turned out to be imprints of the feet of three hominids, one small (G-1) and two larger individuals (G-2 and G-3), keeping pace with each other (Figure 27). The hominids made only two trails because the footprints of one (G-3) of the two larger ones fell in the footprints of the other (G-2), as those of chimpanzees have been observed to do when they follow each other (Leakey & Harris 1987, 491).

On the basis of evidence from the bones of upper and lower limbs of early Australopithecines (McHenry 1986; Senut & Tardieu 1985; Zihlman 1985), there were at least two predominant forms of locomotion about 3 million years ago. One, of *Australopithecus* including 'Lucy', was more ape-like and probably involved the use of the arms for hanging (presumably from branches) and a bipedal gait different from the human one. The other, of *Homo* including the 'First Family', was fully bipedal in the manner of the Laetoli footprints. The postcranial skeleton—those parts that do not include the skull—of Australopithecines was not gradually evolving towards a bipedality of *Homo*, and intermediate between that of apes and humans. Rather it was itself a distinctive gait, closer to apes in its musculature (Berge 1994), yet unlike that of any modern species.

Foley (1992) has shown the energy advantage of bipedalism: a bipedal hominid of given weight could forage over 11 km while a chimpanzee of the same weight would expend the same energy over 4 km. In the savanna where most of the evolution of hominid bipedalism took place (Foley 1987a), there was a need for longer distance ranging to acquire resources. Other things being equal, there would have been a selective advantage to the bipedal animal, although there is little material evidence for behaviour which may have offered a selective advantage to a creature that walked on two legs rather than four.

In addition to the anatomical and physiological adaptations of the limbs involved in ambulation, it has been argued by Falk (1986; 1990) that there seem to have been two distinct responses to bipedalism in the system of blood flow in hominid heads: one among the early and the robust Australopithecines; the other among graciles and humans. Among the early and robust Australopithecines, patterns of blood flow were significantly different from those found among modern apes, which solved the gravitational problems of bipedalism but did not cool the brain. Among graciles and

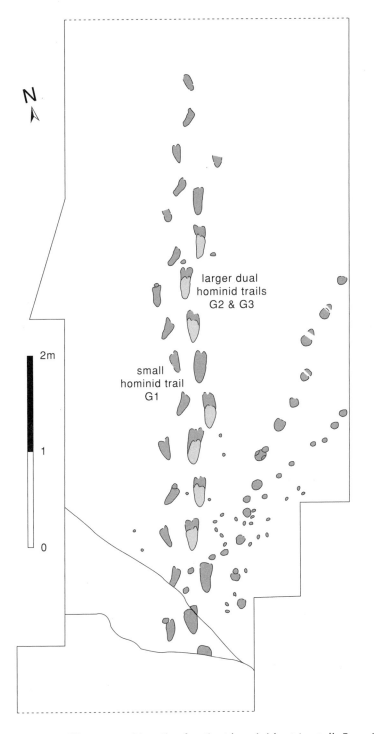

Figure 27   The 3.5 million-year-old trails of extinct hominids at Laetoli. *From* Leakey and Hay 1979.

hominids (including modern humans), the theory is that the novel patterns of blood flow had an important effect in cooling the brain by radiation, not found among the other Australopithecines or among modern apes.

Wheeler (1984; 1994) considered the effects of heat on a primate emerging in the closed tropical forests and subsequently living in more open savannas. Upright posture minimised the surface area exposed to full sun, reducing heat stress by enabling most of the body to be cooler. The only part of the body subjected to excessive heating at midday would have been the head, so that selective brain cooling would extend the range of these hominids both into more open habitats and into hotter parts of the day. The demands of thermo-regulation probably also selected for the hairlessness, to take advantage of cooling by increased sweating, that is now such a marked difference between humans and other apes (Wheeler 1985; 1992). There was a behavioural consequence of hairlessness and bipedalism that could have had a critical influence on the form of adult-infant interaction. These two features led to a need for adult carrying (not just infant clinging) which would have increased the opportunity for joint attention between adults and infants. We suggest this is a key factor in human infant development (Chapter 4) and was critical in the evolutionary emergence of language.

There is a controversial argument for robusts to have preferred forested environments (Shipman & Harris 1988; Vrba 1988). Given the apparently retained adaptations of some of the early Australopithecines for hanging from branches, this might be taken as an argument that the hominids without specialised cooling physiology and anatomy avoided the heat by keeping to the trees (Falk 1990). Falk's argument suggests that the radiator opened up a new niche for hominids allowing them to expand their range. At the same time, the new arrangement of blood flow released a constraint on the expansion of the size of the brain.

The pattern of brain size variation

What, then, of the brain, the organ Gould (1991) calls 'the best available case for predominant exaptation'—the doctrine that structures emerge in evolution before the functions that they now perform—as we saw in discussion of cortical organisation in Chapters 1 and 2. There is an identifiable and consistent pattern for brain size increase from 3.5 million years to the present, and there is also a pattern of body size increase. Interpretation of absolute and relative brain size increase is frequently offered, and Foley (1990) summarised the parameters which have been shown to be positively correlated with relative brain size in primates and other mammals (Table 6).

The variety of explanations for brain size increase supports our conclusion in Chapter 2 that brain size, absolute or relative, does not seem to be a reliable or sufficient indicator of the sorts of abilities that might, in evolutionary terms, have led to the emergence of a distinctively human behaviour such as language. Tobias (1987) argued that the relatively great increase in brain size between the Australopithecines and the earliest *Homo* suggested that language emerged with

Parameter	Significance in hominid evolution
Life History Parameters	
Gestation length	Probably relative unchanged
Lifespan	Considerably extended in modern humans
Neonate weight	Modern humans are relatively altricial, with smaller neonate weight
Weaning age	Greatly reduced in most modern people, especially in food producing societies
Age of first reproduction	Marginally later than African apes; males more variable
Interbirth interval	Similar to gorilla, shorter than chimp
Ecological Parameters	
Home range area	Greatly enlarged
Dietary quality	Higher quality
Maternal metabolic rate	Unknown
Social Parameters	
Group size	Larger in modern humans, probably larger in most hominids
'Social' complexity	Enhanced
Grooming rate	?
Communication	Language, symbolism, etc.

Table 6   Parameters that have been shown to be significantly correlated with relative brain size in primates and other mammals. Significance in hominid evolution refers to changes relative to the African apes and supporting palaeobiological or archaeological evidence. (After Foley 1990).

early *Homo*. The argument can be refuted on many of the grounds on which it was proposed, as well as others deriving from our argument about what language is.

Beyond the simple summary of hominid brain size increase presented in Chapter 2, there is considerable doubt about the reliability of the data themselves and the appropriate analysis of them. Brain size for fossil species is estimated from measurements of cranial capacity. The first difficulty is in the identification of species of even relatively complete specimens. For almost all specimens there is uncertainty about the errors in the estimate of cranial capacity and about the precise date when the creature lived. There is also uncertainty due to the variable relationship between cranial capacity and brain size in living animals. There is still further uncertainty in estimating relative brain size. Finally, even supposing that satisfactory data can be obtained, there is a whole series of difficulties in the statistical analysis of them (Deacon 1990).

Because brain size varies with body size, changes in cranial capacity through time need to be set in the context of changes in body size. There are problems of estimating stature or body weight to calculate relative brain size, due to the fragmentary nature of the fossils when found, and the difficulties of estimating body weight or stature from fragmentary remains of poorly known extinct species. Very few discoveries involve undamaged skeletons; mostly there are fragments of skulls which are reconstructed to form larger incomplete specimens. Very rarely are there bones from several parts of the skeleton in association close enough to allow an interpretation that they derived from a single creature. Usually it is still difficult to estimate stature and body weight from associated bones because of their incompleteness. Estimates of stature and body weight from isolated bones encounter, first, the problem of attribution to species defined primarily from variation in skull form, and, then, of the appropriate comparison for estimating these parameters of body size from such bones. Finally, there are few well preserved skeletons before the last 50 thousand years. In consequence, for most of the period of evolutionary changes in the relation of cranial capacity and body size, it is very rare that there are both estimates of stature or body weight and measurements of cranial capacity for the same individual.

The most explicit argument that brain size increase can be taken to indicate the emergence of language is due to Tobias (1987; 1991), with more cautious anticipations by Holloway (1966; 1969; 1981; 1983) and Falk (1980; 1987). In all cases, the authors rely not only on cranial capacity but on interpretations of the shapes of casts of the inside of the skull (endocasts) to reveal surface features that are more or less similar to those of modern human brains. Holloway's (1969) argument includes the processes involved in making stone tools. We doubt whether the surface of the brain indicates very much about the potential or practice of symbolic communication (Chapter 2), and we will reiterate in a later section our argument against the evidence from stone tools (Davidson & Noble 1993a; Noble & Davidson 1991). First, we discuss the argument about brain size.

Tobias' argument is based on the statistically significant (Blumenberg 1985; Holloway 1973) increase in average brain size between those fossils he identifies as Australopithecines and those he identifies as early *Homo*. But this depends in the first instance on the classifications, not all of which are without dispute (Groves 1989). Further, inspection of the distribution of cranial capacities through time reveals that the Australopithecines, before 2 Myr, had an apparently narrow range of variation, but after 2 Myr the range of variation expanded, with the robusts at the lower end of that range. Most importantly, the ranges appear to overlap (see Figure 28). Closer inspection of Tobias' statistics suggests this is not surprising. Although he shows that the mean for the highly variable *Homo habilis* is more than 11 standard deviations greater than the mean for the robusts, *Australopithecus boisei*, he omits to point out that, considered the other way around, the mean for these scarcely variable robust Australopithecines is only 1.55 standard deviations below the mean for *Homo habilis*.

Tobias attempts to deal with the problem we discussed in Chapter 2 that cranial capacity increases with body size. Measurements of cranial capacity are estimated for skulls from which species were defined, but body size is estimated from postcranial bones (found separately from the skull bones) attributed to those species by some other criteria (which may already involve assumptions about body size).

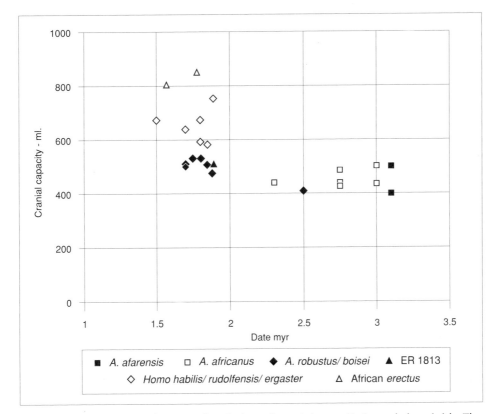

Figure 28 Expansion of range of variation of cranial capacity in early hominids. The specimen known as ER 1813 is shown separately. There is much dispute about its classification as members of the early *Homo* group (Wood 1992a) or as Australopithecines (Falk 1983).

Using average values for the two sets of estimates, Tobias shows that one calculation of relative brain size 'confirms the degree of advancement in brain development' expected. But, again, closer inspection of the pattern of variation suggests otherwise. Here, graphing the data without attention to the species attributions removes the implicit assumptions in assigning limb bones to species that have been defined on the basis of skull characteristics. Plotting the measurements of cranial capacity on the same graph as estimates of stature (Figure 29) shows that, at the time shortly after 2 Myr when the range of cranial capacity expanded, the range of stature also expanded dramatically. Thereafter, stature did not increase greatly, but cranial capacity increased first slowly, then dramatically. As we have already shown, brain size and body size are closely related, so it should be small surprise that the range of cranial capacity increased at the same time as the range of stature. As we will show in Chapter 7, the major increase in relative brain size—in encephalisation— seems to be much later than Tobias is suggesting.

At issue is the selective context for cranial expansion. What did it imply in terms of the abilities permitted by larger brains, and what actually happened in terms of

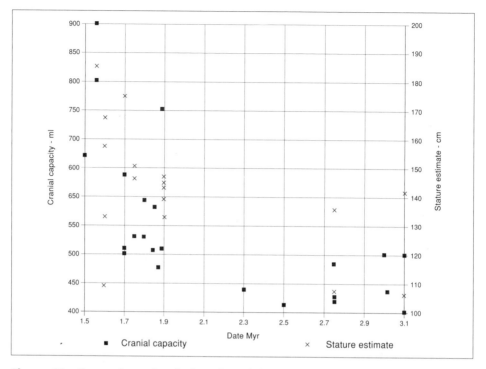

Figure 29 Comparison of variation of cranial capacity and of estimated stature in hominids before 1.5 Myr.

changes in behaviour consequent upon brain expansion? This proves to be a crucial issue in the story we are telling, as many commentators have assumed that absolutely or relatively bigger brains have direct implications for behaviour (e.g. Corballis 1991; Donald 1991; Dunbar 1993; Falk 1990). Tobias (1991) is most generous in his interpretation of the behavioural significance of the stone artefacts of the early hominids, and their discovery at the same sites as animal bones. For him these are signs of the beginnings of culture that would have required language for its transmission. Whatever the guesses or inferences about the impact of brain size increase, in the end it is the evidence of behaviour as revealed through the remains in the archaeological record that allows us to determine its consequences. We will address these issues in two sections, covering diet and tools.

As we indicated in Chapter 2, increase in brain size over the period of hominid evolution has implications in terms of the energy requirements for ontogenetic development and, thus, for foraging behaviour (Foley & Lee 1991). The energy cost of increased encephalisation could be partly met by increasing the quality of foods in the diet. Mothers bear the major costs. They must provide the energy for foetal growth, including brain growth. Spreading the infant's growth over a longer time—delayed development—reduces the need for the mother to provide so much energy so soon, both before and after the baby's birth. In humans the pattern of brain growth relative to body weight, uniquely, continues after birth for a year as it has before birth. Newborn humans have quite large heads, but their brain weight is typically 30% of adult brain weight, compared with about 60% for macaques (Martin 1990). As a result, human infants have a much longer period of dependency than in other primates, though defining precise means of measuring this may be difficult (see Wilson 1975, 348). Just as we suggested with hairlessness and bipedal walking, so too prolonged infant dependency increased the opportunity for joint attention in human development and likely facilitated the evolutionary emergence of language.

We move now to consideration of how, in the course of hominid evolution, diet changed from the generalist fruit and leaf eating diet of the common ancestor to one which was more omnivorous.

The diet of early hominids

There used to be a simple story of early hominid diet and its role in the evolutionary emergence of humans: hunting was the crucial invention which accounted for almost all the uniquenesses of humans (Washburn & Lancaster 1968). One of the prime pieces of evidence was from sites where hominid activities can be identified from the presence of stone tools: namely, the animal bones that are also present. Early views of this conjunction concurred that the hominids had hunted and killed the animals for food (see e.g. Binford 1981; 1983 for discussion of this view).

In the last 25 years, there has been a revolution in the understanding of the materials from which the simple story was told. Non-human primates, both closely and more distantly related to humans, are now known to obtain meat from opportunistic killing of other animals, as we discussed in Chapter 2 (Harding 1981), and chimpanzees obtain substantial amounts of meat from killing (Goodall 1986) and possibly scavenging (Hasegawa et al. 1983) small mammals. Hunting for meat is seen as less distinctive as a human adaptation, because detailed studies of living fisher-hunter-gatherers have shown that, except in extreme northern latitudes, such people do not depend primarily on the meat provided from hunting (Foley 1982; Lee 1968). In addition, there are physiological limits to the amount of energy humans, and probably hominids, can obtain from protein (Speth 1989).

The associations of tools, hominid fossils and animal bones, from the very earliest appearance of stone tools, are no longer thought to be the product of early hominid hunting (Binford 1983; Brain 1981). The savanna provides many opportunities for scavenging from animals that die naturally or at the claws and jaws of other carnivores (Blumenschine 1986; 1991; O'Connell et al. 1988; Schaller & Lowther 1969; Tunnell 1990), and this seems to account for many of the meat procurement practices of hominids (e.g. Stiner 1991; Turner 1992). More detailed understanding (Behrensmeyer 1984; Behrensmeyer & Hill 1980) of the histories of bones in their passage from the bodies of animals to the sediments where archaeologists find them ('taphonomy') suggests that neither hominids nor humans loom very large as agents in the process. Despite these new ways of looking at the theory and evidence of early hominid subsistence, consensus in interpreting the evidence from archaeological sites has been hard to find (Binford 1986; 1988b; Bunn & Kroll 1986; 1988).

Attempts to construct pictures of the habitats of different hominids are not a productive source of definitive evidence about early hominid diets. Any such attempt founders on the problems of taphonomy (White 1988) and also on considerations such as the potential and actual mobility of hominids between habitats.

Some evidence of hominid diets is available from the striations on teeth. This shows that robusts were more like other animals that chew 'hard objects' (Grine & Kay 1988), perhaps nut-like oil seeds (Peters 1987): of the other apes the robusts were most like orang-utans, in terms of tooth wear, and least like gorillas, while graciles were between chimpanzees and gorillas. Walker (1982) suggested that the best interpretation is that robusts ate whole fruits, including casings, pulp and seed. Further progress has been made through chemical analysis of the bones of robust Australopithecines (Sillen 1992). When these analytical techniques are applied to modern animals they show distinctions between herbivores, omnivores and carnivores. The result of the analysis of hominid bones shows that robusts were closer to carnivores than expected.

The quality of the evidence is uneven, with few comparable tooth-wear or chemical studies for other early hominids. Leaving aside the frequent association between stone tools and animal bones, with or without hominid fossils, as inconclusive (Isaac & Crader 1981), there is some evidence from cut-marks on those bones and from wear on the margins of stone tools. Given that there were two species of hominids around at the time most of the sites were used, it is uncertain which one created cut marks or wear patterns or whether both did. For the purposes of our story, it is merely important that eventually the ancestors of humans increased the meat component of their diet over that of the common ancestor. Whether robusts also did so at some time is irrelevant (given that they were not our ancestors), except insofar as it would suggest that meat acquisition alone was not sufficient to account for the selective advantage of human ancestors over their contemporaries among the Australopithecines.

Cut-marks on bones at Olduvai Gorge, in Tanzania, and Koobi Fora, in northern Kenya, showed that stone tools were used on animal parts, and that some of the cutmarks crossed over the tooth marks of carnivores, and others were crossed by them (Bunn 1981; Potts & Shipman 1981). The fact that carnivores were chewing bones that had been cut by hominids is a reminder that the sites where bones and stones are found were not straightforwardly secure living places for hominids—one early *Homo* probably suffered crocodile attack (Davidson & Solomon 1990). Nevertheless, this is clear evidence of some hominid interest in these bones, and although it has become a matter of dispute whether they were obtaining meat or marrow (Binford 1981; Blumenschine 1991), it is unlikely they were obtaining neither. At least, the hominids were scavenging these products arising (or falling) from the attentions of other animals.

Obtaining meat is indicated by studies of the wear on the edges of 1.5 million year old stone flakes found at Koobi Fora (Keeley & Toth 1981), and obtaining marrow may be implied by the presence of a bone at Koobi Fora which could be reconstructed from several dispersed fragments to show the impact scar from the blow which broke it (Bunn et al. 1980). Blumenschine's (1991) analysis of the different skeletal elements at Olduvai Gorge 1.7 million years ago favours an interpretation that, supposing hominids were primary agents of bone accumulation at the site, they were scavenging for marrow and head contents. Heads, particularly, combine fat and protein, a factor likely to be of great significance in seasons when meat sources of protein were otherwise relatively fat-free (Speth & Spielmann 1983). Before we get carried away with the notion that these hominids were practised nutritionists, the evidence from ER 1808, a partial skeleton of *Homo erectus* from Koobi Fora dated to about 1.7 Myr (Feibel et al. 1989), shows a distinctive bone alteration known to result from hypervitaminosis A, an inflammatory condition provoked by consuming the livers of carnivores rich in Vitamin A (Walker et al. 1982; Walker 1982). No other explanation has been offered, and the diagnosis seems to confirm hominid meat-eating.

Puech's studies show wear on teeth characteristic of eating plants, not meat, in early *Homo* from Olduvai (Puech 1984), and early *Homo erectus* from Java (Puech 1983), which suggests meat-eating might not have been universal. Walker's (1982) tooth wear studies showed that meat was not a general part of the hominid diet before *Homo erectus*. Most scholars (Klein 1989) agree that meat began to form a distinctive part of hominid diet, however it was obtained, from early in the Pleistocene. In this, hominids probably contrasted with modern chimpanzees and baboons, the other primates that eat meat (in relatively small quantities). Hominids may, therefore, have been a distinctively meat-eating primate, adding meat and fat to the basic primate plant food diet of the common ancestor. What were the effects on the brain?

It follows from the energy requirements of human brains that hominids must have ensured an increase of energy consumption for increased encephalisation to have occurred. It may be that the early *Homo* species did not achieve this, given the equivocal evidence about the importance of meat in their diet, yet they seem to have laid the foundations. As with the argument about the cooling system for the cranial veins, so with the nutritional argument. First, there was no intent on the part of hominids. They did not know that the radiator cooling system had released a constraint on brain expansion, nor that if this expansion was to happen over the next 2 million years they would need a protein-rich and energy-rich diet, as might most readily be obtained from hunting or scavenging (Hill 1982). Indeed, we might argue that modern humans do not *know* of such a relationship between diet and brain growth either, except by inference from cases of extreme malnutrition and laboratory experiments with rats (Armstrong 1984). Secondly, neither with brain cooling, nor with nutrition for brain growth, did the establishment of these conditions necessarily lead to encephalisation. Other factors were involved, not least the extent of plasticity of the bones of the skull. Finally, discussion of this sort should not be allowed to imply that we are resiling from our position that brain expansion alone did not deliver language, meaning or 'the mind', fully-armed as it were. It was part of a complex mosaic of features implicated in the critical *behavioural* changes. We need to identify the specific circumstances of behavioural change that led to the social construction of 'minded' behaviour.

Tools

Darwin (1889, 51) emphasised the advantage of bipedalism in freeing the hands for tool-making. (We note that the image of 'freeing' connotes entrapment, and has a 'progressivist' flavour not in keeping with notions of evolutionary causation.) Richards (1986) draws attention to the apparent lack of evidence of an immediate use for the 'freed' hands, and that it is necessary to consider the consequences of the recruitment of the feet and legs alone for locomotion. There would have been a number of changes in the connections of the brain consequent upon the loss of manipulative (pedipulative?) function for the feet, and their specialised use for locomotion. We note this to show how the strands of our argument are related (and were anticipated by Darwin), but turn now to the evidence of early tool-making, evidence unknown in Darwin's day, but now a major source of knowledge of early hominid behaviour.

We left the common ancestor in the trees with little more by way of tools than those common among a wide range of species. Teaching of tool-use, we suggested, was not a feature of this animal. Yet with the appearance of stone tools, sometime around 2 Myr, there is an issue of how the descendants learned to make and use them. We suggest that this was crucially influenced by the nature and extent of infant dependency in the emerging hominids. Tobias (1991, 840) is explicit about a sudden change:

> If *A. africanus* was the first tool-maker, and if *A. africanus* had a manifest Broca's area on its endocast, it is conceivable that *A. africanus* ... could first have been capable of spoken language—even before *H. habilis* became dependent on language for survival. ... The development of early stone culture and the cultural transmission of this faculty by rudimentary language ... provided the setting for the splitting of the lineage.

Three elements are fundamental in Tobias's belief: the species attribution of the makers of stone tools; the nature and causes of variation in stone artefacts; and the relationship between those causes and language. In the following section we will examine the strength of the evidence about these elements. We regard the configuration of the brain as relatively minor evidence, given all we have said about 'minded' behaviour, meaning, language and brains.

Which species made the tools?

Until relatively recently, members of the genus *Homo* were thought to be the only creatures to have made and used stone tools, though West African chimpanzees use stone hammers and anvils for cracking nuts. Wright (1972) showed that by providing the right circumstances, assistance and model, orang-utans could be

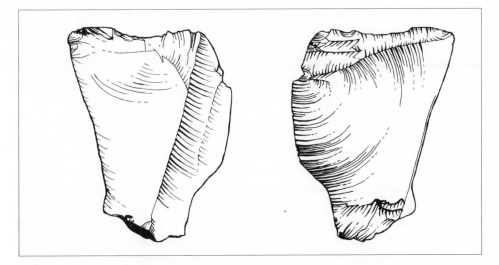

Figure 30 Stone tool handed to Davidson by its maker, 'Kanzi'. The blow used to make this tool was so strong that the flake sheared through the point at which the blow was applied. The flake shows the main physical features by which archaeologists routinely identify stone tools.

induced to make and use stone tools. More recently, the bonobo 'Kanzi' has been shown how to make stone flakes (Toth et al. 1993) (see Figure 30) and, given incentive to do so, has developed new ways of doing it. This seems to suggest that the making of stone tools is not a feature only of the members of the genus *Homo*.

The identification of the species of the first stone tool-maker might be deemed irrelevant, given this new understanding and our stated views of the arbitrariness of the relationship between anatomical behavioural criteria for defining humans, and hence other hominid species. However, if it were established that *Homo* was not the only genus to have spontaneously made stone-tools, it might be taken that stone tools were not such an important piece of evidence for language, unless, of course, Australopithecines spoke too!

The case for Australopithecines making stone tools rests on two pieces of evidence: the claims for stone tools older than 2 million years ago at a time when there are few fossils attributed to *Homo*; and the morphology of some hand bones attributed to the robust Australopithecine, *P. robustus*, which seem to have had the shape to perform the actions necessary to make stone tools.

The evidence for early stone industries is slight. Finds from two sites are concerned: mostly quartz flakes from Omo, north of Lake Turkana (Chavaillon 1976; Merrick & Merrick 1976), now dated about 2.35 Myr (Feibel et al. 1989); trachyte and basalt flakes and cores from several localities at Kada Gona, in the Hadar region of Ethiopia, above and below deposits dated at 2.7 Myr (Harris 1983; Roche & Tiercelin 1977). Supposing the earlier finds are appropriately identified and dated, the early occurrence of stone tools was not necessarily widespread.

Leaving aside the dissenting classifications for some of the Hadar hominids, the oldest claim for the genus *Homo* is for some small skull fragments from the Chemeron Formation, in Kenya, dated at 2.4 Myr (Hill et al. 1992). The Chemeron claim is by no means straightforward, and Wood (1992b) points out that otherwise there is no undisputed claim earlier than 2 Myr. Thus, if the stone tools older than that date are properly attributed (both as being tools and as to date) then the earliest stone tools seem to have been made by a species of Australopithecine.

Susman (1988; 1994) described some hand bones from the South African site of Swartkrans, in a 1.8 Myr layer as sufficiently similar to human bones to allow precision grip, yet sufficiently different in shape from *Homo* to be from a different species. In the same layer, 95% of the reliably identified hominid remains are robusts, so Susman suggests that the hand bones probably came from that animal. Assuming this was the hand that used the tools found with it, this evidence is consistent with the inference from East Africa, that *Homo* was not the only tool maker. Once that is conceded, otherwise problematic artefacts from Pakistan, dated at 2 Myr (Dennell et al. 1988a; 1988b), might have been made by some, unspecified, creature that was not necessarily ancestral to humans.

Nature and causes of variation in stone tools

Making stone tools involves the production of sharp edges by the delivery of a blow to the margin of one rock (a core), usually, but not necessarily, with another rock (a hammer-stone). There are close relationships between, on the one hand, the direction and force of the blow and the shape of the core at the point where it is struck and, on the other, the shape of the flake produced (Cottrell & Kamminga 1987). Once these principles are mastered, which for most knappers does not involve knowledge that these are the principles involved, the shape and variety of forms that can be made by flaking stone are astounding. The techniques used in earliest stone tool making were sufficient to create such forms, but there is no sign that the earliest tool-makers appreciated this. Kanzi's stone tool making obeys the same mechanical principles, such that the flakes produced can be displayed to look like the products of human or hominid flaking. When Kanzi applies a blow to a core at the wrong angle, or with the wrong force, or in the wrong place, either no flake is produced, or one is produced which makes it harder to produce more from that part of the core.

Archaeologists identify patterns in the making of stone tools and give the patterns various names, usually after the site where the pattern was first identified. As happened with fossils, problems about naming attend this practice also. Without wishing to give the impression that early hominids were working in factories, the word used to describe a collection of stone tools showing such a pattern (as recognised by the archaeologist, not necessarily by the maker) is 'industry'. The earliest stone industries have similar characteristics (see Davidson & Noble 1993a) and are grouped together under the name Oldowan (after Olduvai) industry (Figure 31). They are primarily industries in which, by one or more blows struck on cobbles, flakes were produced, as indicated by the results of the use-wear analysis described by Keeley and Toth (1981). The removal of successive flakes from the same margin

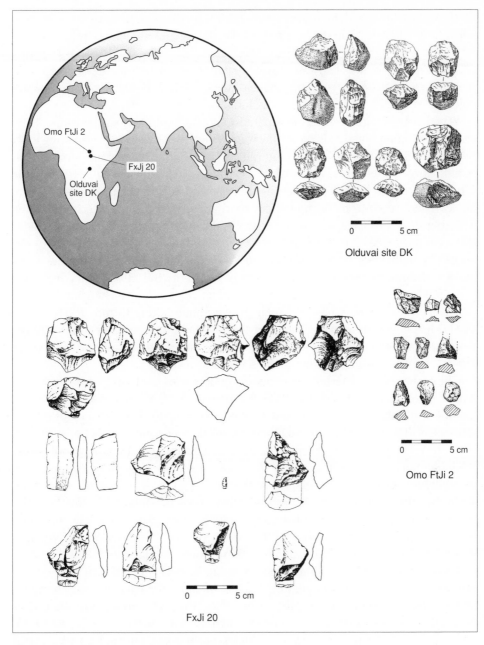

Figure 31 Illustration of Oldowan industry.

of the cobble resulted in a core with quite repetitive patterning of a margin apparently 'sharper' than the original cobble. Such cores are widely referred to as 'choppers', though there is little evidence that they were used to chop. Toth's (1985a) analysis of the Oldowan showed that there was a high degree of determination of form of flake by the initial shape of the core. Other aspects of variation are determined by the nature of the raw material.

Wynn and McGrew (1989) compared Oldowan and chimpanzee tools. They found much comparability between the requirements for chimpanzees making tools by modifying plant parts with requirements for hominids making stone tools. (Chimpanzees use but do not make stone tools.) The authors suggest that the differences result from difference in tasks performed, rather than raw material alone. There seem to be no references to chimpanzees cutting or scraping—the activities that caused the wear on the edges of the tools examined by Keeley. Under these circumstances it is difficult to see the context in which chimpanzees or their ancestors might find flakes useful. It is no coincidence that the earliest stone tools occur with animal bones marked by cuts from such tools. Selection for making sharp stone flakes would occur in the context of a practice of cutting meat from carcases. Other primate predators partition their prey without cutting (Strum 1981; Teleki 1981), but hominids scavenging from the kills of other predators, and, unique among primates in obtaining food from animals larger than themselves (Butynski 1982), may have needed cutting tools in this new niche.

Chimpanzees, when termiting, generally collect grass stems as tools from within 5 m of a termite mound (Goodall 1986, 538), rarely further, while those using stone hammers to crack nuts are inferred to transport them up to 500 m on a regular basis (Boesch & Boesch 1984), but use other options if stone is unavailable or unknown to them. What of hominids needing stone to make cutting and scraping tools? Part of the certainty of identification of the quartz stone tools at Omo is due to the unavailability of that as raw material in the vicinity of the site (Merrick & Merrick 1976), so that one of the supposedly earliest uses of stone tools involved the movement of raw materials 'at least several kilometres'. Much better documented is the availability of raw material for the stone artefacts of Olduvai Gorge, with two known sources of stone 2-5 km and 6-13 km from sites (Hay 1976; Potts 1984).

Potts, using computer simulation of energy costs, argued that there were efficiencies for hominids in creating caches of stone for later use, and bringing animal parts to the caches for processing. This is a useful antidote to the earlier notion that hominids had 'home bases' to which they carried their prey (Isaac 1978), but seems to imply a level of planning which is unnecessary (and indeed involves an implausible amount of logistical planning—implausible because, in accounting for any other aspect of the archaeological record of this period, logistical planning seems unnecessary). McGrew (1992, 204) suggests that other simulations of the cumulative effect over 'hundreds or thousands' of shorter journeys of only tens of metres, as seen in chimpanzees, could produce the apparent concentrations of stones and stone tools seen at early hominid sites. Some support for this is offered by Sept

(1992), who concluded her study of chimpanzee nesting sites with the suggestion that resource availability at particular locations had as much to do with the concentration of chimpanzee activities as did patterns of interaction between individual chimpanzees.

The inferences about chimpanzee stone transport (Boesch & Boesch 1984) were based on the documentation of spatial positions of stones rather than direct observations of chimpanzees carrying them. Likewise, no one has seen an early hominid carrying stone tools, but the probability seems higher that a contemporary observer would have seen it. The prime evidence here is that in addition to the observation of cut marks on bones at sites with stone tools, stone tool cut marks were also observed on bones at sites where there were no stone tools (Glynn Isaac personal communication 1984). While caution must be exercised about the precise causes of the marks, this looks like evidence that hominids carried their tools with them, further confirmed by studies in which knapped stone was fitted back together to reveal that flaked tools had been removed (Toth 1982). We have previously suggested the great selective advantage of habitual stone-carrying for a hominid scavenging from the kills of dangerous predators: searching for stone for a tool is not best done after a kill has been located. The immediacy of operation of this selection suggests that there need not have been deliberate planning involved, merely species specific habit acquired by observational learning. Stone-carriers tended not to fall victim to predators so frequently.

We concur with Wynn and McGrew, and against Tobias, that the Oldowan stone industry shows little sign that it could not have been achieved with the abilities demonstrated by modern apes. In saying that early hominids were like apes, we are not saying they were apes, if by ape is meant only those species of modern primate called apes. These were not chimpanzees or bonobos. We suggest that scavenging meat provided a new context for selective advantage to a hominid that carried cores around to make flakes for cutting meat from the carcase or to break bones for marrow. This does not seem to require human abilities of meaning, 'minded' behaviour or language and more than chimpanzee behaviour.

The role of language in tool-making

Holloway (1969) has been most explicit about the language-like abilities displayed by tool-making. Recruiting Hockett's design features of language (Chapter 2), Holloway suggested that manufacture of stone tools displayed the features of productivity, arbitrariness, duality of patterning and cultural transmission. We reiterate briefly our previous arguments (Noble & Davidson 1991) against these characterisations. The appearance of productivity is provided by the different responses of the raw material to different patterns of application of force. We are usually not in a position to identify whether an individual artefact is a 'deliberate' product or an accidental by-product of the production of some other artefact. Application of force in inappropriate ways may result in no artefact at all, rather than imperfect versions of a planned one, and this reduces the extent to which we can speak, from the archaeological record, of the arbitrariness with which form is imposed on the raw material. Form is strongly dependent on the physics of forces and rocks. Moreover, the comparison with duality of patterning assumes that the 'chopper' was the intended product (like the word) and the flakes removed along the way were meaningless by-products (analogous to phonemes). The opposite seems to be the case, to judge by the use-wear studies (Keeley & Toth 1981), and we call this argument 'the finished artefact fallacy' (Davidson & Noble 1993a; Noble & Davidson 1991).

Finally Holloway asserts that the transmission of tool-making from generation to generation should be regarded as cultural. We have already expressed our concern about using the concept of 'culture' as if there were a way to identify it objectively. The issue, really, is how the practice of stone tool-making passed from one generation to another. We are not attracted to the notion that stone flaking was independently discovered by individuals in each generation, in the manner of Japanese macaques independently discovering potato washing (Visalberghi & Fragaszy 1990). Chimpanzee infants learn tool-use through a mixture of 'social facilitation, observation, imitation, and practice—with a good deal of trial and error thrown in' (Goodall 1986, 561-2), and we have already mentioned the minimal nature of claimed teaching in chimpanzee stone hammer use (Boesch 1991b). Guilmet (1977) drew attention to the socialisation process in learning skills of this nature, but there is little information on the learning of stone knapping among humans. We previously referred to an anecdote in our experience (Noble & Davidson 1989) where a child at a very young age, brought up by a student learning to knap, began to imitate, without teaching, the motor actions of his parent. Such imitation among humans is a familiar part of child-rearing; all that is unusual is that it was knapping which is described in this story. In a human community where knapping was a usual everyday event, it seems plausible that knapping was learned through such imitated motor actions. Ingold (1986) suggested that much craft production is learned in this way without formal teaching, much as children acquire language 'without overt reference to rules'. Hewes (1973) drew attention to the importance of this context, learning through gestural imitation, for the acquisition of gestural communication. Yet we have already noted the poverty of the empirical evidence for imitation in non-human primates. How did this come to be so important in human experience?

Tools and the brain

Much effort and energy has been devoted to the search for signs of the shape of the exterior surface of the cortex of the brain from the examination of endocasts of the interior of the skull. Despite many disputes about individual specimens, there seems to be agreement about distinctive differences between the endocasts of Australopithecines and those of early (and later) *Homo* (Falk 1992). Chief among these are differences in the region where Broca's area is to be found in modern humans, and it is more like humans in all fossils attributed to *Homo* than among the

Australopithecines. In Chapter 2 we drew attention to difficulties in inferring behaviour from such evidence, and we persist in that. The evidence we cited that 'gyrification' (which is probably all that is involved) is precisely determined by brain volume, suggests that the first appearance of the shape by which Broca's area may be identified has more to do with expansion of cranial capacity than with the functions that were performed by this bit of neural tissue. We might, rather, look for confirmation of the functional hypothesis (that changes in the shape of the brain caused behavioural changes) in the evidence of behaviour.

As against our argument that the stone tools do not require an explanation in terms of language abilities, is one that seems to link the earliest stone tools with the sort of changes in the brain said to accompany language: namely, Toth's claim for right-handedness in the making of Oldowan tools (Toth 1985b). This claim has been accepted uncritically by many authors (e.g. Bradshaw & Rogers 1993; Corballis 1991; Falk 1992; Klein 1989; Leakey & Lewin 1992; Savage-Rumbaugh & Lewin 1994). The stepping stones of the full argument are that right-handedness implies hemispheric lateralisation of the brain, with important motor control in the left hemisphere; language is predominantly controlled in the left hemisphere; therefore right-handedness implies language. Lateral dominance is so widespread as to be of less importance in the story, and the evidence for left hemisphere specialisation for language is not so strong as it is said to be (Chapter 1). Here we challenge the claim that the Oldowan tools were necessarily made by right-handed hominids.

The essence of Toth's argument is shown in Figure 32, which shows the successive removal of three flakes from a cobble in plan view as the cobble is held in the left hand and struck from above.

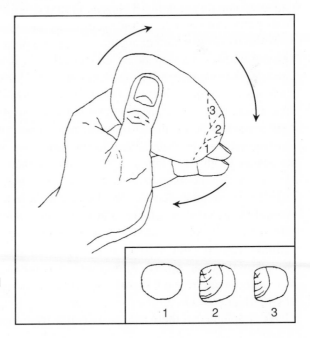

Figure 32 Successive removal of flakes from a cobble by a right-handed person. *From Toth 1985b.*

The argument is that a right-handed person holds the cobble in the left hand and strikes it from above with a hammerstone held in the right. As successive flakes are removed, the cobble is rotated clockwise in the left hand. The first flake has a surface that was originally on the cobble (called the dorsal surface) covered with the weathered skin of the cobble (called cortex). The next flake has a dorsal surface half covered with cortex, and, as shown in Figure 32 this will be the right hand side of the flake. This is true of all successive flakes removed in the same clockwise rotation. When Toth (who is right handed) knapped, to reproduce experimentally the shapes he sees in Oldowan industries, he produced right-oriented flakes on 56% of the occasions. He found that in the sites of Koobi Fora dated between 1.9 and 1.4 million years ago the ratio of right-oriented to left-oriented flakes was 57:43 (he does not give numbers). The similarity of the proportions is such that Toth concludes that the makers (over half a million years, and possibly two or three species) were preferentially right handed.

The argument is difficult to sustain. First, Toth acknowledges that: 'it is only when a sequence of flakes is removed from one face of a core that a non-random pattern becomes evident'. We cannot be sure that this condition applied to these sets of prehistoric stone tools. Indeed, the argument we have been putting that the flakes not the cores were the sought-after tools would suggest otherwise. Sequential removals would be likely if the knappers were seeking to produce a core tool—if it really was a chopper. If they needed a flake, it is more likely that the core would be discarded after one flake was removed, to be picked up again when another was required.

Second, it is not inevitable that the core was struck from above. Hiscock (personal communication 1994) has observed skilled knappers among Australian Aborigines striking a core from below.

Third, in modern human populations preferential right-handedness is present in varying frequencies, depending on the task. For handwriting, given the historical practice of discouraging left-handedness, it may be as much as 90%; for threading a needle it may be as low as 70% (Calvin 1983). Since Toth is right-handed, the appropriate figure for comparison would be to construct a population of, say, 70% right-handers who produced right-oriented flakes in frequencies 56:44, and 30% left-handers who produced them in proportion 44:56. Assuming the condition of sequential production holds, Toth's experimental result suggests that, such an average modern population might produce a combined ratio of 524:476, rather more difficult to establish statistically. Davidson tested the method on samples from Australian archaeological sites and found, in a sample of 100 artefacts, 51 right-oriented and 49 left-oriented. Yet direct skeletal evidence (Peter Brown personal communication), and indirect evidence from the location of traumatic injury (Knuckey 1992) suggests that prehistoric Australian Aborigines were right-handed. Toth's argument does not seem to be very plausible on theoretical, methodological or empirical grounds.

We conclude that there is little evidence from that offered directly or indirectly about brains and tools, separately or together, that unequivocally supports an argument for an early emergence of language.

Social context

The issue with which we conclude this chapter is one we have been foreshadowing: the social context of the emerging behaviour of hominids which ultimately led to language. The issue is not susceptible to analysis due to the impossibility of identifying, to any credible standard, the social behaviour of any prehistoric people. Perhaps for this reason the literature is voluminous, and many of the studies of primates we cited in Chapter 2 were written using chimpanzees or other primates as models for hominid social behaviour. We prefer an approach such as that of Foley and Lee (1989), which seeks to identify the trajectories by which distinctively human patterns may have emerged from a variety of possible earlier forms, including those now used by modern primates. But the difficulty is always one of finding appropriate archaeological evidence for the sorts of social formations that can be defined. For this reason, we will not dwell on the matter here, but reserve the full expression of our view for Chapter 8, the most speculative of this book.

The elements we have identified to this point are, first, the tendency for larger brains to carry with them energy costs and, second, an anatomical advantage for birth at an earlier stage of total brain growth. This in turn increased the length of infant dependency. This context selected for a social formation in which caregivers, probably females, spent more time with their infants. Delay in the learning of locomotion, as well as hairlessness, a feature selected in the context of thermoregulatory advantages in bipedalism, meant that hominid infants probably had to be carried in front of the mother for a longer period than is the case for most other primates. This increased the opportunity for joint attention and observational learning, a feature which is said to be critical to differences in behaviour between wild chimpanzees and 'educated' or 'enculturated' chimpanzees (Tomasello et al. 1994). The contexts in which observational learning could turn into teaching have been reported for chimpanzees (Boesch 1991b), but attempts at teaching nut-cracking using stones did not seem to be very successful, perhaps partly because of the lack of strength of infant chimpanzees. We suggest that increased joint attention might increase the frequency of such episodes, and, in an activity such as stone tool knapping it is not so much the absolute force of the blow as its precise direction and appropriate amount that determines success. Under these circumstances there might be selection for teaching, ultimately applying to communication too.

What if there was no early language origin?

We have suggested that the case for an origin of language around 2 million years ago is difficult to sustain on the presently available evidence. Evidence from brain size increase and changes in brain shape, and from diet and stone tools does not point unequivocally to the need for language. The only other argument for language origins has set a date very much later, within the last 200 000 years. We suspect it is much more recent than that, as we will argue in Chapter 8.

There is a body of materials between these two dates which has often been described as if the makers had language. Hominids had their origin in Africa, but by 1 million years ago, perhaps earlier, they were also present in Asia (Gamble 1993). To accomplish this dispersion from Africa, they may have needed some behaviours they did not use in Africa. As distinct from the relatively unpatterned stone industries of the Oldowan, they used stone flakes, some of which were flaked from cores of highly regular, highly symmetrical, rather standardised form, known as handaxes. Some authors have suggested that these show signs of modern intellect, use of symbols and mathematical regularity. If they did, then we would probably concur the hominids had language.

At the time of an origin for language late in the Upper Pleistocene (see Table 5), there were hominids in temperate latitudes which had pronounced cold seasons. It is widely believed that they constructed shelters and made or used fire. Some scholars believe that there is a history of the use of ochre before the Upper Pleistocene and the modification of objects (other than or as well as handaxes) as symbols. The same scholars would argue that there was a practice of burial at least early in the Upper Pleistocene. In the following chapter we will examine these claims and show how or why the evidence has been inappropriately interpreted, or does not relate to language origins.

CHAPTER 7

BEHAVIOUR THAT LED TO LANGUAGE: NARIOKOTOME TO NEANDERTHAL

We have argued that there is no case that early hominids in East Africa had language or minded behaviour. They were not the same as the common ancestor of humans and African apes: they were bipedal, had larger brains, used stone tools, and incorporated meat and other parts of animals into their diet. In some other behavioural terms, the differences were not great, but their importance is that they marked the first steps in the appearance of modern behaviour. Bipedalism released constraints on brain size and had important effects on how and where these hominids could forage. The increase in brain size may not have been sizeable, but the trend has been continuing for the last two million years. The abilities needed to make stone tools, to carry them around, and to use them were little different from abilities witnessed in the behaviour of modern chimpanzees, but they were the foundation on which later elaborations of tool making and tool use were laid. Animal food became a consistent part of human adaptation, possibly crucial to survival in some of the new environments colonised by the descendants of East African early hominids.

For the bulk of the period from 1.5 Myr to about 100 000 years ago there was little directional change in behaviour. Some of the evidence we shall discuss from this period reflects the increased opportunities for learning and teaching we considered at the end of Chapter 6, but the major changes happened after 100 000 years ago. The contrast is most stark in Europe, where the Neanderthals, the descendants of *Homo erectus*, were replaced around 32 000 years ago by people who used symbols; and there is other archaeological evidence (Mellars 1989b; Mellars & Stringer 1989) that marks the newcomers as language-users (Davidson & Noble 1989). Elsewhere the change is more complex, but a consistent story can be told of the emergence, before 55 000 years ago, of behaviour made possible by language, such as the building of a boat that took people to Australia (Davidson & Noble 1992). This behaviour first emerged among people with skeletal form much more like modern humans than that of other contemporaries who appear never to have behaved in this way. But it was not a simple matter of the modern form making language possible, for there were many millennia during which both modern and archaic forms existed (Grün & Stringer 1991) (see Figure 25), perhaps even side by side in some regions (Stringer & Gamble 1993), with few differences of behaviour between them (Bar-Yosef et al. 1992).

In Table 5 (Chapter 6) we outlined aspects of the chronology of hominids, drawing attention to the subdivisions of the Pleistocene geological period (see also Figure 26, Chapter 6). The events of the last 400 000 years are shown in more detail in Table 7. We will refer to the events of the Middle Pleistocene, which ended at the beginning of the last period of climate as warm as the present (the Last Interglacial), about 125 000 years ago. It is in the period after this, the Upper Pleistocene, that most skeletal remains of Neanderthals and of anatomically modern humans have been found (see Table 4). Neanderthals became extinct (whether or not their genes contributed to modern Europeans) before 30 000 years ago, at the time when there appeared in Europe a whole suite of things (sculptures, bone tools, personal ornaments, burials, stone tools with imposed form, structured hearths) that suggest that symbols and language had emerged. We will refer to the first part of the Upper Pleistocene as the Early Upper Pleistocene. It is in this period that anatomically modern humans and Neanderthals both lived in some regions of the East Mediterranean.

Our earlier argument against gradualism in the emergence of language, that there can be no such thing as 'proto-language' nor some language other than 'language-as-we-know it', might be taken to suggest that the suite of modern behavioural characteristics emerged suddenly and all at the same time. That would be to misunderstand our point. Insofar as such characteristics depended on language in the way we have argued earlier, we will continue to argue against gradualism. On the other hand we are also arguing in an evolutionary framework, so we assume that distinctively modern behaviour came to dominate the world of hominids by natural selection from a range of behaviours exhibited by them. It is thus likely that the archaeological record will show isolated features that look as if they were the product of modern humans and yet could not have been. The argument we are constructing shows how all of that mosaic of features makes up the whole picture of the emergence of human behaviour, and how each is related to the emergence of language in particular.

The *Homo erectus* skeleton from Nariokotome

The recent publication of details of a skeleton of *Homo erectus* allows a good starting point (Walker & Leakey 1993a). This, the most complete early hominid skeleton ever found is the remains of a male, arguably about 11-12 years old (Smith 1993),who died possibly from septicemia following an infected jaw, and fell into a swamp at Nariokotome, on the western side of Lake Turkana, in northern Kenya,

years B.P.	HOMINID FOSSILS	MEAT EATING	STONE TOOLS	BONE TOOLS	FIRE	BURIALS	ART	SHELTER

Table 7 Timescale of the last 400 000 years of hominid and human evolution

about 1.53 million years ago (Walker 1993a). He had no stone tools with him. He was about 160 cm tall, and would probably have reached 185 cm in adulthood, already exhibiting the tall, slender features typical of modern people in arid tropical Africa (Ruff & Walker 1993). His collar bones were of unequal size, strongly suggesting that he was right-handed (Walker & Leakey 1993b). His brain was asymmetrical and showed external features of Broca's area. His cranial capacity was about 880 ml, and might have reached 910 ml in adulthood, giving an EQ of 4.48, almost exactly average for *Homo erectus* (Begun & Walker 1993).

The Nariokotome skeleton is unique, among hominid remains of this age, in having surviving vertebrae. The analysis of the vertebral canal, through which the spinal cord passes in life, showed some similarities with what is known of other primates, along with features unique, among living species, to *Homo sapiens*. The overall size of the spinal cord was not greatly different from that of modern humans, but where modern humans show an expansion of the thoracic area (in the chest area of the spine) when compared with other primates, this skeleton did not. It is suggested that the increased thoracic cord in modern humans may be related either to increased muscular movement or control of the trunk, perhaps related to the efficiency of bipedalism including running, or with increased muscular control of breathing, possibly related to speech production (Evarts 1981, 1113; MacLarnon 1993). Moment-by-moment control of breathing and control of the larynx and facial and other muscles are critical in speech production (Lieberman 1984, 102-120). Calvin (in Walker 1993b) suggests that the enlargement, when it happened, could also have been associated with stabilising the thorax and abdomen for throwing, while Evarts (1981) shows the relation between the thoracic cord and power and precision grips of the hand. We will argue in Chapter 8 that throwing, and hand control, played a crucial part in the story we are telling.

Walker (1993b) considered the indicators criticised in Chapter 6 (enlarged brain relative to Australopithecines, right-handedness, cerebral asymmetry, external features of Broca's area), and concluded that *Homo erectus,* as represented by Nariokotome, did not use language. He goes on (p. 428-9): '[Noble and Davidson's (1991)] review [of language origins] did not cover the morphology of early hominids, but ... those who have done so and then claimed a very early origin for human language and speech are standing on ground that is steadily crumbling away.'

Brain size

The height of the Nariokotome hominid reinforces the point that much of the increase in brain size must be put in relation to the increase in stature at the time. This individual was tall, but his brain was very small, in relation to a modern human population. MacLarnon (1993) points out that in the course of hominid evolution, relative brain size increased much more markedly than the size of the spinal cord. Given the uniqueness of the Nariokotome evidence, we feel that interpretation is difficult at this stage. Were the changes in the thoracic region (perhaps selected by

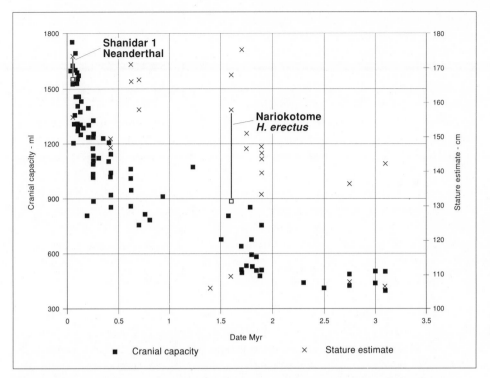

Figure 33 Comparison of variation of cranial capacity and variation of stature in hominids. Only two specimens in this sample have measurements of both: the 1.53 Myr Nariokotome, *Homo erectus*; and the 0.05 Myr Neanderthal, Shanidar 1. Lines joining the points for each of these specimens suggest a very great increase in encephalisation between the two dates.

throwing, and the increased breathing control important in running) sufficient to stimulate the increase in brain size? MacLarnon does not cite the dimensions of any other fossil hominid or human, so it is difficult to judge.

Very few fossils allow a straightforward estimate of both cranial capacity and body size for the same individual. The patterning over the greatest numbers of specimens can be seen by plotting estimated stature on the same graph as the measure of cranial capacity (Figure 33). The Nariokotome individual not only has the greatest stature for his time, but also the largest cranial capacity. The graph shows a pattern of slow and steady increase of cranial capacity from 2 Myr (million years) to about 0.2 Myr, followed by a relatively rapid increase. Stature increases rapidly after 2 Myr and remains more or less steady thereafter. By this representation of the data, there is a great increase in encephalisation after 0.2 Myr.

One consideration in understanding the late increase in encephalisation is the effect of latitude, given that, at any particular part of the cycle of climatic variation, ambient temperatures tend to decline with increasing distance from the equator. That this is an important factor is demonstrated by the success of Ruff and Walker

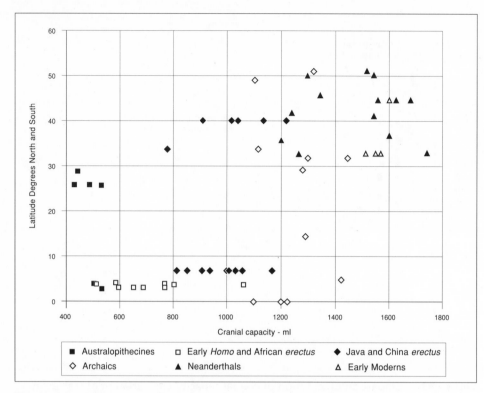

Figure 34 Distribution of hominid cranial capacity by latitude.

(1993) in modelling the body dimensions of the Nariokotome individual according to principles of thermoregulation. Various studies demonstrate some effect of climate on body size (Beals et al.1984): animals of the same species have larger body sizes in the colder parts of their area of distribution; some human populations seem to have reduced body size in the warmer climate of the last 10 000 years (Brown 1987). Plotting hominid cranial capacity against latitude (Figure 34) shows that all of the most recent specimens in this sample are from cooler latitudes. But colonisation of cooler environments is not a straightforward explanation for cranial capacity increase: Australopithecines at different latitudes have overlapping ranges of cranial capacities; *Homo erectus*, Archaics and Neanderthals, in turn, show similar overlap. It seems likely that climate was one factor in the apparent increase in brain size, but samples are too small, and climatic associations too poorly known, to present reliable arguments in more detail than this.

Our argument in Chapters 2 and 6 was that neither absolute nor relative brain size is an adequate indicator of the realised abilities of hominoids, hominids or humans, especially in the light of the argument about symbols, mind and communication in Chapters 3, 4 and 5. The 'mind' is not 'in' the brain, so changes in the brain will not simply reveal its emergence. The difficulty of interpreting patterns of brain size change is reinforced by closer inspection of those patterns in the more recent part of

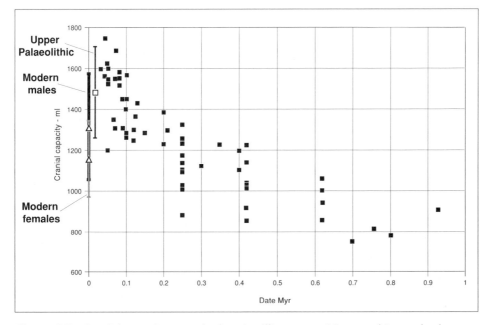

Figure 35 Cranial capacity over the last 1 million years. Mean and 2 standard deviations for the Upper Palaeolithic and for modern males and females from New Britain. *From* Groves 1989, 302.

hominid evolution. Figure 35 suggests that there was a sharp increase in both absolute and relative cranial capacity in the last 200 000 years. None of the fossil specimens after that date has a cranial capacity less than 1200 ml. Figure 35 also shows the male and female means (with 2 standard deviations) for a modern population (from New Britain). These ranges suggest that the majority of earlier hominid cranial capacities of the last one million years fall within a modern range of variation, though values above 1250 ml are rarely reached before 200 000 years ago. We repeat the point made in Chapter 6 that there are huge uncertainties in the prehistoric data.

Given the arguments we have expressed so far, it seems fair to conclude that, in explaining modern human behaviour, attention is inappropriately concentrated on absolute and relative brain size increase. The average size of modern human brains for the sample from New Britain is 1240 ml (Groves 1989, 302), an increase of about 600 ml over 2 million years (less than one third of a millilitre per millennium). It is unknown whether this resulted in more neurons, larger neurons, more dendrites or lower neuron density or some combination of these effects, nor what selective advantage there may have been to such small increases (though there was surely *some*). Reorganisation of structures in the brain undoubtedly took place during this evolution, especially given the somewhat different patterns of areas of association for naturalistic calls of monkeys and those of human speech (Burling 1993; Deacon 1992). Deacon has argued that 'quantitative reorganisation of the known [brain] circuits can provide a plausible model for the circuit reorganization that underlies the shift from stereotypic calls to human language'. Selection may well favour larger brains, but language functions did not emerge simply as a consequence of the brain reaching a certain size.

Deacon (1992, 154) nonetheless argues: (1) that the pattern of brain size increase since 2 million years supports 'selection with respect to language' from that date; (2) that there is consistent directional selection from that period onwards to the appearance of archaic *Homo sapiens*; and (3) that 'during the evolution of distinct lineages of *Homo sapiens*, including the Neanderthals ... selection on brain function did not produce any further major neurological changes.' All three claims are open to question: (1) as the Nariokotome vertebral column demonstrates, there were many changes to be incorporated in the whole evolving nervous system, not just those related to language; (2) Leigh's (1992) statistical analysis of the cranial capacity of *Homo erectus* suggests the pattern of change is complex. Depending on the method of analysis and the choice of appropriate samples, there is little consistent directional increase over time for that group of hominids; and (3) Figure 35 suggests that the period from the appearance of archaic *Homo sapiens* (the last 0.2 Myr) was precisely the period of most demonstrable and rapid cranial capacity increase.

Given that much of the change of brain shape appears to relate to increase in size, it would be extraordinary if there were no changes in relationship within the brain in the period of rapid increase in cranial capacity. Deacon suggests that 'the incredible cultural transitions that took place around the same period as the disappearance of the Neanderthals will be best explained in terms of cultural evolution rather than sudden neurologically mediated language evolution'. We agree with the statement, although Deacon makes it in support of an early language origin. We have been arguing that language is not (just) 'neurologically mediated'. Secondly, we are arguing that these 'cultural' transitions are themselves the best evidence that there was a sudden appearance of language in this period. Let us now turn to that evidence.

Colonisation

Amid all the discussion and dispute about the naming of species of early hominid, and the interpretation of fossil bones or archaeological materials to infer the behaviour of those species, one fact is generally agreed: the earliest hominids have been found in Africa, and their descendants are also found outside Africa. Colonisation of all the major habitats of the world is one of the distinctive characteristics of humans, and the process began with our hominid ancestors, perhaps even with the Australopithecines and early *Homo* colonising southern Africa from their origin in east Africa (Foley 1987a).

The spread is generally represented as a move out of Africa, but is best perceived as a gradual expansion of ranges which took this unusual, bipedal, stone-tool-using,

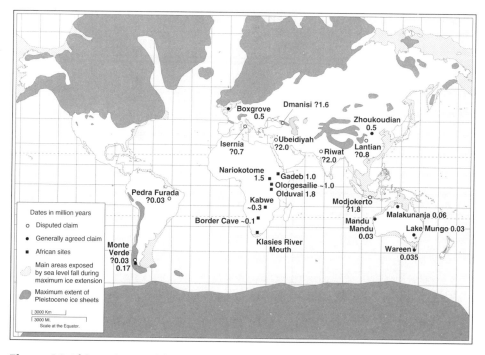

Figure 36 African sites and first hominid colonisation outside Africa, showing sites with disputed chronology and sites with agreed chronology.

meat-eating primate beyond its previous range into land and environments that *we* can best describe as 'beyond Africa'. The creatures themselves would not have known that they had crossed a geographical barrier, at least at the moment of moving beyond Africa, and we should not confuse a move with a migration. This was not colonial expansion such as that associated with Columbus, Quiros or Cook, nor migration of refugees fleeing inter-tribal conflict or genocidal persecution. Nor can we believe that this was a single event, lacking, as it does, any single stimulus.

Gamble (1993) recently summarised the evidence for first colonisation by hominids outside Africa. Key sites with their approximate dates are shown in Table 8 and Figure 36. The current consensus is that at some date about 1 million years ago our ancestors began to spread into other parts of the world. Such dispersals took hominids into new environments and new climates, so that by 0.75 million years ago, they were living in a wider range of environments than any other primate. Recent finds suggest that dispersal outside Africa may have been earlier than the consensus would have it: Dennell and colleagues (1988a; 1988b) argue for 2 million year old stone tools, at Riwat, in modern Pakistan; Franzen (1985) argues that there may have been Australopithecines in Java from a much earlier radiation out of Africa; recent dates from Java have been taken to indicate *Homo erectus* there at 1.8 Myr (Swisher et al. 1994), though not all scholars are agreed that the dates indicate the time of death of the hominids (de Vos & Sondaar 1994); a jaw, attributed to

AGE (years)	Africa	SW Asia	South and Southeast Asia	East Asia
1 800 000	Olduvai		??Riwat ??Modjokerto	
	Nariokotome			
1 500 000	Chesowanja			
1 000 000		'Ubeidiyah		Lantian
500 000	Kabwe			Zhoukoudian
100 000	Border Cave Klasies River Mouth	Tabun		
0		Qafzeh Kebara		

Table 8 Early hominid and human sites in different continents.

Homo erectus, has been found at the site of Dmanisi, in Georgia, possibly dated to 1.6 Myr (Gabunia & Vekna 1995). If these dates were confirmed, they would tend to support the claim of dates of 2 Myr for the site of 'Ubeidiyah, in the Jordan Valley (Repenning & Fejfar 1982). All these claims are isolated, difficult to explain, and open to other interpretation, but future discoveries may show them as part of a pattern requiring revision of current understanding. Against them is a recent view that hominids cannot be shown to have been in Europe much earlier than 0.5 Myr (Roebroeks 1994).

The dispersal of hominids should be considered in the light of evidence for the movement of other meat-eating species, particularly in the context of opportunities for scavenging provided by other carnivorous, but not carcase destroying, animals (Turner 1984; 1992). On this basis, there were good opportunities for hominids colonising Europe before 1.5 Myr, and after 0.5 Myr. In the period from 1.5 Myr to

Australasia	Europe	Americas	Novelties
	Dmanisi?		
			??Fire??
	Isernia la Pineta? Heidelberg?		
	Boxgrove High Lodge Bilzingsleben Terra Amata La Cotte de St Brelade Grotte Vaufrey		?Fire
	Tata		
Malakunanja II Mandu Mandu	Hohlenstein Stadel Sungir	Pedra Furada Monte Verde	Sea-crossing Imposed form "Art"

0.5 Myr hominids might have had sporadic success, but would have been competing for food with other animals that scavenged carcases from meat-eaters. The very fact that those scavengers survived in Europe suggests that hominid behaviour did not exclude them by successful competition for the same resources.

The regions outside Africa first colonised by hominids were the temperate grasslands which, while more seasonal and generally cooler, share the pattern of a high annual turnover of biological energy with the savannas where hominids emerged (Foley 1987a). These are conditions for which the most successful colonisers would have been carnivores. Gamble (1986) suggested that the earliest European hominids had strong ecological limitations, shunning the forests of the warmest interglacial episodes as well as the extreme cold of periglacial areas during glacial maxima (Soffer & Gamble 1990). They should be considered as primates well adapted to intermediate environments covering the largest areas and lasting the longest periods of time. Recent challenge to this argument (Roebroeks et al. 1992) seems more likely to have identified how close to the limits of their ecological tolerance these hominids came, rather than to have established that they were successful colonists of all land systems. It is only after the last Glacial maximum that there is evidence for successful colonisation of the densest forests (of the present interglacial in Europe), and the coldest tundras (of Siberia and North America), and by then recognisably modern human behaviour was well established.

There were two barriers to early colonisation by hominids, those into Australia and into the Americas. These provide insights about how to interpret the colonisations by earlier hominids, as well as about their realised abilities.

At times of low sea-level (during glacial maxima, see Figure 26) Australia formed a single continent (Sahul) with the main island of Papua New Guinea and Irian Jaya, but Sahul was always separate from the islands of south-east Asia which formed another land mass (Sunda) at those times. There is no evidence that any of the anthropoids (macaques), hominoids (orang-utans or gibbons) or hominids (*Homo erectus*) of south-east Asia ever crossed the sea barrier to set foot in Australia (Davidson & Noble 1992). We believe that the breakthrough which enabled humans to make the sea-crossing involved the abilities to plan ahead that are made possible by language.

The first colonisation of Sahul, before 55 kyr (Roberts et al. 1990), may have been an incidental consequence of sea-going (rather than a planned voyage of discovery) but it was not an accidental result of humans drifting on logs or rafts of vegetation (Irwin 1992). It required a boat, not least because sea-crossings also took people to islands off the north-west coast of the continent (New Britain and Buka) shortly after the first colonisation (Allen 1989). The building of a boat requires planning, the selection of actions that are not intrinsic to the *use* of a boat for purposes of its production. Planning of this sort, as we stressed in Chapter 4, depends on language to guide such actions to their end point. Support for this view of the realised abilities of the first colonists of Australia is provided by the material evidence from the earliest sites within Australia. Although the record of flaked stone artefacts is relatively unspectacular, there are signs that the first Australians had artefacts (ground-edged and hafted stone axes) with form determined by more than the mechanical requirements of making them (Davidson & Noble 1993a), as well as indications of symbolic decoration (Davidson & Noble 1992; Morse 1993) as early as any in the world (Figure 37).

The case of the colonisation of the Americas is more complicated. Here, the issue is the crossing of a cold barrier to enter through Alaska, joined by a sub-continental land mass at the low sea-level of the last glacial period until 14 kyr (Gamble 1993). When the land bridge existed, there was, of course, no perception of a barrier in the way there was for hominids coming to the end of the world in Sunda, nor was there any greater sense of migration than for the first hominids moving out of Africa. There is no agreement about the rate or mode of colonisation of the Americas: some stick firmly to a belief that there is no secure evidence earlier than 15 kyr; others

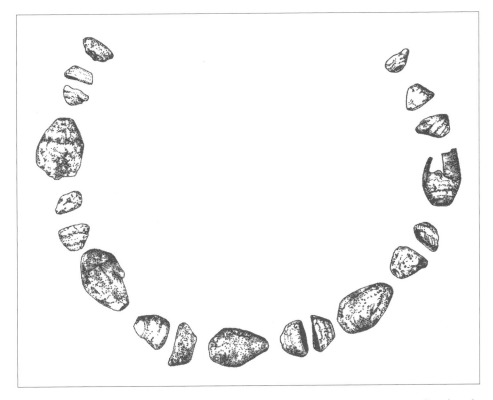

Figure 37 Pierced shells from Mandu Mandu rockshelter, Western Australia, dated at 32 kyr.

accept a series of claims of varying validity for human presence from as early as 35 kyr (Guidon & Delibrias 1986). There is a long history of claims for old dates in the Americas being found wanting (Lynch 1990), and no one has presented convincing evidence for hominids other than humans in any of the Americas. Once humans arrived in Alaska during the last Glacial period, the possibility of dispersion into more southern parts of the continent appears blocked by the mountain glaciers in the Rocky Mountains and the continental ice sheet. One proposal about how this barrier was avoided is the coastal route (Fladmark 1979), perhaps including boats. This would, of course, involve the same planning as the boat used to get to Australia, and with little possibility that it appeared any earlier than that one.

Unless the absence of hominids is merely an accidental consequence of the security of obtaining food in Siberia (i.e., the pickings were too rich to move on) (Velichko & Kurenkova 1990), the major issue is the difficulty of logistics on the edges of the Arctic (shelter, clothing, fire, storage of supplies for winter). The absence of people in northern Europe at the time of the last Glacial maximum suggests that even after the date we are suggesting for the emergence of planning, making provision to survive the extremes of a glacial margin winter was not straightforward. By this argument, colonisation of the Americas was only possible after such logistics were worked out, and they were not worked out anywhere in the world before the last Glacial maximum. Such a view suggests that, earlier than the first colonisation of Australia, in colonising different parts of the world, hominids were not behaving in ways that required language and 'mindedness'.

This rapid sketch of the end of the process of colonisation almost completely avoids what is one of the fiercest and most intractable battles in the current literature of physical anthropology: the emergence of modern human skeletal morphology. On the one hand are those who believe that in each region colonised by *Homo erectus* it evolved into the modern regional variant of *Homo sapiens* (e.g. Frayer et al. 1993); on the other are those who believe that *Homo sapiens* emerged in Africa from *Homo erectus*, and eventually displaced *Homo erectus* in all regions (with or without genetic mixture) (e.g. Aiello 1993; Stringer 1992). Since we have nailed our standard firmly to the mast of behavioural evolution rather than biological determination of that behaviour, we will continue to skirt this battle-ground.

Hunting and other subsistence

If the emergence of modern skeletal form is a current arena for vicious academic debate, previous hostilities surrounded the subsistence behaviour of earlier hominids as we discussed in Chapter 6. The matter is of importance because out of these subsistence practices emerged the behaviour of modern fisher-gatherer-hunters and also modern pastoralists and agriculturalists.

For modern humans, food is obtained by agriculture and animal farming, or by fishing, gathering and hunting. Both types of procurement involve sets of rights to the resources of the environment (Ingold 1987) which often conflict when the two compete. Such rights are institutionalised through negotiation using language and other symbols. We should beware the stereotype that there was an evolutionary progress from fishing, gathering and hunting to farming (Davidson 1989b; Foley 1988); rather, the conflict between institutional arrangements of appropriation leads to the destruction or restriction of the rights of non-agricultural peoples. Davidson (in press) has argued that changing patterns of symbolism through 'art', after the emergence of language, reflect the process of institutionalisation of the rights associated with human foraging and relations to the land and its resources.

The issue to be faced here is how hominids broadened their diet and became the most predatory primate. We will deal in turn with the theoretical implications of some ecological differences between carnivores and herbivores; with the empirical evidence that meat eating became more important from at least the time of the Nariokotome individual; and with the changing patterns of organisation of acquisition of meat during the evolution of the genus *Homo*.

Seen across a wide spectrum of mammalian species, herbivores and predators show consistent patterns of difference in biology and ecology (Foley 1987a; Shipman & Walker 1989). In particular, in adapting to a predatory niche, selection would favour hominids which were faster (all the better to run down, or avoid becoming, prey) and had more endurance (Carrier 1984). Sweating is widespread among Old World Anthropoids, and hominid running doubtless recruited this exaptively, further enhancing its significance through the thermoregulatory advantages of hairlessness (Wheeler 1985). The adaptation to running would require adjustments to the breathing and respiration systems. Support for this argument is provided by the stress related robustness (hypertrophy) of the lower limb bones of early *Homo* and later hominids (Trinkaus 1987). In addition, carnivores that interact peacefully with each other in the pursuit of prey are more successful than solitary animals (Shipman & Walker 1989), a feature that motivated our discussion of cooperation among apes in Chapter 2. Unfortunately, such interactions cannot be measured through archaeological evidence.

Meat-eaters generally have teeth well-suited to cutting meat (Shipman & Walker 1989), something that is difficult to derive exaptively from a primate common ancestor. Hominids moving into a more carnivorous niche would have been favoured if they used cutting tools, evidenced by the discovery of meat-polish on the edges of some of the earliest stone tools of *Homo erectus* (Keeley & Toth 1981).

Meat-eaters have low population densities, for otherwise they would tend to destroy their food-supply (Shipman & Walker 1989). In the evolutionary emergence of greater primate carnivory, we might expect that one option would be greater tendency to migrate and high mobility.

Finally, in the theoretical survey by Shipman and Walker, the length of time from conception to birth (gestation) scales to body size (mass) for both herbivores and carnivores. For carnivores with body mass greater than 1 kg, gestation time is shorter than for herbivores of similar weight. Carnivores are more altricial—the young are born more helpless and are dependent on their parents for longer. With hominids, gestation length has shortened in relation to brain size, because infants born at the same stage of brain growth as other primates would require a huge birth canal in the mother. This, in turn would lead to changes in gait. The dimensions of the pelvis of the Nariokotome skeleton (taking into account that it was male) suggest that the distinctive human gait was already in place in *Homo erectus* (Shipman & Walker 1989). Among humans, brain growth continues at the foetal rate outside the mother's body to a greater extent than among other primates. Selection has led to 'secondary atriciality'—prolonged dependence (compared with other primates) outside the mother's body (Jones et al. 1992)—in line with, but distinct from, the pattern for carnivores. The pelvis of the Nariokotome skeleton suggests such dependence was already a feature of hominid infancy.

Anatomical, archaeological and developmental evidence all indicates that *Homo erectus* had increased meat consumption by comparison with other primates. Some of these adaptations had consequences for other aspects of behaviour: the use of flaked stone tools; the process of dispersal; and the greater involvement of adults as caregivers in the maturation of offspring, particularly interacting with the postnatal development of the brain. Meat became a major component of the diet of hominids from *Homo erectus* onwards.

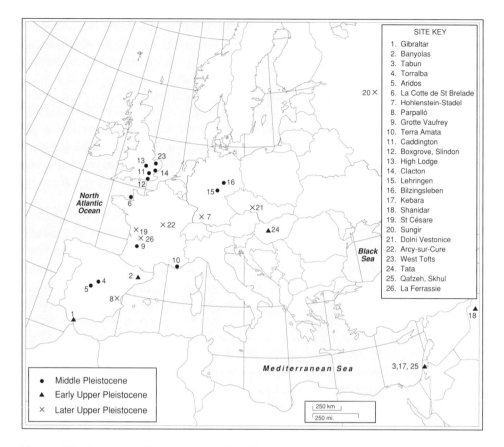

Figure 38 Location of European and Mediterranean sites mentioned in the text, from Middle and Upper Pleistocene.

Data from wear marks on teeth after *Homo erectus* are not abundant, and interpretation is not straightforward. Analysis of specimens from Africa, Europe and Asia shows variation between examples from different time periods (species), between those from different environments and between individuals from the same site (Puech et al. 1983). European Neanderthals show some sign of meat-eating, as does an early modern human from Kabwe in Africa (Puech et al. 1980). A Neanderthal juvenile from Gibraltar (in southern Spain) (see Figure 38) showed signs of meat-eating, with tooth abrasion most similar to that found among recent Eskimos or Fuegians (Lalueza Fox & Pérez-Pérez 1993), while the possibly contemporary Banyolas mandible (from northern Spain) showed an abrasive vegetable diet (Lalueza Fox et al. 1993). While these results appear equivocal, the analysis of use-wear on stone tools is unambiguous. At almost all sites where stone tools show traces of use, there are artefacts with the distinctive polish caused by cutting meat, and others used on animal skins (Anderson-Gerfaud 1990; Beyries 1987; Frame 1986; Keeley 1980; 1981; Shea 1989), as well as blood residues on the margins of stone tools from Tabun (Loy & Hardy 1992), in a layer now dated at around 150 000 years ago (Grün et al. 1991).

From our earlier arguments, the significance of the dietary shift was in the fact that meat was procured, not primarily in how it was. Scavenging may have been for the leftovers from other carnivores that were of nutritional value to hominids— heads and marrow; or, it might have involved getting to the carcase more quickly than other scavengers, for meatier parts; it may have been the primary source of food, or of meat, or only one of a number of strategies for obtaining animal protein and fat (Chase 1988). Hunting might be similarly broken down into cooperative or individual action by the hunters; capture of individual prey or multiple prey; confrontation hunting or killing at a distance (Geist 1978); it might involve immediate consumption or the removal of meat or of body parts with meat to a secure place or a 'home base'. Either scavenging or hunting might be opportunistic or systematic, and either activity might occur with or without the efficiencies that could accrue from attending to repetitive cues from the environment (vultures indicate a dead animal, fresh tracks indicate the passage of prey).

We were careful in Chapter 2 to point out the absurdity of denying the word hunting to the predatory activities of chimpanzees. It seems equally absurd to deny that hominids had the capacity to run down and kill certain classes of animals. The question for later periods is the extent of prior intent in hunting among hominids.

Some of the classic textbook examples from earlier prehistory are no longer considered as hunting: the giant baboon bones from Olorgesaile, in Kenya (between 1.7 Myr and 0.5 Myr) (Shipman et al. 1981) are not now believed to have been accumulated and broken by hominids (Koch 1990); the site of Torralba, (undated, but perhaps 0.2 Myr in Spain) claimed to show the use of fire to drive elephants into a bog where they could be dispatched and butchered (Howell 1964) on closer analysis shows opportunistic exploitation of horses and deer with probable expedient scavenging of leftovers (Binford 1987; Klein 1987). Elephant (and other large animal) carcases may have been exploited by hominids of these times, as at Olorgesaile (Potts 1989) or Aridos (in Spain probably contemporary with Torralba) (Villa 1990), or at La Cotte de St Brelade (in Jersey, dated from about 0.25 Myr to 0.19 Myr) (Callow 1986a), where on separate occasions mammoths and rhinoceros seem to have been driven off a cliff (Scott 1986). Klein suggests that in southern Africa, hominids (probably *Homo erectus*) rarely killed the large ungulates, bones of which are common at the sites where stone tools are found. Later, about 100 000 years ago, at Klasies River Mouth in South Africa, probably associated with the earliest hominids of modern skeletal form, animal protein and fat were obtained by hunting small to medium sized animals and scavenging the largest ones (Binford 1984; Klein 1976).

One recent survey of the evidence of Neanderthals suggests that there is little evidence for systematically organised hunting as practised by modern humans (Stringer & Gamble 1993). The results are not all straightforward: where one scholar sees scavenging by hominids, another cannot (Binford 1988a; Grayson &

Delpech 1994). There are disagreements about the extent of carnivore involvement in adding to or deleting from bone accumulations (in Spain: Davidson 1989c; Lindly 1988). Further insight is provided by the few studies that consider the changes during the Early Upper Pleistocene. Stiner (1990) showed that, in Italy, only sites after the Early Upper Pleistocene show the patterning associated with documented cases of modern human hunting by ambush or trap. It would appear that modern human behaviour led to the consistent capture of prime age animals (Davidson 1989c). Similarly, some Early Upper Pleistocene sites have evidence of scavenging of heads; others are the result of hunting. Only relatively recent sites have faunal collections consistently showing successful hunting (Stiner 1991).

Klein (1980; 1987) showed differences between early and later sites of southern Africa, both associated with hominids of modern human skeletal form. He suggested that only after the Early Upper Pleistocene had people probably developed projectiles or snares and traps that enabled them to procure large or dangerous animals with safety. As with the construction of a boat, making a trap or a multi-part weapon entails a means of representing the end product of one's ongoing actions—the process we call planning.

One outcome of this survey is that, in two regions, human behaviour after the end of the Early Upper Pleistocene was organised differently from earlier hominid behaviour. The differences seem to be explicable in terms of planning and the technology of procurement. What is fundamental to understanding the process of emergence of modern human behaviour is that in the South African case both the hominids and the humans had modern anatomy, while in Europe the hominids were Neanderthals and the behaviourally distinct humans were different from them anatomically. The evidence from the east Mediterranean region seems to offer the third situation, where Neanderthals (though some suggest they are inappropriately so-called) and hominids with modern human anatomy had similar stone tools, killed similar species of animals and behaved rather similarly. Attempts to interpret differences in season of killing the prey (Lieberman & Shea 1994) do not seem to show conclusively that the behaviour of the two anatomical forms was different. The behaviour associated with the emergence of language was not obviously, or simply, derived from anatomical changes.

Handaxes and other tools

Hominid behaviour in the period from the appearance of *Homo erectus* to the appearance of modern human behaviour is generally characterised by archaeologists as involving two successive stone tool industries (the Acheulean and the Mousterian), with some minor variations (early non-Acheulean industries on the periphery of the distribution of Acheulean industries, and the Clactonian flake industry) (Foley 1987b). We have previously discussed how these industries did not require the sort of planning and meaning-making that we are pursuing in this chapter (Davidson & Noble 1993a). Recent reviews suggest that the standard story we

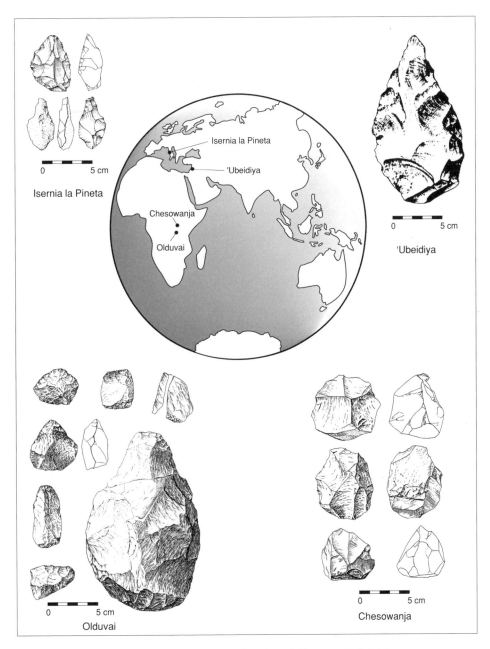

Figure 39 Stone industries, including Acheulean bifaces, 1.5–0.5 Myr.

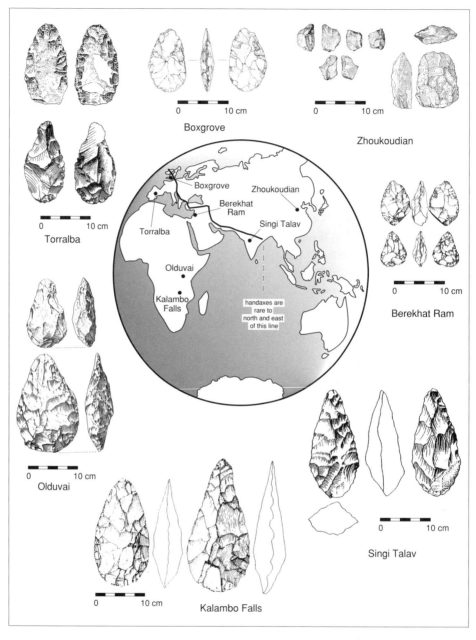

Figure 40 Stone industries around the world, 0.5–0.125 Myr.

discussed previously is on the brink of major reassessment (Villa 1991). We believe this reassessment will make our previous argument less contentious.

The succession of stone industries?

The earliest stone industries (Chapter 6) were the relatively unpatterned ones called Oldowan, where flakes were struck from cobbles, and produced a distinctive end-product (a 'chopper') when successive flakes were removed from the same margin of a core. After about 1.4 Myr (Asfaw et al. 1992), distinctive industries (called Acheulean) emerged in which many flakes were removed from several margins and from both faces of a core. These cores are called Acheulean handaxes or bifaces. Acheulean industries overlap Oldowan industries in time (Clark et al. 1994; Leakey 1971), and may grade through an industry known as Developed Oldowan (Gowlett 1988; Stiles 1979). The handaxes or bifacial cores were often highly regular, highly symmetrical, rather standardised in form (see Figures 39 and 40).

The standard story is that from the earliest appearance of Acheulean industries to about 90 000 years ago (Bischoff et al. 1992) hominids produced flakes from handaxes at sites throughout most of the world. These industries are generally associated with *Homo erectus*, though there is some disagreement about whether European hominids should be called by that name. (In keeping with our scepticism about the reality of the species names used by palaeoanthropologists, it seems to us highly unlikely that a single stone industry, if patterned by 'culture', could have been produced by two different species.) In the Early Upper Pleistocene, the best documented stone industry is that most usually associated with Neanderthals and called Mousterian. Patterning in Mousterian industries is primarily a result of modification of flake edges (retouching) during use (Dibble 1987; 1989), together with the practice among archaeologists of partitioning of ranges of continuous variation into discrete named artefact types (Barton 1990).

Recent evidence shows that this story has problems. The British site of High Lodge (dated at about 0.5 Myr) (Ashton et al. 1992) shows that industries classified as Mousterian occurred in the same climatic episode in the Middle Pleistocene as Acheulean industries at Boxgrove (Roberts 1986; 1994). At La Cotte de St Brelade (Callow 1986a; 1986b) Mousterian industries were earlier than the Acheulean ones at the same site, and from the same period as the Mousterian at the southwest French site, Grotte Vaufrey (Rigaud 1988). This undermines the traditional sequential view of these industries and supports arguments against conscious design of artefact form by the makers.

The stone industry from High Lodge has retouched flakes (Figure 41). The very early date for High Lodge shows that the practice of retouching flakes was very persistent—hardly a cultural practice restricted in time and space—and primarily dependent on the contingencies of available flakes and necessary actions. As with the Oldowan, modification results from contingent function and the final form depends on both the initial form and on its lifetime of functions. Gamble (1986, 178) considered the early industries of Europe all together, arguing that they 'have little

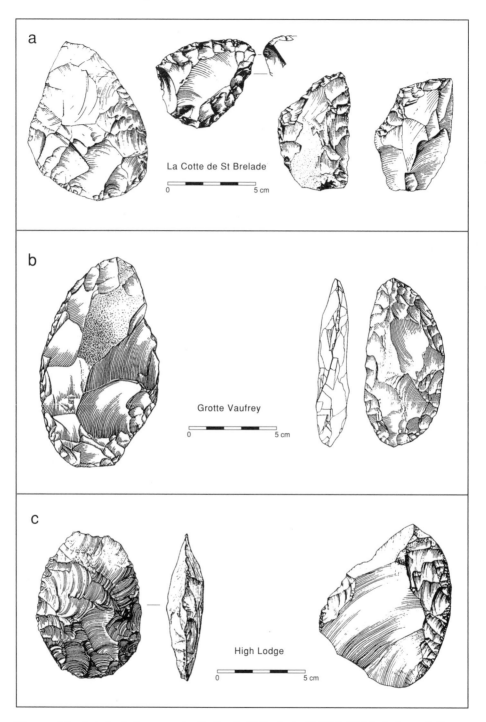

Figure 41 Artefacts from **a** La Cotte de St Brelade (0.25-0.19 Myr), *from* Callow 1986a, **b** Grotte Vaufrey, *from* Rigaud 1988, and **c** High Lodge (>0.5 Myr), *from* Ashton et al. 1992.

temporal ordering and resemble nothing so much as a well stirred minestrone soup of types and techniques that coagulate into industries on the end of the taxonomist's spoon'. This coagulation is another example of the power of naming·with reification of the named entities.

Acheulean handaxes: geometry, aesthetics and planning?

Acheulean handaxes have been the subject of speculation since their first discovery, but most recently attention has been focussed on the appearance of design in their manufacture. Some authors have suggested that the standardisation and symmetry imply modern intellect, use of symbols and appreciation of mathematical regularity (Gowlett 1984). If true, we would probably admit the hominids had language, though Dibble (1989) has effectively shown the fallacy of much of that argument. Wynn (1979; 1993; 1990) sought to use criteria for ontogenetic development devised by Piaget to determine that Acheulean hominids must have had the abilities Piaget associated with the intelligence of adult modern humans (Wynn 1979). More recently, leaving aside Piaget's scheme, Wynn has argued that if the shape of handaxes was intentional then the hominids had a concept of symmetry, and the attendant requirements of conceptualising the actions needed to produce it. We are uncertain how this can be tested. It is possible to analyse those objects recognised as handaxes to reveal symmetry, and, following that, to identify the ways a modern knapper would set out to achieve it. But how to evaluate the assumption of prehistoric intentionality?

Crucial evidence is provided by fitting back together the flakes originally left at sites. Bradley and Sampson (1978) analysed several such conjoin sets from the British site of Caddington, and found several knapping errors (40% of the attempts to 'make bifaces' had broken through applying too much force). Another specimen was flaked and then discarded before 'completion' as a handaxe, implying rather less planning and foresight than Wynn proposes. At least ten flakes are missing from the conjoin set associated with this piece, suggesting that the flakes were sought, rather than a biface. Finally, one other conjoin set was sufficiently complete to allow a cast to be made of the core that had been removed when the flakes were abandoned (Figure 42). It shows that while the core was bifacial, it was not symmetrical. We can only guess whether it would have (or did) become symmetrical in subsequent use as a source of more flakes.

At Boxgrove, only two artefacts were reported to conjoin onto handaxes, while much larger conjoin sets resulted either from the removal of flakes from non-bifacial cores, or from the removal of the soft outer cortex of the nodules (rounded lumps of stone) being obtained at the site (Bergman & Roberts 1988). Davidson's examination of a collection of artefacts from the neighbouring site of Slindon showed a similar collection of flakes made in removing the outer cortex of flint nodules, together with other flint flakes and cores and a non-flint handaxe. As hominids at both sites had access to flint nodules in the same geological formation, an explanation has to be found for the non-flint handaxe at Slindon. We suggest that

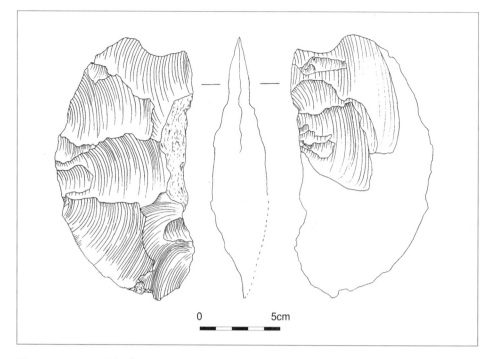

Figure 42 Mould of core removed from knapping areas at Caddington. *From* Bradley & Sampson 1978.

this, like the flint handaxes at Boxgrove, was abandoned when hominids at the site were able to obtain new flint to prepare cores (by removing the cortex from nodules). These might, in turn, have been turned into handaxes by repeated flaking. The flint handaxes at Boxgrove should not be regarded as a stockpile resulting from the flaking that happened at the site, but as discards at the end of their useful life. In a pattern of activity where hominids were carrying stone tools with them when they arrived at a source of raw material suitable for resupplying, they might discard the tool that had been used many times. Sometimes it was from a different source (as at Slindon), sometimes from the same one (as at Boxgrove).

This evidence seems to suggest that these hominids were as interested in the flakes as in the symmetry or proportions of the end-product. How does this fit with the evidence from other times and places?

Acheulean handaxe: tool or source of tools?

The apparent intent shown by the form of Acheulean (and other) handaxes has been taken to imply that production of handaxes was the objective of knapping. This may not be the whole story, or even the right one. We have previously suggested that talking about the shape of handaxes involves the 'finished artefact fallacy' (Davidson & Noble 1993a). There is empirical support for this claim that archaeologists have been considering as intended final products artefacts that are better considered as

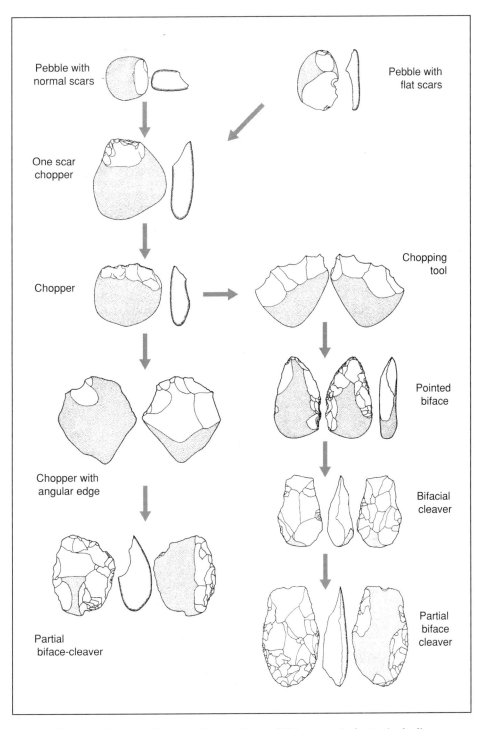

Figure 43   Continuity of forms of Lower Palaeolithic stone industry including bifaces. Modified *from* Villa 1983.

'finished with' than as 'finished'. Villa shows at Terra Amata (in southern France, dated at 230 000 years ago by thermoluminescence, or 380 000 years ago by Electron Spin Reonance) continuity of forms classified as discontinuous by typology (Figure 43). This shows that bifaces are only recognised by archaeologists when they have the characteristics said (by Wynn and many others) to be the forms of finished artefacts intended by the knappers. Archaeologists have invented names for all sorts of other shapes that might have been produced along the way, and call them all 'tools'.

Binford (1972) showed that there were different patterns of occurrence of handaxes and of flakes and flake-tools in Acheulean industries. Many Acheulean examples of butchery had large numbers of sharp flakes associated, and relatively few handaxes (Clark and Haynes 1970). Recent work at Olorgesaile also shows that Acheulean flakes were used in butchery (Potts 1989), just as they were in the Oldowan (Keeley & Toth 1981).

These observations present two problems: first, why is the evidence for the polish caused by cutting meat only remarkable for its consistency, not its abundance; and second, why are there some sites with very large concentrations of handaxes? The first is certainly affected by the analytical problem that there has been a tendency only to look at tools identified by the modification of their edges by the removal of further small flakes (retouching) (Frame 1986), despite the fact that there is evidence that meat polish is more abundant on unretouched than retouched flakes at some sites (Beyries 1987; Keeley 1980). Some handaxes show use-wear from cutting meat (Keeley 1993), but in general the edge may be unsuitable except for heavy duty butchery. The unretouched flakes removed from handaxes, on the other hand, provided the sharpest edges that can be made, and repeated flaking could produce more when one becomes dulled by the accumulation of fat and meat. This may also mean that some unretouched flakes were discarded during butchery before they could acquire meat-polish.

The sharp margins of the handaxe actually make it unsuitable for use *as* an axe held (necessarily with power grip) in the hand. But this is a feature which enters into one answer to the second question. Whether they were ever intended to be thrown, it is true that the symmetry ensures the aerodynamic efficiency of handaxes (O'Brien 1981). Many of the sites with large numbers of handaxes were near watercourses. These might be the result of hydraulic sorting in active stream channels which deposited the similarly sized and shaped handaxes in one part of the stream channel, and the lighter flakes in others. On the other hand, Calvin (1993) has pointed out how effective would be a strategy of throwing handaxes into a herd of animals drinking at the bank of stream or waterhole. Once an animal had been felled, the hominids might have retrieved the meat rather than the handaxe that fell into the water. This would be unsurprising if the classic handaxe shape represents a core near the end of its useful life.

There is also reason to question the standard view (Jones et al. 1992, 352-353) that the form of Acheulean bifaces dominated the production of stone tools from 1.4

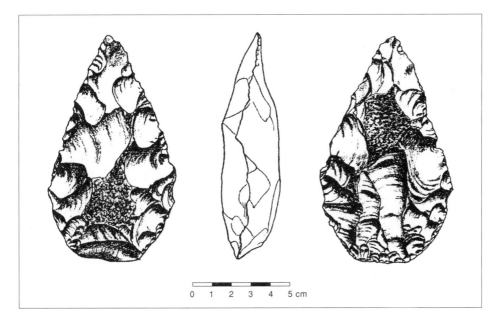

Figure 44   A 'handaxe' from the Barkly Tableland, Northern Territory (Australia). *From* Rainey 1991.

Myr to 90 000 years ago. The reality is that this has not been continuous either in time or space. There is more than a hint that perceptions of the importance of handaxes are biased by the interest in them by archaeologists. Bifaces were certainly produced outside the Acheulean tradition. They have been found in some parts of Australia (Rainey 1991) (Figure 44), that are symmetrical about a plane and about the plan of that plane. As Australia was first colonised after the 'end' of the Acheulean tradition, the features that link these objects to the Acheulean result from something other than a common tradition of producing stone flakes and cores. It seems likely that common processes involve aspects of economy of flaking or use rather than intentions to produce a particular form.

Importantly, bifacial handaxes seem not to have been widely produced in east Asia (but were not entirely absent). Many factors might contribute to this difference (Schick 1994; Schick & Toth 1993, 276-279), and it may be a response to the availability of bamboo as raw material for tools. In parts of Europe, there is a longstanding recognition of flake industries apparently without handaxes, called the Clactonian. At some sites, however, this industry seems very like Acheulean but that handaxes had not been found (Ashton et al. 1994). Mithen (1994), following Wymer (1988), has pointed out that Acheulean industries tend to be found in open country, while the flake industries tend to wooded environments. This observation fits with the handaxe throwing hypothesis.

Mithen (1994) (and commentators) suggest that the flake industries result from individual learning of knapping skills, while the continuity of making more complex forms such as handaxes results from enhanced social learning in larger groups.

We suggested in Chapter 6 that the conditions of increased altriciality of hominids led to increased occasions for joint attention with caregivers, and increased opportunities for observational learning. The repeated forms of stone artefacts such as handaxes seem likely to be the result of learned motor actions rather than deliberate design or 'planned' attempts to reproduce a 'mental template' of the ideal form. The contexts of learning stone knapping may have been favourable for the selection of 'scaffolding' behaviour such as that claimed as teaching among chimpanzees.

The Levallois technique: why it is not important

At some time (probably 300 000 years ago or more) during the period of hominids making tools of the Acheulean industry, there appeared a technique called Levallois which, in the traditional interpretation, has the appearance of planning much more than any earlier stone tool making. The technique was used in both Acheulean and Mousterian industries. The standard interpretation is that a core was prepared in such a way that a flake of predetermined shape could be removed (Boëda 1988; Bordes 1961). We have already pointed out that this interpretation is sometimes paradoxical, given instances of the final flake being discarded with the prepared core (Davidson & Noble 1993a; Schafer 1990; Van Peer 1992). In addition, the basic form of the core from which these supposedly important flakes were struck was present from the earliest stone industries at Olduvai Gorge (Davidson & Noble 1993a; Leakey 1971), so it does not seem likely that such cores represented a novelty in planning beginning at the time the Levallois technique is said to appear. Rather, such cores had been used for producing flakes almost from the very beginning, and continued to be so used even after knappers began to strike large flakes from them.

The hypothesis that cores were shaped to produce a final flake of predetermined (planned) form suggests (from a present-day perspective) a wastefulness of knapping effort and raw material that seems implausible. Support for this position is given by conjoining studies (Van Peer 1992). The logic of the interpretation of the Levallois technique suggests that cores were knapped to produce a single flake that was removed for use. If this is true, conjoining of the many preparation flakes, and the core, should commonly be possible. Van Peer's study shows that there are frequent conjoins, but not only do Levallois flakes appear to remain with the cores, conjoining is only possible by allowing for other flakes that have been removed. The same is true at Grotte Vaufrey (Geneste 1988). It is the flakes produced along the way that were used, rather than, particularly, the 'predetermined' flake. In addition, among unretouched artefacts, more Levallois flakes did not show signs of use, while more of the non-Levallois flakes showed them (Beyries 1987). In some studies, as few as 12% of the Levallois artefacts showed such signs (Shea 1989). This seems a curious end to a wasteful plan. Finally, Dibble (1989) suggested that there was a reasonable expectation that the supposed predetermination of the shape of Levallois flakes should produce greater standardisation of flake dimensions than among flakes from bifaces or other flakes. He found that this was not true.

Modern experimental knappers attempting to reproduce what they think was the intention of the prehistoric knappers sometimes find that Levallois products are difficult to reproduce (Hayden 1993). It may be that this is because the prehistoric knappers had no such intention. Other experimental knappers have found that Levallois flakes are produced as unintentional products of biface manufacture, and have reported them from prehistoric handaxe knapping floors, including a specimen that conjoins to a handaxe (Bradley & Sampson 1978; 1986). The case for 'planning' in industries with Levallois technique needs to be more carefully made.

Variation in the Mousterian

Causes of variation in the stone tool industries associated with Neanderthals, called the Mousterian by those who do not accept Gamble's lumping together of early European stone industries, have been amongst the most debated issues in archaeology (Rolland & Dibble 1990). François Bordes (e.g. Bordes & de Sonneville-Bordes 1970), chiefly responsible for systematising the naming of the tool types and the different sorts of Mousterian industries, attributed the variation of relative frequencies of flaked stone artefacts to the style of tools preferred by different ethnic groups circulating around the southwestern region of France. Binford and Binford (1966) objected that tools were for using, and sought to explain the artefact frequencies in terms of different tool-kits. As Rolland and Dibble suggest, both approaches rested on invalid assumptions about the reality of the categories of objects named by archaeologists, and then about the reality of the groups of artefacts named in the next stage of analysis. Dibble (1987; 1989) has shown that many of the tool types defined as separate entities by Bordes (and those who use his classification scheme) are produced during the use-life of a single flake as it is successively transformed by reduction of edges by retouching when the edge is no longer serviceable. Beyries (1987) shows that the forms distinguished by typologists do not have consistent patterns of use-wear. This does not seem to be the production of forms for particular functions, rather it confirms the suggestion made above of contingent use of flakes according to the tasks at hand. Most recently, Rolland and Dibble (1990) have argued that much of the variation results from raw material availability and intensity of reduction and use of the tools. Again, these results indicate that hominids were not 'planning' their tool making strategies but adjusting to local circumstances as resource availability and need demanded. The stone tools of hominids before what we are calling the emergence of modern human behaviour do not indicate planning or other features that suggest we should attribute them with language.

Raw material movements

The raw material for making stone tools is only available at particular locations, so that different patterns for obtaining raw material have been taken to indicate planning depth (Féblot-Augustins 1993; Potts 1988; Roebroeks et al. 1988; Whallon 1989). As we noted in Chapter 6, the evidence is that hominids were carrying stone

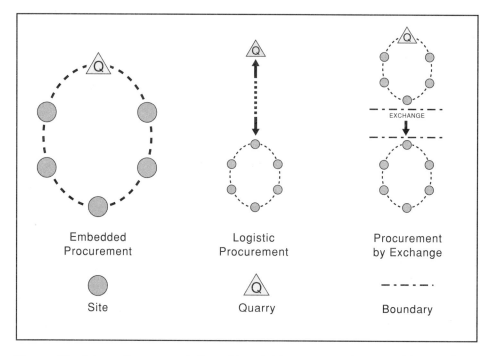

Figure 45   Schematic representation of hominid movements between 'sites' and quarries in different systems of raw material procurement.

around with them from the very earliest use of stone tools, and, in any activities involving potentially fatal interaction with other predators or scavengers, natural selection would favour hominids that did so. If this was not the case, there would be very little archaeological record at all. How and where hominids obtained their supplies of raw material for stone tools is less certain. As Potts (1988) argued for Olduvai Gorge, Roebroeks and his colleagues have suggested 'economical' 'organisation' for the supply of raw material in Middle Palaeolithic sites, on the basis of evidence that 'retouched items were discarded at much larger distances from the source than non-retouched items' in several regions of Europe, as well as North Africa and the East Mediterranean regions (Rolland & Dibble 1990).

There are fundamental differences in organisation of activities represented by the different means of acquisition of raw material. The simplest level involves the acquisition of raw material during the everyday movements characteristic of all foraging hominids. We might call this embedded procurement—procurement incidental to some other activity (Figure 45). We believe that there is little need to infer any more complex procurement than this for any period earlier than the emergence of language. More complex is logistic procurement, where special purpose trips were made to obtain particular raw materials. This label might be attached to the inferred movements of chimpanzees to recover hammers for nut-cracking (Boesch & Boesch 1984). Obtaining raw material by exchange or trade is not claimed for any situation earlier than the emergence of modern human behaviour.

Most work, hitherto, has not considered these fundamental distinctions about raw material procurement, but has concentrated on the distances between source and site (Roebroeks et al. 1988). The most detailed analysis (Geneste 1988) suggests that there are significantly fewer retouched artefacts made on local materials (within 5 km of the site) than on those from more distant sources (more than 30 km from site). This is what we would expect in a situation where tools were routinely carried with the foragers for contingent use, and replaced as opportunities arose. It is not a strong case for planned or organised stone procurement. Indeed, for periods earlier than the emergence of modern human behaviour, the case still needs to be made for *organisation* of raw material procurement, rather than variation resulting from the contingencies of use of places and resources (Kuhn 1991; Stiner & Kuhn 1992).

Tool novelties that indicate the emergence of modern human behaviour

Through all of the discussion of tools we must remember that stone was not the only material being used. While we emphasise the presence of meat polish on the earliest stone tools, some have polish from cutting plants, but three others have wood-working use-wear (Keeley & Toth 1981). The incidence of wooden tools is underestimated by the destruction of most wooden objects, but use-wear studies are consistent in finding that stone tools, particularly scrapers, were used to work wood (Anderson-Gerfaud 1990; Beyries 1987; Keeley 1980; Shea 1989). This evidence is reinforced by the very rare examples of surviving wooden tools. Most remarkable among these are the two instances of 'spears', from Clacton (England), dated about 300 000 years ago (Oakley et al. 1977), and from Lehringen (Germany), 120 000 years ago (Thieme & Veil 1985). Gamble interprets both of these as possible 'snow-probes' for identifying carcases buried beneath snow (Gamble 1986), though we have no problem with identifying them as spears. Whether they were spears or snow-probes in any contingency of use, the issue for our argument is the degree of planning involved in their production.

We have argued against the planning of the form of stone artefacts for the Middle and Early Late Pleistocene. Do not the wooden tools imply precisely that sort of planning? The extent of planning can be exaggerated. McNabb (1989) has shown that the form of point produced on wood depends on the starting conditions (shape of wood, type of edge). It seems likely that 'pointed sticks' were produced rather than deliberately designed spears of a particular type. Given that scraping has been a hominid activity for 2 million years, hominids show similarity to chimpanzees in the simplicity of the tool produced, though the use of one tool to make another one clearly distinguishes between humans and chimpanzees (McGrew 1987; Noble & Davidson 1991).

What is most remarkable, given the shaping shown by the two wooden spears, is the absence of bone worked in similar ways earlier than the emergence of modern

Figure 46 Flaked bone tools from Bilzingsleben. (Photograph by Davidson, courtesy of Dietrich Mania).

human behaviour. Bone survives much better than wood in the archaeological record, yet bone tools before the end of the Early Upper Pleistocene are only made by flaking (Mania 1983) (Figure 46), hence, like stone, subject to the constraints of mechanics in the shapes that can be produced. Bone tools made by grinding, not flaking, first appear after the Early Upper Pleistocene in Europe and the East Mediterranean (Mellars 1989a), possibly at the same time in South Africa (Singer & Wymer 1982) and occur in the oldest layers at several sites in Australia (Davidson & Noble 1992). Grinding allows the production of shapes relatively independent of the mechanical constraints attendant upon flaking. Hayden (1993) is dismissive of the significance of this: 'There is no empirical or even common sense basis for [the] claim that the manufacture of bone tools requires a different or more complex conceptualization process than the manufacture of stone tools. ... It takes little imagination and virtually no skill to produce a bone awl or spatula, or most other bone implements.' The empirical evidence is that such tools were *not* produced earlier in prehistory and not by any hominids other than modern humans, some early claims having been overinterpreted (Davidson 1990). It seems more likely that this novel achievement does represent a conceptualisation of the form being aimed at that had not been achieved before.

The evidence of ground bone tools occurs at the same time (and in some of the same sites) as the earliest appearance of carving of bone and ivory to make three-dimensional figures of animals and imaginary creatures (see Figure 9, Chapter 3) (Hahn 1972; 1986). It could be that this was simply the transfer into a durable medium of a skill applied to wood, but we believe otherwise. The techniques to make bone tools had been present, in principle, since the scraping of the first wooden tools, but had not been applied to bone, just as the techniques to make the highly standardised stone tools made by humans had been present for more than a million years. It seems much more likely that the lack of 'imagination' Hayden speaks of—what we would call the lack of a concept of the final, intended form—constrained hominids in the production of tool forms.

The same story can be told in stone artefacts. Most modification of tools as late as the Early Upper Pleistocene was modification of the working edge in the contingencies of use. After the Early Upper Pleistocene, stone tools were made with what Mellars (1989a) calls 'imposed form', often shown by the modification of non-working edges, as in the backed pieces from the Chatelperronian from France or the Howieson's Poort industry in South Africa (see Davidson & Noble 1993a). Each of these features of the changing technology across the period of emergence of modern human behaviour might have some simpler explanation (in which case we would find it difficult to identify the emergence of modern human behaviour at all), but their conjunction in time is suggestive that for the first time, several features of hominid behaviour cannot be so easily explained as by the presence of humans, now using language and capable of visualising forms of tools and innovating in a number of ways.

By now the story is becoming familiar. We have examined the data in the two major classes of evidence for prehistoric human behaviour, those concerning acquisition of food from animals and the tools involved (with animals and other things). There is little sign of behaviour that necessarily required the sort of planning and foresight we attribute to the use of language. At least one of the methodological problems in both cases is the power of naming that we have alluded to throughout this work. Having shown this for the major categories of evidence, we need not detain ourselves overlong with the evidence from several other categories—fire, shelter, and burial—for which the data are more inconsistent and equally difficult to interpret.

Fire

Recent review shows how tenuous are the claims for early use of or control of fire in Africa, Asia and Europe (James 1989) before the appearance of Neanderthals. Archaeologists tend to concentrate on these claims, sometimes because of the spectacular images they suggest. We have already noted that claims for the use of fire in hunting elephants at Torralba and Ambrona can no longer be accepted, but Gamble (1993) revives speculation about fire use by early hominids by suggesting it was necessary to defrost frozen mammoth meat! The reality is somewhat different. Archaeologists have worked hard looking for fires (e.g. Barbetti 1986), but have found it difficult to distinguish between natural fires and those for which hominids were responsible (Clark & Harris 1985). There are some early sites with evidence of burning (Callow et al. 1986), some of which seem likely to have involved hominids, but there are many more sites with no charcoal and no other evidence of fires. Initially modest evidence (and modest claims) have become more exaggerated with the telling. At Terra Amata, there are quite detailed observations of the features claimed to be fireplaces (Villa 1983, 79-80). These consisted of: 'an area of reddened sand about 30 cm wide, with traces of charcoal and reddened pebbles ... indicating the location of a hearth. There seems to have been nearby a small pile of pebbles ... Above and in the same area ... concentrations of charcoal were observed ... suggesting repeated use of the same fireplace'.

As with claims from most early sites (Klein 1989, 218), this could result from natural fires, but, in any case, Villa's reports of the original observations are transformed at the hands of later commentators. Thus, Schick and Toth (1993, 280) state that 'depressions with burned material were discovered with rocks on one side, suggesting a hearth with a windbreak (facing the direction of the prevailing winds today).' The issue is clouded if judgement is to be based on anything other than the primary evidence.

How might hominids have obtained fire? The inconsistent pattern of occurrence at early sites, once the dubious claims have been eliminated, does not suggest that hominids were adept at making fire. If they were obtaining it from natural fires, little other than response to immediate contingencies is indicated. McGrew (1989a) even suggests that chimpanzees might be able to 'manage' fire once they have access to it.

If hominids are argued to be making fire, we must consider how they did so and how they discovered how to do so. Little attention has been paid in the archaeological literature to the physics of making fire. Two circumstances seem to be required: the production of heat by friction or spark, and the presence of a suitable combustible substance in contact with that heat. We doubt that the sparks produced from flaking stone are suitable: they may not be hot enough, and would not retain heat long enough to burn grass. Friction is a better candidate, but all known ethnographic examples involve wood-on-wood friction. Cutting wood with bamboo tools might be a suitable candidate for the accidental discovery of fire making, and once discovered this might be a practice as easily learned and reproduced as stone tool making.

There is some suggestion that localised burnt areas perhaps associated with Neanderthals occasionally look like prepared fireplaces (Straus 1989), but generally these are isolated and unusual (Stringer & Gamble 1993). More usual for the earliest sites with evidence of repeated burning is that there are layers of ash without any patterning in the distribution of other archaeological evidence around them, as at Klasies River Mouth in South Africa (Singer & Wymer 1982). An exception is the site of Kebara (Bar-Yosef & Vandermeersch 1991; Bar-Yosef et al. 1992), where among the layers of repeated burning were smaller areas of localised burning that might be interpreted as hearths. It looks unlikely that there was general control of production of fire earlier than the emergence of other features of modern human behaviour.

Shelter

Fire is suggested as an essential element of the colonisation of cold environments. It is one aspect of the control of microenvironments: the construction of shelter is another. Production of nests is one of the things we allowed to the common ancestor, though protection from cold, rain or heat does not seem to be a prime function of the sort of nests made by other primates. There is rare evidence of overhead cover in apes, but only in response to immediate contingencies (Groves & Sabater Pí 1985).

Archaeological evidence for the construction of shelters is subject to the same limitations as other claims for human uniqueness in the evidence of hominid behaviour: claims are often exaggerated. An arrangement of small stones at the DK site in Olduvai Gorge (one of the oldest sites there) was claimed to be the remains of the stones at the base of a hut made from saplings and branches (Leakey 1971). The claim has been shown to be unlikely, not least because it occurs at the site with the largest number of signs (teeth) that live crocodiles were there and at the time hominids were there also (Davidson & Solomon 1990). Likewise, much has been made of the claim for a hut at Terra Amata (de Lumley 1969), but the evidence is tenuous. Villa (1983) describes it as consisting of patches of discolouration in the sand interpreted as postholes, with from one to four examples each in seven strata, implying successive discrete occupation of similar huts. Villa's successful conjoining of artefacts from different strata suggests that the apparent integrity of each of these occupations is not as great as the original excavators claimed. The hut appears more like wishful thinking than good evidence of shelter.

One supporting aspect of the Terra Amata interpretation is the limitation on the distribution of materials. The hut interpretation attributes this to a barrier created by the walls of the hut. On the other hand, limits to distribution of materials are created also by the mechanics of actions and the rubbish they leave. There is experimental evidence to show how far stone flakes are dispersed when knappers are standing or sitting (Newcomer & Sieveking 1980), and such limited dispersals (Binford 1978) probably account for some of the apparent boundaries to these and other archaeological distributions, including that claimed at Bilzingsleben (Mania 1983).

The earliest unimpeachable structured shelters were the huts constructed from mammoth bones and mandibles on the Russian and Ukranian plain dated 30 000 to 20 000 years ago, facilities implying planning after the emergence of language (see Gamble 1986, 263-268). The issue urgently needs synthesis such as James (1989) has done for the evidence for fire. As we would expect, the construction of effective artificial shelter cannot be confirmed at any date earlier than the emergence of modern human behaviour.

Burial

There have been two recent syntheses of Neanderthal burial (Gargett 1989; Smirnov 1989), Gargett seeking to question the reliability of the evidence, and Smirnov taking it for granted. We tend to side with Gargett, for reasons we will outline briefly. Aside from the Nariokotome skeleton there have been hardly any other hominid remains, before Neanderthals, where different anatomical elements can be easily attributed to the same skeleton. The apparently sudden appearance of several examples scattered across the distribution of Neanderthals is the prime reason for believing that these hominids were the first to bury their dead. And those who believe the argument for burial seek to account for it by the appearance of self-awareness, hygiene or olfactory sensitivity. Some go so far as to posit the appearance of religious belief. Such accounts do not provide a mechanism for the appearance of these novel aspects of consciousness, though we suggest they are all primarily products of evaluations based on language.

Gargett (1989) argued that the circumstances of survival of Neanderthal skeletons in caves have as much to do with how sediments formed in caves as they do with the behaviour of living Neanderthals. We have suggested (Noble & Davidson 1989) that careful assessment would reduce the number of bodies to be accounted for, and illustrated this by the example of Shanidar Cave, where the word 'burial' is still used to refer to the skeletal remains of Neanderthals generally acknowledged to have died when the cave roof collapsed onto them. Pollens and other parts of flowers (the ones mentioned at the end of Chapter 3) were found in sediment around one skeleton, of an elderly male, suggesting to the excavator that other Neanderthals made offerings of these flowers (Solecki 1975). Keeley (1993) has suggested that there is evidence from the Acheulean site of Hoxne for the gathering of plant material for bedding—a behaviour akin to nest-building. Such a practice would provide a simple explanation (Noble & Davidson 1989) for the pollen and flowers found at Shanidar. On this interpretation, the individual was killed where he slept when rocks from the roof fell onto him.

There is general agreement that, while the burials of modern humans sometimes (but not always) contain objects that are likely to have been buried with the corpse, Neanderthal skeletons are only accompanied by things that are indistinguishable from the other artefacts and objects to be found in the sediments of the cave (Harrold 1980). One of the problems is that so many of the skeletons were excavated a long time ago, before excavation methods had been refined, and before the subtleties of interpretation were defined. Of the two most recently excavated Neanderthal skeletons, no one has claimed a burial pit for the St Césaire individual (the 'last Neanderthal' dated at 32 000 years, by thermoluminescence which might give a radiocarbon date several thousand years more recent), while the Kebara 2 skeleton (dated around 60 000 years by thermoluminescence) is shown in a depression in the sediment, but there is no sign that that depression was filled in to cover the body (Bar-Yosef et al. 1992, Figure 13).

Gamble (1993) points out that there are no claims for intentional burial of Neanderthals from sites outside caves. There are open air burials among the earliest burials of modern people (e.g. Lake Mungo, Sungir, Dolni Vestonice). This observation tends to support Gargett's argument. We have also to take into account that the geomorphic phenomenon is not new—cave sediments had been forming and deforming long before Neanderthals—but survival of relatively complete skeletons is. Gamble suggests that this relates to successful competition with carnivores: Neanderthal 'burials' occur in regions where there were no longer abundant carnivores to devour the corpse, and are absent from regions where there still were (such as Eastern Europe). This interpretation gains confirmation from the absence of burials of archaic or modern hominids in Africa, and the presence of human burials in relatively carnivore-free Australia (Lake Mungo) as early as those in Europe. Some of the earliest open-site burials in Europe (Dolni Vestonice and Sungir) occur in precisely those regions where there are no Neanderthal 'burials' in or out of caves. Discovery of one Neanderthal 'burial' outside a cave would do more than anything else to provide convincing evidence that the act of burial involved disposal of the dead by other hominids, and not merely by natural processes. We do not believe that the existing evidence is adequate to support an argument from burial to self-awareness, still less to religion. It cannot inform us about the emergence of modern human behaviour.

The question of early symbols

There is recent synthesis about claims for early symbolism (Chase & Dibble 1987; Davidson 1990; Duff et al.1992; Hayden 1993; Lindly & Clark 1990; Marshack 1989; Schepartz 1993; Taborin 1990). Marshack (1989) has drawn attention to several isolated objects that, properly interpreted, might indicate a gradual appearance of the use of symbols in enduring material. Chase and Dibble (1987) began the process of examining such claims sceptically, concluding that there was no good evidence of symbolic behaviour among Neanderthals. Examination of several of the objects championed by Marshack leaves no doubt that they have been wrongly interpreted (Davidson 1990; 1991) and their form can, generally, be accounted for by alteration in the jaws of carnivores or by other natural processes (Chase 1990). Taborin (1990) concurs, that the signs of decoration appear for the first time in the sequence at Arcy-sur-Cure after the likely appearance of modern human behaviour. Lindly and Clark (1990, 238-9) show that, in addition, 'as Chase and Dibble have reported for archaic *H. sapiens*, the daily activities of pre-Upper Paleolithic morphologically modern humans had no archaeologically discernible symbolic component.' They acknowledge, however, that there is 'equivocal, but scarce' (p.237) evidence from southern Africa (at Klasies River Mouth and Border Cave); this evidence seems, to us and to others (e.g. Mellars 1990), much less equivocal than any of the claims for the Neanderthal sites of Europe.

One claim is that makers of Acheulean handaxes, earlier than Neanderthals,

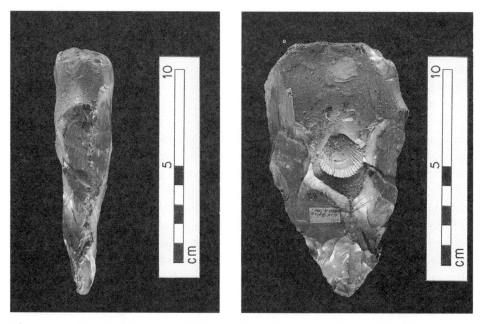

Figure 47 Handaxe from West Tofts, southern Britain (see Figure 40) with fossil shells visible in the cortex of the nodule. The shell is preserved because flaking from the margins has not reached the centre of the artefact (courtesy of the Cambridge University Museum of Archaeology and Anthropology).

deliberately avoided flaking fossil shells off the surface of handaxes (Oakley 1981). This has recently been repeated by others (Bradshaw & Rogers 1993; Hayden 1993) (Figure 47). There are two points here. First, fossil shells are preserved in the cortex of the nodule from which flakes had been struck. Such fossils may be presumed to be frequent features of the cortex of flint nodules, yet there are (so far as we know) only two examples 'preserved' on handaxes. It must have been a far more frequent occurrence that fossils were available to be seen by *Homo erectus* with no attention being paid. Secondly, and in support of the initial scepticism, one of these handaxes has edge angles such that the removal of more flakes is very difficult. The survival of the fossil seems much more likely to be due to the difficulty of further flaking than to any intent on the part of the knapper. This also accounts for the 'central' position of both fossils.

Davidson's (1990) first-hand inspection of some of the early supposedly symbolic objects casts doubt on the existence of any objects that cannot be explained in some other way for the European Neanderthals and hence, perhaps for other parts of the world. Those objects that remain unexplained, such as the fragment of apparently deliberately shaped mammoth tooth from Tata (Hungary), dated perhaps as old as 98 000 years ago, are unique and difficult to construe as part of a system where convention determined the form of symbols. Symbols must be repeated to establish the existence of such convention (Chase & Dibble 1992). It is also claimed that the Tata tooth is covered with ochre (Marshack 1976), though this is not visible now even under magnification.

Ochre

The supposed ochre on the Tata tooth tends to enhance the claim for planned activity that is not explained by reaction to immediate contingencies, and some scholars believe that there is a history of the use of ochre before the Upper Pleistocene. Many of the earliest claims have been examined by Butzer (Butzer 1980; Wreschner 1980) and shown to be irrelevant. Examples from Lower and Middle Palaeolithic sites are not ochre, but red rocks over-interpreted by the excavators. As with the case for shelter, there is need for a critical synthesis of the evidence. The most explicit claim, that there were 75 ochre 'crayons' at Terra Amata, has never been adequately published, and the most detailed publication about the site (Villa 1983) does not even mention them. We suspect that, as with other evidence from Terra Amata, the specific claim cannot be justified.

An example of the difficulty of evaluating claims about ochre is given by the Gadeb Acheulean sites in Ethiopia. Here Clark and Kurashina (1979, 35) found: 'heavily weathered basalt fragments which, when rubbed, give a red pigment. None of the pieces show unquestionable evidence of rubbing but the possibility should not be ignored'. This observation solidifies in the conclusion to a claim that the hominids 'may have been experimenting with pigment' (p. 39), while it was only the archaeologists who were!

Claims for ochre increase in Upper Pleistocene sites, with many assertions about its presence with Mousterian industries. Hayden (1993), for example reports 'widespread occurrence of ocre 'crayons' and 'pencils' and occasional large amounts of ocre powder', but does not cite a single primary source for such claims. Some pieces of ochre associated with Mousterian industries were undoubtedly worked (Vandermeersch 1966), though it is not clear for what purpose. In the East Mediterranean, the sites with skeletons of early modern human form associated with Mousterian industries (Qafzeh and Skhul) have ochre, while those that have Neanderthal skeletons (Kebara) do not (Bar-Yosef 1992).

Once humans crossed into Australia, they were using ochre for some purpose, and at more than one site (Davidson & Noble 1992), with large fragments of haematite (red ochre) that show signs of having been ground down. The ochre story needs more modern discoveries accurately assessed before it can be taken to show signs of earlier use of pigment symbolically.

Vocal tracts

Finally we return briefly to the question of anatomy, made more lively by the recent discovery of the earliest surviving hyoid bone (Arensburg et al.1990; Lieberman et al. 1992). This bone (located in the throat), found with the Neanderthal skeleton at Kebara (Israel), is significantly larger than those of modern Arabs in all dimensions

(Arensburg et al. 1989), though sufficiently similar in proportions to suggest that this bone, at least, was not an impediment to the production of vocal utterance. There is not enough known from prehistoric specimens to enable understanding of how this large size might have influenced the production of vocalisations. It is, however, irrelevant to the discussion of language, since we are suggesting that what is important is the symbolic nature of utterance rather than its production involving the throat.

This position also enables us to avoid the controversial view that the vocal abilities of Neanderthals and humans were fundamentally different (Lieberman 1984), when there are strong disagreements about the interpretation of the anatomical evidence in this area (Duchin 1990; Gibson & Jessee 1993; Houghton 1993; Lieberman et al. 1992; Milo & Quiatt 1993). Part of Lieberman's argument is that the Neanderthal throat would not have been as well suited to the production of the vowels a, i and u. Our argument (in Chapter 2) is that the whole set of fine and precise muscular control of vocalisations of modern humans allows not only a wide range of vowel sounds (though Spanish only has five) but more importantly a whole set of consonants, such as other primates *do not* utter.

The essential point here is that it seems likely that *language* could have emerged in a creature that was not as able as us vocally, but that given the advantages of a vocal-auditory channel for communication, selection might favour those that communicated more effectively by that means. If language itself conferred selective advantage, as we believe, then its emergence might provide a context for the selection of different morphology of the oral cavity.

The emerging behaviour of hominids which ultimately led to language

It was on these behavioural bases that language as we know it emerged, with consequent implications for symbol use, minded behaviour and communication that we identified in Chapters 3, 4 and 5. How do the pieces all fit together? We have tried to concentrate on those areas and aspects where the evidence is most easily assessed, which has led, perhaps, to over-emphasis on the early hominids, and on the evidence from Neanderthals and other hominids in their region of distribution. We do not expect that the general pattern of the story will be very different once better behavioural evidence is available from other parts of the world. The regional focus might change, perhaps to southern Africa, but not the general elements of the story.

We have shown the evidence of bipedalism, and cranial thermoregulation leading to absolutely and relatively increasing brain size, with different stages of increase in encephalisation. Brain size increased most markedly long after hominids began to walk fully bipedally, and to have skeletal proportions much like those of modern humans. The major stage of brain size increase took place within the last 200 000 years, without major modification to the pelvis. This increase seems only to have been possible through an evolution of the relation between brain growth and gestation length, such that humans, of all primates, have the longest period of brain growth outside the mother. In consequence, human infants are dependent on caregivers for a higher proportion of their infancy, and much brain development takes place during this critical period. Hairlessness, unidentifiable archaeologically, but inferred as part of the thermoregulatory package, also leads to the need for mothers actively to carry their children, face-to-face, more than among hairy apes. We suggest that this leads to increased incidence of joint attention between mother and infant and more opportunities for learning.

The other great change was meat-eating. We have argued that it was not so important whether hominids were scavengers or killers of prey, as that they were eaters of meat. Bipedalism, however, would have adapted them for running , aided by their propensity to sweat, and humans are adept at running down prey. This adaptation would doubtless bring with it selection for improved efficiency and control of respiratory functions.

Meat provided high quality, high density food that was necessary for the growth of an energy-expensive organ such as the brain. Other consequences of carnivory were the selection for close interaction between individuals, for cutting tools and for high mobility and low population density. Moreover, carnivory made mobility and migration advantageous and opened up the possibility of acquiring food in many different environments, leading to occupation of regions beyond the African tropics.

By one million years ago hominids were present in and beyond Africa as scavengers and opportunistic hunters, using stone tools to cut meat and plants, and to scrape skin and wood. They were relatively successful primates, in the sense that they were persistently present in most of the regions they ever visited, though we suspect they were never consistently present there.

There is a marked absence of directional change in behaviour after initial spread beyond Africa when we consider most aspects of the evidence: obtaining meat involved scavenging and opportunistic hunting at all periods and all regions; stone tool carrying was the first great behavioural adaptation of early hominids, but thereafter, making stone tools (and probably wooden ones) involved a limited set of motor actions (producing some stereotypical products) and the solution of problems arising from immediate contingencies; fire may have been obtained from natural fires where possible, but there is little sign of repeated management and less of fire-making and control; there is also little sign that hominids were able to construct shelters or behave in any other way that suggests the planning and foresight we attribute to the reflectivity that flows from language. There were some environmental barriers to these successful primates imposed by this lack of planning: they could not cross wide water barriers, and could not successfully colonise very cold environments that required logistic organisation critical to survival. They probably could not cope well in heavily forested environments.

What made them dominant primates, consistently present in all environments, including those where logistic planning was essential to survival, and those that could only be reached through planned travel? Evolutionary change in the hominid skeleton during the last 2 million years is well known, but little of it is closely connected to archaeological evidence of behavioural changes. The presence in the East Mediterranean region in the Early Upper Pleistocene of hominids of archaic and others of more modern skeletal form, both showing signs of similar behaviour, suggests that biology alone had little to do with the changes involved. This interpretation is confirmed by the evidence for behavioural change among hominids (and humans) with modern skeletal form in South Africa. The process observable in Europe was of a different nature: behavioural change was probably a result of replacement by biologically different humans.

They became dominant, we suggest, because among the variable populations of hominids, some with skeletal anatomy more like the modern form, and some with less modern skeletons, language arose. This was a product of behavioural discoveries rather than biological events. The evolutionary changes in biology had set up the circumstances in which the behaviour of language would have the form it does: use of the vocal-auditory channel with prolonged learning during infancy in a social context. The nature of language as a symbolic communication system 'created' the human mind, capable of logistics and planning apt for all environments, of reifying concepts, of distinguishing 'us' from 'them', of the invention of the supernatural, of investigating its own workings and the past.

What was involved in this recent discovery?

CHAPTER 8

THE ORIGIN OF SYMBOL-MAKING

The story we have been telling

The story of the evolutionary origin of the human mind could be told as one of those 'incredible journeys' into the complex weave of nerve cells that make up the human brain. The mysteriousness guaranteed by such a way of tackling things may look appropriate to the subject matter of the tale. How is it that humans are self-consciously aware of circumstances that confront them? It is this fact of human life that, among other things, explains why, sometimes, we anxiously agonise about events and, sometimes, joyfully reminisce over, appreciate and anticipate them. But the very immediacy of these experiences affecting how we are as people makes the 'incredible journey' into nerve cells seem, at best, incomplete.

From the outset we have preferred to keep firmly in *our* minds the fact that lives are lived in these immediacies of feeling and awareness because they are lived in a material world counted, to put it somewhat colourlessly, in terms of objects, other creatures and their doings. The practice of archaeology takes that, of course, for granted; psychology, by contrast, sometimes loses sight of the worldly sources of experience, concentrating attention on the cognitive capacities of the experiencer—hence the 'incredible journey' option beckons. In the opening chapter of this volume we explained what it is we are trying to explain—that the mark of modern human behaviour is its self-awareness, its 'mindedness'. It behoves students of psychology or archaeology to try to account for this, and our explanation is that language provides the key. It is by means of language that people can describe what they perceive, reflect on that, recognise themselves as part of and as the perceivers of their perceived world (Merleau-Ponty 1964[1947]), agonise, reminisce, and make plans.

Language has this power because its constituent signs are symbols (in considering the nature of language we eschew an analogous 'incredible journey' into the realm of phonemes and syllables). Symbols are entities that stand, by convention, for things other than themselves. The words and phrases of a language are those sorts of things. Language users know that their communicative utterances have meanings, that the terms they use are things that refer to other things, to events, states of affairs, including their own states of feeling and awareness. We have not said much about how changes in the very uses of language, in their evolutionary history, have enabled people to elaborate stories of their being and awareness. Nor have we said anything in detail about how such stories may have been derived and what they have produced in terms of the evolution of human practices. That can be a feature of the next project. Our primary aim has been to account for how the foundation of these elaborations emerged. To do so, great care has had to be exercised in defining what the 'modern' human nature is whose evolutionary emergence is to be explained. That is why the centre of the text (Chapters 3, 4 and 5) is an extended theoretical analysis—including relevant empirical reference—of symbol, mind and the character of 'minded', meaning-laden, perceiving (Coulter & Parsons 1990; Toulmin 1982).

The 'book-ends' of that analysis are the empirical data of the archaeology of human origins: what may be reconstructed about the common ancestor of modern humans and their contemporary primate relatives (Chapter 2); what is known of the evolutionary history of the ancient ancestors of modern humans deriving from that common one (Chapter 6), and what is known about our more immediate ancestors (Chapter 7). The theme which emerges consistently, from both theoretical and empirical inquiry, is that *behaviour* is at stake in the story of the evolution of the human mind. The practices of creatures in relation to the physical and social resources available to them are the means by which they come to 'make up their minds' (Olson 1989). While brain cells are intrinsic to behaviour, as phonemes to language, selection on behaviour, including linguistic behaviour, and hence the brain cells that permit it, is where the action is. In this final chapter we offer proposals about the behavioural steps involved in discovery, by our ancestors, of the symbolic potential of communicative signs.

The archaeological evidence reviewed in the two preceding chapters allows the proposition that for some time subsequent to the evolution of morphologies approximating the form of modern human beings, behaviours expressed by them had crucial similarities to those observed among other modern primates. The essence of these similarities is that those behaviours occurred as responses to unfolding contingencies, rather than as the execution of pre-figured plans. The term 'plan', as used by Parker and Milbrath (1993) (Chapter 4) includes reference to controlled action—for example, reaching and grasping (von Hofsten 1989). Our preference as regards 'planning' is to limit its use to sequences of actions carried out consciously toward a predetermined goal. While controlled action need not be 'conscious' (see, for example, Latash 1993, 214–7) its effects may nonetheless have consequences for subsequent behaviour. Alterations to the forms of cores, as stones are flaked, open up possibilities for one over another set of subsequent actions involving that flaked stone. If a core is flaked to the point where further flaking is, literally, unhandy, it may be discarded. Nonetheless, its very ease of one-handed grasping makes it more readily able to be pitched. The practice of hurling missiles at rivals and predators is observed among modern chimpanzees (Goodall 1986). We can securely presume such a practice in hominids among whom the evidence of stone carrying is also well established.

For a relatively brief time in evolutionary terms, the archaeological record shows evidence of behaviour involving stone and other natural materials (ochre, bone) that is critically different from what we have been reviewing. Actions are being taken upon materials that show evidence of forward planning to achieve a goal. Undertaking such behaviour entails being able to articulate that goal and the steps needed to reach it. Even if the initial achievement of a sequence-based outcome is accidental, the capacity to note the outcome and to recreate the steps leading to its re-achievement depends on the same ability. The evidence in the archaeological record of human evolution of the last 60 000 years is of behaviour undertaken according to plan. The arrival in the Australian region may have been an accident, but it is not one that could have happened in the absence of the use of sea-going vessels constructed according to plan. Archaeologically, this is the earliest evidence of modern human behaviour (Davidson & Noble 1992).

There is no knowing exactly how long prior to the first colonisation of Australia such plan-based behaviour had been expressed. On the basis of linguistic analysis it has been argued (Nicholls 1992) that the people who first went there originated from a common (modern human) ancestor whose other descendants radiated across Europe (and that a second radiation characterises the divergence of Australian from North American human groups). DNA analysis may not provide unequivocal evidence for an origin of modern human genes in Africa (Bowcock et al. 1994; Harpending et al. 1993; Templeton 1993), or it may (Penny et al. 1994), but all interpretations allow agreement that colonisation of Australia and Papua New Guinea occurred early in the global radiation of modern humans. We may speculate that a period of 10 000 years, from the time of common origin, is sufficient to allow for the appearance of modern humans on the southernmost coastlines of Asia. Finally, it can be said that there is no archaeological evidence for the expression of modern human behaviour anywhere else before about 100 000 years ago. Hence, we conclude that sometime between about 100 000 and 70 000 years before the present the behaviour emerged which has become identified as linguistic.

Throwing, pointing, gesturing

In this chapter we set out an argument about how that behaviour emerged and advance a second argument, namely, about why it was selected. Language may seem indispensable to the conduct of modern human life, yet all other living creatures, including the closest primate relatives of modern humans, survive without such capacity. The mere emergence of this behaviour is, thus, no guarantee of its fitness. Selection for its maintenance relied, in our view, on particular consequences of the change in awareness its emergence induced. Since speakers know that their utterances convey meanings, and know they are making them, they can exercise control over what they say. The capacity to control information contrasts with the expression of it involuntarily, behaviour more typical of chimpanzees (Menzel 1971). Control of information, for example, about resources has advantage for those 'in the know'. We return to this matter later.

Stone-throwing seems an unpromising starting place, yet it forms part of the argument about how signs came to have the potential to be used as symbols. We pick up aspects of arguments rehearsed by William Calvin, but take the direction of argument along a different path at critical points (Noble & Davidson 1991). Calvin argued (e.g., 1982; 1991; 1993), following Darlington (1975; see also Knüsel 1992) that throwing is a practice whose evolution could account for changes in brain size and organisation. As we saw in Chapter 7, it may have been important in the evolution of the modern spinal cord. In Calvin's view, the neural circuitry in the brain needed for reliable control of a throwing launch would be good for enhanced control of the timing of extension and flexion of adjacent muscle groups, some of which are involved in vocal utterance (Abbs & Connor 1989). Goodall reports (Lawick-Goodall 1968b) that, among chimpanzees, the throws sometimes appeared to be made using a definite aim, although very few (5 of 44) objects thrown actually hit another creature, those that did being thrown a distance of less than 6 feet. Timing control using forelimbs by chimpanzees is argued as having some similarities to that of modern humans (Ott et al. 1994), in contrast to that of baboons, whose common ancestry with hominoids is more remote.

The essence of Calvin's argument is the natural selection of the neural organisation that supports increasing control of forceful (hence effective) stone throwing. To be effective, increased force—which means increased velocity—entails a narrowing of the time window for release of the missile so that its trajectory stays on target—assuming here, a target on the ground. Too early or too late a release means the missile heads skyward or earthward, rather than retaining a flight path which makes it likely to hit a distant target. Timing control—the coordination of a large set of muscles in torso, shoulder, arm and hand (Turvey 1990)—is thus critical. And it is increasingly so as the velocity of the releaser mechanism rises, hence as the 'time window' for effective release narrows. The releaser mechanism in this case is one or other forelimb of a bipedal hominid. Calvin offers a scenario in which such throwing is selected because of its advantage in improving predation. We are noncommittal on that point; throwing with greater force and precision may (or may also) be effective in driving off rival predators during scavenging bouts. The issue is the plausibility of the argument that such throwing offers selective advantage, hence that timing circuitry in the brain for increasing force and precision, will be naturally selected. More precise control for throwing would also lead to more precise control of the forces for timing and sequencing in the knapping of stone.

Calvin invokes a model for timing precision (Enright 1980) based on a principle of mutual coupling among a set of individual neurons generating action potentials (the form of electrical output in nerve cells that we described in Chapters 4 and 5). Through mutual coupling, discharge in any one neuron triggers the rest. By such a principle the temporal irregularity of discharge of action potentials in any one neuron is averaged out by the *statistical* regularity of a discharge occurring in any one of the set of such neurons. The greater the number of neurons making up such a set, the greater the regularity that can result. This model may be appropriate to the conditions for coordinated muscle control being considered; the more general issue (e.g., Georgopoulos, Schwartz & Kettner 1986; Kalaska & Crammond 1992) is that voluntary control seems to depend on output from networks of nerve cell clusters in the motor cortex, that the control system is widely distributed in that brain region (Evarts 1981), and that it is variable in its organisation in response to specific features of task demands (Gracco 1990). It is inevitable that the more diverse the repertoire of motor acts, the more populous must be the central neural system to control them. Thus, improved throwing, and more precise and forceful manipulation otherwise, may, through greater foraging success, select for the enlarged brain circuitry needed to express it.

Hammond (1990) reports results of a series of experiments in which people carried out repetitive tapping tasks using the preferred and non-preferred hands. While participants could tap as rapidly with either hand, greater irregularity in the intervals between taps was observed in the non-preferred hand, indicating less precise timing control of that hand. Hammond went on to argue that this factor also explains the lesser efficiency of that hand in corrective manœuvres at the terminal phase of various aiming tasks. The significance of timing control for effective aiming at a target accords with Calvin's argument, as does Hammond's larger case for linking timing control of the limbs to that of the vocal tract. Selection of the hand/ arm which, through finer motor control, yields more effective results from throwing, may account for the close connection found between handedness and the brain hemisphere associated with both vocal utterance and control of facial and mouth muscles more generally (Hammond 1990, 60–61). We note in this context that although the relationships between spoken and gestural utterance in contemporary human life are complex, it is consistently observed that disturbances to one are accompanied by disturbances to the other (Glosser & Wiener 1990). Peters (1990) has argued that the same neural system—the supplementary motor area—is responsible for control of hands and voice at the level of initiation and coordination of voluntary activity.

On the basis of advantages in the form of improvements in throwing and knapping, we can plausibly argue for selection for greater manual control in hominid ancestors. What might drive selection for improved vocal control, which is what seems to have happened (Deacon 1992)? Our position is that increased vocal control is not readily explained in the absence of an account of how communication itself becomes elaborated. We can do nothing with mysterious stories, as that by

Burling mentioned in Chapter 1, about talking as a form of self-address which just shows up. The contexts for communication to increase in salience can only be speculated about. What follows is a chain of speculation which is not offered as *the* story. Rather we are satisfied that each element in the speculative chain does not violate interpretations of either the archaeological or modern-day behavioural evidence. We also argue that better speculative accounts will not be free to overlook the conceptual issues we identify, even if every link in our chain is found to be mistaken in one way or another.

Voice and hand-arm gesture are not independent. Such gestures come in various shapes and types. MacNeill (1992) argues for gesture and speech to be seen as elements in an overall system of expressivity; he includes both representational or imitative (iconic) forms, and forms of pointing, in his classification of gestures. Some theorists (e.g., Hewes 1974; Kendon 1991) argue that iconic gesture is one of the foundations of the evolutionary emergence of language. Iconic gestures offer something of a puzzle to linguists. Burling (1993) considers that they represent a virtually species-specific type of human expression. They are not altogether linguistic, but neither are they in the category of 'gesture-calling' which we discussed in Chapter 5 and elsewhere. Burling notes that some chimpanzees come close to making gestures that imitate others, and 'Kanzi' has been reported to make a 'pointing' gesture (Savage-Rumbaugh 1984). As we discussed in Chapter 4, Tomasello, Kruger and Rattner (1993) have drawn a distinction between the imitation found among such 'enculturated' primates and the emulation expressed by these animals in the wild.

We have said previously (Davidson & Noble 1993b) that by the very fact of being a common feature of human communication, yet witnessed only rarely among other primates, iconic calls and gestures are just the sort of behaviour on which natural selection could have operated. On this same score, we note that a rare occurrence among monkeys and chimpanzees is to respond to a vocal or gestural utterance with another one (Fouts et al. 1984; Seyfarth et al. 1980); these too are behaviours forming the potential for the natural selection of imitation as a general feature. The essence of imitation in the first place is replication of the behaviour of a co-present model. Imitation can only be recognised, at its inception, by the feature of co-presence of the model being imitated. As we sought to establish in concluding Chapter 4, the ingredient of co-action is the key to the 'socialising of attention' which occurs in the lives of modern human infants, providing a scaffolding by means of which they may appropriate meaning and reference. The evolutionary emergence we have documented (Chapters 2, 6 and 7), since the time of the common ancestor, of bipedalism, hairlessness, cranial thermoregulation, increased brain size, carnivory, and secondary altriciality in a tool-making primate, created the context for joint attention and imitative learning. Gesture figures strongly in this process among modern humans (see, e.g., Volterra & Erting 1990), and a foundational gesture among infants is that which adult observers gloss as 'pointing' (Hannan 1987).

We gather these various elements together not to retail a recapitulationist story but as preparation for one that takes targeted throwing, pointing, and gesturing, when they occur in the presence of conspecifics, as plausible evolutionary steps enabling communicative signs to become used symbolically.

Lock and colleagues (1990) conclude that the action observable in infants as pointing begins as a set of activities involving extension of the forelimb with no clear motivation (such as failed grasping, or a precocious form of demand). The appearance of this action in human infants may not be very different from how it appeared in 'Kanzi'; the critical difference is what others make of it. Savage-Rumbaugh reports (1984) that Kanzi's pointing behaviour was not reacted to, when witnessed by Kanzi's wildborn foster-parent. Language-using human adults inevitably construe certain of their infants' limb actions as efforts to point, and selectively reinforce those actions that better resemble 'real' points, thereby drawing the infant's behaviour into their conceptual and motivational world. Call and Tomasello (1994) experimented using an orang-utan raised from an early age in the company of humans using Sign language (see Miles 1990) and found reliable evidence that the animal understood the function of pointing to indicate the whereabouts of various items under novel conditions of production and comprehension. In contrast, another orang-utan, which was not thus 'enculturated' was limited more to the use of pointing in specific conditions akin to its previous training in making this gesture in relation to food items.

In the evolutionary emergence and selection of pointing, this behaviour, like language itself, cannot first emerge by means of the same social scaffolding. We have proposed, rather, that if throwing at a target is selected for, an inevitable posture, as a feature of the end-phase of the throw, is orientation of the arm to the target (Noble & Davidson 1989). For an observer, this posture directly indicates the whereabouts of a target. The posture achieves the communication of information. Were it imitated as a posture in appropriate circumstances, it would come to signal the presence and whereabouts of potential predators, prey or antagonists without revealing the presence and whereabouts of the signaller to that predator, prey or antagonist.

There seem to be advantages delivered by this spin-off product of target-oriented throwing in terms of improved food-getting and avoidance of predators. We note that our concerns are with bipedal hominids and, on the basis of speculation about increasingly effective throwing (plus whatever other manipulative acts with stone may be altered through increased timing control), with an explanation for relative increase in encephalisation. The behaviours under discussion are as purposive as the behaviours of chimpanzees cracking nuts with stones or fishing for termites with grass stems. We see no reason to expect that, as behaviours, they require anything more in the way of consciousness *of* the control needed for their execution. The critical point is that the increased control, together with other contextual changes, could take these creatures on a behavioural path ever more divergent from their chimpanzee relatives; there is no basis, yet, to require us to invoke a qualitative difference in awareness. Language users can gloss the behaviours as 'aimed throwing' and 'pointing', but we should be careful not to assume that hominids too were aware of such meanings of their actions. The meaning is a product of our use of language, not of the acts we describe as aimed throwing and pointing (see Chapter 5). As with the chimpanzees, we are not in a position to know if or what meanings any such behaviours had for those producing them at the time.

The prominence of pointing actions is redoubled if increasing hairlessness increases the likelihood that infant hominids are carried facing the adults, as we proposed in Chapter 6 when discussing feasible transformations in interactional contexts for learning. Once the action of sustained extension of the arm towards a target has emerged, arm extensions by infant hominids may evoke an imitative reaction by adults; hence the behaviour is shaped and increasingly expressed from a young age. Pointing the hand at a target from a young age is practice for aiming, and serves in the improvement of throwing and of knapping. Removing flakes from cores involves aiming, and eye-hand coordination (Abrams et al. 1990) is essential for all such tasks.

The next links in the chain take us to realms of sheer speculation, but they are not outlandish as possibilities, since they rest on feedback loops that continually improve eye-hand coordinations. We assume competition for meat with other predators and scavengers as a source of selective pressure. Control of musculature needed for pointing is a basis for sustained pointing that follows the path of a moving target. The new information this behaviour signals to others is that a target animal is retreating or advancing, provoking pursuit or flight. A further advantage arises if a distinctive feature of the target is outlined by a moving hand or arm, an action that may distinguish predator from prey for others at the scene. What might induce such elaboration is unknown. We can surmise increased chances for fluidity of forelimb control if the behaviour is practised from infancy. Newport and Supalla (1980) report that children learning Sign language from non-fluent adult signers produce morphologically more complex versions than those of their models. Volterra, Beronesi and Massoni (1990) observed a parallel phenomenon in the gestural utterances of a deaf child of non-signing adults who used conventional and ad hoc gestures in interacting with him. These examples, from language-based communicative contexts, are remote from the one we are trying to speculate about, but may be seen as indicative of what could occur.

Whatever we might postulate as a framework for its emergence, the information available to conspecifics by such choreography is substantial: it reveals the presence, location, travel path, and the 'category' of a target animal. If expressed along with suppression of vocalising, the foraging success of those engaging in it is enhanced. The listed items of data are not radically different from what the vervet monkeys convey with their cries; and vervets suppress those utterances if they are alone when encountering a predator. We emphasise that we are considering the activity of a primate very different from vervet monkeys; but the order of complexity of the behaviours selected for has features akin to theirs.

Tracing: the invention of signifiers

The behaviour which really makes the difference is the next one. Repetition or imitation of an elaborated ('iconic') gesture in a context beyond its use in the activity of hunting down the prey might, by accident or incidentally, lead to the leaving of a trace in a plastic medium. Such a medium is the mud-bank of a watercourse where scavenging and/or predatory activity would likely be concentrated. In a circumstance where slain prey is being divided, repetition of the gesture associated with the appearance of its form could, on occasion, leave such finger marks. Our reasoning is this. Creatures leave marks under all sorts of circumstances—the Laetoli trails are a famous such case. Marks in bone occur many thousands of years before the appearance of modern human morphology and before the signs of symbols. Though these have been claimed as deliberately made (Mania & Mania 1988), we argue (Davidson 1989; Davidson 1990; Davidson & Noble 1993a) that some are an unintended by-product of the action of cutting with sharp-edged stone flakes on flesh-bearing bone, while others did not involve hominids at all. The hominid marks are among the signs of increasing control of motor sequences, but they offer no evidence that those leaving the marks *noticed* them.

The difference in the speculative scenario we have been developing is that a trace made incidentally is nonetheless incidental to an imitative action which calls attention to the presence of predators or prey, feasibly a context of fear and excitement. We have argued that secondary altriciality produces conditions for imitative learning to be a regular feature of the ontogenetic development of infant hominids. Hence imitation was more salient among hominids than apes. There is the prospect for the appearance resulting from this sort of trace—the trace of an imitative gesture—to be itself noticed, by the trace-maker and others who witness (thence imitate) its production. This is because the gesture that produced the trace is associated with the prey animal whose appearance provoked it. Any re-tracing of the form of the trace reproduces a gesture associated with a distinctive feature of the landscape whilst at the same time creating a new entity for visual perceptual attention.

Why concentrate on this concatenation of elements? The issue we address is that of making the 'sign' an entity in itself. We have argued throughout that other modern primates, in their own ecologies, may be observed to communicate using vocal and gestural signs, but that there is no evidence to support a proposition of their *appreciating* that such signs have the functions they achieve. The signs themselves go unnoticed; they are seen or heard 'through' to what they signify.

Signs that themselves go unnoticed function in something like the way that signs do in a 'conditioning' experiment (chapter 3). In that context a formerly neutral signal, such as a sound (Pavlov's bell) or visual shape, eventually serves to evoke salivation from a hungry animal (Pavlov's dog) after the signal has been regularly associated with a salient stimulus such as food. The signal is detected, but all of the animal's attention is oriented to what it signifies (the food). There is no assumption that the conditioning signal (which could correspond to a word in English) is understood by the animal as a symbol which stands for—refers to—the food. In the same way, we argue there is no assumption that imitative gestures, seen in a context of predation, are seen *as* referential signs. The concept which is key to our argument has been distinguished by Terrace (1985) as the capacity to *understand* that entities can be referred to by use of their jointly known names. 'Naming' is not to be confused with the conditioned association of a signal with an appearance. In learning to apply names to things, the form of orientation is one of seeing the named entity as identified by that name. Attention is both to the object as something that bears a title (Noble 1993b, and Chapter 5), and to the sign which *is* that title. Such reference can eventually be accomplished whether or not the named entity is immediately perceivable. This is because the name is understood as the item which achieves the reference.

In his dissection of the nature of the linguistic sign, Saussure was at pains to distinguish between the concepts of signifier and signified. In our discussions of that (Chapters 1 and 4) we sought to replace the mentalistic basis of Saussure's critique with the more concrete point that the term signi*fied* may be understood as referring to the entity named, signi*fier* refers to the name itself. The distinction emphasises the point that signifiers (the things that act as names) are as real (for language users) as signifieds (the things named). Our argument overall is that appreciating the reality of signifiers has to arise in order that they can be made detachable from immediate contexts of association, carried off as it were (dis-placed) to other contexts, yet appreciated as continuing to refer to now absent signifieds. The trace, in 'freezing' the gesture (Gibson 1966, 229–230), makes the signifier a new environmental entity so that its existence is created as something in itself, yet as existing in simultaneous relationship to both sign-maker and signified. Some such reorientation of attention *away* from the signified is needed in order to realize the existence of the sign as signifier. Howsoever that is accomplished, once done, the sign becomes usable symbolically, as a name. Its form, initially iconic, could be reduced or otherwise modified and have increasingly arbitrary formal relation with its referent, such reductions being enabled so long as all common users were party to new encodings—remained in the 'language game'.

From the occasion of discovery/invention of signs as signifiers, any vocal utterances associated with manual gestures would be similarly transformed in their use and also become symbols. More flexible vocal and airway control is feasibly selected for, given the advantages of communication using the voice. Such advan-tage might arise from the more persistent use of the forelimbs for carrying, tool use, handling, etc. (Lieberman 1984, 324–6), in addition to their use for gesture-making.

We are agnostic on the issue of whether single (manual-vocal) gesture names might be the first phase in an evolutionary series, culminating in the syntactical features found in all contemporary languages (e.g., Butterworth, Comrie & Dahl 1984). Greenfield (1991) argues that there are signs of syntax in the utterances of 'enculturated' modern primates, and that there are parallels in the growth of syntactic hierarchical organization of utterances and the use of tools in modern human children, during their first 2 years after birth. This argument might suggest the possibility of syntactic hierarchy in utterance sequencing as an early feature of prehistoric use of symbols. From the scenario we have postulated it may not be implausible that two-sign utterances, indicating actor-performing-action, were an early accomplishment; nonetheless, we refrain from further comment on this question here.

Selection for linguistic behaviour

Of more particular concern is the context for selection of the behaviour whose form of emergence we have been speculating upon. We may 'rationally' suppose that a capacity for reference, to use and understand utterances at the symbolic level, brings advantages in terms of information exchange, planning and the like. The general expectation is that the emergence of language made communication somehow 'better'. Another force at work, though, is the rapidity with which symbols can be modified in their form, yet go on being meaningful for so long as the modifications are jointly appreciated, i.e., within a given community—the feature of arbitrariness of linguistic symbols, including the feature of reduction from Peircian iconic to symbolic form (Chapters 3 and 5). With the emergence of such 'idiosyncratic' meanings ('codes'), as groups become isolated from each other, comes the emergence of unreliable reference (Davidson & Noble 1992; Noble & Davidson 1993), the breakdown of unambiguous communication. Failures and misunderstandings between groups due to this would increase the importance of personally worn or expressed emblems to allow speakers to know that meanings were common among those similarly marked. Such distinctive emblems, arising within human groups, would also constrain the flow of communication between bearers of dissimilar emblems. 'In-group' and 'out-group' membership (Sherif 1966) may be signalled, indeed, by passwords (shibboleths) and other markers, so that the boundaries of reliable meanings may be distinguished. Davidson (in press) explores the implications of personal ornament in the archaeological record around the world after the appearance of other modern human behaviours.

A consequence of experiencing the occurrence of unreliable communication is that strategies come into play, in the context of language use, which make the withholding of information, or the production of deliberately misleading information, advantageous. These possible forms of exploitation, entirely recognisable in contemporary human dealings, are the rapidly appreciated fruits of the consciousness that is delivered by seeing that symbols are one's own expressive products, and may be used deceptively for purposes of social control (Orwell 1968). This function of language—for lying—stands among its other functions in the everyday political, religious and aesthetic activities of human life.

It may be thought 'unbecoming' to identify the construction of falsehood, the artful use of discourse, as a selective advantage. A key sign of mindedness is nevertheless exactly identified by such control (Whiten & Byrne 1988), as is the related capacity to entertain the thought that the other person harbours a false belief (Baron-Cohen et al. 1993), hence that such a belief may be planted in them. Given the potency of language in this respect, human groups without the capacity to use signs symbolically would lose out fairly thoroughly to those who could. A related consequence is the parallel division in genetic and linguistic groupings (Barbujani & Sokal 1990) which can be accounted for through the isolation of communities across whose memberships communication is untrustworthy. Competition between, and cooperation within, human groupings, entails the refinement of linguistic and related practices. Human mentality, understood as co-extensive with language in use among us, is thus itself an evolving feature of the natural world.

Concluding

So where have we got to? That question has two senses: what terminus have we arrived at in presenting our argument; and where might human beings have got to in the evolution of their 'mental powers and capacities'? In answer to the first sense of the question, we have asserted that 'the mental' equates to language in human life, hence makes for the uniqueness of human mentality. But we have also argued that language must be conceptualised as a form of interactive behaviour. It is the human nature of the *interactive* context in the case of bonobo 'Kanzi' that engenders the powers and capacities of mind expressed by that creature, in turn raising a question about Kanzi's being human (Chapter 3). More naturally 'minded' human beings are participants in and contributors to a wide range of 'discursive ecologies' (Chapter 5, and Noble 1993b). We add that the form and features of any individual 'mind' can be read as a history of the discourses that person has committed to. This view of mind recognises its existence through its expression, and its inseparability from the embodied and contextualised agent of that expression.

According to one commentator (Danesi 1993) the 18th century Italian theorist, Giambattista Vico, would endorse this conclusion, though Vico (1928[1725]) postulated that language originates from the imagination, as against our argument (Davidson & Noble 1989) that imagination is among language's several fruits. We mention Vico because he is also relevant to the second sense of the question, namely, where have humans 'got to' in the evolution (consequent upon first emergence) of their mental powers. Vico is identified as the originator of the concept of the 'primitive mind', a category we noted in Chapter 5. He considered that the myths and legends of ancient peoples are legitimate accounts of their real-world experience, reflecting the forms of mindedness of the narrators. Where human beings have 'got to' in the evolution of mindedness is not something we aim to *pronounce* upon. With Vico, we take it that the world of expressed theory, narrative and related artefacts, is the place to search for the nature of the mind whose evolution proceeds from the point of language's first emergence.

Darwin, like Vico before him, could only speculate about the emergence of human mindedness, though he was surely right, in the statement we quoted at the start of the book, about implications for psychology ('I see open fields for far more important researches'), as, we believe, Vico was right about language being the key to human mentality. It has subsequently been possible to constrain speculation about human evolution by attending to the archaeological evidence that records it. But an archaeological record does not speak for itself; it must be interpreted—a theoretical framework needs to be articulated so that the record may be understood coherently. We have argued that the record of artefacts, the products of behaviour, provides the real evolutionary answers. We argue this because the mindedness we seek to explain is also argued as manifest in behaviour.

Among strongly contested areas in the archaeology of human prehistory is the import of stone artefacts used as tools (Chapter 7). Understanding the true signifi-cance of stone tools in the story of modern human emergence bears upon the significance of all products of modern human ingenuity. The computer, an astound-ing contemporary human artefact, is mistaken as a model of brain and/or mind (Chapter 5). No one, we assume, would make the mistake of seeing a stone tool as such a model, though there is much debate about the mentality needed to produce different forms of prehistoric stone artefact. In our argument, the sort of planning needed to make a ground-edged and hafted hand-tool is the platform for the sort of planning needed to build a boat, and ultimately, a computer. None of these artefacts can work as models of mind, because the planning in question springs from interactive behaviour based on the use of communicative signs symbolically. The products of such planning nonetheless powerfully reflect back on the mentality of their producers (the computer as model for mind). The nature of the uniquely human behaviour of symbol use, in connection with its application to available material resources, is surely an 'open field for important researches on the origin of man and his history'.

REFERENCES

Abrams, R. A., Meyer, D. E. & Kornblum, S. 1990. Eye-hand coordination: Oculomotor control in rapid aimed limb movements. *Journal of Experimental Psychology: Human Perception & Performance*, 16, 248–267.

Abbs, J. H. & Connor, N. P. 1989. *Motor coordination for functional human behaviors*. Amsterdam: North-Holland.

Adams, M. J. & Bruck, M. 1993. Word recognition. *Reading and Writing*, 5, 113–139.

Aiello, L. C. 1993. The fossil evidence for modern human origins in Africa. *American Anthropologist*, 95, 73–96.

Aiello, L. C. 1994. Variable but singular. *Nature*, 368, 399–400.

Allen, J. 1989. When did humans first colonize Australia? *Search*, 20, 149–154.

Anderson, J. R. 1985. *Cognitive psychology and its implications* (2nd ed.). New York: Freeman.

Anderson-Gerfaud, P. 1990. Aspects of behaviour in the Middle Palaeolithic. In P. Mellars (Eds.), *The emergence of modern humans* (pp. 389–418). Edinburgh: Edinburgh University Press.

Andrews, P. 1995. Ecological apes and ancestors. *Nature*, 376, 555–556.

Arensburg, B., Shepartz, L. A., Tillier, A. M., Vandermeersch, B. & Rak, Y. 1990. A reappraisal of the anatomical basis for speech in Middle Palaeolithic hominids. *American Journal of Physical Anthropology*, 83, 137–146.

Arensburg, B., Tillier, A. M., Vandermeersch, B., Duday, H., Schepartz, L. A. & Rak, Y. 1989. A Middle Palaeolithic human hyoid bone. *Nature*, 388, 758–760.

Armstrong, E. 1984. Comment on Beals, Smith and Dodd (1984). *Current Anthropology*, 25, 318–319.

Armstrong, E., Zilles, K. & Schleicher, A. 1993. Cortical folding and the evolution of the human brain. *Journal of Human Evolution*, 25, 387–392.

Asfaw, B., Beyene, Y., Suwa, G., Walter, R. C., White, T. D., WoldeGabriel, G. &

Yemane, T. 1992. The earliest Acheulean from Konso-Gardula. *Nature*, 360, 732–735.

Ashton, N. M., Cook, J., Lewis, S. G. & Rose, J. (Ed.). 1992. *High Lodge*. London: British Museum Press.

Ashton, N., McNabb, J., Irving, B., Lewis, S. & Parfitt, S. 1994. Contemporaneity of Clactonian and Acheulian flint industries at Barnham, Suffolk. *Antiquity*, 68, 585–589.

Atkinson, R. L., Atkinson, R. C., Smith, E. E. & Bem, D. J. 1993. *Introduction to psychology* (11th ed.). Fort Worth: Harcourt Brace Jovanovich.

Austin, J. L. 1961. *Philosophical papers* (edited by J. O. Urmson and G. J. Warnock). Oxford: Oxford University Press.

Bahn, P. 1986. No sex please, we're Aurignacians. *Rock Art Research*, 3, 99–120.

Baker, C. & Battison, R. (Ed.). 1980. *Sign language and the deaf community*. Silver Spring, MD: National Association of the Deaf.

Baker, G. P. & Hacker, P. M. S. 1984. *Language, sense & nonsense*. Oxford: Blackwell.

Bakhtin, M. M. 1981[1975]. Discourse in the novel. In M. Holquist (Ed.), *The dialogic imagination* (pp. 259–422). Austin: University of Texas Press.

Bar-Yosef, O. & Vandermeersch, B. (Ed.). 1991. *Le squelette moustérien de Kébara 2*. Paris: Éditions du Centre National de la Recherche Scientifique.

Bar-Yosef, O. 1992. The role of western Asia in modern human origins. *Philosophical Transactions of the Royal Society of London B*, 337, 193–200.

Bar-Yosef, O., Vandermeersch, B., Arensburg, B., Belfer-Cohen, A., Goldberg, P., Laville, H., Meignen, L., Rak, Y., Speth, J. D., Tchernov, E., Tillier, A.-M. & Weiner, S. 1992. The excavations in Kebara Cave, Mt. Carmel. *Current Anthropology*, 33, 497–550.

Barbetti, M. 1986. Traces of fire in the archaeological record. *Journal of Human Evolution*, 15, 771–781.

Barbujani, G. & Sokal, R. R. 1990. Zones of sharp genetic change in Europe are also linguistic boundaries. *Proceedings of the National Academy of Sciences of the United States of America*, 87, 1816–1819.

Baron-Cohen, S., Tager-Flusberg, H. & Cohen, D. (Eds.). 1993. *Understanding other minds*. Oxford: Oxford University Press.

Barton, C. M. 1990. Beyond style and function. *American Anthropologist*, 92, 57–72.

Bates, E., Thal, D. & Marchman, V. 1991. Symbols and syntax: A Darwinian approach to language development. In N. A. Krasnegor, D. M. Rumbaugh, R. L. Schiefelbusch & M. Studdert-Kennedy (Eds.), *Biological and behavioral determinants of language development* (pp. 29–65). Hillsdale, NJ: Erlbaum.

Bauchot, R. 1982. Brain organisation and taxonomic relationships in insectivora and primates. In E. Armstrong & D. Falk (Eds.), *Primate brain evolution* (pp. 163–175). New York: Plenum Press.

Bauer, R. H. 1993. Lateralization of neural control for vocalization by the frog (*Rana pipiens*). *Psychobiology*, 21, 243–248.

Beals, K. L., Smith, C. L. & Dodd, S. M. 1984. Brain size, cranial morphology, climate, and time machines. *Current Anthropology*, 25, 301–330.

Beck, B. B. 1980. Animal tool behavior. New York: Garland STPM Press.

Begun, D. R. & Walker, A. 1993. The endocast. In A. Walker & R. E. F. Leakey (Eds.), *The Nariokotome* Homo erectus *skeleton* (pp. 326–358). Cambridge, Massachusetts: Harvard University Press.

Begun, D. R. 1993. Response to Shea and Inouye. *Science*, 259, 294.

Behrensmeyer, A. K. 1984. Taphonomy and the fossil record. *American Scientist*, 72, 558–566.

Behrensmeyer, A. K. & Hill, A. P. 1980. *Fossils in the making.* Chicago: The University of Chicago Press.

Bentrup, F.W. 1979. Reception and transduction of electrical amd mechanical stimuli. In W. Haupt and M. E. Feinleib (Eds) *Physiology of movements, Encyclopedia of plant physiology, vol 7* (pp. 42–70). Berlin: Springer-Verlag.

Berge, C. 1994. How did the australopithecines walk? *Journal of Human Evolution*, 26, 259–273.

Berger, P. L. & Luckmann, T. 1966. *The social construction of reality.* Harmondsworth: Penguin.

Bergman, C. A. & Roberts, M. B. 1988. Flaking technology at the Acheulean site of Boxgrove, West Sussex (England). *Revue archéologique de Picardie*, 1–2, 105–113.

Beyries, S. 1987. *Variabilité de l'industrie lithique au Moustérien.* Oxford: British Archaeological Reports International Series 328.

Bickerton, D. 1990. *Language and species.* Chicago: University of Chicago Press.

Biederman, I. 1987. Recognition-by-components. *Psychological Review*, 94, 115–147.

Binford, L. R. 1972. Contemporary model building. In D. L. Clarke (Eds.), *Models in archaeology.* London: Methuen.

Binford, L. R. 1978. Dimensional analysis of behavior and site structure. *American Antiquity*, 45, 4–20.

Binford, L. R. 1981. *Bones.* New York: Academic Press.

Binford, L. R. 1983. *In pursuit of the past.* London: Thames and Hudson.

Binford, L. R. 1984. *Faunal remains from Klasies River Mouth.* New York: Academic Press.

Binford, L. R. 1986. Comment on Bunn and Kroll's "systematic butchery by Plio-Pleistocene hominids at Olduvai Gorge". *Current Anthropology*, 27, 444–446.

Binford, L. R. 1987. Were there elephant hunters at Torralba? In M. H. Nitecki & D. V. Nitecki (Eds.), *The evolution of hunting* (pp. 47–105). New York: Plenum Press.

Binford, L. R. 1988a. Étude taphonomique des restes fauniques de la Grotte Vaufrey, Couche VIII. In J.-P. Riguad (Ed.), *La Grotte Vaufrey à Cenac et Saint-Julien (Dordogne)* (pp. 535–564). Société Préhistorique Française.

Binford, L. R. 1988b. Fact and fiction about the *Zinjanthropus* floor. *Current Anthropology*, 29, 123–135.

Binford, L. R. & Binford, S. R. 1966. A preliminary analysis of functional variability in the Mousterian of Levallois facies. *American Anthropologist*, 68, 238–295.

Bischoff, J. L., Garcia, J. F. & Straus, L. G. 1992. Uranium-series isochron dating at El Castillo cave (Cantabria, Spain). *Journal of Archaeological Science*, 19, 49–62.

Bloch, M. 1991. Language, anthropology and cognitive science. *Man*, 26, 183–198.

Blumberg, M. S. & Alberts, J. R. 1992. Functions and effects in animal communication. *Animal Behaviour*, 44, 382–383.

Blumenberg, B. 1985. Population characteristics of extinct hominid endocranial volume. *American Journal of Physical Anthropology*, 68, 269–279.

Blumenschine, R. J. 1986. *Early hominid scavenging opportunities*. Oxford: British Archaeological Reports International Series.

Blumenschine, R. J. 1991. Hominid carnivory and foraging strategies, and the socio-economic function of early archaeological sites. *Philosophical Transactions of the Royal Society of London B*, 334, 211–221.

Boas, F. 1955. *Primitive art*. New York: Dover.

Boëda, E. 1988. Le concept Levallois et evaluation de son champ d'application. *Études et Recherches Archéologiques de l'Université de Liège*, 31, 13–26.

Boehm, C. 1992. Vocal communication of Pan troglodytes. In J. Wind, B. Chiarelli, B. Bichakjian, A. Nocentini & A. Jonker (Eds.), *Language origin* (pp. 323–350). Dordrecht: Kluwer Academic Publishers.

Boesch, C. 1991a. Symbolic communication in wild chimpanzees? *Human Evolution*, 6, 81–90.

Boesch, C. 1991b. Teaching in wild chimpanzees. *Animal Behaviour*, 41, 530–532.

Boesch, C. 1993. Aspects of transmission of tool-use in wild chimpanzees. In K. Gibson & T. Ingold (Eds.), *Tools, language and cognition in human evolution* (pp. 171–183). Cambridge: Cambridge University Press.

Boesch, C. 1994. Chimpanzee—red colobus monkeys. *Animal Behaviour*, 47, 1135–1148.

Boesch, C. & Boesch, H. 1981. Sex differences in the use of natural hammers by wild chimpanzees. *Journal of Human Evolution*, 10, 565–583.

Boesch, C. & Boesch, H. 1984. Mental map in wild chimpanzees. *Primates*, 25, 160–170.

Boesch, C. & Boesch, H. 1989. Hunting behavior of wild chimpanzees in the Taï National Park. *American Journal of Physical Anthropology*, 78, 547–573.

Boesch, C. & Boesch, H. 1990. Tool use and tool making in wild chimpanzees. *Folia Primatologica*, 54, 86–99.

Bolton, N. 1977. *Concept formation*. Oxford: Pergamon Press.

Bordes, F. 1961. *Typologie du Paléolithique Ancien et Moyen*. Bordeaux: Delmas.

Bordes, F. & de Sonneville-Bordes, D. 1970. The significance of variability in Palaeolithic assemblages. *World Archaeology*, 2, 61–73.

Bowcock, A. M., Ruiz-Linares, A., Tomfohrde, J., Kidd, J. R. & Cavalli-Sforza, L. L. 1994. High resolution of human evolutionary trees with polymorphic microsatellites. *Nature*, 368, 455–457.

Bradley, B. & Sampson, C. G. 1978. Artifacts from the Cottages Site. In C. G. Sampson (Eds.), *Paleoecology and archeology of an Acheulian site at Caddington, England* (pp. 83–137). Dallas: Department of Anthropology, Southern Methodist University.

Bradley, B. & Sampson, C. G. 1986. Analysis by replication of two Acheulian artefact assemblages. In G. N. Bailey & P. Callow (Eds.), *Stone Age prehistory* (pp. 29–45). Cambridge: Cambridge University Press.

Bradshaw, J. L. & Rogers, L. J. 1993. *The evolution of lateral asymmetries, language, tool use, and intellect.* Sydney: Academic Press, Inc.

Brain, C. K. 1981. *The hunters or the hunted?* Chicago: University of Chicago Press.

Brannigan, C. R. & Humphries, D. A. 1972. Human non-verbal behaviour. In N. Blurton-Jones (Eds.), *Ethological studies of child behaviour* (pp. 37–64). Cambridge: Cambridge University Press.

Brockelman, W. Y. 1984. Social behaviour of gibbons. In H. Preuschoft, D. J. Chivers, W. Y. Brockelman & N. Creel (Eds.), *The lesser apes* (pp. 285–290). Edinburgh: Edinburgh University Press.

Brown, F. H. 1982. Correlation of Tulu Bor Tuff at Koobi Fora with the Sidi Hakoma Tuff at Hadar, Ethiopia. *Nature, 300,* 631–633.

Brown, P. 1987. Pleistocene homogeneity and Holocene size reduction. *Archaeology in Oceania, 22* (41–71).

Brown, P. 1990. Osteological definitions of 'anatomically modern' *Homo sapiens*: A test using modern and terminal Pleistocene *Homo sapiens. Proceeding of the Australasian Society for Human Biology, 3,* 31–74.

Bruner, J. 1983. *Child's talk.* New York: Norton.

Bruner, J. 1985. Vygotsky: A historical and conceptual perspective. In J. V. Wertsch (Eds.), *Culture, communication and cognition: Vygotskian perspectives.* Cambridge: Cambridge University Press.

Bruner, J. 1990. *Acts of meaning.* Cambridge, Mass.: Harvard University Press.

Bunn, H. T. 1981. Archaeological evidence for meat-eating by Plio/Pleistocene hominids from Koobi Fora and Olduvai Gorge. *Nature, 291,* 574–577.

Bunn, H. T., Harris, J. W. K., Isaac, G. L., Kaufulu, Z., Kroll, E., Schick, K., Toth, N. & Behrensmeyer, A. K. 1980. FxJj 50. *World Archaeology, 12,* 109–136.

Bunn, H. T. & Kroll, E. M. 1986. Systematic butchery by Plio/Pleistocene hominids at Olduvai Gorge, Tanzania. *Current Anthropology, 27,* 431–452.

Bunn, H. T. & Kroll, E. M. 1988. Reply to fact and fiction about the *Zinjanthropus* floor. *Current Anthropology, 29,* 135–149.

Burling, R. 1993. Primate calls, human language, and nonverbal communication. *Current Anthropology, 34,* 25–53.

Busse, C. D. 1978. Do chimpanzees hunt cooperatively? *American Naturalist, 112,* 767–770.

Butters, N. & Cermak, L. S. 1980. *Alcoholic Korsakoff's Syndrome.* New York: Academic Press.

Butterworth, B., Comrie, B. & Dahl, Ö. (Ed.). 1984. *Explanations for language universals.* Berlin: Mouton.

Butterworth, G. 1991. The ontogeny and phylogeny of joint visual attention. In A. Whiten (Eds.), *Natural theories of mind* (pp. 223–232). Oxford: Blackwell.

Butterworth, G. & Grover, L. 1988. The origins of referential communication in human infancy. In L. Weiskrantz (Eds.), *Thought without language* (pp. 5–24). Oxford: Clarendon Press.

Butynski, T. M. 1982. Vertebrate predation by primates. *Journal of Human Evolution*, 11, 421–430.

Butzer, K. W. 1980. Comment on Wreschner (1980). *Current Anthropology*, 21, 635.

Byrne, B. 1991. Experimental analysis of the child's discovery of the alphabetic principle. In L. Rieben & C. A. Perfetti (Eds.), *Learning to read* (pp. 75–84). Hillsdale, NJ: Lawrence Erlbaum Associates.

Byrne, B. 1992. Studies in the acquisition procedure for reading. In P. B. Gough, L. C. Ehri & R. Treiman (Eds.), *Reading acquisition* (pp. 1–34). Hillsdale, NJ: Erlbaum.

Byrne, R. W. 1994. The evolution of intelligence. In P. J. B. Slater & T. R. Halliday (Eds.), *Behaviour and evolution*. Cambridge: Cambridge University Press.

Byrne, R. W. & Byrne, J. M. 1991. Hand preferences in the skilled gathering tasks of Mountain Gorillas (*Gorilla gorilla berengei*). *Cortex*, 27, 521–546.

Byrne, R. W. & Whiten, A. 1988. *Machiavellian intelligence*. Oxford: Clarendon Press.

Call, J. & Tomasello, M. 1994. The production and comprehension of referential pointing by orang-utans (*Pongo pygmaeus*). *Journal of Comparative Psychology*, 108, 307–317.

Callow, P. 1986a. Interpreting the La Cotte sequence. In P. Callow & J. Cornford (Eds.), *La Cotte de St. Brelade 1961–1978* (pp. 73–82). Norwich: Geo Books.

Callow, P. 1986b. The La Cotte industries and the European Lower and Middle Palaeolithic. In P. Callow & J. Cornford (Eds.), *La Cotte de St. Brelade 1961–1978* (pp. 377–388). Norwich: Geo Books.

Callow, P., Walton, D. & Shell, C. 1986. The use of fire at La Cotte de St. Brelade. In P. Callow & J. Cornford (Eds.), *La Cotte de St. Brelade 1961–1978* (pp. 193–195). Norwich: Geo Books.

Calvin, W. H. 1982. Did throwing stones shape hominid brain evolution? *Ethology and Sociobiology*, 3, 115–124.

Calvin, W. H. 1983. *The throwing madonna*. New York: McGraw-Hill.

Calvin, W. H. 1991. *The ascent of mind*. New York: Bantam Books.

Calvin, W. H. 1993. The unitary hypothesis. In K. R. Gibson & T. Ingold (Eds.), *Tools, language and cognition in human evolution* (pp. 230–250). Cambridge: Cambridge University Press.

Cameron, D. W. 1993. The Pliocene hominid and protochimpanzee behavioral morphotypes. *Journal of Anthropological Archaeology*, 12, 386–414.

Capron, H. L. 1987. *Computers: Tools for an information age*. Menlo Park, California: Benjamin/Cummings.

Caro, T. M. & Hauser, M. D. 1992. Is there teaching in nonhuman animals? *Quarterly Review of Biology*, 67, 151–.

Carpenter, M., Tomasello, M. & Savage-Rumbaugh, S. 1995. Joint attention and imitative learning in children, chimpanzees, and enculturated chimpanzees. *Social Development*, 4, 217–237.

Carrier, D. R. 1984. The energetic paradox of human running and hominid evolution. *Current Anthropology*, 25, 483–495.

Cartmill, M. 1974. Rethinking primate origins. *Science*, 184, 436–443.

Chamberlain, A. T. & Wood, B. A. 1987. Early hominid phylogeny. *Journal of Human Evolution*, 16, 119–133.

Chapman, M. & Dixon, R. A. 1987. Inner processes and outward criteria. In M. Chapman & R. A. Dixon (Eds.), *Meaning and the growth of understanding* (pp. 103–127). Berlin: Springer.

Chase, P. G. 1988. Scavenging and hunting in the Middle Paleolithic. In H. Dibble & A. Montet-White (Eds.), *Upper Pleistocene prehistory of western Eurasia* (pp. 225–232). Philadelphia: University Museum, University of Pennsylvania.

Chase, P. G. 1990. Sifflets du Paléolithique moyen(?). *Bulletin de la Société Préhistorique Française*, 87, 165–167.

Chase, P. G. 1991. Symbols and Paleolithic artifacts. *Journal of Anthropological Archaeology*, 10, 193–214.

Chase, P. G. 1993. Archaeology and the cognitive sciences in the study of human evolution. *Behavioral and Brain Sciences*, 16, 752–753.

Chase, P. G. 1994. On symbols and the Palaeolithic. *Current Anthropology*, 35, 617–629.

Chase, P. G. & Dibble, H. L. 1987. Middle Palaeolithic symbolism. *Journal of Anthropological Archaeology*, 6, 263–296.

Chase, P. G. & Dibble, H. L. 1992. Scientific archaeology and the origins of symbolism. *Cambridge Archaeological Journal*, 2, 43–51.

Chavaillon, J. 1976. Evidence for the technical practices of early Pleistocene hominids, Shungura Formation, Lower Omo Valley, Ethiopia. In Y. Coppens, F. C. Howell, G. L. Isaac & R. E. F. Leakey (Eds.), *Earliest Man and environments in the Lake Rudolf basin* (pp. 565–573). Chicago: University of Chicago Press.

Cheney, D. L. & Seyfarth, R. M. 1990. *How monkeys see the world*. Chicago: University of Chicago Press.

Cheney, D. L. & Seyfarth, R. M. 1991. Reading minds or reading behaviour? Tests for a theory of mind in monkeys. In A. Whiten (Eds.), *Natural theories of mind* (pp. 175–194). Oxford: Blackwell.

Chivers, D. J. & Hladik, C.-M. 1984. Diet and gut morphology in primates. In D. J. Chivers, B. A. Wood & A. Bilsborough (Eds.), *Food acquisition and processing in primates* (pp. 213–230). New York: Plenum Press.

Chomsky, N. 1964. Current issues in linguistic theory. In J. A. Fodor & J. J. Katz (Eds.), *The structure of language* (pp. 50–118). Englewood Cliffs, NJ: Prentice-Hall.

Chomsky, N. 1980. *Rules and representations*. New York: Columbia University Press.

Chomsky, N. 1986. *Knowledge of language*. New York: Praeger.

Churchland, P. S. 1986. *Neurophilosophy*. Cambridge, Mass.: MIT Press.

Clark, J. D. & Harris, J. W. K. 1985. Fire and its roles in early hominid lifeways. *African Archaeological Review*, 3, 3–27.

Clark, J. D. & Haynes, C. V. 1970. An elephant butchery site at Mwanganda's Village, Karonogo, Malawi, and its relevance for Palaeolithic archaeology. *World Archaeology*, 1, 390–411.

Clark, J. D. & Kurashina, H. 1979. Hominid occupation of the east-central high-lands of Ethiopia in the Plio-Pleistocene. *Nature*, 282, 33–39.

Clark, J. D., de Heinzelin, J., Schick, K. D., Hart, W. K., White, T. D., WoldeGabriel, G., Walter, R. C., Suwa, G., Asfaw, B., Vrba, E. & H.-Selassie, Y. 1994. African *Homo erectus. Science*, 264, 1907–1910.

Clutton-Brock, J. 1987. *A natural history of domesticated animals.* London: Cambridge University Press/British Museum (Natural History).

Clutton-Brock, T. H. & Harvey, P. H. 1980. Primates, brains and ecology. *Journal of Zoology, London*, 190, 309–323.

Cohen, N. J. & Squire, L. R. 1980. Preserved learning and retention of pattern-analyzing skill in amnesia. *Science*, 210, 207–210.

Conkey, M. 1987. New approaches in the search for meaning? *Journal of Field Archaeology*, 14, 413–430.

Conroy, L. P. 1993. Female figurines of the Upper Palaeolithic and the emergence of gender. In H. du Cros & L. Smith (Eds.), *Women in archaeology. A feminist critique* (pp. 153–160). Canberra: Australian National University.

Corballis, M. C. 1991. *The lopsided ape.* New York: Oxford University Press.

Coren, S. & Porac, C. 1983. Subjective contours and apparent depth. *Perception & Psychophysics*, 33, 197–200.

Coruccini, R. S. 1992. Bootstrap approaches to estimating confidence intervals for molecular dissimilarities and resultant trees. *Journal of Human Evolution*, 23, 481–493.

Costall, A. 1984. Are theories of perception necessary? *Journal of the Experimental Analysis of Behavior*, 41, 109–115.

Costall, A. 1985. How meaning covers the traces. In N. H. Freeman & M. V. Cox (Eds.), *Visual order* (pp. 17–30). Cambridge: Cambridge University Press.

Costall, A. 1991. 'Graceful degradation'. In A. Still & A. Costall (Eds.), *Against cognitivism* (pp. 151–169). New York: Harvester Wheatsheaf.

Cottrell, B. & Kamminga, J. 1987. The formation of flakes. *American Antiquity*, 52, 675–708.

Coulter, J. 1979a. The brain as agent. *Human Studies*, 2, 335–348.

Coulter, J. 1979b. *The social construction of mind.* London: MacMillan.

Coulter, J. 1983. *Rethinking cognitive theory.* London: MacMillan.

Coulter, J. 1984. On comprehension and "mental representation". In G. N. Gilbert & C. Heath (Eds.), *Social action and artificial intelligence* (pp. 8–23). Nottingham: Gower.

Coulter, J. 1987. Recognition in Wittgenstein and contemporary thought. In M. Chapman & R. A. Dixon (Eds.), *Meaning and the growth of understanding* (pp. 85–102). Berlin: Springer-Verlag.

Coulter, J. 1989. *Mind in action.* Cambridge: Polity Press.

Coulter, J. 1991a. The informed neuron: Issues in the use of information theory in the behavioral sciences. In W. Rapaport (Ed.), *Cognitive Science Technical Reports.* Buffalo, N.Y.: State University of New York Press.

Coulter, J. 1991b. Is the "new sentence problem" a genuine problem? *Theory & Psychology*, 1, 317–336.

Coulter, J. & Parsons, E. D. 1990. The praxiology of perception: Visual orientations and practical action. *Inquiry*, 33, 251–272.

Crain, S. 1991. Language acquisition in the absence of experience. *Behavioral and Brain Sciences*, 14, 597–650.

Crystal, D. 1987. *The Cambridge encyclopedia of language*. Cambridge: Cambridge University Press.

Cutting, J. E. & Kozlowski, L. T. 1977. Recognising friends by their walk. *Bulletin of the Psychonomic Society*, 9, 353–356.

Cutting, J. E., Proffitt, D. R. & Kozlowski, L. T. 1978. A biomechanical invariant for gait perception. *Journal of Experimental Psychology: Human Perception and Performance*, 4, 357–372.

Danesi, M. 1993. *Vico, metaphor, and the origin of language*. Bloomington, Indiana: Indiana University Press.

Darlington, P. J. 1975. Group selection, altruism, reinforcement, and throwing in human evolution. *Proceedings of the National Academy of Sciences of the United States of America*, 72, 3748–3752.

Darwin, C. 1872. *The expression of the emotions in man and animals*. London: Murray.

Darwin, C. 1875a. *Insectivorous plants*. London: Murray.

Darwin, C. 1875b. *The movements and habits of climbing plants* (2nd ed.). London: Murray.

Darwin, C. 1968[1859]. *The origin of species*. Harmondsworth: Penguin.

Darwin, C. 1981[1871]. *The descent of man, and selection in relation to sex*. Princeton, NJ: Princeton University Press.

Davidson, I. 1988. The naming of parts. In B. Meehan & R. Jones (Eds.), *Archaeology with ethnography* (pp. 17–32). Canberra: Australian National University.

Davidson, I. 1989a. Comment on "Deliberate engravings on bone artefacts of Homo erectus". *Rock Art Research*, 5, 100–101.

Davidson, I. 1989b. Is intensification a condition of the fisher-hunter-gatherer way of life? *Archaeology in Oceania*, 24, 75–78.

Davidson, I. 1989c. *La economía del final del Paleolítico en la España oriental*. Valencia: Diputación Provincial.

Davidson, I. 1990. Bilzingsleben and early marking. *Rock Art Research*, 7, 52–56.

Davidson, I. 1991. The archaeology of language origins. *Antiquity*, 65, 39–48.

Davidson, I. 1992. There's no art—to find the mind's construction—in offence. *Cambridge Archaeological Journal*, 2, 52–57.

Davidson, I. in press. The power of pictures. In M. Conkey, O. Soffer & D. Stratmann (Eds.), *Beyond art: Pleistocene image and symbol*. California Academy of Sciences.

Davidson, I. & Noble, W. 1989. The archaeology of perception. *Current Anthropology*, 30, 125–155.

Davidson, I. & Noble, W. 1992. Why the first colonisation of the Australian region is the earliest evidence of modern human behaviour. *Archaeology in Oceania*, 27, 135–142.

Davidson, I. & Noble, W. 1993a. Tools and language in human evolution. In K. R.

Gibson & T. Ingold (Eds.), *Tools, language and cognition in human evolution* (pp. 363–388). Cambridge: Cambridge University Press.

Davidson, I. & Noble, W. 1993b. On the evolution of language. *Current Anthropology*, 34, 165–166.

Davidson, I. & Solomon, S. 1990. Was OH7 the victim of a crocodile attack? In S. Solomon, I. Davidson & D. Watson (Eds.), *Problem solving in taphonomy* (pp. 198–206). St Lucia, Queensland: Anthropology Museum, University of Queensland.

Davis, S. J. M. 1987. *The archaeology of animals*. London: Batsford.

Davis, W. 1986. The origins of image making. *Current Anthropology*, 27, 193–215.

de Vos, J. & Sondaar, P. 1994. Dating hominid sites in Indonesia. *Science*, 266, 1726–1727.

Deacon, T. W. 1988. Human brain evolution: I. Evolution of language circuits. In H. J. Jerison & I. Jerison (Eds.), *Intelligence and evolutionary biology* (pp. 363–381). Berlin: Springer-Verlag.

Deacon, T. W. 1990. Fallacies of progression in theories of brain-size evolution. *International Journal of Primatology*, 11(3), 193–236.

Deacon, T. W. 1992. The neural circuitry underlying primate calls and human language. In J. Wind, B. Chiarelli, B. Bichaklian, A. Nocentine & A. Jonkers (Eds.), *Language origin* (pp. 121–162). Dordrecht: Kluwer Academic Publishers.

Delluc, B. & Delluc, G. 1978. Les manifestations graphiques aurignaciennes sur support rocheux des environs des Eyzies. *Gallia Préhistoire*, 21, 213–438.

DeMatteo, A. 1977. Visual imagery and visual analogues in American Sign Language. In L. A. Friedman (Eds.), *On the other hand* (pp. 109–136). New York: Academic Press.

Dennell, R. W., Rendell, H. & Hailwood, E. 1988a. Late Pliocene artifacts from Northern Pakistan. *Current Anthropology*, 29, 495–498.

Dennell, R. W., Rendell, H. & Hailwood, E. 1988b. Early tool making in Asia: two million year old artefacts in Pakistan. *Antiquity*, 62, 98–106.

Dennett, D. 1979. *Brainstorms: Philosophical essays on mind and psychology*. Hassocks: Harvester Press.

Dennett, D. 1983. Intentional systems in cognitive ethology. *The Behavioral and Brain Sciences*, 6, 343–390.

Dennett, D. 1987. *The intentional stance*. Cambridge, Mass.: MIT/Bradford Books.

Dennett, D. 1991. *Consciousness explained*. London: Allen Lane/Penguin.

Deregowski, J. B. 1980. *Illusions, patterns and pictures*. London: Academic Press.

Deregowski, J. B. 1984. *Distortion in art*. London: Routledge & Kegan Paul.

Deregowski, J. B., Muldrow, E. S. & Muldrow, W. F. 1972. Pictorial recognition in a remote Ethiopian population. *Perception*, 1, 417–425.

Descartes, R. 1988[1637]a. Discourse on the method. In *Descartes: Selected philosophical writings* (pp. 20–56). Cambridge: Cambridge University Press.

Descartes, R. 1988[1637]b. Optics. In *Descartes: Selected philosophical writings* (pp. 57–72). Cambridge: Cambridge University Press.

Descartes, R. 1988[1641]. Meditations on first philosophy. In *Descartes: Selected philosophical writings* (pp. 73–159). Cambridge: Cambridge University Press.

Descartes, R. 1988[1644]. Principles of philosophy. In *Descartes: Selected philosophical writings* (pp. 160–212). Cambridge: Cambridge University Press.

Dewart, L. 1989. *Evolution and consciousness*. Toronto: University of Toronto Press.

Diamond, J. 1991. *The Rise and Fall of the Third Chimpanzee*. London: Vintage Books.

Dibble, H. L. 1987. Reduction sequences in the manufacture of Mousterian implements of France. In O. Soffer (Eds.), *The Pleistocene Old World* (pp. 33–44). New York: Plenum Press.

Dibble, H. L. 1989. The implications of stone tool types for the presence of language during the Lower and Middle Paleolithic. In P. Mellars and C. Stringer (Eds.), *The human revolution* (pp. 415–431). Edinburgh: Edinburgh University Press.

Donald, M. 1991. *Origins of the modern mind*. Cambridge, Massachusetts: Harvard University Press.

Donald, M. 1993. Précis of "Origins of the modern mind: Three stages in the evolution of culture and cognition". *Behavioral and Brain Sciences*, 16, 737–791.

Doran, D. M. 1993. Comparative locomotor behavior of chimpanzees and bonobos. *American Journal of Physical Anthropology*, 91, 83–98.

Dretske, F. 1981. *Knowledge and the flow of information*. Cambridge, Mass.: MIT/Bradford Books.

Dreyfus, H. L. 1972. *What computers can't do*. New York: Harper & Row.

Dreyfus, H. L. 1993. *What computers still can't do*. Cambridge, Mass.: The MIT Press.

Duchin, L. E. 1990. The evolution of articulate speech. *Journal of Human Evolution*, 19, 687–697.

Duff, A. I., Clark, G. A. & Chadderton, T. J. 1992. Symbolism in the Early Palaeolithic. *Cambridge Archaeological Journal*, 2, 211–229.

Dunbar, R. I. M. 1988. *Primate social systems*. London: Croom Helm.

Dunbar, R. I. M. 1993. Coevolution of neocortical size, group size and language in humans. *Behavioral and Brain Sciences*, 16(4), 681–735.

Edelman, G. M. 1992. *Bright air, brilliant fire*. Basic Books.

Efron, R. 1990. *The decline and fall of hemispheric specialization*. Hillsdale, NJ: Erlbaum.

Elias, N. 1989. The symbol theory. *Theory, Culture & Society*, 6, 169–217, 339–383, 499–537.

Enright, J. T. 1980. Temporal precision in circadian systems. *Science*, 209, 1542–1545.

Erneling, C. E. 1993. *Understanding language acquisition*. Albany: State University of New York Press.

Evans, C. S., Evans, L. & Marler, P. 1993. On the meaning of alarm calls. *Animal Behaviour*, 46, 23–38.

Evarts, E. V. 1981. Role of motor cortex in voluntary movements in primates. In J. M. Brookhart, V. B. Mountcastle & V. B. Brooks (Eds.), *Handbook of physiology,*

Section I: The nervous system, Volume II. Motor control, Part 2. (pp. 1083–1120). Bethesda, MD: American Physiological Society.

Falk, D. 1980. Language, handedness, and primate brains. *American Anthropologist*, 82, 72–78.

Falk, D. 1983. Cerebral cortices of East African early hominids. *Science*, 221, 1072–1074.

Falk, D. 1986. Evolution of cranial blood drainage in hominids. *American Journal of Physical Anthropology*, 70, 311–324.

Falk, D. 1987a. Brain lateralization in primates and its evolution in hominids. *Yearbook of Physical Anthropology*, 30, 107–125.

Falk, D. 1987b. Hominid paleoneurology. *Annual Review of Anthropology*, 16, 13–30.

Falk, D. 1990. Brain evolution in *Homo. American Journal of Physical Anthropology*, 13, 333–381.

Falk, D. 1992. *Braindance.* New York: Henry Holt.

Fant, L. J. 1972. *Ameslan.* Silver Springs, MD: National Association of the Deaf.

Féblot-Augustins, J. 1993. Mobility strategies in the late Middle Palaeolithic of Central Europe and Western Europe. *Journal of Anthropological Archaeology*, 12, 211–265.

Fedigan, L. M. 1982. *Primate paradigms.* Montreal: Eden Press.

Feibel, C. S., Brown, F. H. & McDougall, I. 1989. Stratigraphic context of fossil hominids from the Omo Group deposits. *American Journal of Physical Anthropology*, 78, 595–622.

Feraud, G., York, D., Hall, C. M., Goren, N. & Schwarcz, H. P. 1983. 40 Ar/39Ar age limit for an Acheulian site in Israel. *Nature*, 304, 263–265.

Fernald, A. & Simon, T. 1984. Expanded intonation contours in mothers' speech to newborns. *Developmental Psychology*, 20, 104–113.

Firth, R. 1973. *Symbols public and private.* London: Allen & Unwin.

Fladmark, K. R. 1979. Routes. *American Antiquity*, 44, 55–69.

Flanagan, O. J. 1992. *Consciousness reconsidered.* Cambridge, MA: MIT Press/ Bradford.

Flew, A. 1971. *An introduction to western philosophy.* London: Thames and Hudson.

Fodor, J. A. 1975. *The language of thought.* Cambridge, MA: Harvard University Press.

Fodor, J. A. 1983. *The modularity of mind.* Cambridge, Mass.: MIT Press.

Fodor, J. A. & Pylyshyn, Z. W. 1988. Connectionism and cognitive architecture. *Cognition*, 28, 3–71.

Foley, R. A. 1982. A reconsideration of the role of predation on large mammals in tropical hunter-gatherer adaptation. *Man*, 17, 383–402.

Foley, R. A. 1987a. *Another unique species.* Harlow, Essex: Longman.

Foley, R. A. 1987b. Hominid species and stone-tool assemblages. *Antiquity*, 61, 380–392.

Foley, R. A. 1988. Hominids, humans and hunter-gatherers. In T. Ingold, D. Riches & J. Woodburn (Eds.), *Hunters and gatherers, Volume 1* (pp. 207–221). Oxford: Berg.

Foley, R. A. 1989. The evolution of hominid social behaviour. In V. Standen & R. A. Foley (Eds.), *Comparative socioecology* (pp. 473–494). Oxford: Blackwell Scientific Publications.

Foley, R. A. 1990. The causes of brain enlargement in human evolution. *Behavioral and Brain Sciences*, 13, 354–356.

Foley, R. A. 1992. Evolutionary ecology of fossil hominids. In E. A. Smith & B. Winterhalder (Eds.), *Evolutionary ecology and human behavior* (pp. 131–164). New York: Aldine de Gruyter.

Foley, R. A. 1994. Speciation, extinction and climatic change in hominid evolution. *Journal of Human Evolution*, 26, 275–289.

Foley, R. A. & Lahr, M. M. 1992. Beyond "Out of Africa". *Journal of Human Evolution*, 22, 523–529.

Foley, R. A. & Lee, P. C. 1989. Finite social space, evolutionary pathways, and reconstructing hominid behavior. *Science*, 243, 901–906.

Foley, R. A. & Lee, P. C. 1991. Ecology and energetics of encephalization in hominid evolution. *Philosophical Transactions of the Royal Society of London B*, 334, 223–232.

Folomkina, S. & Weise, H. 1963. *The learner's English-Russian dictionary*. Cambridge, Mass.: MIT Press

Fossey, D. 1972. Vocalizations of the mountain gorilla (*Gorilla gorilla beringei*). *Animal Behaviour*, 20, 36–53.

Fossey, D. 1983. *Gorillas in the mist*. London: Hodder and Stoughton.

Fossey, D. & Harcourt, A. H. 1977. Feeding ecology of free-ranging Mountain Gorilla (*Gorilla gorilla beringei*). In T. H. Clutton-Brock (Eds.), *Primate ecology* (pp. 415–447). London: Academic Press.

Fouts, R. S., Fouts, D. H. & Schoenfeld, D. 1984. Sign language conversational interaction between chimpanzees. *Sign Language Studies*, 42, 1–12.

Frame, H. 1986. Microscopic use-wear traces. In P. Callow & J. Cornford (Eds.), *La Cotte de St. Brelade 1961–1978* (pp. 353–362). Norwich: Geo Books.

Fraser, H. 1992. *The subject of speech perception*. London: Macmillan.

Frayer, D. W., Wolpoff, M. H., Thorne, A. G., Smith, F. H. & Pope, G. G. 1993. Theories of modern human origins. *American Anthropologist*, 95(1), 14–50.

Friedman, W. F. 1977. *History of the use of codes*. California: Aegean Park Press.

Frisch, K. v. 1954. *The dancing bees* (Ilse, D., Trans.). London: Methuen.

Fromkin, V. & Rodman, R. 1978. *An introduction to language* (2nd ed.). New York: Holt, Rinehart and Winston.

Galaburda, A. M. & Pandya, D. N. 1982. Role of architectonics and connections in the study of primate brain evolution. In E. Armstrong & D. Falk (Eds.), *Primate brain evolution* (pp. 203–216). New York: Plenum Press.

Galdikas, B. M. F. 1982. Orang-utan tool-use in Tanjung Puting Reserve, Central Indonesian Borneo (Kalimantan Tengah). *Journal of Human Evolution*, 10, 19–33.

Galilei, G. 1953[1632]. *Dialogue concerning the two chief world systems, Ptolemaic & Copernican* (Drake, S., Trans.). Berkeley: University of California Press.

Gamble, C. 1986. *The Palaeolithic settlement of Europe*. Cambridge: Cambridge University Press.

Gamble, C. 1993. *Timewalkers*. Stroud, Gloucestershire: Alan Sutton.

Gardner, H. 1985. *The mind's new science*. New York: Basic Books.

Gardner, R. A. & Gardner, B. T. 1968. Teaching sign language to a chimpanzee. *Science*, 165, 664–672.

Gardner, R. A. & Gardner, B. T. 1980. Comparative psychology and language acquisition. In T. A. Sebeok & J. Umiker-Sebeok (Eds.), *Speaking of apes* (pp. 287–330). New York: Plenum.

Gargett, R. H. 1989. Grave shortcomings. *Current Anthropology*, 30, 157–190.

Gebo, D. L. 1992. Plantigrady and foot adaptation in African apes. *American Journal of Physical Anthropology*, 89, 29–58.

Geertz, C. 1964. The transition to humanity. In S. Tax (Eds.), *Horizons of anthropology* Chicago: Aldine.

Geist, V. 1978. *Life strategies, human evolution, environmental design*. New York: Springer-Verlag.

Geneste, J.-M. 1988. Les industries de la Grotte Vaufrey. In J.-P. Riguad (Eds.), *La Grotte Vaufrey à Cenac et Saint-Julien (Dordogne)* (pp. 441–517). Société Préhistorique Française.

Georgopoulos, A. P., Schwartz, A. B. & Kettner, R. E. 1986. Neuronal population coding of movement direction. *Science*, 233, 1416–1419.

Ghiglieri, M. P. 1989. Hominoid sociobiology and hominid social evolution. In P. G. Heltne & L. A. Marquardt (Eds.), *Understanding chimpanzees* (pp. 370–379). Cambridge, Massachusetts: Harvard University Press.

Gibson, J. J. 1950. *The perception of the visual world*. Boston: Houghton-Mifflin.

Gibson, J. J. 1966. *The senses considered as perceptual systems*. Boston: Houghton-Mifflin.

Gibson, J. J. 1967. New reasons for realism. *Synthese*, 17, 173–201.

Gibson, J. J. 1971. The information available in pictures. *Leonardo*, 4, 27–35.

Gibson, J. J. 1979. *The ecological approach to visual perception*. Boston: Houghton-Mifflin.

Gibson, K. R. 1986. Cognition, brain size and the extraction of embedded resources. In J. G. Else & P. C. Lee (Eds.), *Primate ontogeny, cognitive and social behavior* (pp. 93–105). Cambridge: Cambridge University Press.

Gibson, K. R. 1990. Tool use,imitation, and deception in a captive cebus monkey. In S. T. Parker & K. R. Gibson (Eds.), *"Language" and intelligence in monkeys and apes* (pp. 205–218). Cambridge: Cambridge University Press.

Gibson, K. R. & Jessee, S. 1993. Comment on Milo and Quiatt (1993). *Current Anthropology*, 34, 585.

Gimbutas, M. 1982. *The goddesses and gods of old Europe*. Berkeley, CA: University of California Press.

Glosser, G. & Wiener, M. 1990. Gestures and speech. In G. R. Hammond (Eds.), *Cerebral control of speech and limb movements* (pp. 257–277). Amsterdam: North-Holland.

Godelier, M. 1977[1971]. Myth and history. In *Perspectives in Marxist anthropology* (pp. 204–220). Cambridge: Cambridge University Press.

Goffman, E. 1955. Embarrassment and social organization. *American Journal of Sociology*, 62, 264–271.

Goffman, E. 1956. *The presentation of self in everyday life*. Edinburgh: University of Edinburgh, Social Sciences Research Centre.

Goffman, E. 1963. *Behavior in public places*. New York: The Free Press of Glencoe.

Goldin-Meadow, S. 1993. When does gesture become language? In K. R. Gibson & T. Ingold (Eds.), *Tools, Language and Cognition in Human Evolution* (pp. 63–85). Cambridge: Cambridge University Press.

Goldin-Meadow, S. & Feldman, H. 1977. The development of language-like communication without a language model. *Science*, 197, 401.

Gombrich, E. H. 1960. *Art and illusion*. London: Phaidon.

Goodall, A. G. 1977. Feeding and ranging behaviour of a Mountain Gorilla group (*Gorilla gorilla beringei*) in the Tshibinda-Kahuzi region (Zaire). In T. H. Clutton-Brock (Eds.), *Primate ecology* (pp. 449–479). London: New York.

Goodall, J. 1964. Tool-use and aimed throwing in a community of free ranging chimpanzees. *Nature*, 201, 1264–1266.

Goodall, J. 1986. *The Chimpanzees of Gombe*. Cambridge, MA: The Belknap Press of Harvard University Press.

Goode, D. A. 1980. The world of the congenitally deaf-blind. In J. Jacobs (Eds.), *Mental retardation* (pp. 187–207). Springfield, Illinois: Thomas.

Goodman, M., Bailey, W. J., Hayasaka, K., Stanhope, M. J., Slightom, J. & Czelusniak, J. 1994. Molecular evidence on primate phylogeny from DNA sequences. *American Journal of Physical Anthropology*, 94, 3–24.

Goody, J. 1987. *The interface between the written and the oral*. Cambridge: Cambridge University Press.

Goren-Inbar, N. 1986. A figurine from the Acheulian site of Berekhat Ram. *Mitekufat Haeven*, 19, 7–12.

Gould, S. J. 1977. *Ontogeny and phylogeny*. Cambridge, Mass.: Harvard University Press.

Gould, S. J. 1991. Exaptation. *Journal of Social Issues*, 47, 43–65.

Gould, S. J. & Vrba, E. S. 1982. Exaptation. *Paleobiology*, 8, 4–15.

Gowlett, J. A. J. 1984. Mental abilities of early Man. In R. Foley (Ed.), *Hominid evolution and community ecology* (pp. 167–192). London: Academic Press.

Gowlett, J. A. J. 1988. A case of Developed Oldowan in the Acheulean? *World Archaeology*, 20, 13–26.

Gowlett, J. A. J. 1992. Tools—the Palaeolithic record. In S. Jones, R. Martin & D. Pilbeam (Eds.), *The Cambridge encyclopedia of human evolution* (pp. 350–360). Cambridge: Cambridge University Press.

Gracco, V. L. 1990. Characteristics of speech as a motor control system. In G. R. Hammond (Eds.), *Cerebral control of speech and limb movements* (pp. 3–28). Amsterdam: North-Holland.

Grayson, D. K. & Delpech, F. 1994. The evidence for Middle Palaeolithic scavenging from Couche VII, Grotte Vaufrey (Dordogne, France). *Journal of Archaeological Science*, 21, 359–375.

Greenfield, P. M. 1980. Toward an operational and logical analysis of intentionality. In D. R. Olson (Eds.), *The social foundations of language and thought* (pp. 254–279). New York: Norton.

Greenfield, P. M. 1991. Language, tools and brain. *Behavioral and Brain Sciences*, 14, 531–595.

Greenfield, P. M. & Savage-Rumbaugh, E. S. 1990. Grammatical combination in *Pan paniscus*. In S. T. Parker & K. R. Gibson (Eds.), *"Language" and intelligence in monkeys and apes* (pp. 540–578). Cambridge: Cambridge University Press.

Greenfield, P. M. & Savage-Rumbaugh, E. S. 1993. Comparing communicative competence in child and chimp. *Journal of Child Language*, 20, 1–26.

Gregory, R. L. 1974. *Concepts and mechanisms of perception*. London: Duckworth.

Gregory, R. L. (Ed.). 1987. *The Oxford companion to the mind*. Oxford: Oxford University Press.

Grice, H. P. 1969. Utterer's meaning and intentions. *Philosophical Review*, 78, 147–177.

Grine, F. E. & Kay, R. F. 1988. Early hominid diets from quantitative image analysis of dental microwear. *Nature*, 333, 765–768.

Groves, C. P. 1970. *Gorillas*. London: Arthur Baker.

Groves, C. P. 1989. *A theory of human and primate evolution*. Oxford: Clarendon Press.

Groves, C. P. & Sabater Pí, J. 1985. From ape's nest to human fix-point. *Man*, 20, 22–47.

Gruber, H. E. & Barrett, P. H. 1974. *Darwin on man*. New York: Dutton.

Grün, R. & Stringer, C. B. 1991. Electron spin resonance dating of the evolution of modern humans. *Archaeometry*, 33, 153–199.

Grün, R., Stringer, C. B. & Schwarcz, H. P. 1991. ESR dating of teeth from Garrod's Tabun cave collection. *Journal of Human Evolution*, 20, 231–248.

Guidon, N. & Delibrias, G. 1986. Carbon-14 dates point to Man in the Americas 32,000 years ago. *Nature*, 321, 769–771.

Guilford, T. & Dawkins, M. S. 1991. Receiver psychology and the evolution of animal signals. *Animal Behaviour*, 42, 1–14.

Guilford, T. & Dawkins, M. S. 1992. Understanding signal design. *Animal Behaviour*, 44, 384–385.

Guilmet, G. M. 1977. The evolution of tool-using and tool-making behaviour. *Man*, 12, 33–47.

Hacking, I. 1983. *Representing and intervening*. Cambridge: Cambridge University Press.

Hagen, M. (Ed.). 1980. *The perception of pictures vol. 1*. New York: Academic Press.

Hagen, M. 1986. *Varieties of realism*. Cambridge: Cambridge University Press.

Hahn, J. 1972. Aurignacian signs, pendants and art objects in Central and Eastern Europe. *World Archaeology*, 3(3), 252–266.

Hahn, J. 1986. *Kraft und aggression*. Tübingen: Institut Für Urgeschichte der Universität Tübingen.

Haimoff, E. H. 1984. Acoustic and organizational features of gibbon songs. In H. Preuschoft, D. J. Chivers, W. Y. Brockelman & N. Creel (Eds.), *The lesser apes* (pp. 333–352). Edinburgh: Edinburgh University Press.

Halliday, T. 1983. Information and communication. In T. R. Halliday & P. J. B. Slater (Eds.), *Animal Behaviour* (pp. 43–81). Oxford: Blackwell.

Halverson, J. 1987. Art for art's sake in the Palaeolithic. *Current Anthropology*, 28, 63–89.

Halverson, J. 1992a. Paleolithic art and cognition. *The Journal of Psychology*, 126, 221–236.

Halverson, J. 1992b. The first pictures. *Perception*, 21, 389–404.

Hammond, G. R. 1990. Manual performance assymetries. In G. R. Hammond (Eds.), *Cerebral control of speech and limb movements* (pp. 59–77). Amsterdam: North-Holland.

Hannan, T. E. 1987. A cross-sequential assessment of the occurrences of pointing in 3- to 12-month-old human infants. *Infant Behavior and Development*, 10, 11–22.

Harding, R. S. O. 1981. An order of omnivores. In R. S. O. Harding & G. Teleki (Eds.), *Omnivorous primates* (pp. 191–214). New York: Columbia University Press.

Harpending, H. C., Sherry, S. T., Rogers, A. R. & Stoneking, M. 1993. The genetic structure of ancient human populations. *Current Anthropology*, 34, 483–496.

Harré, R. & Secord, P. F. 1972. *The explanation of social behaviour*. Oxford: Blackwell.

Harris, J. W. K. 1983. Cultural beginnings. *African Archaeological Review*, 1, 3–31.

Harris, R. 1987. *Reading Saussure* London: Duckworth.

Harris, R. 1988. *Language, Saussure and Wittgenstein*. London: Routledge.

Harrold, F. 1980. A comparative analysis of Eurasian Palaeolithic burials. *World Archaeology*, 12, 195–211.

Hasegawa, T., Hiraiwa, M., Nishida, T. & Takasaki, H. 1983. New evidence of scavenging behaviour in wild chimpanzees. *Current Anthropology*, 24, 231–232.

Hay, R. L. 1976. *Geology of Olduvai Gorge*. Berkeley: University of California Press.

Hayden, B. 1993. The cultural capacities of Neanderthals. *American Anthropologist*, 24, 113–146.

Hayes, K. & Hayes, C. 1952. Imitation in a home-raised chimpanzee. *Journal of Comparative and Physiological Psychology*, 45, 450–459.

Heil, J. 1981. Does cognitive psychology rest on a mistake? *Mind*, 90, 321–342.

Hewes, G. W. 1973. Primate communication and the gestural origin of language. *Current Anthropology*, 14, 5–24.

Hewes, G. W. 1974. Gesture language in culture contact. *Sign Language Studies*, 4, 1–34.

Heyes, C. M. 1994. Social cognition in primates. In N. J. Mackintosh (Ed.), *Handbook of perception and cognition* (pp. 281–305). New York: Academic Press.

Hill, A., Ward, S., Deino, A., Curtis, G. & Drake, R. 1992. Earliest *Homo*. *Nature*, 355, 719–722.

Hill, K. 1982. Hunting and human evolution. *Journal of Human Evolution*, 11, 521–544.

Hladik, C.-M. 1977. Chimpanzees of Gabon and Chimpanzees of Gombe. In T. H. Clutton-Brock (Ed.), *Primate ecology* (pp. 481–501). London: Academic Press.

Hockett, C. F. 1960. The origin of speech. *Scientific American*, 203(9), 89–96.

Hockett, C. F. & Altmann, S. A. 1968. A note on design features. In T. A. Sebeok (Ed.), *Animal communication* (pp. 61–72). Bloomington: Indiana University Press.

Hockett, C. F. & Ascher, R. 1964. The human revolution. *Current Anthropology*, 5(3), 135–168.

Hodge, R. & Kress, G. 1988. *Social semiotics*. Cambridge: Polity Press.

Hofman, M. A. 1983. Energy metabolism, brain size, and longevity in mammals. *Quarterly Review of Biology*, 58(4), 495–512.

Holloway, R. L. 1966. Cranial capacity, neural reorganization, and hominid evolution. *American Anthropologist*, 68, 103–121.

Holloway, R. L. 1969. Culture: A human domain. *Current Anthropology*, 10, 395–412.

Holloway, R. L. 1973. New endocranial values for the East African early hominids. *Nature*, 243, 97–99.

Holloway, R. L. 1981. Culture, symbols, and human brain evolution. *Dialectical Anthropology*, 5, 287–303.

Holloway, R. L. 1983. Human palaeontological evidence relevant to language behaviour. *Human Neurobiology*, 2, 105–114.

Holquist, M. 1981. The politics of representation. In S. J. Greenblatt (Eds.), *Allegory and representation* (pp. 163–183). Baltimore: Johns Hopkins University Press.

Hopkins, C. D. 1983. Sensory mechanisms in animal communication. In T. R. Halliday & P. J. B. Slater (Eds.), *Animal Behaviour* (pp. 114–155). Oxford: Blackwell.

Hopkins, W. D. & Savage-Rumbaugh, E. S. 1991. Vocal communication as a function of differential rearing experiences in Pan paniscus. *International Journal of Primatology*, 12, 559–583.

Houghton, P. 1993. Neanderthal supralaryngeal vocal tract. *American Journal of Physical Anthropology*, 90, 139–146.

Howell, F. C. 1964. *Early Man*. New York: Time-Life Books.

Hubel, D. H. & Wiesel, T. N. 1968. Receptive fields and functional architecture of monkey striate cortex. *Journal of Physiology*, 195, 215–243.

Hubel, D. H. & Wiesel, T. N. 1970. Stereoscopic vision in macaque monkey. *Nature*, 225, 41–42.

Hunt, K. D. 1992. Positional behavior of *Pan trogodytes* in the Mahale mountans and Gombe stream National Parks, Tanzania. *American Journal of Physical Anthropology*, 87, 83–105.

Hunt, K. D. 1994. The evolution of human bipedality. *Journal of Human Evolution*, 26, 183–202.

Huxley, T. H. 1906. *Man's place in nature and other essays*. London: J.M. Dent and Sons.

Ingold, T. 1986. *Evolution and social life*. Cambridge: Cambridge University Press.

Ingold, T. 1987. *The appropriation of nature*. Iowa City: University of Iowa Press.

Ingold, T. 1989. The social and environmental relations of human beings and other animals. In V. Standen & R. A. Foley (Eds.), *Comparative socioecology* (pp. 495–512). Oxford: Blackwell Scientific Publications.

Ingold, T. 1993a. Tool-use, sociality and intelligence. In K. R. Gibson & T. Ingold (Eds.), *Tools, Language and Cognition in Human Evolution* (pp. 429–445). Cambridge: Cambridge University Press.

Ingold, T. 1993b. Tools, techniques and technology. In K. R. Gibson & T. Ingold (Eds.), *Tools, language and cognition in human evolution* (pp. 337–345). Cambridge: Cambridge University Press.

Irwin, G. 1992. *The prehistoric exploration and colonisation of the Pacific.* Cambridge: Cambridge University Press.

Isaac, G. L. 1978. The food-sharing behavior of protohuman hominids. *Scientific American,* 238, 90–108.

Isaac, G. L. & Crader, D. C. 1981. To what extent were early hominids carnivorous? In R. S. O. Harding & G. Teleki (Eds.), *Omnivorous primates* (pp. 37–103). New York: Columbia University Press.

Jablonski, N. G. & Chaplin, G. 1992. The origin of hominid bipedalism reexamined. *Archaeology in Oceania,* 27, 153–160.

James, S. R. 1989. Hominid use of fire in the Lower and Middle Pleistocene. *Current Anthropology,* 30, 1–26.

James, W. 1981[1890]. *The principles of psychology.* Cambridge, Mass.: Harvard University Press.

Jarman, P. J. 1974. The social organisation of antelope in relation to their ecology. *Behaviour,* 48, 215–266.

Jaynes, J. 1977. *The origin of consciousness in the breakdown of the bicameral mind.* Boston: Houghton Mifflin.

Jayyusi, L. 1984. *Categorization and the moral order.* Boston: Routledge & Kegan Paul.

Jerison, H. J. 1973. *Evolution of the brain and intelligence.* New York: Academic Press.

Jerison, H. J. 1982. Allometry, brain size, cortical surface, and convolutedness. In E. Armstrong & D. Falk (Eds.), *Primate brain evolution* (pp. 77–84). New York: Plenum Press.

Joanette, Y., Goulet, P. & Hannequin, D. 1990. *Right hemisphere and verbal communication.* New York: Springer-Verlag.

Johanson, D. C. & Edey, M. 1981. *Lucy.* New York: Simon and Schuster.

Johanson, D. C. & Shreeve, J. 1991. *Lucy's child.* London: Penguin Books.

Johanson, D. C. & Taieb, M. 1976. Plio-Pleistocene hominid discoveries in Hadar, Ethiopia. *Nature,* 260, 293–297.

Johanson, D. C., White, T. D. & Coppens, Y. 1978. A new species of the genus *Australopithecus* (Primates: Hominidae) from the Pliocene of Eastern Africa. *Kirtlandia,* 28, 1–14.

Jolly, A. 1972. *The evolution of primate behavior.* New York: Macmillan.

Jones, S., Martin, R. & Pilbeam, D. (Ed.). 1992. *The Cambridge encyclopedia of human evolution.* Cambridge: Cambridge University Press.

Jung, C. G. 1976. *The symbolic life.* London: Routledge & Kegan Paul.

Kalaska, J. F. & Crammond, D. J. 1992. Cerebral cortical mechanisms of reaching movements. *Science,* 255, 1517–1523.

Kanizsa, G. 1974. Contours without gradients or cognitive contours? *Italian Journal of Psychology*, 1, 93–113.

Kano, T. 1979. A pilot study on the ecology of Pygmy Chimpanzees, *Pan paniscus*. In D. A. Hamburg & E. R. McCown (Eds.), *The great apes* (pp. 123–135). Menlo Park: The Benjamin/Cummings Publishing Company.

Kaplan, G. & Rogers, L. 1994. *Orang-utans in Borneo*. Armidale, NSW: University of New England Press.

Keeley, L. H. 1980. *Experimental determination of stone tool uses*. Chicago: The University of Chicago Press.

Keeley, L. H. 1993. Microwear analysis of lithics. In R. Singer, B. G. Gladfelter & J. J. Wymer (Eds.), *The Lower Palaeolithic site at Hoxne, England* (pp. 129–138). Chicago: The University of Chicago Press.

Keeley, L. H. & Toth, N. 1981. Microwear polishes on early stone tools from Koobi Fora, Kenya. *Nature*, 293, 464–465.

Kendon, A. 1981. Current issues in the study of "nonverbal communication". In A. Kendon (Eds.), *Nonverbal Communication, Interaction, and Gesture* (pp. 1–53). The Hague: Mouton.

Kendon, A. 1991. Some considerations for a theory of language origins. *Man*, 26, 199–221.

Kendon, A. 1993. Human gesture. In K. R. Gibson & T. Ingold (Eds.), *Tools, language and cognition in human evolution* (pp. 43–62). Cambridge: Cambridge University Press.

Kimbel, W. H., Johanson, D. C. & Rak, Y. 1994. The first skull and other new discoveries of *Australopithecus afarensis* at Hadar, Ethiopia. *Nature*, 368, 449–451.

King, B. J. 1991. Social information transfer in monkeys, apes, and hominids. *Yearbook of Physical Anthropology*, 34, 97–115.

Klein, R. G. 1976. The mammalian fauna of the Klasies River Mouth sites, southern Cape Province. *South African Archaeological Bulletin*, 31, 75–98.

Klein, R. G. 1980. Environmental and ecological implications of large mammals from the Upper Pleistocene and Holocene sites in Southern Africa. *Annals of the South African Museum*, 81, 223–283.

Klein, R. G. 1987. Reconstructing how early people exploited animals. In M. H. Nitecki & D. V. Nitecki (Eds.), *The evolution of hunting* (pp. 11–45). New York: Plenum Press.

Klein, R. G. 1989. *The human career*. Chicago: The University of Chicago Press.

Klima, E. & Bellugi, U. 1979. *The signs of language*. Cambridge, Mass.: Harvard University Press.

Knuckey, G. 1992. Patterns of fracture upon Aboriginal crania from the recent past. In N. W. Bruce (Eds.), *Living with civilisation* (pp. 47–58). Perth: Centre for Human Biology, University of Western Australia.

Knüsel, C. J. 1992. The throwing hypothesis and hominid origins. *Human Evolution*, 7, 1–7.

Koch, C. P. 1990. Bone breakage, differential preservation and *Theropithecus* butchery at Olorgesaile, Kenya. In S. Solomon, I. Davidson & D. Watson (Eds.),

Problem solving in taphonomy (pp. 158–166). St. Lucia, Queensland: Anthropology Museum, University of Queensland.

Kortlandt, A. 1986. The use of stone tools by wild-living chimpanzees and earliest hominids. *Journal of Human Evolution*, 15, 77–132.

Krebs, J. R. & Dawkins, R. 1984. Animal signals. In J. R. Krebs & N. B. Davies (Eds.), *Behavioural Ecology* (pp. 380–402). Oxford: Blackwell.

Kroeber, A. L. 1928. Sub-human cultural beginnings. *Quarterly Review of Biology*, 3, 325–342.

Kroeber, A. L. & Kluckhohn, C. 1954. *Culture: A critical review of concepts and definitions.* New York: Vintage Books.

Kuhn, S. L. 1991. New problems, old glasses. In G. A. Clark (Eds.), *Perspectives on the past* (pp. 243–257). Philadelphia: University of Pennsylvania Press.

Kuhn, T. 1970. *The structure of scientific revolutions* (2nd ed.). Chicago: University of Chicago Press.

Ladefoged, P. 1975. *A course in phonetics.* New York: Harcourt Brace Jovanovich.

Lalueza Fox, C. & Pérez-Pérez, A. 1993. The diet of the Neanderthal child Gibraltar 2 (Devil's Tower) through the study of the vestibular striation pattern. *Journal of Human Evolution*, 24, 29–41.

Lalueza Fox, C., Pérez-Pérez, A. & Turbón, D. 1993. Microscopic study of the Banyoles mandible (Girona, Spain). *Journal of Human Evolution*, 24, 281–300.

Langacker, R. W. 1987. *Foundations of cognitive grammar, volume I.* Stanford, California: Stanford University Press.

Latash, M. L. 1993. *Control of human movement.* Champaign, Ill.: Human Kinetics Publishers.

Lawick-Goodall, J. van 1968a. A preliminary report on expressive movements and communication in the Gombe Stream chimpanzees. In P. C. Jay (Ed.), *Primates* (pp. 259–374). New York: Holt, Rinehart and Winston.

Lawick-Goodall, J. van 1968b. The behaviour of free-living chimpanzees in the Gombe Stream Reserve. *Animal Behaviour Monographs*, 1, 161–311.

Leakey, M. D. 1966. A review of the Oldowan culture from Olduvai Gorge, Tanzania. *Nature*, 210, 462–466.

Leakey, M. D. 1971. *Olduvai Gorge.* Cambridge: Cambridge University Press.

Leakey, M. D. & Hay, R. L. 1979. Pliocene footprints in the Laetolil Beds at Laetoli, northern Tanzania. *Nature*, 278, 317–323.

Leakey, R. & Lewin, R. 1992. *Origins Reconsidered.* London: Little Brown.

Lee, R. B. 1968. What hunters do for a living, or, how to make out on scarce resources. In R. B. Lee & I. DeVore (Eds.), *Man the Hunter* (pp. 30–48). Chicago: Aldine.

Leigh, S. R. 1992. Cranial capacity evolution in *Homo erectus* and early *Homo sapiens. American Journal of Physical anthropology*, 87, 1–13.

Leighton, D. R. 1986. Gibbons: territoriality and monogamy. In B. B. Smuts, D. L. Cheney, R. M. Seyfarth, R. W. Wrangham & T. T. Struhsaker (Eds.), *Primate societies* (pp. 135–145). Chicago: The University of Chicago Press.

Lenneberg, E. H. 1967. *Biological foundations of language.* New York: Wiley.

Lévi-Strauss, C. 1966. *The savage mind.* London: Weidenfeld and Nicolson.

Lewin, R. 1989. *Bones of contention*. Harmondsworth: Penguin Books.

Lewis-Williams, J. D. & Dowson, T. A. 1988. The signs of all times. *Current Anthropology*, 29, 201–245.

Liberman, I. Y. & Liberman, A. M. 1992. Whole language vs code emphasis. In P. B. Gough, L. C. Ehri & R. Treiman (Eds.), *Reading acquisition* (pp. 343–366). Hillsdale, NJ: Erlbaum.

Lieberman, D. & Shea, J. J. 1994. Behavioral differences between Archaic and Modern humans in the Levantine Mousterian. *American Anthropologist*, 96(2), 300–332.

Lieberman, P. 1984. *The biology and evolution of language*. Cambridge, Massachusetts: Harvard University Press.

Lieberman, P., Laitman, J. T., Reidenberg, J. S. & Gannon, P. J. 1992. The anatomy, physiology, acoustics and perception of speech. *Journal of Human Evolution*, 23, 447–467.

Lieberman, S. J. 1980. Of clay pebbles, hollow clay balls, and writing. *American Journal of Archaeology*, 84, 339–358.

Lindly, J. M. 1988. Hominid and carnivore activity at Middle and Upper Paleolithic cave sites in eastern Spain. *Munibe*, 40, 45–70.

Lindly, J. M. & Clark, G. A. 1990. Symbolism and modern human origins. *Current Anthropology*, 31, 233–61.

Liska, J. 1986. Symbols: the missing link? In J. G. Else & L. C. (Eds.), *Primate Ontogeny, Cognition and Social Behaviour* (pp. 169–178). Cambridge: Cambridge University Press.

Lloyd, J. E. 1971. Bioluminescent communication in insects. *Annual Review of Entomology*, 16, 97–122.

Lock, A. 1978. The emergence of language. In A. Lock (Eds.), *Action, gesture and symbol* (pp. 3–18). London: Academic Press.

Lock, A. 1980. *The guided reinvention of language*. London: Academic Press.

Lock, A., Young, A., Service, V. & Chandler, P. 1990. Some observations on the origins of the pointing gesture. In V. Volterra & C. J. Erting (Eds.), *From gesture to language in hearing and deaf children* (pp. 42–55). Berlin: Springer-Verlag.

Lorblanchet, M. 1977. From naturalism to abstraction in European prehistoric rock art. In P. J. Ucko (Eds.), *Form in indigenous art*. Duckworth: London.

Lovejoy, O. 1981. The origin of man. *Science*, 211, 341–350.

Loy, T. H. & Hardy, B. L. 1992. Blood residue analysis of 90,000-year old stone tools from Tabun Cave, Israel. *Antiquity*, 66, 24–35.

Lumley, H. D. 1969. A paleolithic camp site at Nice. *Scientific American*, 220, 42–50.

Lynch, T. F. 1990. Glacial-age Man in South America? *American Antiquity*, 55(1), 12–36.

MacKinnon, J. 1974. The behaviour and ecology of wild orang-utans (*Pongo pygmaeus*). *Animal Behaviour*, 22, 3–74.

Macksey, K. 1986. *Technology in war*. New York: Prentice Hall.

MacLarnon, A. 1993. The vertebral canal. In A. Walker & R. E. F. Leakey (Eds.), *The Nariokotome Homo erectus skeleton* (pp. 359–390). Cambridge, Massachusetts: Harvard University Press.

MacLean, C. 1979. *The wolf children*. Harmondworth: Penguin.

Malatesta, C. Z. & Haviland, J. 1982. Learning display rules. *Child Development*, 53, 991–1003.

Mania, D. & Mania, U. 1988. Deliberate engravings on bone artefacts of Homo erectus. *Rock Art Research*, 5, 91–109.

Mania, D. 1983. Autochthone Lagerplatzstrukturen im altpaläolithischen Fundhorizont auf der Steinrinne bei Bilzingsleben. *Ethnographische-Archäologische Zeitschrifte*, 24, 296–303.

Marchant, L. F. & McGrew, W. C. 1991. Laterality of function in apes. *Journal of Human Evolution*, 21, 425–438.

Margolis, J. 1987. Wittgenstein's "forms of life". In M. Chapman & R. A. Dixon (Eds.), *Meaning and the growth of understanding* (pp. 129–150). Berlin: Springer-Verlag.

Marks, J. 1994. Blood will tell (won't it?). *American Journal of Physical Anthropology*, 94, 59–79.

Marler, P. 1967. Animal communication signals. *Science*, 157, 769–774.

Marler, P. 1976. Social organization, communication and graded signals the chimpanzee and the gorilla. In P. P. G. Bateson & R. A. Hinde (Eds.), *Growing points in ethology* (pp. 239–280). Cambridge: Cambridge University Press.

Marler, P. & Tenaza, R. 1977. Signalling behavior of apes with special reference to vocalization. In T. A. Sebeok (Eds.), *How animals communicate* (pp. 965–1033). Bloomington: Indiana University Press.

Marshack, A. 1972. The roots of civilization. New York: McGraw-Hill.

Marshack, A. 1976. Some symbolic implications of the Palaeolithic symbolic evidence for the origin of language. *Current Anthropology*, 17, 274–282.

Marshack, A. 1989. Evolution of the human capacity. *Yearbook of Physical Anthropology*, 32, 1–34.

Martin, R. D. 1990. *Primate origins and evolution*. London: Chapman and Hall.

Martinson, D. G., Pisias, N. G., Hays, J. D., Imbrie, J., Moore, T. C. & Shackleton, N. J. 1987. Age dating and the orbital theory of the ice ages. *Quaternary Research*, 27, 1–29.

Masataka, N. 1992. Motherese in a signed language. *Infant Behavior and Development*, 15, 453–460.

Mayr, E. 1969. *Principles of systematic zoology*. New York: McGraw-Hill.

McClelland, J. L., Rumelhart, D. E. & Hinton, G. E. 1986. The appeal of parallel distributed processing. In D. E. Rumelhart & J. L. McClelland (Eds.), *Parallel distributed processing* (pp. 3–44). Cambridge, Mass.: MIT Press.

McFarland, D. 1985. *Animal behaviour*. Harlow: Longman Scientific and Technical.

McGrew, W. C. 1987. Tools to get food. *Journal of Anthropological Research*, 43, 247–258.

McGrew, W. C. 1989a. Comment on James (1989). *Current Anthropology*, 30, 16–17.

McGrew, W. C. 1989b. Why is ape tool use so confusing? In V. Standen & R. A. Foley (Eds.), *Comparative socioecology* (pp. 457–472). Oxford: Blackwell Scientific Publications.

McGrew, W. C. 1991. Chimpanzee material culture. In R. A. Foley (Ed.), *The origins of human behaviour* London: Unwin Hyman.

McGrew, W. C. 1992. *Chimpanzee material culture.* Cambridge: Cambridge University Press.

McGrew, W. C. 1993. The intelligent use of tools. In K. Gibson & T. Ingold (Eds.), *Tools, language and cognition in human evolution* (pp. 151–170). Cambridge: Cambridge University Press.

McGrew, W. C. & Marchant, L. F. 1992. Chimpanzees, tools, and termites. *Current Anthropology,* 33, 114–119.

McGrew, W. C. & Tutin, C. E. G. 1978. Evidence for a social custom in wild chimpanzees? *Man: the Journal of the Royal Anthropological Institute,* 13, 234–251.

McGrew, W. C., Tutin, C. & Baldwin, P. 1979. Chimpanzees, tools, and termites. *Man,* 14, 185–214.

McHenry, H. M. 1986. The first biped. *Journal of Human Evolution,* 15, 177–191.

McKenzie, B. & Over, R. 1983. Young infants fail to imitate facial and manual gestures. *Infant Behavior and Development,* 6, 85–95.

McNabb, J. 1989. Sticks and stones. *Proceedings of the Prehistoric Society,* 55, 251–271.

McNeill, D. 1992. *Hand and mind.* Chicago: University of Chicago Press.

Mead, G. H. 1934. *Mind, self, and society.* Chicago: University of Chicago Press.

Mellars, P. A. 1989a. Technological changes across the Middle-Upper Palaeolithic transition. In P. Mellars & C. B. Stringer (Eds.), *The human revolution* (pp. 338–365). Edinburgh: Edinburgh University Press.

Mellars, P. A. 1989b. Major issues in the emergence of modern humans. *Current Anthropology,* 30, 349–85.

Mellars, P. A. 1990. Comment on Lindly and Clark (1990). *Current Anthropology,* 31, 245–246.

Mellars, P. A. & Stringer, C. (Ed.). 1989. *The human revolution.* Edinburgh: Edinburgh University Press.

Meltzoff, A. & Gopnik, A. 1993. The role of imitation in understanding persons and developing a theory of mind. In S. Baron-Cohen, H. Tager-Flusberg & D. Cohen (Eds.), *Understanding other minds* (pp. 335–366). Oxford: Oxford University Press.

Meltzoff, A. N. & Moore, M. K. 1983. Newborn infants imitate adult facial gestures. *Child Development,* 54, 702–709.

Menzel, E. W. 1971. Communication about the environment in a group of young chimpanzees. *Folia Primatologica,* 15, 220–232.

Menzel, E. W. 1974. A group of young chimpanzees in a one-acre field. In A. M. Schrier & F. Stollnitz (Eds.), *Behavior of Nonhuman Primates* (pp. 83–153). New York: Academic Press.

Merleau-Ponty, M. 1964[1947]. *The primacy of perception.* Evanston, Ill.: Northwestern University Press.

Merrick, H. V. & Merrick, J. P. S. 1976. Archeological occurrences of earlier Pleistocene age from the Shungura Formation. In Y. Coppens, F. C. Howell, G. L. Isaac & R. E. F. Leakey (Eds.), *Earliest Man and environments in the Lake Rudolf basin* (pp. 574–584). Chicago: The University of Chicago Press.

Michaels, C. F. & Carello, C. 1981. *Direct perception.* Englewood Cliffs, N.J.: Prentice-Hall.

Miles, H. L. W. 1990. The cognitive foundations for reference in a signing orang-utan. In S. T. Parker & K. R. Gibson (Eds.), *"Language" and intelligence in monkeys and apes* (pp. 511–539). Cambridge: Cambridge University Press.

Miller, G. A. 1981. *Language and speech.* San Francisco: W.H. Freeman.

Miller, K. G. & Fairbanks, R. G. 1985. Cainozoic delta^{18}O record of climate and sea level. *South African Journal of Science,* 81, 248–249.

Mills, J. A. 1994. Evolutionary theory and psychology. *Theory & Psychology,* 4, 155–160.

Milo, R. & Quiatt, D. 1993. Glottogenesis and anatomically modern *Homo sapiens. Current Anthropology,* 34, 569–598.

Mitani, J. 1985. Sexual selection and adult male orang-utan long calls. *Animal Behaviour,* 33, 272–283.

Mitani, J. C. 1992. Singing behavior of male gibbons. In T. Nishida, W. C. McGrew, P. Marler, M. Pickford & F. DeWaal (Eds.), *Topics in primatology. Volume 1. Human origins* (pp. 199–210). Tokyo: University of Tokyo Press.

Mitani, J. C. in press. Comparative field studies of African ape vocal behavior. In W. C. McGrew, T. Nishida & L. Marchant (Eds.), *Ape societies.* Cambridge: Cambridge University Press.

Mitani, J., Hasegawa, T., Gros-Louis, J., Marler, P. & Byrne, R. 1992. Dialects in wild chimpanzees? *American Journal of Primatology,* 27, 233–243.

Mithen, S. 1994. Technology and society during the Middle Pleistocene. *Cambridge Archaeological Journal,* 4, 3–32.

Moran, G., Krupka, A., Tutton, A. & Symons, D. 1987. Patterns of maternal and infant imitation during play. *Infant Behavior and Development,* 10, 477–491.

Morphy, H. 1991. *Ancestral connections.* Chicago: University of Chicago Press.

Morse, K. 1993. Shell beads from Mandu Mandu rockshelter, Cape Range Peninsula, Western Australia, before 30,000 bp. *Antiquity,* 67, 877–883.

Nagell, K., Olguin, R. S. & Tomasello, M. 1993. Processes of social learning in the imitative learning of chimpanzees and human children. *Journal of Comparative Psychology,* 107, 174–186.

Nagel, T. 1974. What is it like to be a bat? *Philosophical Review,* 83, 435–450.

Narins, P. M. & Capranica, R. R. 1976. Sexual differences in the auditory system of the tree frog *Eleutherodactylus coqui. Science,* 192, 378–380.

Neisser, U. 1967. *Cognitive psychology.* New York: Appleton-Century-Crofts.

Newcomer, M. H. & Sieveking, G. d. G. 1980. Experimental flake scatter-patterns. *Journal of Field Archaeology,* 7, 345–352.

Newport, E. L. & Supalla, T. 1980. Clues from the acquisition of signed and spoken language. In U. Bellugi & M. Studdert-Kennedy (Eds.), *Signed and spoken language* (pp. 187–211). Weinheim: Verlag Chemie.

Nicholls, J. 1992. *Linguistic diversity in space and time.* Chicago: University of Chicago Press.

Nishida, T. 1980. The leaf-clipping display. *Journal of Human Evolution,* 9, 117–128.

Nishida, T. 1986. Local traditions and cultural transmission. In B. B. Smuts, D. L. Cheney, R. M. Seyfarth, R. W. Wrangham & T. T. Struhsaker (Eds.), *Primate societies* (pp. 462–474). Chicago: The University of Chicago Press.

Noble, W. 1981. Gibsonian theory and the pragmatist perspective. *Journal for the Theory of Social Behaviour*, 11, 65–85.

Noble, W. 1987. Perception and language: Towards a complete ecological psychology. In A. Costall & A. Still (Eds.), *Cognitive psychology in question* (pp. 128–141). Brighton: Harvester.

Noble, W. 1992. Language, thought and confusion. *Man*. 27, 637–642.

Noble, W. 1993a. What kind of approach to language fits Gibson's approach to perception? *Theory & Psychology*, 3, 57–78.

Noble, W. 1993b. Meaning and the "discursive ecology": Further to the debate on ecological perceptual theory. *Journal for the Theory of Social Behaviour*, 23, 375–398.

Noble, W. & Davidson, I. 1989. On depiction and language. *Current Anthropology*, 30, 337–342.

Noble, W. & Davidson, I. 1991. The evolutionary emergence of modern human behaviour. *Man*, 26, 223–253.

Noble, W. & Davidson, I. 1993. Tracing the emergence of modern human behavior. *Journal of Anthropological Archaeology*, 12, 121–149.

O'Brien, E. 1981. The projectile capabilities of an Acheulian handaxe from Olorgesailie. *Current Anthropology*, 22, 76–79.

O'Connell, D. C. 1988. *Critical essays on language use and psychology.* New York: Springer.

O'Connell, J. F., Hawkes, K. & Jones, K. B. 1988. Hadza scavenging. *Current Anthropology*, 29, 356–363.

Oakley, K. P. 1981. Emergence of higher thought 3.0–0.2 Ma B.P. *Philosophical Transactions of the Royal Society of London B*, 292, 205–211.

Oakley, K. P., Andrews, P., Keeley, L. H. & Clark, J. D. 1977. A reappraisal of the Clacton spearpoint. *Proceedings of the Prehistoric Society*, 43, 13–30.

Oates, J. F. 1986. Food distribution and foraging behavior. In B. B. Smuts, D. L. Cheney, R. M. Seyfarth, R. W. Wrangham & T. T. Struhsaker (Eds.), *Primate Societies* (pp. 197–109). Chicago: The Unviersity of Chicago Press.

Olson, D. R. 1986. The cognitive consequences of literacy. *Canadian Psychology*, 27, 109–121.

Olson, D. R. 1988. Representation and misrepresentation. Conference on *Implicit and explicit knowledge*, Tel Aviv.

Olson, D. R. 1989. Making up your mind. *Canadian Psychology*, 30, 617–627.

Olson, D. R. 1994. *The world on paper.* Cambridge: Cambridge University Press.

Olson, T. R. 1985. Cranial morphology and systematics of the Hadar Formation hominids and *Australopithecus africanus.* In E. Delson (Eds.), *Ancestors* (pp. 102–109). New York: Alan R. Liss.

Ong, W. J. 1982. *Orality and literacy.* London: Methuen.

Orwell, G. 1968. *The collected essays, journalism and letters of George Orwell.* London: Secker & Warburg.

Ott, I., Schleidt, M. & Kien, J. 1994. Temporal organisation of action in baboons. *Brain, Behaviour and Evolution*, 44, 101–107.

Palmer, A. 1987. Cognitivism and computer simulation. In A. Costall & A. Still (Eds.), *Cognitive psychology in question* (pp. 55–69). Brighton: Harvester.

Papousek, M. & Papousek, H. 1991. The meanings of melodies in motherese in tone and stress languages. *Infant Behavior and Development*, 14, 415–440.

Pardoe, C. 1991. Competing paradigms and ancient human remains. *Archaeology in Oceania*, 26, 79–85.

Parker, S. T. & Milbrath, C. 1993. Higher intelligence, propositional language, and culture as adaptations for planning. In K. R. Gibson & T. Ingold (Eds.), *Tools, language and cognition in human evolution* (pp. 314–333). Cambridge: Cambridge University Press.

Patla, A. E. (Ed.). 1991. *Adaptability of human gait: Implications for the control of locomotion*. Amsterdam: North-Holland.

Patterson, F. G. & Linden, E. 1981. *The education of Koko*. New York: Holt, Rinehart and Winston.

Pavlov, I. P. 1927. *Conditioned reflexes* (Anrep, G. V., Trans.). Humphrey Milford: Oxford University Press.

Peirce, C. S. 1955[1931]. *Logic as semiotic*. New York: Dover.

Pelcin, A. 1994. A geological explanation for the Berekhat Ram figurine. *Current Anthropology*, 35, 674–675.

Penny, D., Steel, M., Wadell, P. J. & Hendy, M. 1994. Quantitative evaluation of large DNA data sets: the "Out-of-Africa" hypothesis. In *Fifth Australasian Archaeometry Conference*. Armidale: University of New England.

Perkins, W. H. & Kent, R. D. 1986. *Functional anatomy of speech, language, and hearing*. San Diego: College-Hill Press.

Peters, C. R. 1987. Nut-like oil seeds. *American Journal of Physical Anthropology*, 73, 333–363.

Peters, M. 1990. Interaction of vocal and manual movements. In G. R. Hammond (Eds.), *Cerebral control of speech and limb movements*. Amsterdam: North-Holland.

Piaget, J. 1954. *The construction of reality in the child*. New York: Basic Books.

Piaget, J. 1959. *The language and thought of the child* (3rd ed.). London: Routledge & Kegan Paul.

Pinker, S. 1992. Review of "Language and species" by Derek Bickerton. *Language*, 68, 375–382.

Pinker, S. & Bloom, P. 1990. Natural language and natural selection. *Behavioral and Brain Sciences*, 13, 707–784.

Potts, R. 1984. Home bases and early hominids. *American Scientist*, 72, 338–347.

Potts, R. 1988. *Early hominid activities at Olduvai*. New York: Aldine.

Potts, R. 1989. Olorgesailie. *Journal of Human Evolution*, 18, 477–484.

Potts, R. & Shipman, P. 1981. Cutmarks made by stone tools on bones from Olduvai Gorge, Tanzania. *Nature*, 291, 577–580.

Premack, D. G. 1976. *Language and intelligence in ape and Man*. Hillsdale, NJ: Erlbaum.

Premack, D. G. 1988. Minds with and without language. In L. Weiskrantz (Ed.), *Thought without language* (pp. 46–65). Oxford: Clarendon Press.

Premack, D. G. & Premack, A. J. 1983. *The mind of an ape.* New York: Norton.

Premack, D. G. & Woodruff, G. 1978. Does the chimpanzee have a theory of mind? *Behavioral and Brain Sciences,* 1, 515–526.

Priest, S. 1991. *Theories of the mind.* London: Penguin.

Puech, P.-F. 1983. Tooth wear, diet, and the artifacts of Java Man. *Current Anthropology,* 24, 381–382.

Puech, P.-F. 1984. Acidic-food choice in *Homo habilis* at Olduvai. *Current Anthropology,* 25, 349–350.

Puech, P.-F., Albertini, H. & Mills, N. T. W. 1980. Dental destruction in Broken Hill Man. *Journal of Human Evolution,* 9, 33–39.

Puech, P.-F., Albertini, H. & Serratrice, C. 1983. Tooth microwear and dietary patterns in early hominids from Laetoli, Hadar and Olduvai. *Journal of Human Evolution,* 12, 721–729.

Pylyshyn, Z. W. 1984. *Computation and cognition.* Cambridge, Mass: The MIT Press.

Quiatt, D. & Huffman, M. A. 1993. On home bases, nesting sites, activity centres, and new analytic perspectives. *Current Anthropology,* 34, 68–70.

Quiatt, D. & Reynolds, V. 1993. *Primate behaviour.* Cambridge: Cambridge University Press.

Quine, W. v. O. 1960. *Word and object.* Cambridge, Mass.: Technology Press of M.I.T.

Quine, W. v. O. 1969. Natural kinds. In *Ontological relativity and other essays* (pp. 114–138). New York: Columbia University Press.

Rainey, A. 1991. Some Australian bifaces. *Lithics,* 12, 33–36.

Razran, G. 1965. Empirical codifications and specific theoretical implications of compound-stimulus conditioning: Perception. In W. F. Prokasy (Ed.), *Classical conditioning* (pp. 226–248). New York: Appleton-Century-Crofts.

Reader, J. 1981. *Missing links.* London: History Book Club.

Repenning, C. A. & Fejfar, O. 1982. Evidence for earlier date of 'Ubeidiya, Israel. *Nature,* 299, 344–347.

Reynolds, P. C. 1993. The complementation theory of language and tool use. In F. R. Gibson & T. Ingold (Eds.), *Tools, Language and Cognition in Human Evolution* (pp. 407–428). Cambridge: Cambridge University Press.

Richards, G. 1986. Freed hands or enslaved feet? *Journal of Human Evolution,* 15, 143–150.

Richman, D. P., Stewart, R. M., Hutchinson, J. W. & Caviness, V. S. 1975. Mechanical model of brain convolutional development. *Science,* 189, 18–21.

Rigaud, J.-P. (Ed.). 1988. *La Grotte Vaufrey à Cenac et Saint-Julien (Dordogne).* Mémoires de la Société Préhistorique Française 19.

Rightmire, G. P. 1993. Variation among early *Homo* crania from Olduvai Gorge and the Koobi Fora Region. *American Journal of Physical Anthropology,* 90, 1–33.

Ristau, C. A. 1991. Before mindreading. In A. Whiten (Eds.), *Natural Theories of Mind* (pp. 209–222). Oxford: Blackwell.

Roberts, M. B. 1986. Excavations of the Lower Palaeolithic site at Amey's Eartham pit, Boxgrove, West Sussex. *Proceedings of the Prehistoric Society,* 52, 215–245.

Roberts, R. G., Jones, R. & Smith, M. A. 1990. Thermoluminescence dating of a 50,000-year-old human occupation site in northern Australia. *Nature*, 345, 153–156.

Roberts, M. B., Stringer, C. B. & Parfitt, S. A. 1994. A hominid tibia from Middle Pleistocene sediments at Boxgrove, UK. *Nature*, 369, 311–313.

Roche, H. & Tiercelin, J.-J. 1977. Découverte d'une industrie lithique ancienne *in situ* dans la formation d'Hadar, Afar Centrale, Ethiopie. *Comptes Rendus de l'Academie des Sciènces de Paris, D*, 284, 1871–1874.

Rodman, P. S. 1977. Feeding behaviour of orang-utans of the Kutai Nature Reserve, East Kalimantan. In T. H. Clutton-Brock (Eds.), *Primate ecology* (pp. 383–413). London: Academic Press.

Roebroeks, W. 1994. Updating the earliest occupation of Europe. *Current Anthropology*, 35, 301–305.

Roebroeks, W., Conard, N. J. & van Kolfschoten, T. 1992. Dense forests, cold steppes, and the Palaeolithic settlement of northern Europe. *Current Anthropology*, 33, 551–586.

Roebroeks, W., Kolen, J. & Rensink, E. 1988. Planning depth, anticipation and the organization of Middle Palaeolithic technology. *Helinium*, 28, 17–34.

Rogers, J. 1993. The phylogenetic relationships among *Homo*, *Pan* and *Gorilla*. *Journal of Human Evolution*, 25, 201–215.

Rogers, J. 1994. Levels of the genealogical hierarchy and the problem of hominoid phylogeny. *American Journal of Physical Anthropology*, 94, 81–88.

Rolland, N. & Dibble, H. L. 1990. A new synthesis of Middle Paleolithic variability. *American Antiquity*, 55, 480–499.

Rosen, S. & Howell, P. 1991. *Signals and systems for speech and hearing.* London: Academic Press.

Rowlands, M. 1994. Connectionism and the language of thought. *British Journal for the Philosophy of Science*, 45, 485–503.

Rozin, P. 1976. The evolution of intelligence and access to the cognitive unconscious. In J. M. Sprague & A. N. Epstein (Eds.), *Progress in psychobiology and physiological psychology* (pp. 245–280). New York: Academic Press.

Ruff, C. B. & Walker, A. 1993. Body size and body shape. In A. Walker & R. E. F. Leakey (Eds.), *The Nariokotome Homo erectus skeleton* (pp. 234–265). Cambridge, Massachusetts: Harvard University Press.

Rumbaugh, D. M., Hopkins, W. D., Washburn, D. A. & Savage–Rumbaugh, E. S. 1991. Comparative perspectives of brain, cognition, and language. In N. A. Krasnegor, D. M. Rumbaugh, R. L. Schiefelbusch & M. Studdert–Kennedy (Eds.), *Biological and behavioral determinants of language development.* Hillsdale, New Jersey: Lawrence Erlbaum Associates.

Russell, B. 1993[1946]. *History of western philosophy.* London: Routledge.

Ruvolo, M. 1994. Molecular evolutionary processes and conflicting gene trees. *American Journal of Physical Anthropology*, 94, 89–113.

Ryle, G. 1949. *The concept of mind.* London: Hutchinson.

Ryle, G. 1967[1951]. Ludwig Wittgenstein. In K. T. Fann (Eds.), *Ludwig Wittgenstein* (pp. 116–124). New Jersey: Humanities Press.

Sacks, H. 1992[1966]. Button-button who's got the button? In G. Jefferson (Ed.), *Lectures on conversation, vol. I* (pp. 363–369). Oxford: Blackwell.

Sapir, E. 1921. *Language: An introduction to the study of speech*. New York: Harcourt Brace Jovanovich.

Saussure, F. d. 1983[1916]. *Course in general linguistics* (Harris, R., Trans.). London: Duckworth.

Savage-Rumbaugh, E. S. 1984. Pan paniscus and Pan troglodytes: Contrasts in preverbal communicative competence. In R. L. Susman (Eds.), *The pygmy chimpanzee: Evolutionary biology and behavior* (pp. 395–413). New York: Plenum Press.

Savage-Rumbaugh, S. & Lewin, R. 1994. *Kanzi*. New York: McGraw-Hill.

Savage-Rumbaugh, E. S., McDonald, K., Sevcik, R., Hopkins, W. & Rupert, E. 1986. Spontaneous symbol acquisition and communicative use by pygmy chimpanzee (*Pan paniscus*). *Journal of Experimental Psychology: General*, 115, 211–235.

Savage-Rumbaugh, E. S., Romski, M. A., Hopkins, W. D. & Sevcik, R. A. 1989. Symbol acquisition and use by *Pan troglodytes, Pan paniscus, Homo sapiens*. In P. G. Heltne & L. A. Marquardt (Eds.), *Understanding chimpanzees* (pp. 266–295). Cambridge, Massachusetts: Harvard University Press.

Savage-Rumbaugh, E. S., Rumbaugh, D. M., Smith, S. T. & Lawson, J. 1980. Reference: the linguistic essential. *Science*, 210, 922–925.

Savage-Rumbaugh, E. S. & Rumbaugh, D. 1993. The emergence of language. In K. R. Gibson & T. Ingold (Eds.), *Tools, language and cognition in human evolution* (pp. 86–109). Cambridge: Cambridge University Press.

Sawaguchi, T. 1992. The size of neocortex in relation to ecology and social structure in monkeys and apes. *Folia Primatologica*, 58, 131–145.

Schafer, J. 1990. Conjoining of artefacts and consideration of raw material. In *The big puzzle. Proceedings of the international symposium on refitting stone artefacts* (pp. 83–100). Bonn: Holos.

Schaller, G. & Lowther, G. R. 1969. The relevance of carnivore behaviour to the study of early hominids. *Southwestern Journal of Anthropology*, 25, 307–341.

Schaller, G. B. 1963. *The Mountain gorilla*. Chicago: The University of Chicago Press.

Schank, R. C. & Abelson, R. 1977. *Scripts, plans, goals and understanding*. Hillsdale, NJ: Erlbaum.

Schepartz, L. A. 1993. Language and modern human origins. *Yearbook of Physical Anthropology*, 36, 91–126.

Schick, K. D. & Toth, N. 1993. *Making silent stones speak*. New York: Simon and Schuster.

Schick, K. D. 1994. The Movius Line reconsidered. In R. S. Coruccini & R. L. Ciochon (Eds.), *Integrative paths to the past* (pp. 569–596). Englewood Cliffs, NJ: Prentice Hall.

Schieffelin, B. B. 1979. Getting it together: An ethnographic approach to the study of the development of communicative competence. In E. Ochs & B. B. Schieffelin (Eds.), *Developmental pragmatics* (pp. 73–108). New York: Academic Press.

Schiffman, H. R. 1990. *Sensation and perception* (3rd ed.). New York: Wiley.

Schmandt-Besserat, D. 1978. The earliest precursor of writing. *Scientific American*, 238, 38–47.

Schwartz, J. H. 1987. *The red ape*. Boston: Houghton Mifflin.

Scott, K. 1986. The bone assemblages of Layers 3 and 6. In P. Callow & J. Cornford (Eds.), *La Cotte de St. Brelade 1961–1978* (pp. 159–183). Norwich: Geo Books.

Searle, J. R. 1980. Minds, brains, and programs. *Behavioral and Brain Sciences*, 3, 417–424.

Searle, J. R. 1992. *The rediscovery of the mind*. Cambridge, Mass.: MIT Press.

Sekuler, R. & Blake, R. 1990. *Perception* (2nd ed.). New York: McGraw-Hill.

Senut, B. & Tardieu, C. 1985. Functional aspects of Plio-Pleistocene hominid limb bones. In E. Delson (Eds.), *Ancestors* (pp. 193–201). New York: Alan R. Liss.

Sept, J. M. 1992. Was there no place like home? *Current Anthropology*, 33, 187–207.

Seyfarth, R. M. 1986. Vocal communication and its relation to language. In B. B. Smuts, D. L. Cheney, R. M. Seyfarth, R. W. Wrangham & T. T. Struhsaker (Eds.), *Primate societies* Chicago: The University of Chicago Press.

Seyfarth, R. M., Cheney, D. L. & Marler, P. 1980. Monkey responses to three different alarm calls. *Science*, 210, 801–803.

Shackleton, N. J., Bacckman, J., Zimmerman, H., Kent, D. V., Hall, M. A., Roberts, D. G., Schnitker, D., Baldauf, J. G., Desprairies, A., Homrighausen, R., Huddlestun, P., Keene, J. B., Kaltenback, A. J., Krumsiek, K. A. O., Morton, A. C., Murray, J. W. & Westberg-Smith, J. 1984. Oxygen isotope calibration of the onset of ice-rafting and history of glaciation in the North Atlantic region. *Nature*, 307, 620–623.

Shannon, C. & Weaver, W. 1949. *The mathematical theory of communication*. Urbana, Ill.: University of Illinois Press.

Shaw, G. B. 1948. Preface to *The magnificent birth of language* by R. A. Wilson. New York: Philosophical Library.

Shea, B. T. & Inouye, S. E. 1993. Knuckle-walking ancestors. *Science*, 259, 293–294.

Shea, J. J. 1989. A functional study of the lithic industries associated with hominid fossils in the Kebara and Qafzeh caves, Israel. In P. Mellars & C. B. Stringer (Eds.), *The human revolution* (pp. 611–625). Edinburgh: Edinburgh University Press.

Sherif, M. 1966. *Group conflict and cooperation*. London: Routledge and Kegan Paul.

Shipman, P. L. & Harris, J. M. 1988. Habitat preference and paleoecology of *Australopithecus boisei* in eastern Africa. In F. E. Grine (Ed.), *Evolutionary history of the "robust" Australopithecines* (pp. 343–381). New York: Aldine de Gruyter.

Shipman, P. L. & Walker, A. 1989. The costs of becoming a predator. *Journal of Human Evolution*, 18, 373–392.

Shipman, P. L., Bosler, W. & Davis, K. L. 1981. Butchering of giant geladas at an Acheulian site. *Current Anthropology*, 22, 257–268.

Shorey, H. H. 1976. *Animal communication by pheromones.* New York: Academic Press.

Shropshire, W., Jr 1979. Stimulus perception. In W. Haupt & M. E. Geinleib (Eds), *Physiology of movements. Encyclopedia of plant physiology, vol. 7* (pp. 10–41). Berlin: Springer-Verlag.

Sillen, A. 1992. Strontium-calcium ratios (Sr/Ca) of *Australopithecus robustus* and associated fauna from Swartkrans. *Journal of Human Evolution*, 23, 495–516.

Singer, R. & Wymer, J. 1982. *The Middle Stone Age at Klasies River Mouth in South Africa.* Chicago: The University of Chicago Press.

Skelton, R. R. & McHenry, H. M. 1992. Evolutionary relationships among early hominids. *Journal of Human Evolution*, 23, 309–349.

Slater, P. J. B. 1983. The study of communication. In T. R. Halliday & P. J. B. Slater (Eds.), *Animal Behaviour* (pp. 9–42). Oxford: Blackwell.

Smirnov, Y. 1989. Intentional human burial. *Journal of World Prehistory*, 3, 199–233.

Smith, B. H. 1993. The physiological age of KNM-WT 15000. In A. Walker & R. E. F. Leakey (Eds.), *The Nariokotome Homo erectus skeleton* (pp. 195–220). Cambridge, Massachusetts: Harvard University Press.

Smuts, B. B., Cheney, D. L., Seyfarth, R. M., Wrangham, R. W. & Struhsaker, T. T. 1986. *Primate societies.* Chicago: The University of Chicago Press.

Snowdon, C. T. 1990. Language capacities of nonhuman animals. *Yearbook of Physical Anthropology*, 33, 215–243.

Soffer, O. & Gamble, C. S. (Ed.). 1990. *The world at 18 000 bp. Volume 1.* London: Unwin Hyman.

Sokoloff, L. 1981. Circulation and energy metabolism of the brain. In G. J. Siegel, R. W. Albers, B. W. Agranoff & R. Katzman (Eds.), *Basic neurochemistry.* Boston: Little, Brown.

Solecki, R. S. 1975. Shanidar IV, a Neanderthal flower burial in Northern Iraq. *Science*, 190, 880–881.

Solecki, R. S. 1961. Three adult Neanderwartal skeletons from Shanidar Cave, northern Iraq. *Sumer*, 17, 17–112.

Speth, J. D. 1989. Early hominid hunting and scavenging. *Journal of Human Evolution*, 18, 329–343.

Speth, J. D. & Spielmann, K. A. 1983. Energy source, protein metabolism, and hunter-gatherer subsistence strategy. *Journal of Anthropological Archaeology*, 2, 1–31.

Stanford, C. B., Wallis, J., Matama, H. & Goodall, J. 1994. Patterns of predation by chimpanzees on red colobus monkeys in Gombe National Park, 1982–1991. *American Journal of Physical Anthropology*, 94, 213–228.

Stevens, C. F. 1973. Neuronal properties. In E. C. Carterette & M. P. Friedman (Eds.), *Handbook of perception: Biology of perceptual systems* (pp. 21–38). New York: Academic Press.

Stich, S. 1992. What is a theory of mental representation? *Mind*, 101, 243–261.

Stiles, D. 1979. Early Acheulean and Developed Oldowan. *Current Anthropology*, 20, 126–129.

Still, A. & Costall, A. 1991. Mutual elimination of dualism in Vygotsky and Gibson. In A. Still & A. Costall (Eds.), *Against cognitivism* (pp. 225–236). New York: Harvester-Wheatsheaf.

Stiner, M. C. 1990. The use of mortality patterns in archaeological studies of hominid predatory adaptations. *Journal of Anthropological Archaeology*, 9, 305–351.

Stiner, M. C. 1991. Food procurement and transport by human and non-human predators. *Journal of Archaeological Science*, 18, 455–482.

Stiner, M. C. & Kuhn, S. L. 1992. Subsistence, technology, and adaptive variation in Middle Palaeolithic Italy. *American Anthropologist*, 94, 306–339.

Straus, L. G. 1989. On early hominid use of fire. *Current Anthropology*, 30, 488–491.

Stringer, C. B. 1987. A numerical cladistic analysis for the genus *Homo*. *Journal of Human Evolution*, 16, 135–146.

Stringer, C. B. 1992. Replacement, continuity and the origin of *Homo sapiens*. In G. Bräuer & F. H. Smith (Eds.), *Continuity or replacement* (pp. 9–24). Rotterdam: A.A. Balkema.

Stringer, C. B. & Andrews, P. 1988. Genetic and fossil evidence for the origin of modern humans. *Science*, 239, 1263–1268.

Stringer, C. B. & Gamble, C. 1993. *In search of the Neanderthals*. London: Thames and Hudson.

Strum, S. C. 1981. Processes and products of change. In R. S. O. Harding & G. Teleki (Eds.), *Omnivorous primates* (pp. 255–302). New York: Columbia University Press.

Sugarjito, J. & Nuhuda, N. 1981. Meat eating behavior in wild orang-utans. *Primates*, 22, 414–416.

Susman, R. L. 1987. Pygmy chimpanzees and common chimpanzees. In W. G. Kinzey (Ed.), *The evolution of human behavior* (pp. 72–86). Albany, NY: State University of New York Press.

Susman, R. L. 1988. Hand of *Paranthropus robustus* from Member 1, Swartkrans. *Science*, 240, 781–784.

Susman, R. L. 1994. Fossil evidence for early hominid tool use. *Science*, 265, 1570–1573.

Swisher, C. C., Curtis, G. H., Jacob, T., Getty, A. G., Suprijo, A. & Widiasmoro 1994. Age of the earliest known hominids in Java, Indonesia. *Science*, 263, 1118–1121.

Szalay, F. S. 1975. Where to draw the nonprimate-primate taxonomic boundary. *Folia Primatologica*, 23, 158–163.

Szalay, F. S. & Delson, E. 1979. *Evolutionary history of the primates*. New York: Academic Press.

Taborin, Y. 1990. Les prémices de la parure. In C. Farizy (Eds.), *Paléolithique Moyen recent et Paléolithique Supérieur ancien en Europe* (pp. 335–344). Nemours: Musée de Préhistoire d'Ile de France.

Tardieu, C., Aurengo, A. & Tadieu, B. 1993. New method of three-dimensional analysis of bipedal locomotion for the study of displacements of the body and body-parts centers of mass in Man and the non-human primates. *American Journal of Physical Anthropology*, 90, 455–476.

Tattersall, I. 1992. Species concepts and species identification in human evolution. *Journal of Human Evolution*, 22, 341–349.

Teleki, G. 1973. *The predatory behavior of wild chimpanzees*. Lewisburg: Bucknell University Press.

Teleki, G. 1981. The omnivorous diet and eclectic feeding habits of chimpanzees in Gombe National Park, Tanzania. In R. S. O. Harding & G. Teleki (Eds.), *Omnivorous primates*. New York: Columbia University Press.

Templeton, A. R. 1993. The "Eve" hypothesis. *American Anthropologist*, 95, 51–72.

Terrace, H. S. 1985. In the beginning was the "name". *American Psychologist*, 40, 1011–1028.

Thieme, H. & Veil, S. 1985. Neue Untersuchungen zum eemzeitlichen Elefanten-Jagdplatz Lehringen, Ldkr. Verden. *Die Kunde N.F.*, 36, 11–58.

Tobias, P. V. 1988. The brain of *Homo habilis*. *Journal of Human Evolution*, 16, 741–761.

Tobias, P. V. 1991. *Olduvai Gorge*. Cambridge: Cambridge University Press.

Tomasello, M. 1990. Cultural transmission in the tool use and communicatory signaling of chimpanzees. In S. T. Parker & K. R. Gibson (Eds.), *"Language" and intelligence in monkeys and apes* (pp. 274–311). Cambridge: Cambridge University Press.

Tomasello, M., Davis-Dasilva, M., Camak, L. & Bard, K. 1987. Observational learning of tool use by young chimpanzees. *Human Evolution*, 2, 175–183.

Tomasello, M., Kruger, A. C. & Ratner, H. H. 1993. Cultural learning. *Behavioral and Brain Sciences*, 16, 495–552.

Tomasello, M., Savage-Rumbaugh, E. S. & Kruger, A. 1994. Imitative learning of actions on objects by children, chimpanzees, and enculturated chimpanzees. *Child Development*, 64, 1688–1705.

Toth, N. 1982. *The Stone technologies of early hominids at Koobi Fora, Kenya*. Ann Arbor: University Microfilms International.

Toth, N. 1985a. The Oldowan reassessed: a close look at early stone artifacts. *Journal of Archaeological Science*, 12, 101–120.

Toth, N. 1985b. Archaeological evidence for preferential right-handedness in the Lower and Middle Pleistocene, and its possible implications. *Journal of Human Evolution*, 14, 607–614.

Toth, N., Schick, K., Savage-Rumbaugh, E. S., Sevcik, R. A. & Rumbaugh, D. 1993. *Pan* the tool-maker. *Journal of Archaeological Science*, 20, 81–91.

Toulmin, S. 1972. *Human understanding, volume I*. Oxford: Clarendon Press.

Toulmin, S. 1982. The genealogy of "consciousness". In P. F. Secord (Ed.), *Explaining human behaviour* (pp. 53–70). Beverly Hills: Sage.

Trehub, S. E., Unyk, A. M. & Trainor, L. J. 1993. Adults identify infant-directed music across cultures. *Infant Behavior and Development*, 16, 193–211.

Trinkaus, E. 1987. Bodies, brawn, brains and noses. In M. H. Nitecki & D. V. Nitecki (Eds.), *The evolution of human hunting* (pp. 107–145). New York: Plenum Press.

Tunnell, G. G. 1990. Systematic scavenging: minimal energy expenditure at Olare Orok in the Serengeti ecosystem. In S. Solomon, I. Davidson & D. Watson

(Eds.), *Problem solving in taphonomy.* Tempus Vol. 2 (pp. 167–196). St Lucia, Queensland: Anthropology Museum, University of Queensland.

Turner, A. 1984. Hominids and fellow travellers: human migration into high latitudes as part of a large mammal community. In R. A. Foley (Eds.), *Hominid evolution and community ecology* (pp. 193–217). London: Academic Press.

Turner, A. 1992. Large carnivores and earliest European hominids. *Journal of Human Evolution,* 22, 109–126.

Turvey, M. T. 1990. Coordination. *American Psychologist,* 45, 938–953.

Turvey, M. T., Shaw, R. E., Reed, E. S. & Mace, W. M. 1981. Ecological laws of perceiving and acting: In reply to Fodor and Pylyshyn. *Cognition,* 9, 237–304.

Tutin, C. E. G., Fernandez, M., Williamson, M. E. & McGrew, W. C. 1991. Foraging profiles of sympatric lowland gorillas and chimpanzees in the Lope Reserve, Gabon. *Philosophical Transactions of the Royal Society of London B,* 334, 179–186.

Tuttle, R. H. 1986. *Apes of the world.* Park Ridge, NJ: Noyes Publications.

Tuttle, R. H. 1987. Kinesiological inferences and evolutionary implications from Laetoli bipedal trails G-1, G-2/3, and A. In M. D. Leakey & J. M. Harris (Eds.), *Laetoli* (pp. 503–523). Oxford: Clarendon Press.

Tuttle, R. H. 1988. What's new in African paleoanthropology. *Annual Review of Anthropology,* 17, 391–426.

Tyson, E. 1699. *Orang-Outang, sive Homo Sylvestris: or, the anatomy of a pygmie compared with that of a monkey, an ape and a man.* London: T. Bennett and D. Brown.

Van Peer, P. 1992. *The Levallois reduction strategy.* Madison, Wisconsin: Prehistory Press.

Vandermeersch, B. 1966. Découverte d'un objet en ocre avec traces d'utilisation dans e Moustérien de Qafzeh (Israël). *Bulletin de la Société Préhistorique Française,* 66, 157–158.

Vauclair, J. 1990. Primate cognition. In S. T. Parker & K. R. Gibson (Eds.), *"Language" and intelligence in monkeys and apes* (pp. 312–329). Cambridge: Cambridge University Press.

Velichko, A. A. & Kurenkova, E. I. 1990. Environmental conditions and human occupation of northern Eurasia during the Late Valdai. In O. Soffer & C. S. Gamble (Eds.), *The World at 18 000 bp. Volume 1* (pp. 255–265). London: Unwin Hyman.

Verbrugge, R. R. 1985. Language and event perception. In W. H. Warren & R. E. Shaw (Eds.), *Persistence and change* (pp. 157–194). Hillsdale, NJ: Erlbaum.

Vico, G. 1928[1725]. *La scienza nuova.* Bari: Laterza.

Villa, P. 1983. *Terra Amata and the Middle Pleistocene archaeological record of Southern France.* Berkeley: University of California Press.

Villa, P. 1990. Torralba and Aridos. *Journal of Human Evolution,* 19, 299–309.

Villa, P. 1991. Middle Pleistocene prehistory in southwestern Europe. *Journal of Anthropological Research,* 47, 177–217.

Villaverde Bonilla, V. 1994. *Arte Paleolitico de la Cova del Parpallo.* Valencia: Servei d'Investigacio Prehistorica, Diputacio de Valencia.

Visalberghi, E. & Fragaszy, D. 1990. Do monkeys ape? In S. T. Parker & K. R.

Gibson (Eds.), *"Language" and intelligence in monkeys and apes* (pp. 247–273). Cambridge: Cambridge University Press.

Visalberghi, E. 1993. Capuchin monkeys. In K. R. Gibson & T. Ingold (Eds.), *Tools, language and cognition in human evolution* (pp. 138–150). Cambridge: Cambridge University Press.

Visalberghi, E., Fragaszy, D. & Savage-Rumbaugh, S. n.d. Performance in a tool-using task by common chimpanzees (*Pan trogodytes*), bonobos (*Pan paniscus*), orang-utans (*Pongo pygmaeus*), and capuchin monkeys (*Cebus apella*).

Voloshinov, V. N. 1973[1929]. *Marxism and the philosophy of language* (L. Matejka and I. R. Titunik, Trans.). New York: Seminar Press.

Volterra, V. & Erting, C. J. (Eds.). 1990. *From gesture to language in hearing and deaf children*. Berlin: Springer-Verlag.

Volterra, V., Beronesi, S. & Massoni, P. 1990. How does gestural communication become language? In V. Volterra & C. J. Erting (Eds.), *From gesture to language in hearing and deaf children* (pp. 205–216). Berlin: Springer-Verlag.

von Hofsten, C. 1989. Mastering reaching and grasping. In S. A. Wallace (Ed.), *Perspectives on the coordination of movement* (pp. 223–258). Amsterdam: North-Holland.

Vrba, E. S. 1988. Late Pliocene climatic events and hominid evolution. In F. E. Grine (Eds.), *Evolutionary history of the "robust" Australopithecines* (pp. 405–426). New York: Aldine de Gruyter.

Vygotsky, L. S. 1962[1934]. *Thought and language*. Cambridge, Mass.: MIT Press.

Walker, A. 1993a. Taphonomy. In A. Walker & R. E. F. Leakey (Eds.), *The Nariokotome Homo erectus skeleton* (pp. 40–53). Cambridge, Massachusetts: Harvard University Press.

Walker, A. 1993b. Perspectives on the Nariokotome discovery. In A. Walker & R. E. F. Leakey (Eds.), *The Nariokotome Homo erectus skeleton* (pp. 411–430). Cambridge, Massachusetts: Harvard University Press.

Walker, A. & Leakey, R. E. F. (Eds.). 1993a. *The Nariokotome Homo erectus skeleton*. Cambridge, Masschusetts: Harvard University Press.

Walker, A. & Leakey, R. E. F. 1993b. The postcranial bones. In A. Walker & R. E. F. Leakey (Eds.), *The Nariokotome Homo erectus skeleton* (pp. 95–160). Cambridge, Massachusetts: Harvard University Press.

Walker, A., Zimmerman, M. R. & Leakey, R. E. F. 1982. A possible case of hypervitaminosis A in *Homo erectus. Nature*, 296, 248–250.

Walker, A. C. 1982. Dietary hypotheses and human evolution. *Philosophical Transactions of the Royal Society of London B*, 292, 57–64.

Walker, S. 1983. *Animal thought*. London: Routledge & Kegan Paul.

Warren, W. H., Jr & Verbrugge, R. R. 1984. Auditory perception of breaking and bouncing events: a case study in ecological acoustics. *Journal of Experimental Psychology: Human Perception and Performance*, 10, 704–712.

Wartofsky, M. W. 1980. Visual scenarios. In M. H. Hagen (Ed.), *The perception of pictures, II* (pp. 131–152). New York: Academic Press.

Washburn, L. W. & Lancaster, C. S. 1968. The evolution of hunting. In R. B. Lee & I. DeVore (Eds.), *Man the Hunter* (pp. 293–303). Chicago: Aldine.

Waterman, P. G. 1984. Food acquisition and processing as a function of plant chemistry. In D. J. Chivers, B. A. Wood & A. Bilsborough (Eds.), *Food Acquisition and Processing in Primates* (pp. 177–211). New York: Plenum Press.

Watts, D. P. 1988. Ant eating behavior of mountain gorillas. *Primates*, 30, 121–125.

Wenner, A. M. 1971. *The bee language controversy*. Boulder, Colorado: Educational Programs Improvement Corporation.

Wertsch, J. V. 1991. *Voices of the mind*. London: Harvester-Wheatsheaf.

Wertsch, J. V. & Stone, C. A. 1985. The concept of internalization in Vygotsky's account of the genesis of higher mentla functions. In J. V. Wertsch (Eds.), *Culture, communication and cognition* (pp. 162–179). Cambridge: Cambridge University Press.

Westergaard, G. C. & Suomi, S. J. 1994. The use and modification of bone tools by capuchin monkeys. *Current Anthropology*, 35, 75–77.

Whallon, R. 1989. Elements of cultural change in the later Palaeolithic. In P. Mellars & C. B. Stringer (Eds.), *The human revolution* (pp. 433–454). Edinburgh: Edinburgh University Press.

Wheeler, P. E. 1984. The evolution of bipedality and loss of functional body hair in hominids. *Journal of Human Evolution*, 13, 91–98.

Wheeler, P. E. 1985. The loss of functional body hair in man. *Journal of Human Evolution*, 14, 23–28.

Wheeler, P. E. 1992. The influence of the loss of functional body hair on the water budgets of early hominids. *Journal of Human Evolution*, 23, 379–388.

Wheeler, P. E. 1994. The thermoregulatory advantages of heat storage and shade-seeking behaviour to hominids foraging in equatorial savannah environments. *Journal of Human Evolution*, 26, 339–350.

White, J. 1967. *The birth and rebirth of pictorial space*. New York: Harper & Row.

White, L. A. 1942. On the use of tools by primates. *Journal of Comparative Psychology*, 34, 369–374.

White, L. A. 1959. The concept of culture. *American Anthropologist*, 61, 227–251.

White, T. D. 1988. The comparative biology of "robust" *Australopithecus*: clues from context. In F. E. Grine (Eds.), *Evolutionary history of the "robust" Australopithecines*. New York: Aldine de Gruyter.

Whiten, A. & Byrne, R. W. 1988. Tactical deception in primates. *Behavioral and Brain Sciences*, 11, 233–273.

Whiten, A. 1993. Evolving a theory of mind. In S. Baron-Cohen, H. Tager-Flusberg & D. Cohen (Eds.), *Understanding other minds* (pp. 367–396). Oxford: Oxford University Press.

Wilson, E. O. 1975. *Sociobiology*. Cambridge, Massachusetts: Belknap Press.

Wittgenstein, L. 1958. *Philosophical investigations*. Oxford: Blackwell.

Wittgenstein, L. 1961[1922]. *Tractatus logico-philosophicus*. London: Routledge & Kegan Paul.

Wobst, H. M. 1977. Stylistic behavior and information exchange. In C. E. Cleland (Eds.), *For the Director* (pp. 317–342). Ann Arbor: Museum of Anthropology, University of Michigan.

WoldeGabriel, G., White, T. D., Suwa, G., Renne, P., de Heinzelin, J., Hart, W. K. & Heiken, G. 1994. Ecological and temporal placement of early Pliocene hominids at Aramis, Ethiopia. *Nature*, 371, 330–333.

Wood, B. A. 1992a. Origin and evolution of the genus *Homo. Nature*, 355, 783–790.

Wood, B. A. 1992b. Old bones match old stones. *Nature*, 355, 678–679.

Wood, B. A. 1994. The oldest hominid yet. *Nature*, 280–281.

Wrangham, R. W. 1974. Artificial feeding of chimpanzees and baboons in their natural habitat. *Animal Behavior*, 22, 83–93.

Wrangham, R. W. 1977. Feeding behaviour of chimpanzees in Gombe National Park, Tanzania. In T. H. Clutton-Brock (Eds.), *Primate ecology* (pp. 503–538). London: Academic Press.

Wrangham, R. W. 1987. The significance of African apes for reconstructing human social evolution. In W. G. Kinzey (Eds.), *The evolution of human behavior.* New York: State University of New York Press.

Wrangham, R. W. & Riss, E. van Z. B. 1990. Rates of predation on mammals by Gombe chimpanzees, 1972–1975. *Primates*, 31, 157–170.

Wreschner, E. E. 1980. Red ochre and human evolution. *Current Anthropology*, 21(5), 631–644.

Wright, R. V. S. 1972. Imitative learning of a flaked tool technology. *Mankind*, 8, 296–306.

Wymer, J. 1988. Palaeolithic archaeology and the British Quaternary sequence. *Quaternary Science Reviews*, 7, 79–98.

Wynn, T. 1979. The intelligence of later Acheulean hominids. *Man*, 14, 371–391.

Wynn, T. 1993. Two developments in the mind of *Homo erectus. Journal of Anthropological Archaeology*, 12, 299–322.

Wynn, T. & McGrew, W. C. 1989. An ape's eye view of the Oldowan. *Man*, 24, 383–398.

Wynn, T. & Tierson, F. 1990. Regional comparison of the shapes of later Acheulean handaxes. *American Anthropologist*, 92, 73–84.

Zihlman, A. 1985. *Australopithecus afarensis*. In P. V. Tobias (Eds.), *Hominid evolution* (pp. 213–220). New York: Alan R. Liss.

Zihlman, A. L., Cronin, J. E., Cramer, D. L. & Sarich, V. M. 1978. Pygmy chimpanzee as a possible prototype for the common ancestor of humans, chimpanzees and gorillas. *Nature*, 275, 744–746.

Zimansky, P. 1993. Review of "Before writing (vols I and II)" by Denise Schmandt-Besserat. *Journal of Field Archaeology*, 20, 513–517.

Zukow, P. G. 1990. Socio-perceptual bases for the emergence of language. *Developmental Psychobiology*, 23, 705–726.

INDEX